PATRICIAN L

The Public and Private Life of Sir Henri-Gustave Joly de Lotbinière, 1829–1908

Patrician Liberal examines the life and career of a neglected figure in Canadian history, Sir Henri-Gustave Joly de Lotbinière. This book provides a detailed account of Joly's political career as Quebec premier, Cabinet minister in the Laurier government, and lieutenant-governor of British Columbia, as well as his public role as a French-speaking Protestant promoter of national unity, a leading spokesperson for the Canadian forest conservation movement, a Quebec seigneur, and father to a large and devoted family.

Joly's life serves as a prism through which author J.I. Little elucidates important themes in Quebec and Canadian society, economy, politics, and culture during the Victorian and Edwardian eras. As Little reveals, Joly's story is particularly fascinating for how closely the conflicting forces in his life – religious, cultural, and social – mirrored those of a Canadian society straining to forge a cohesive and distinctive national identity.

J.I. LITTLE is a professor in the Department of History at Simon Fraser University, author of *Loyalties in Conflict: A Canadian Borderland in War and Rebellion, 1812–1840*, and co-author of *An Illustrated History of Quebec: Tradition and Modernity*.

Patrician Liberal

The Public and Private Life of Sir Henri-Gustave Joly de Lotbinière, 1829–1908

J. I. LITTLE

UNIVERSITY OF TORONTO PRESS
Toronto Buffalo London

ISBN 978-1-4426-4699-5 (cloth)
ISBN 978-1-4426-1477-2 (paper)

Publication cataloguing information is available from Library
and Archives Canada.

University of Toronto Press acknowledges the financial assistance
to its publishing program of the Canada Council for the Arts
and the Ontario Arts Council.

University of Toronto Press acknowledges the financial
support of the Government of Canada through the Canada Book Fund
for its publishing activities.

This book has been published with the help of a grant from the Canadian
Federation for the Humanities and Social Sciences, through the Awards
to Scholarly Publications Program, using funds provided by the Social
Sciences and Humanities Research Council of Canada.

To the memory of my grandmother, Edith Taylor McCrea,
seigneur's daughter and lumberman's wife

Contents

List of Illustrations

Preface

Given that I have spent most of my career as a social historian examining such themes as colonization, religion, institutional reform, and political culture at a regional level, this biography of a prominent national figure represents a rather sharp shift in focus on my part. I am of the generation who, as Geoff Eley writes in his semi-autobiographical *A Crooked Line*, dismissed the writing of individual biographies as old-fashioned and trivializing, replaced by "the pursuit of structural or broadly contextualized materialist analysis." But the subsequent rise of cultural history, with its turn to subjectivity, has led to a resurgence of interest in biography, though with the goal – as Eley also notes – of revisiting individual lives "as complex texts in which the same large questions that inspired the social historians were embedded."[1] Inspired by microhistorian Giovanni Levi's insight that scale does not have its own independent existence,[2] I was drawn to the challenge of examining the generalized and the abstract through the lens of the personal and the particular. In searching for a subject, I was fortunate to discover the personal papers of a historically neglected and complex figure, Henri-Gustave Joly de Lotbinière, whose extensive correspondence had not previously been exploited, despite being available in the national archives of Quebec as well as Canada.

Having grown up in a small, partially English-speaking community to the immediate south of Lotbinière, and having come of age in the Trudeau era, I was intrigued by Joly because of his biculturalism and Canadian nationalism. It was my interest in environmental history, however, that initially drew me to him as a subject because of his role as a pioneer conservationist. A favourable bias towards one's subject may be an occupational hazard of the biographer, but my main goal has been less to gain a place for Joly de Lotbinière in the nation's pantheon of great men than to interpret what his life and career revealed about Quebec and Canadian society, economy, politics, and culture during the Victorian and Edwardian eras.

This study therefore falls somewhere between biography, defined by Jill Lepore as "largely founded on a belief in the singularity and significance of an individual's life and his contribution to history," and microhistory, which Lepore states "is founded upon almost the opposite assumption: however singular a person's life may be, the value of examining it lies not in its uniqueness, but in its exemplariness, in how that individual's life serves as an allegory for broader issues affecting the culture as a whole."[3] But this statement echoes the common misconception that, in being concerned about larger historical questions, microhistory must necessarily approach the local as a case study, or the individual as a representative figure. Rather, as Michael Gardiner states, microhistory emphasizes 'the role of social contradictions in generating social change.'[4] Thus, Joly's ideology was a product of his birth into Quebec's old Catholic seigneurial elite, on his mother's side, as well as his upbringing in the commercial and liberal Paris of his father's Protestant family. Therefore, his role as father, businessman, and public figure can only be understood as a product of those very different social and cultural influences. Perhaps the best label for this study is what Alice Kessler-Harris refers to as anti-biography. In her words, "Rather than offering history as background, or introducing it in order to locate an individual in time," the anti-biography asks "how the individual life helps us to make sense of a piece of the historical process."[5] In paying considerable attention to Joly's private life, for example, my goal is not only to understand him as an individual but also to explore how the private informed the public, as well as vice versa.[6]

Although this book is a life story that follows a chronological narrative line, each chapter does have a distinct thematic focus. In addition to investigating Joly's public role as long-term leader of the provincial Liberals and short-term premier of Quebec, bicultural promoter of national unity, leading spokesman for the Canadian forest conservation movement, reform-oriented member of the Laurier government in Ottawa, and influential lieutenant governor of British Columbia, this study examines his family relations as well as his role as seigneur and lumber producer. Focussing on a single individual has enabled me to trace the common thread that connects these disparate themes, beginning with the evolution and role of social class and the relationship between the private and the public, the personal and the political.

Particular attention is paid to how Joly reconciled the conflicting forces that he was subjected to personally and that strained society as a whole, for he embodied the cultural duality of Canada as well as the tension between land-based aristocratic values and urban bourgeois ones. This tension contributed to the mutual estrangement of Joly's parents and to the early death in India of his reckless younger brother, but Joly himself was able to benefit from his somewhat unique position by keeping a foot in both the traditional rural and the modern urban worlds, as well as the French-Canadian and English-Canadian ones. He was not only a French-speaking Protestant, but also a Canadian who had grown up in Paris and a social conservative who was also a political liberal. From a psychological perspective, it seems clear that Joly's somewhat unstable social and cultural identity goes a long way towards explaining his search for security as well as his protective impulse, as manifested in his attachment to family and dedication to provincial rights, national unity, efficient honest government, and the conservation of natural resources for future generations.

Liberal as these goals were, they also reflected Joly's patrician sense of noblesse oblige, and it was his gentlemanly deportment and skills in diplomacy as well as his family pedigree that made him such a respected figure in a young country that was still in the early stages of forging a cohesive and distinctive national identity. In fact, there are basic similarities between Joly's political ideology and the Red Toryism that was identified in the 1960s as distinctively Canadian, for that political ideology (which has since been overwhelmed by "neoconservatism") favoured traditional values and institutions, the decentralization of state power, small business, and volunteerism to solve social problems such as poverty. Gad Horowitz, applying Louis Hartz's fragment thesis, claimed that Red Toryism resulted from the impact of the Tory Loyalist "touch" on the dominant bourgeois liberal ideology. The example of Joly suggests that Red Toryism was not necessarily as exclusive to English Canada as Horowitz and others have assumed.[7] The fact remains, however, that Joly would never consider joining a Conservative Party that he associated with unprincipled profligacy, intolerance, and corruption. Joly's Protestantism, his attachment to family, and his distaste for political cronyism also placed strict limits on his public career, so that today he is a largely forgotten historical figure in a country that remains sharply divided along linguistic lines.

A word on usage: In the interest of brevity as well as accuracy, I generally refer to Joly de Lotbinière simply as Joly, for he did not formally
adopt the longer name until 1888. Units of measurement are sometimes
left in their original imperial measurement form, especially when referring to ratios such as crop yields, but I have included a short list of
conversions. The word *sic* is used to mark grammatical errors and non-
standard spellings within direct quotations only when they might otherwise be viewed as my own typographical or spelling errors. Finally,
I have translated the longer and more difficult French quotes, but also
included the originals in the text.

Acknowledgments

This study is based largely on the voluminous Joly de Lotbinière collection of confidential correspondence and other material, one that fills fourteen microfilm reels, nine of which are Henri-Gustave's own records.[1] A number of people have made my task not only possible but also enjoyable. Mylène Richard and Hélène Leclerc of le Domaine Joly de Lotbinière welcomed me twice to this fascinating historic site and provided access to its photographic archives as well as invaluable information on the family. I am also grateful to them for their comments on the first chapter. Sean Wilkinson was my excellent research assistant, and Brian Young applied his critical pen to the introduction, forcing me to clarify my interpretation of a man who defies easy categorization. He was also kind enough to allow me to read his forthcoming book on Quebec's patrician Taschereau and McCord families. Bob McDonald critiqued the chapters on Ottawa and British Columbia, and I drew on the expertise of Benoît Grenier and Donald Fyson for information on the seigneurial and legal systems, respectively. Nicolas Kenny provided advice on the translations, Nikki Strong-Boag was a sympathetic and insightful reader of the entire manuscript, and I benefited greatly from the very careful critical analysis of the three anonymous assessors. Needless to say, none of these individuals can be held responsible for my interpretation of their comments. I also drew on the cheerful assistance of Pierre-Louis Lapointe and others at the Bibliothèque et Archives nationales du Québec, Nancy Blake and Sonny Wong of the Simon Fraser University Library's interlibrary loans department, and Stephen DeMuth of the university's Instructional Media Centre, who produced the map of Lotbinière. Len Husband of the University of Toronto Press was, yet again, a source of level-headed encouragement, and Emily Johnston and David Zielonka guided me through the editing process. Many thanks to all concerned. Research for this book was funded by a Standard Research Grant from the Social Sciences and Humanities Research Council of Canada, and I am particularly grateful for the two-semester research leave stipend, which greatly expedited the entire process. Publication was made possible by a subsidy from the Canadian Federation for the Humanities and Social Sciences through its Awards to Scholarly Publications Program. Finally, as always, my greatest debt is to my wife, Andrea, who provides the support, love, and connection with our community that adds a semblance of balance to my life.

Conversion Standards

£1 currency or 1 Louis d'or = 24 francs or livres ancien cours or livres
  tournois of 20 sols
1 sol = 12 deniers
1 denier = 1 penny
£1 cy = 20 shillings; 1 s. = 12 pence
1 league = 5.56 kilometres
1 arpent = 0.4 hectares
1 square arpent = 0.84 acres
1 hectare = 2.47 acres
1 minot = 1.07 imperial bushels = 39 litres
1 square mile = 2.59 square kilometres
1 cubic foot = 0.03 cubic meters

Canadian Genealogical Line

Louis-Théandré Chartier de Lotbinière (1612–after 1680)
René-Lous Chartier de Lotbinière (1641–1709)
Eustache Chartier de Lotbinière (1688–1749)
Michel Chartier de Lotbinière (1723–98)
Michel-Eustache-Gaspard-Alain Chartier de Lotbinière (1748–1822)
Julie-Christine Chartier de Lotbinière (1810–87) m Gaspard-Pierre-
  Gustave Joly (1798–1865)

Joly Offspring

Henri-Gustave (1829–1908) m Margaretta Josepha (Lucy) Gowen
Amélie-Ursule (1831–1922) m Henry George Savage
Edmond de Lotbinière (1832–57)
Julie-Charlotte (1835–35)
Arthur (1838–38?)

Offspring of Henri-Gustave and Lucy

Julia Josepha (1858–1942) m St George Boswell
Edmond Gustave (1859–1911) m Lucy Geils Campbell
Louisa-Maud (1861–62)
Alain Chartier (1862–1944) m Marion Helen Campbell
Margaretha Anna (1864–1949) m Herbert Colborne Nanton
Matilda Florence (1867–1903) m Henry Smith Greenwood
Henri Gustave (1868–1960) m Mildred Louisa Grenfell

Ethel Blanche (1872–1935) m Dudley Acland Mills
John Livesey (1872–75)
Ernest Edgar (1874–75)
Justine de Lotbinière (1875–78)

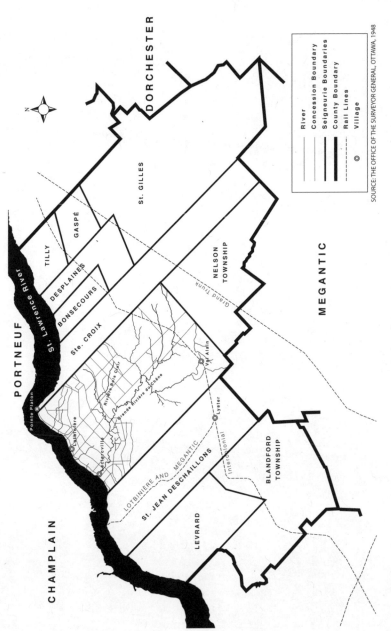

CHAMPLAIN

PORTNEUF

St. Lawrence River

DORCHESTER

St. GILLES

GASPÉ

TILLY

DESPLAINES

BONSECOURS

Ste. CROIX

NELSON TOWNSHIP

Pointe Platon

Deschênes

Lotbinière

Leclercville

Rivière Belle Chute

Grande Rivière duchêne

St. Alain

Lyster

Intercolonial

Grand Trunk

LOTBINIÈRE AND MEGANTIC

St. JEAN DESCHAILLONS

LEVRARD

BLANDFORD TOWNSHIP

MEGANTIC

LOTBINIÈRE COUNTY

N

River
Concession Boundary
Seigneurie Boundaries
County Boundary
Rail Lines
Village

SOURCE: THE OFFICE OF THE SURVEYOR GENERAL, OTTAWA, 1948

PATRICIAN LIBERAL

Introduction

Early in 1908, the year of Quebec City's extravagant tercentenary celebration,[1] the municipal council announced that it would rename Haldimand Street, within the walls of the old city, in Sir Henri-Gustave Joly de Lotbinière's honour. Rather ironically, given that he had dedicated much of his life to resolving conflicts between French-speaking and English-speaking Canadians, this announcement resulted in a controversy along those same lines, for it was greeted with protest by the city's English-speaking elite. Although the *Daily Telegraph* agreed that "the name of 'De Lotbiniere' is illustrious in the history of Canada and of Quebec, and none has worn it with more honor and distinction to himself and the Ancient Capital, as well as to the country at large, than Sir Henri," it argued that Joly himself would be opposed to the removal of "so useful a reminder of such a distinguished figure in our annals as Governor Haldimand." Better to replace one of the names chosen from the "almost exhausted" calendar of saints, which strangers found so confusing, or a more generic name such as Garden Street or Rampart Street, thereby not offending any "susceptibilities."[2] A member of the long-established Literary and Historical Society agreed, adding the additional argument that Haldimand Street was not suitable because of its small size: "Surely the name de Lotbiniere deserves a nobler prominence."[3] Another local newspaper suggested that Haldimand's name was suitable to "the narrow and less frequented street in the old Upper Town eloquent of the past," but the name Lotbinière should be given to one of the more modern streets, "say near the building of that Legislature of which he was so long a distinguished member."[4] This advice – which nicely illustrated the tension in Joly's life between tradition and modernity – was heeded, for Haldimand Street has survived in Old

Quebec, and the name Lotbinière is to be found on the street fronting the provincial legislature.

Such an honour may seem somewhat surprising, given that Joly had quit the legislature in protest twenty-three years earlier and that his premiership had been brief and controversial. But even if Joly was not in the first rank of importance as a Canadian or Quebec politician, he did serve as provincial party leader for sixteen years, he managed to govern effectively if briefly during a particularly difficult period of Quebec's history, and he was rewarded with a knighthood for his efforts to ease tensions between French and English Canada during the critical years following the Riel crisis. He was also Canada's most prominent forest conservation advocate, a capable reform-oriented member of the Laurier administration, and undoubtedly the most influential lieutenant governor British Columbia has ever had. Very few Canadians could boast such a varied and useful career, yet unlike Quebec contemporaries such as Israël Tarte, Hector-Louis Langevin, Adolphe Chapleau, Godfroy Langlois, Honoré Mercier, Louis-Antoine Dessaulles, and Wilfrid Laurier, Joly has not previously been the subject of a book-length biography. In the introductory remarks to his excellent monograph on the first ten years of Quebec's provincial governance, Marcel Hamelin (author of the *Dictionary of Canadian Biography* article on Joly) does not even include Joly among the political figures who deserve further study.[5] Perhaps not surprisingly, then, Joly is completely ignored in Yvan Lamonde's lengthy volume on the social history of ideas in pre-twentieth-century Quebec.[6]

One probable reason that Quebec historians have not paid more attention to Joly is that he was a Canadian nationalist, first and foremost, going so far as to break publicly with his Liberal colleagues over their political exploitation of Riel's execution in 1885. Furthermore, he became more sympathetic to British imperialism as he grew older, and he and his family became too assimilated into the English-speaking world to fit comfortably into what Jocelyn Letourneau refers to as Quebec's grand narrative.[7] The fact that Joly was a descendant of New France's office-holding and seigneurial elite may be yet another reason that he has not received more attention, for Quebec historians of the post–Quiet Revolution generation have been fixated on the rise of modernity.[8] Fernande Roy's seminal study argues that the influence of Church-inspired conservatism was quite limited even in pre-1960 Quebec and that the prevailing ideology was liberalism, the ultimate goal of which was the defence of private property.[9] Although he was a

Protestant who promoted a number of progressive reforms, as we shall see, Joly did not fit this mould because his liberalism was compromised by his paternalism and his social conservatism.

Though failing to identify liberalism as an ideology, Marcel Hamelin made essentially the same point as Roy when he wrote that, in contrast to the provincial press, "des préoccupations idéologiques n'apparaissent que rarement chez la majorité des hommes politiques québécois."[10] But a younger generation of historians has begun to present a more sophisticated interpretation of political ideology in the province. Éric Bédard has recently argued convincingly that the prominent French-speaking reform politicians of the post-Rebellion era were essentially anti-republican and anti-American conservatives who believed that the Catholic Church played a crucial role in sustaining the social order and whose liberalism was centred not on the individual but on the national community.[11] Although Hamelin claims that *agriculturisme* was rarely mentioned in the Legislative Assembly after Confederation, it cannot be denied that provincial governments funded colonization roads, subsidized colonization societies, and promoted railway construction in the name of expanding the agricultural frontier. Even though the main aim of the colonization movement was not to resist Quebec's industrialization and urbanization as historians once assumed, but to stem the flow of French-Canadian families to the factory towns of southern New England, it was inspired by the Catholic Church in a visionary expansionist campaign that idealized rural life.[12] The Church's influence was such that, as Brian Young has shown, the codifiers of Quebec's civil code in 1866 felt compelled to recognize its dominant status as well as buttress patriarchal power in relation to marriage and the family. More recently, Bruce Curtis has demonstrated that the same conservative ruralist impulse influenced Joseph-Charles Taché's design in 1871 of the first scientific census for the new national state.[13]

Roy would be correct in replying that in none of these cases did conservative nationalism challenge the fundamental liberal ethos of individual property rights or free enterprise,[14] an ethos that Joly certainly shared. But as Arno Mayer has argued for pre-1914 Europe in general, and Eugen Weber for rural France in particular, central values of the Ancien Régime persisted well into the industrial era.[15] Wealth and prestige may not have been as tied to noble status and land ownership in Quebec as they were in much of Europe, but there was no successful revolution in Quebec, and not all members of the seigneurial class became impoverished and inconsequential after the Conquest, as historians

such as Alfred Dubuc and Fernand Ouellet have implied.[16] Members of
the Canadian nobility sold thirty-three seigneuries between 1782 and
1840,[17] but the fact remains that Joly was far from the only member of
the landed elite to play an important role in Quebec politics and society during the nineteenth and twentieth centuries. As Daniel Salée has
pointed out, "generations of Taschereaus, Massons, and Casgrains provided more than their share of Ministers, high-ranking civil servants,
magistrates, lieutenant-governors, and bishops."[18]

Young's recent research supports Salée, for Young argues that the patrician elite maintained a particularly strong influence in the Quebec
City area as it became increasingly eclipsed by Montreal. In his words,
"their social instincts were shaped by seigniorial privilege, inherited
landed wealth, position in Anglican or Roman Catholic hierarchies,
local status (as opposed to international recognition) and forms of
power filtered through honours, profession, militia, or voluntary associations."[19] A relevant term might be the one Cameron Nish borrowed
from Molière's satirical play to describe the elite of New France, namely
bourgeois-gentilhomme.[20] Although Nish attempted, somewhat unsuccessfully, to demonstrate that members of the seigneurial class were
fundamentally bourgeois, the fact is that what Young refers to as "feudal vestiges" survived well into the Victorian and Edwardian eras.[21]

The degree to which Joly was perceived to be a gentleman in the
traditional sense is illustrated by the description penned by Senator
Laurent-Olivier David for the *Courrier de Montréal* in 1875:

> Good build and a kind face, noble and distinguished deportment, curly-
> haired, graying, thick moustache, looks like a serviceman on leave. A
> pleasant and gifted speaker, an elegant, easy, polished original and caustic
> orator, quick-witted; knows how to skilfully let fly remarks, always care-
> ful not to offend an adversary. A quick, curious, and highly cultured mind,
> prefers useful and practical things to grand concepts and profound theo-
> ries. A strict and upright conscience, free of prejudices and weaknesses,
> resisting the seduction and trickery of politics. Wealthy, very wealthy and
> proportionately charitable, always ready to give to the destitute and all
> good causes.

To complete his portrayal of Joly as a landed aristocrat, David added
that he was "more content on his vast estates, among his many workers with their calloused hands and tanned faces, than in chic drawing
rooms or the Chamber of Deputies."[22]

Linked to the theme of social class, a central thread in the ensuing chapters is ideology, or what Bédard refers to more loosely as "un certain rapport du monde,"[23] but this is not primarily an intellectual history. As Patrice Dutil notes in the introduction to his biography of one of Joly's Liberal colleagues, Godfroy Langlois, "'ideology' cannot be firmly grasped unless the politics that express it, or fail to express it, are understood." Dutil adds, "Political intrigues show us how ideologies really work."[24] Political history is a central theme of this study, but ideology is also more than politics, particularly for a man such as Joly, for whom home, family, and religion were at least as important as public life. European political historians have shifted their attention towards the small scale and the "private," rejecting the history of the state as an abstract entity on the grounds that it is "a story of empty appearances" that exaggerates the state's monopoly over power.[25] Canadian historians are still obsessed by the rise of the modern state, but they are at least beginning to write political biographies that transcend the divide between the public and the private. A pioneering example is Young's revisionist study of George-Étienne Cartier in which politics takes a back seat to the subject's business and personal life.[26] As an upstanding family man (in contrast to Cartier), Joly was less patently ambitious and more dedicated to public life out of a paternalistic sense of duty. Giorgi Chittolini notes that in the world of private relations can be found "a complex web of regulation and discipline" operating quite independently of the world of formal power,[27] but it does not follow that Joly's public face was much different from his private one. Our title refers to Joly's public and private *life* rather than *lives*, not because the private was public as in today's invasive popular culture, but because the two spheres formed a seamless web as far as Joly was concerned, even if he was careful not to take advantage of his public life for private ends. In short, our examination of his private life – including his role as seigneur and businessman – sheds light on his public life, as well as vice versa.

The fact that Joly was the product of two quite different worlds – patrician Catholic Quebec on his mother's side and bourgeois Protestant France (in a somewhat paradoxical reversal of the old world and the new) on that of his father – meant that he experienced in a particularly acute sense the conflicting pressures exerted by the transition from pre-industrial to industrial society. But that tension should not be exaggerated, for (to translate a French saying) Joly appears always to have felt comfortable in his own skin. Richard Bushman's study of refinement in the republican United States is instructive in this respect,

for he finds that after the turn of the nineteenth century, the culture
of gentility – as reflected in popular manners, housing styles, garden
landscapes, and so on – began exercising increasing influence over
much of the population. To explain this apparent paradox, Bushman
suggests that "capitalism and gentility were allies in forming the modern economy" because "a capitalist economy requires both frantic getting and energetic spending."[28] Joly was actually quite parsimonious,
as we shall see, but this did not prevent him from conforming to the
image of a landed gentleman.

Nor does Joly appear to have been greatly conflicted by the fact
that he was immersed in two distinct linguistic cultures, as someone
raised in a French-speaking environment but with English-speaking
relatives on his mother's side, as well as an English-speaking wife.
In fact, his dual religious heritage was more significant than his linguistic background at a time when marriages between Catholics and
Protestants were rare and the country was torn by sectarian conflicts,
but Joly reconciled that dichotomy in his own mind by adhering to a
moderate Anglicanism. Joly's duality both helped and hindered his
political career. It ensured support from Quebec's influential Anglo-
Protestant bourgeoisie, but also a degree of mistrust by the province's
French-speaking majority, for whom Catholicism was an intrinsic part
of their cultural identity. As a Canadian nationalist who sympathized
with the British imperial connection, Joly was a more logical candidate for the House of Commons than for the provincial Assembly, yet
(aside from the brief era of the dual mandate after Confederation) he
resisted running at the federal level until late in life. Influential though
he was, Joly was too proud, too ethical, and too lacking in the common
touch to become a political force of the first rank, and he willingly
stepped aside for the more flamboyant Honoré Mercier as leader of
the provincial Liberals. He was also content to play the role of efficient
administrator in the Laurier government and behind-the-scenes diplomat in Victoria.

Supporters of the biographical approach have traditionally stressed
the importance of individual agency and contingency in history,[29] and
this volume does aim to present Joly as a living and active human being rather than an object of abstract forces, but a study of his political
career also serves the broader purpose of shedding light on the tensions within Confederation and how they were accommodated, though
never resolved. This is not a case study of a representative figure, then,
but neither is it focused on the achievements of a particular individual.

On a more strictly ideological level, Joly's life helps us to appreciate in relatively concrete terms the tensions and contradictions within Canada's increasingly dominant liberal value system, or what Ian McKay refers to as this country's prevailing liberal order.[30] Joly certainly valued individual liberty, economic progress, and private property (the three key features of the liberal order), but the fact that he clung to the land and to the aristocratic ethos that was part of his family heritage reveals how strongly he believed in the preservation of the traditional social order as well as the social obligations that came with being a patrician. Canadian historians have generally associated paternalism in the public arena with the pre-Rebellion era and with authoritarian Tories such as Upper Canada's Governor Sir Francis Bond Head, but the winning of responsible government meant that initiatives such as penal reform and aboriginal relocation (two of Bond Head's pet projects) became more closely associated with the expanding powers of the modern state.[31] From this perspective, paternalism and liberalism were not as mutually exclusive as has been assumed.

Not only has Canada had a strong Red Tory tradition, as already noted, but Daniel Samson also has pointed to Nova Scotia's influential agricultural reformer John Young, a disciple of Scotland's Sir John Sinclair, as a man whose conservative radicalism "looked backward as much as forward, invoking the Tory myth of stability, elite emulation, and a harmonious order, while at the same time urging innovation and 'enterprise.'"[32] Thus, it was not particularly difficult for Joly to reconcile his defence of the Catholic Church's official status in Quebec with his advocacy of more state support for public schools, or his economic liberalism with his promotion of greater state involvement in forest conservation. From his perspective, the state should be a protector of the public good, and what Elsbeth Heaman refers to as conservative rights,[33] as well as a guardian of individual property rights. Joly's rather paternalistic liberalism, then, was broader than what the definition offered by Roy and McKay encompasses,[34] and it clearly resonated with many Canadians during a period when the certainties of the pre-industrial world were being turned upside down.

In chapter 1 we briefly examine Joly's deep patrician roots in New France and Lower Canada, beginning with Louis-Théandre Chartier de Lotbinière, who arrived in Canada in 1651. The five generations of Chartiers de Lotbinière were all highly ranked public officials, and it was the second of them, René-Louis, who was granted the seigneury that would remain in the family's hands until the mid-twentieth century.

But the seigneury's land was poorly drained, and it served largely as a source of social status rather than as an economic or political power base until Henri-Gustave's parents became the first seigneurs to live on it. The first chapter closes with an examination of how the Swiss-born Pierre-Gustave Joly developed a thriving lumber business on the seigneury of Lotbinière despite his troubled relationship with the *censitaires* who became the suppliers of logs for his sawmills.

Chapter 2 focuses on Henri-Gustave's close relations with his wife, Margaretta Josepha Gowen, and their children, most of whom did not become integrated into Quebec society, despite their education in local French-language institutions and their family links with Quebec City's English-speaking bourgeoisie. Rather, several sons and daughters became tied to the British military, through profession or marriage, in a neat symbiosis between the traditions of the Ancien Régime elite and the opportunities provided by the modern British Empire. Of the seven offspring who survived to maturity, only the eldest daughter and eldest son would remain in Quebec, with the latter following in his father's footsteps as his law partner and junior business associate, though never managing to emerge from his shadow. The dominant theme of this chapter is paternalism, a word with class as well as gender connotations, and the theme reappears repeatedly in the chapters on Joly's public career.

In chapter 3 we examine the impact of the "abolition" of seigneurial tenure in 1854, a topic that has remained largely unexplored by Quebec's historians. Our rather paradoxical finding is that this legislation actually entrenched the Joly family more firmly in their Lotbinière property. Henri-Gustave was identified as a seigneur throughout his life, and the fact that he was no longer obliged to grant lots to censitaires after 1854 ensured that he would have a secure supply of raw material for his lumber business, as well as a dependent labour force. By continuing the careful forest management of his father, Henri-Gustave was able to support his family in some comfort while effectively practicing what we now refer to as sustained-yield forestry. Local farmers' reliance on winter logging on the seigneury's forest reserve may not have contributed to Pierre-Gustave Joly's popularity, but it certainly helped to ensure that his son, Henri-Gustave, would have a dependable power base for his political career. This constituency was crucial because, as a Paris-educated Protestant, Henri-Gustave could never completely overcome his outsider status in French-speaking Quebec, nor did he become entirely assimilated into the English-speaking business community, despite marrying into it and playing a prominent role in the Anglican Church.

Chapter 4 examines Joly's opposition to Confederation, his role as leader of the provincial Liberals, and his consistent opposition to fiscal profligacy and political corruption, as well as his support for mildly reformist social policies. Chapter 5 reviews the one aspect of Joly's life that has received detailed attention from historians, his role as provincial premier between March 1878 and October 1879. This was a period of economic crisis when Joly's organizational skills earned him widespread respect, but his economizing policies proved to be no match for Conservative obstructionism and bribery. As a political reformer, Joly practiced a paternalism of a different order than that of old Tories such as Governor Bond Head, who countenanced corruption and violence as a means to an end,[35] and these two political chapters underscore Joly's insistence that government operate within its means, and without becoming beholden to wealthy party funders. This insistence served both as an asset and as a handicap to his public career.

In chapter 6 we examine how – having resigned from provincial politics as a result of the Riel crisis in 1885 – Joly eventually returned to the public stage in a somewhat futile attempt to repair relations between English and French Canada, thereby earning a knighthood in 1895. The other focus of his attention during this decade or so was the forest conservation movement, for which he became Canada's leading spokesman, as we see in chapter 7. Once again, rather than causing him to vacillate between two apparently contradictory value systems, Joly's paternalism and his belief in liberal reform tended to complement each other in initiatives such as Arbour Day and his insistence that wood lots be preserved, fire regulations be enforced, and the export of pulpwood from Canada be banned.

The same balancing act is examined in chapter 8, which focuses on Joly's role as minister of internal revenue in the Laurier government between 1896 and 1900. A diligent and effective administrator, Joly never fully accepted the broker-based patronage system that replaced the old patron-client relationship after the institutionalization of the party system in the 1840s.[36] As a patrician paternalist, he fought off his Liberal colleagues' demands that employees of his department who were suspected to be Conservative supporters be replaced with the party faithful. But he also contributed to the state formation project that is generally assumed to have replaced the paternalist system of government, by instituting a greater degree of uniformity in the country's weights and measures system. While intensifying the government's campaign against the illicit production of alcohol, however, Joly was too sensitive to the Catholic Church's stance to become an advocate of prohibition.

Finally, in chapter 9 we turn to the public role that perhaps best suited Joly's patrician status and diplomatic temperament, namely that of lieutenant governor of British Columbia. This was no sinecure, especially for a man of Joly's advanced years, for he was largely responsible for introducing the party system that stabilized governance in the fractious west coast province. In short, the example of Sir Henri-Gustave Joly de Lotbinière suggests that the new urban and industrial order of the Victorian and Edwardian eras did not sweep away the social, economic, and political influence of the old patrician elite as easily or as quickly as historians of Quebec and Canada have tended to assume and that the paternalist ethos was not necessarily incompatible with liberal reform.[37]

Chapter One

Blood and Soil

Henri-Gustave Joly's passport, issued in 1873, identified him as a "born British subject," five feet eleven inches in height, with blue eyes, grey hair, pale complexion, and straight nose.[1] The fact that he had actually been born in his father's mother country of France reflects how thoroughly Joly had come to identify himself with the British empire by the 1870s. Contemporaries described his appearance and demeanour as that of the archetypal aristocrat. Thus, the French-born journalist and essayist Auguste Achintre wrote in 1871 that Joly reminded him of the portraits one found in galleries of eighteenth-century gentlemen, portraits that evoked "un parfum d'aristocratie bon ton" and reflected "tout ce que l'âge passé avait de moeurs charmantes et d'habitudes délicates."[2] With his handlebar moustache and long thick sideburns, Joly had the "allure svelte d'un officier de cavalrie," to quote the conservative Quebec historian Robert Rumilly.[3] Quite conscious of his distinguished heritage, Joly was strongly attached to the seigneury that signified his patrician status. Although he and his wife kept a house and later an apartment in Quebec City, where he had a law practice (becoming a Queen's Councillor in 1878)[4] and where he sat in the legislature for many years, they and their children lived in Lotbinière during the summer months. Joly also continued to maintain a strong interest in the management of his landed estate while living in Ottawa and Victoria.

Given that family lineage has traditionally been traced through the male line, it may seem anomalous that Joly's public image was largely based on his maternal inheritance, but his father was a foreigner, and it was his mother who had inherited the seigneury of Lotbinière. Joly's was not a case of deep ancestral connection to the land and its people, however, for his parents were the first seigneurs to live in Lotbinière, and he himself spent his youth attending school and university in Paris. But the family did have a multigenerational link to Lotbinière, which had been granted to Joly's great-great-great-grandfather, and the role of seigneur did confer social status even after the outdated land tenure system technically ceased to exist in 1854. Surprisingly little research has been done on the impact of this reform at the local community level, but we shall see that in the case of Lotbinière the former seigneur continued to exercise as much influence and power as ever.

The Chartier de Lotbinière Legacy

Historians of New France long denied that the nobility dominated the colony as it did the mother country, but they now recognize that the feudal system was deeply entrenched in Canada.[5] Recent research has revealed that a minimum of 239 nobles spent at least some time in New France, the vast majority as military officers from the middle or minor nobility, and that they developed as a distinctive social class.[6] The Chartiers de Lotbinière were not military nobility but they were related through marriage to some of France's greatest families – the Chateaubriands, La Rochefoucaults, and Polignacs – and they established themselves early as important office holders in Canada.[7] Louis-Théandre Chartier de Lotbinière, the first member of the family to sail to New France, was the son of the famous René-Pierre Chartier, doctor in ordinary to Louis XIII and the ladies of the court, as well as professor of surgery at the Collège Royal. Louis-Théandre arrived in Canada in 1651, the same year that his relative by marriage, Jean de Lauson, became governor. The kinship ensured Chartier de Lotbinière's appointment as attorney in the colony's first properly constituted court, the Seneschal's Court. He later became the court's lieutenant general for civil and criminal affairs, then the colony's attorney general, and finally, lieutenant general of the newly established Provost's Court.[8]

Chartier de Lotbinière's son, René-Louis, was appointed deputy attorney general to the Sovereign Council at the young age of twenty-eight; he then was appointed councillor for life in 1675 but resigned to take over his father's higher-paid position in the Provost's Court two years later. He would hold this position for the next twenty-six years. Promoted to lieutenant colonel of the Quebec militia in 1673, de Lotbinière accompanied Governor La Barre as commanding officer of the regiment that failed in its expedition against the Iroquois in 1684. Six years later, he led the defence of Quebec against the siege by Phips.

His appointment as chief councillor in 1703 made him the fourth most important person in the colony after the governor, the intendant, and the bishop, and he served in the intendant's place during the latter's absences.[9]

René-Louis Chartier de Lotbinière was still a young man when he received the seigneury that was named in honour of his family in 1672. With the seigneury measuring two and a quarter leagues (12.5 kilometres) along the south shore of the St Lawrence, by two leagues (11.1 kilometres) deep, Lotbinière's eastern edge lay approximately sixty-five kilometres to the west of Quebec City. The north shore of the St Lawrence was being settled more quickly because much of the south shore was vulnerable to overland Iroquois attack and was not easily accessible from the river due to its high cliffs. Behind these elevations, Lotbinière generally consisted of low-lying swampy land drained by small rivers that were suitable in a few places for mill sites and for timber drives during the spring floods.[10] (See map at the front of this book.) As a result, much of the seigneury was never settled, and the chief source of income for the seigneurs would eventually be its forests, not rents from the censitaires who were dependent originally on the fishery and later on winter logging to supplement their agricultural activities.

Despite René-Louis Chartier de Lotbinière's failure to attract the settlers officially required, an additional grant in 1685 and a purchase in 1686 expanded his seigneury by one and a quarter leagues (7.0 kilometres) to the west. Four leagues in depth (22.2 kilometres) were added by Governor Frontenac in 1693, thereby tripling the original size of the seigneury, though this additional land would be held as a 433-square-kilometre timber reserve. These boundaries would remain fixed thereafter, making Lotbinière one of the few fiefs to survive in one piece and in the hands of the same family until the seigneurial system was abolished in 1854.[11] The local residents would, thereafter, continue for many years to pay annual rents to the former seigneurs, and Lotbinière would remain in Joly de Lotbinière family possession until it was expropriated by the province in 1967.

By the time René-Louis Chartier de Lotbinière died in 1709, a chapel and gristmill had been constructed, but there were still only twenty-one censitaires, attracted largely by the offshore abundance of fish and eels.[12] René-Louis's third son, Eustache, would in 1713 acquire his siblings' shares of the property. Although he was only twenty years old when his father died, Eustache was being groomed to assume the important posts of his father and grandfather. He was already an ensign in the colonial regular troops, and he would be named to the Superior Council a year later, in 1710.[13]

The seigneury finally became an official parish known as Saint-Louis in 1722, and its first curé (parish priest) arrived two years later when there were fifty-one censitaires, all but nine of whom were located on lots fronting the St Lawrence. Forty arpents (sixteen hectares) of the domaine, which was the land reserved for the seigneur's own use,[14] were under cultivation at this time, but the manor house was not resided in by the seigneur, who was preoccupied by the colony's fur trade as well as his role in the Superior Council. De Lotbinière, whose wife died in 1723, leaving five children under the age of eleven, was ordained as canon and archdeacon only three years later. Becoming vicar general to Bishop Saint-Vallier soon afterward, he forbade the parishioners of Lotbinière to sing songs or circulate defamatory libels against each other on pain of being refused the sacraments, but his attention was focused more on his continuing role in the Superior Council as well as administration of the diocese during the long absences of the successive bishops.[15]

Because de Lotbinière's two older sons also became priests, it was his youngest son, Michel, who inherited the seigneury at the age of twenty-six in 1749. Having married the daughter of the king's engineer, Chaussegros de Léry, Michel Chartier de Lotbinière broke with the family tradition of winning fame on the bench by going to France to study military engineering. Upon his return in 1753 he helped his father-in-law to repair the fortifications of Quebec and two years later he was placed in charge of building Fort Carillon at the south end of Lake Champlain. De Lotbinière failed to receive further promotions, but he worked on Quebec's defence works prior to its capitulation in 1759, and he was ordered to fortify Ile aux Noix the following year in a vain attempt to stop the British advance from the south.[16] Over a century later, Colonel Thomas Bland Strange, the commanding officer of the Quebec Citadel, would refer to this service at a banquet in honour of his friend, Henri-Gustave Joly, whose French-Canadian identity was then under attack by political opponents:

> Mais, qu'est-ce qu'être Canadien-français? ... Est-ce que vous avez oublié que ses nobles ancêtres ont servi leur patrie dans les conseils de l'État et sur les champs de bataille pendant des centaines d'années? Est-ce que vous ne vous rappelez pas que dans ses veines coule le noble sang

des sieurs de Lotbinière et de Vaudreuil? que c'est au talent de M. de
e.g.Lotbinière, ingénieur-militaire de France, que l'on doit le plan des fortifications du champ de bataille qui nous a valu la glorieuse victoire de
Carillon?[17]

(But what is it to be a French Canadian? ... Have you forgotten that for
hundreds of years his noble ancestors served their country in the councils
of state and on the fields of battle? Do you not remember that in his veins
runs the noble blood of the sieurs de Lobtinière and Vaudreuil? That it is
to the talent of M. de Lotbinière, military engineer of France, that is owed
the plan for the battle-field fortifications that won you the glorious victory
of Carillon?)

Meanwhile, the seigneury lay neglected both before and after the
British Conquest. According to a census taken in 1762, Lotbinière had
a population of approximately 400 persons, or seventy-nine families, a
rather small increase from the fifty-one censitaire families in 1724.[18] Ex-
iled to France as a result of the defeat on the Plains of Abraham, Michel
Chartier de Lotbinière chose, after failing to revive his military career,[19]
to return to the colony. He had purchased five seigneuries, including
three from his cousin Marquis de Vaudreuil, the former governor who
had already granted him another seigneury southwest of Lake Champlain in 1758. Unable to convince the British government to recognize
his rights to the two seigneuries that were located south of the border
with New York, de Lotbinière sailed back to France in 1776. There he
lobbied to have that country enter the war on the side of the rebelling
American colonies. After the war, the Americans refused to recognize
his land claims, but the French government provided him with an annual pension of £1,200 and conferred the title of marquis on him in
1784. The ever-restless de Lotbinière moved back to Canada in 1790 and
then to New York in 1796, where he died in a yellow fever epidemic two
years later.[20]
  Meanwhile, his son, Michel-Eustache-Gaspard-Alain, proved to be
much more successful in currying favour with the colonial authorities,
for he rushed to the defence of the colony when the American War of
Independence broke out in 1776.[21] His role in the war ended after he
was taken prisoner at St-Jean-sur-Richelieu and held for eleven months
in Pennsylvania, where he became seriously ill, but his loyalty earned
him the rank of captain and a half-pay salary for the rest of his life.[22]
Keeping a safe distance from his father, Gaspard-Alain continued

after the war to be favoured by Governor Carleton, who became Lord Dorchester. De Lotbinière became a justice of the peace in 1785 and, after protesting vigorously in 1791 and 1793 against the suppression of the French language in the newly established Legislative Assembly of Lower Canada, he was elected that assembly's speaker in 1794. A year later he was appointed to the Legislative Council, which placed him in position to be granted 12,961 acres (5,184 hectares) of freehold township land outside the bounds of the seigneuries. He became a lieutenant colonel of the militia in 1794 and a colonel in 1803, and he would command two battalions during the War of 1812.[23] Gaspard-Alain Chartier de Lotbinière therefore fails to support the assumption of Robert Larin and Yves Drolet that the Canadian nobility declined in numbers because they were unable to preserve a distinction based on military service.[24]

It had appeared that there would be no direct heirs, but de Lotbinière's wife died in 1799, and four years later, at the age of fifty-four, he married the much younger Mary Charlotte Munro, daughter of the Loyalist speaker of Upper Canada's Legislative Council. John Munro had been a colonel and justice of the peace in New York, and according to family legend, his wife rode hundreds of miles with one of the children across enemy lines in order to carry dispatches that were sewn into the lining of her clothing.[25] Of the six offspring of Gaspard-Alain Chartier de Lotbinière and Mary Charlotte Munro, only three daughters would reach maturity.[26]

Gaspard-Alain Chartier de Lotbinière's will sheds light on his values and preoccupations as a member of the landed nobility in the post-Conquest era. In 1798, the year before his first wife died, he had been described as a scandalous lecher whose residence served as a miniature bordello,[27] but he now asked that a monument be erected in the chapel where he was to be buried, simply stating that he had been a good son, a good husband, and a good father and that he had loved his country and served his king with zeal. The inheritance would be divided equally among his three daughters and their younger siblings, should any be born before his death, with provision made for their mother, whose marriage to him had specified separation of goods. His wife was to serve as the tutor of their daughters, but only as long as she remained a widow, and the executors were to have the right to inspect the children's education. They were to take particular care should one or more sons be born before the aging de Lotbinière died because "une faiblesse sur l'éducation de mes garçons feroit leur malheur et englouteroit ma famille dans l'obscurité la plus vile." Given that he did not expect to still be living when his daughters married, de Lotbinière declared that each daughter must have her mother's blessing on her choice of marriage partner; otherwise, the daughter would have only the use value of her inheritance rather than full ownership, though this would pass on to her offspring after her death. There was, however, a chance for appeal to a family council of seven on the grounds that their mother's refusal was capricious. Mme de Lotbinière was to have use of the Vaudreuil manor house, or the one in town if she so chose, as well as all the furnishings and a generous pension. In short, the will reflected de Lotbinière's strong emotional ties to his wife and daughters, but the fact that they were females meant that their freedom to marry, in the case of the widow, or to choose freely, in the case of the daughters, was subordinated to the long-term interests of the family line.[28]

Meanwhile, the post-war era finally saw the population of Lotbinière seigneury begin to increase, with 713 souls and approximately 140 households in 1790, which was double the number of 1762.[29] De Lotbinière opened new sections of the seigneury to settlement in the following years, reporting to the surveyor general in 1814 that it had been surveyed into seven concessions with 580 ninety-arpent (thirty-six-hectare) lots, 504 of which were arable.[30] As a result, the population had reportedly reached 342 families by the time of de Lotbinière's death in 1822.[31] The absentee de Lotbinière had come into conflict, however, with those who opposed the construction in 1815 of a road to the new gristmill on the Rivière du Chêne at the western end of the seigneury. This was an important project because land clearances had reduced the flow of the domaine's mill stream, and the gristmill was the main source of seigneurial income. Unfortunately for de Lotbinière, delays in the construction of the road and bridge meant that revenue from his new mill did not cover the interest costs of its construction, and, according to the parish historian, the recalcitrance of the censitaires in paying their rents forced him into a debt of £800 with the local curé.[32] De Lotbinière's heirs would have a total debt of £3,365 to pay off, including £900 to their mother by virtue of her marriage contract and £146 for their father's monument. But the arrears they were owed in rents from the three seigneuries amounted to twice that amount, at £6,620, and the inheritance also included 4,800 acres (1,943 hectares) of freehold land, a house in Montreal, and a building lot near the St Louis gate in Quebec City.[33]

De Lotbinière's will dictated that his estate was to be managed on behalf of his three daughters by the Montreal notary Joseph Papineau, until each reached the age of twenty-five. Although their mother had converted to Catholicism prior to her marriage, two of the daughters would marry English-speaking Protestants.[34] The third, Julie-Christine (whose godparents were both from the seigneurial elite),[35] married a French-speaking Protestant named Gaspard-Pierre-Gustave Joly in 1828, when she was only nineteen years old and he was thirty. An admirer recalled, upon Julie-Christine's death, "I often saw her as a beautiful young lady, in fact an angel floating upon earth. I well remember the morning she was married (almost 59 years ago) how lovely she looked, how bright and happy she appeared. I saw your father also on that occasion ... he wore a beautifully fitting claret colored coat, and looked every inch the gentleman he was."[36] One of French Canada's oldest noble families had, in the formal sense, come to an end, yet the three Chartier de Lotbinière heirs would cling to their seigneurial privileges, and in the case of Mme Joly, those privileges would be exploited more intensively than in the past.

The Joly Legacy

Born in Geneva, Gaspard-Pierre-Gustave Joly was from Épernay in France's Marne department, where his paternal family had established an export business specializing in the wine trade. Affable, wealthy, and well-educated, Joly had highly placed friends, such as the diplomat Napoleon Lannes, Duke of Montebello,[37] and he had proven to be a star attraction in the salons of Montreal. Joly travelled widely on family business, including to Sweden, Poland, Germany, Austria, and England, but he and his wife, Julie-Christine, decided to live in Lower Canada after taking an extended European honeymoon. Before they returned home, their first child, Henri-Gustave, was born in Épernay on December 5, 1829. He would be followed in quick succession in Lower Canada by two sisters, one of whom died in infancy, and two brothers, one of whom died soon after being born while the family was back in France in 1838.[38]

In the meantime, the division of the Chartier de Lotbinière inheritance among the three surviving daughters had been delayed by the requirement for an inspection of the three seigneuries by representatives of all the concerned parties, as well as three arbitrators. Finally, in 1829, the division took place at a meeting in Montreal at which Julie-Christine, who had married with separate property,[39] was legally represented by Joseph Papineau's prominent politician son, Louis-Joseph. The seigneury of Rigaud was 63,504 arpents (25,402 hectares) in size, of which 21,430 arpents (8,572 hectares) had been granted to censitaires, producing an estimated £595 Halifax currency per year in various rents. Vaudreuil was considerably smaller, at 49,392 arpents (19,757 hectares), but the larger number of 25,344 arpents (10,138 hectares) had been granted, producing £675 in rents. Vaudreuil also had several other advantages, including a number of small hay-producing islands, a manor house, and a domaine near the mill and church, making it suitable for subdivision into village lots. As for Lotbinière, it was by far the largest in size at 148,176 arpents (59,270 hectares), of which 452 lots totalling 46,298 arpents (18,519 hectares) had been granted to censitaires with the obligation to pay the relatively low equivalent of £154 per year in wheat and money (plus nine capons). There was also an additional estimated revenue of £125 from the two seigneurial gristmills and an equivalent amount from the *lods et ventes* (sales tax), for a total annual value of £405.[40] Attached to Lotbinière for inheritance purposes was the Quebec City property valued at £800 as well as the obligation to pay £10 per year to the *fabrique* (parish council or vestry) and £50 annually to Mme de Lotbinière, but no part of the succession's other debts.

The strategy adopted was for each of the three parties to bid on the three main properties as they were drawn by lot, and when Lotbinière was drawn first, Julie-Christine was allowed to claim it with no competing bids from her sisters.[41] At face value, this was an odd choice, given how much more arable the other two seigneuries were, as reflected in their rents. But Joly, who was also present at the meeting, presumably appreciated the value of the Lotbinières' still largely untapped timber reserves. According to Surveyor General Joseph Bouchette's report in 1832, Lotbinière was "well stocked with fine elm, ash, maple, beech, plane, wild cherry and other timber: the banks of the rivers du Chêne, Huron and Boisclere [sic] produce pine of first rate growth."[42] A sawmill had been constructed as early as 1716,[43] and Bouchette reported that six were in operation in 1832, but there was still plenty of raw material. A survey completed in 1836 found that on the 83,000 ungranted acres there was a per-acre average of 7,816 feet of pine, 2,993 feet of spruce, and 2,618 feet of hemlock in one-inch boards of first-quality timber, plus a quantity of valuable cedar, ash, birch, tamarack, maple, and second-quality timber that could prove useful for local settlers. The previous year 58,000 spruce trees and 500 pines had been cut within a half mile of the river banks.[44]

Joly may not have had legal ownership of the seigneury, but the marriage contract signed by his wife stated that he would "enjoy the Honorific rights" attached to it. Furthermore, after Joseph Papineau transferred his management rights to Joly and Julie-Christine (her father's will dictated that she would not assume full ownership of her inheritance until she reached the age of twenty-five), she relinquished sole responsibility to her husband.[45] Shortly before Joly and his bride left on their European honeymoon, he announced to the censitaires that he was willing to let bygones be bygones as far as past cutting of wood on the seigneur's property was concerned, but those who continued to do so would be pursued rigorously in court.[46] To ensure that he would have a loyal seigneurial agent, Joly appointed his uncle to the position, but Lieutenant Colonel Fehr de Brunner would become an infirm dependent for most of his remaining fifteen years of life.[47]

Arrears in rents on the Lotbinière seigneury had reached £1,854 by 1828, and the following year the local curé petitioned the government for aid, claiming that of the 300 families in his parish, eighty-three did not have enough grain to last until the next harvest, forty-nine had enough food for only a month, and thirty-four had no means of subsistence.[48] One of Fehr de Brunner's first steps was, nevertheless, to post a notice on the church door inviting debtors to meet with him in order to make arrangements for payment in instalments with products such as hay, straw, potatoes, oats, or cattle.[49] The gristmill on the domaine had to be replaced, and the one on the Rivière du Chêne was also found to be seriously neglected, with the dam having rotted and the large water wheel in ruins, but investments in infrastructure would hardly be profitable during a decade of successive crop failures.[50] To help compensate, Joly began to crack down on those who were cutting trees on ungranted land, announcing as well that for every eleven fish caught, one had to be given to the seigneur.[51]

Having had the bounds of the seigneury surveyed, Joly built a sawmill in 1833 (at a cost of £425) near the gristmill on the Rivière du Chêne, and a larger one a year later (at a cost of £725) near the mouth of the same river, thereby fostering the birth of the village of Leclercville.[52] In 1834, as well, Joly signed a contract with forty-four farmers from Lotbinière and ten from neighbouring Ste Croix to cut more than 20,000 spruce logs on the ungranted part of the seigneury.[53] Each farmer contractor, known as an entrepreneur, was responsible for a distinct territory. An average of 370 logs each is not a large number, but the contractors obviously worked with small crews who spent relatively short periods of time in the woods.[54] By the winter of 1843-4, the number of logs to be cut by forty-one of these contractors had dropped to 13,900,[55] and in 1848 thirty-nine local farmers and their partners were to cut and deliver only 10,000 white spruce logs. The previous year, however, Joly had informed his agent that "le bois ne manque pas" and instructed him to have 30,000 to 40,000 thousand logs cut.[56]

Throughout this period the terms of the contracts remained much the same. No large trees could be left uncut on the excuse that they were too heavy to haul; any logs found to be defective would not be paid for even in part; and those men cutting near the smaller streams had to deliver their logs to the Rivière du Chêne with the first spring floods on pain of a 33 percent reduction in payment. Furthermore, even though the entrepreneurs had to supply their own tools, horses, and provisions, as well as build their own shanties, the contracts treated them like employees by stating that there would be three inspections, or *collages*, from January to March (to ensure that they were maintaining a satisfactory pace of production) and by dictating that at least one man had to be provided for every 400 logs to be floated down the smaller streams. Furthermore, no entrepreneur could agree to drive anyone else's logs downstream unless he had hired someone to do the same for him. Any logs not delivered by the specified date would not be paid for even though the seigneurial agent could have them floated down the river after that date. Two-thirds of the payment would be made after the last inspection and the rest a month after the logs had been dropped in the river, provided all terms of the contract had been fulfilled. Illustrating how crucial the spring drive was, a clause was added in 1849 stating that the seigneurial agent could replace any men he judged to be incapable of the job, at the expense of the entrepreneurs.[57] Finally, as an incentive to keep the streams clear for the drive, Joly also authorized his agent to make small advances to contractors for that purpose.[58]

The rather strict and restrictive terms of Joly's contracts were similar to those imposed on subcontractors by the large timber limit holders in the Mauricie region, where the same system originated in 1835 but remained marginal prior to 1875.[59] These terms also reflect the fact that population pressure on the land was placing Lower Canada's seigneurs in an increasingly dominant position, with the result that they raised rates, added new charges, accepted bribes, sold back rents to debt collectors, and evicted more readily than in the past. Many also began renting land rather than conceding it *en roture* (effectively, in perpetuity for a fixed annual levy) so that by the 1830s approximately 30 percent of the farms in the seigneurial lowlands were under limited-term rental contracts.[60] The Joly family does not appear to have engaged in the latter practice, nor did they exact statute labour on their domain, but they did introduce new charges and protect the lumber resource for themselves. A contract printed in 1830 that remained standard until the end of the seigneurial regime in 1854 imposed a number of onerous requirements on the grantee. The annual *cens et rentes*, in this case for a three- by twenty-five-arpent (thirty-hectare) lot, was three Spanish dollars and three *minots* of wheat. Since the *cens et rentes* charged could not be raised in the future, seigneurs commonly included products such as wheat to protect themselves against inflation. According to the 1831 census report, the average *cens et rente* in Lotbinière was 125 deniers, equivalent to about half a pound currency or two dollars, which was not far below the 131 deniers average for the province as a whole.[61]

Such a small sum would seem not to be a particularly onerous burden, but it was far from the only one. The obligations to clear property lines, erect fences, and dig drainage ditches, as well as allow the construction of roads and bridges, were for the public benefit and could also be found in freehold zones.[62] In addition, however, whenever he sold his *roture* (lot), each censitaire had to pay a sales tax known as the *lods et ventes* (sometimes translated as mutation fine), which amounted to one-twelfth of the price obtained.[63] To ensure that the vendor did not attempt to report a lower price, the seigneur's *droit de retrait* gave him the right to reclaim the property for the reported sale price. Censitaires were also restricted to using the seigneurial (banal) gristmill on pain of having their grain seized and a fine levied. More legally questionable were the Lotbinière clauses stating that no part of the *roture* could be alienated in mortmain, which meant that land could not be sold or bequeathed to the Catholic Church and thereby escape future *lods et ventes*, and that no mills of any kind could be built without the seigneur's written permission, even though there were reportedly six sawmills owned by various individuals in 1814.[64] Indeed, all sites for churches, presbyteries, manors, and public works were also reserved, and there would be no payment to censitaires for any lumber, stone, gravel, lime, or other materials needed for their construction.[65] Mines and quarries (reserved by the Crown during the French regime)[66] were to be the exclusive property of the seigneur, who would enjoy the right of access to such sites without compensation. Furthermore, no oak could be cut, and a later contract stated that no trees of any kind could be sold by a censitaire before establishing residency and improving at least ten arpents (four hectares).[67] Finally, the seigneur reserved the right to hunt and fish on the land that had been granted, but the grantee could not hunt beyond its borders without permission.[68]

Citing seigneurs who "used their holdings to engage in the capitalist adventure," geographer Serge Courville argues that the seigneury "was not a rigid structure but a living organism reacting to the general economic climate" and that it "was a framework for industrial growth."[69] As he admits, however, development under this system of tenure depended heavily on the entrepreneurship of the seigneurs, for they monopolized much of the means of production.[70] In the case of Lotbinière, this control soon led to conflict with the local population, even though Bouchette claimed in 1832 that the "industrious tenants" of Lotbinière were "good cultivators" who produced "abundant crops of grain, etc."[71] When a new *terrier* (seigneurial census) was drafted that same year, and censitaires who were in arrears were taken to court (even though the contracts now stated that failure to pay the *cens et rentes* would result in forfeiture without trial),[72] a number of the censitaires reacted by sending a protest petition to the Legislative Assembly. In a letter published in *Le Canadien*, Joly claimed that a certain unnamed individual, acting as an agent of a committee director from outside the parish, had been going from village to village and house to house with petition in hand, announcing that twenty-eight parishes had joined the crusade against the seigneurs.[73] The focus of the complaints, however, appears to have been Lotbinière, and it was probably no coincidence that Joly asked the Quebec immigration agent that year to send him some British settlers.[74]

According to Joly, the petitioners demanded first that he grant land to all applicants and that the *cens et rentes* be fixed at one to one-and-a-half sols per arpent, with concessions made at a higher rate reduced to that level. Rural resentment of the seigneurs was clearly not confined to the areas near Montreal where the rebellion broke out in 1837, for the Lotbinière petitioners also demanded that the *droit de mouture* (seigneur's gristmill monopoly) and the *lods et ventes* be abolished, that the seigneur be prevented from building sawmills and cutting trees on ungranted land without permission from the censitaires, and that the *droit de retrait* and the exclusive right to hunt and fish (which was not entirely exclusive, as noted previously), as well as other feudal rights, be abolished without compensation.[75] In addition to citing the French government in their favour, the petitioners referred to natural rights, leading Joly to allude to "la foule brutale" and "le droit du plus fort." He then asked whether the members of the Legislative Assembly, having jealously defended the laws and customs guaranteed to the French-speaking population by the English government, would countenance the spoliation of rights that had been uncontested for centuries, rights as clear and positive as human laws and the passage of time could sanction. Resorting to the nationalist argument favoured by his prominent Patriote friend, Louis-Joseph Papineau, Joly asked if the legislators did not fear that "en sapant nos institutions par leur base" the entire edifice would fall on their heads.[76] The fact was, however, that Joly had no particular interest in the seigneury as an institution. Three years later, in 1835, he had the large tract granted by Governor Frontenac, which was known as the Augmentation of Lotbinière and officially estimated at £8,643.12s in value, commuted to freehold tenure (it would later be known as Joly township, at least informally). In fact, Joly would have done the same for the entire seigneury had it not been for the prohibitive costs involved.[77]

Meanwhile, a special committee of the Legislative Assembly chaired by the prominent Patriote A. N. Morin proceeded with an inquiry into the petition of the Lotbinière censitaires, as well as the situation in several other seigneuries.[78] Witnesses complained that Joly illegally charged premiums (*pots-de-vin*) for land grants, dispossessed without compensation those who had made improvements as squatters, and refused to grant land in certain areas while charging exorbitant *cens et rentes* in others. The local surveyor noted, however, that the *pots-de-vin* were required only for previously settled lots, which would be reasonable considering their greater value, and that the *cens et rentes* for the settled lots were the same as for unimproved lots. In addition, Joly claimed that during the previous three months he had granted and promised to grant more than fifty lots, including to some of the signatories to the petition.[79] He also argued that the annual charge of only one louis (one pound or four dollars) for sixty excellent arpents (twenty-four hectares), half in grain and half in money, meant that by selling the eggs from three or four hens during the summer, a censitaire could pay for a lot that would support him and his family, as well as provide for his heirs. Finally, he claimed, grantees were allowed to take several years before beginning their payments.

Witnesses also complained that the seigneur was cutting serviceable timber on unconceded lands, to which Joly replied that he had the right to do so and that logs had not been taken from settled parts of the seigneury. Furthermore, Joly argued, hundreds of habitants had asked him for employment in his *chantiers* and expressed satisfaction with the opportunity to earn wages during the dead season of winter. Joly also argued that the timber reserves required by each deed until ten arpents (four hectares) were improved were not for his benefit, but for that of the censitaires themselves; claimants in neighbouring seigneuries sometimes destroyed all the serviceable timber, leaving no building materials for the individuals who subsequently purchased the land from them with the intention of settling on it. Joly added that the petitioners had nothing to complain about as far as the two gristmills were concerned, for during the previous two years he had invested several thousand pounds in order to ensure that they were in good order, and there were none better in the neighbouring seigneuries. Responding to the complaint that the roads were impassable, Joly declared that he had built a road at his own expense to the new concessions and asked sarcastically whether the petitioners expected that from the single sol per arpent they deigned to pay for their land each year, the seigneur should repair their roads and contribute to "leur paresse et à leur incurie." As for the banal rights, the *droit de retrait*, the right of fishing and hunting, and so on, Joly simply added that these were not unique to Lotbinière but were the general law of the country.[80]

The seigneurial committee ended its labours by making no recommendations, blaming the failure of the governor general to provide certain important documents and pointing to the sensitivity of the property rights issue. Despite their protest, 503 of the Lotbinière censitaires settled with the seigneur in April 1836 for a total of £798 in back payments,[81] but economic conditions and the political climate were not favourable as the colony moved towards rebellion. Julie-Christine had recently granted Joly full power to administer her affairs,[82] and he confided to his father in France the same year that he had decided to sell the seigneury. He auctioned off all the livestock and equipment on the seigneurial farm in June 1836, before departing for Paris to escape what Papineau claimed were "des attaques injustes dans des gazettes uniquement parce qu'il était seigneur."[83] The family remained there for several years, and even though Joly had supported the moderate John Neilson in his break with Papineau, this did not cause ill feelings between him and the fiery Patriote leader.[84] In fact, Joly carried letters back and forth from Paris to Lower Canada for the Papineaus when they went into exile, and the two families socialized with each other regularly during the early 1840s when the Jolys were living in the same house as their friend, the famous liberal philosopher Félicité de Lamennais.[85]

What business activities Joly was involved in while in Paris is not known, but his correspondence makes no reference to the wine business that was managed by his brother, Moïse-Salomon.[86] Purportedly to improve his health but obviously also because it offered the opportunity to assert his will in what was becoming an increasingly uncertain world from his perspective,[87] Pierre-Gustave travelled alone to Greece and the Middle East in 1839–40. Not only did he write a perceptive and unsentimental travel narrative,[88] but as one of the first persons to purchase a complete set of Louis J. M. Daguerre's image-imprinting equipment, and having signed a contract with the famous Paris optician Noël Paymal Lerebours, Joly produced ninety-two daguerreotypes during his travels. These included the first such image of the Parthenon as well as images of the Sphinx, the Cheops pyramid, the Colossus of Memnon in Egypt, the city of Jerusalem, the Dead Sea, and several scenes in Lebanon. While in Upper Egypt, Joly transported the more than 100 pounds of equipment by *dahabeah* (Nile river boat) and donkey. Lerebours reproduced several of Joly's daguerreotypes in the book titled *Excursions daguerriennes: Vues et monuments les plus remarquables du globe,* and the French architect Hector Horeau also published several engravings from Joly's images in *Panorama d'Égypte et de Nubie.* Modernizing as the technology was, the aim was to preserve a visual memory of ancient sites that were threatened by natural catastrophe and souvenir hunters.[89] Joly's pioneering photographs and interest in exotic countries earned him an invitation to join the recently established Société Orientale in 1843.[90]

Joly had spared no expense on his Middle Eastern journey, sailing first class and staying in the best hotels available,[91] but before departing on another lengthy journey in 1841, he provided his wife with a detailed financial statement in which he reported that he had lost more than half his fortune that same year. And he added that if he died before returning, it would be difficult for her to acquire more than a small part of what remained. His still-considerable assets amounted to 171,674 francs or approximately $41,200 in Canadian currency of the time.[92] Aside from the 70,000 francs tied up in the lumber business, Joly claimed against the estate the 10,000 francs he had paid the Crown to convert part of the seigneury into freehold tenure in 1825, plus 35,000 francs as the value of the large sawmill he had built at the Rivière du Chêne and 15,000 francs for the sawmill at the Portage. Joly had also paid 8,000 francs to purchase land from three censitaires in order to create the farm on the 360-arpent (144-hectare) seigneurial domaine, as well as smaller amounts of money for land attached to the mills. Finally, he expected to inherit 20,000 francs from his father. For reasons that are not clear, Joly did not claim the money he had invested in the gristmills as a debt owed him by the seigneury, but nearly half of his claimed assets were debts owed by his wife for investments he had made in the property. The only debt he owed at the time was 6,000 francs to his sister.

Joly counselled that in the case of his death the sawmill business be liquidated because even though careful management could result in profits as high as 40,000 francs a year, its speculative nature meant that it could also entail serious losses. One advantage to closing the mills would be that the seigneury's forests would gain in value more quickly, and Joly advised that strict conservation measures be enforced to protect them. Finally, he noted that all his movable assets belonged to his wife by marriage contract (it actually specified only the household furniture, carriages, horses, and other personal items), and that she was also entitled to a *douaire* (in fact, it was an annuity) of £200 (4,200 francs) per year.[93] For the sake of their heirs, however, he asked her to remember the pressure he had been under to agree to this condition and to remember that she had promised to take into consideration the enormous sacrifices he had made to increase the revenues of her seigneury. He also reminded her that he could have mortgaged the property in order to raise the sums invested but had used his own money instead.[94] As a result, a seigneury that was now worth a million francs owed only the £800 (17,000 francs) that had been borrowed by her father. The value of the seigneury lay primarily in its forests, for the rents brought in only 12,000 to 13,000 francs a year, and the censitaires were 30,000 to 40,000 francs in arrears. Julie-Christine also still owned the three-and-a-half-arpent (1.4-hectare) property by the St Louis gate in Quebec City that Joly valued at 25,000 francs. He claimed that in the current circumstances he did not have the courage to make a will, but he added that if he survived, he hoped to be able to ensure a better future for their children. Should he not return, Joly counselled his wife to see, above all, to their education, not allowing her expenditures to jeopardize their future and not forgetting him for another.[95]

Joly was obviously restless in Paris. His otherwise rather non-reflexive Middle Eastern travel journal had concluded with a candid self-appraisal that suggests a complex and somewhat mercurial personality: "Mélancolique par habitude, gai par contact. Opiniâtre parfois, faible souvent. Assez bon jugement, peu d'esprit, froid mais sensible." Reflecting his dissatisfaction with himself and his current position, Joly added, "Assez bon prince, du reste, mais sans carrière, sans avenir; tournant dans un cercle, non pas des vices, mais vicieux. Qui peut aimer un pareil être?"[96] To renew his sense of purpose, and despite his plea of poverty to his wife, Joly became involved in a speculative French

Guiana colonization project during the early 1840s. Jules Lechevalier and several others had acquired an 18,000-hectare land grant from the colonial government in 1839 on condition that their company drain, clear, and cultivate 300 hectares a year until 6,000 hectares had been improved. Joly and the wealthy collector, historian, and bibliographer Henri Ternaux-Compans[97] joined forces with Lechevalier in 1843 after the latter had decided to take advantage of the French government's desire to discover how best to mitigate the economic impact of the inevitable emancipation of its plantation colony slaves. Each of the three partners of the Société d'études pour la colonisation de la Guyanne française was to invest 100,000 francs on the understanding that the French government would contribute 200,000 francs. The society was to exist for only five years, and the three partners would receive only 5 percent annually plus expenses on their investment (only Lechevalier would receive a salary), for the ultimate altruistic aim was to launch a land company owned principally by the colonists themselves.[98]

According to a letter written by Louis-Joseph Papineau to his wife in 1843, however, Joly soon became impatient with the delays and decided to return to Canada (leaving Henri-Gustave behind to attend school) instead of remaining involved in the project.[99] As a result, the Guianian society's contract was terminated several months after it was established, with Lechevalier owing Joly the sum of 2,066 francs.[100] The experience did not entirely crush Joly's colonialist enthusiasm, however, for in 1845 he became a titular (that is, fourth-class) member of the Paris-based Institut d'Afrique, an organization whose goal was "de protéger, d'éclairer et d'émanciper la race africaine" and to promote commerce and industry as well as the arts, letters, and sciences in that continent.[101]

But Joly's principal goal now was to increase the value of the Lotbinière seigneury sufficiently to make a profitable sale and then resettle in one of the French provinces in two or three years' time.[102] He had a close relationship with his mother and sister, and Julie-Christine had been far from eager to return to her homeland, but they felt that they needed to make the sacrifice for the sake of their children's future.[103] Joly's mother made it clear in the letter Papineau carried to him in Canada in 1845 that she relied on him, given that he had a brother overloaded with family business responsibilities, and a somewhat reckless sister. Madame Joly added that she would have sent him a cargo of the latest brochures on political, scientific, and industrial matters, "mais je puis espérer que ma chère Julie, et ma bonne et gentille Amélie [Joly's daughter] se chargeront plus agréablement que tous nos savants accademiques [*sic*] de faire passer les heures froides et sombres du Canada."[104]

Joly now directed his considerable energies towards improving Lotbinière, socially as well as economically. In 1845 he offered to build a parish school (an offer that was gratefully accepted by the local school commissioners) and also organized the First Battalion of the Lotbinière county militia.[105] During the following two years he built two new gristmills at a cost of £420, as well as a thirty-foot public wharf at Pointe Platon (site of the future manor house) at a cost of £300 plus the timber.[106] He also granted permission for a local farmer to build a sawmill on the Rivière Bois Clair, specifying that the farmer was to ensure that none of the logs would be from the ungranted land of the seigneury.[107] But much of his energy was devoted to boosting north shore railway construction from Upper Canada to Quebec City, and to the rather impractical idea of having the future south shore line terminate at Pointe Platon where freight and passengers would be transported across the St Lawrence to Portneuf, which would be linked by rail to Quebec City. The option of extending the south-shore line to Lévis, he warned, would cause the old capital to be completely eclipsed by Montreal and ports on the Atlantic coast.[108] This is, in effect, what happened after the south shore line was built from Richmond in the Eastern Townships to Lévis, passing a mile and a half south of the Lotbinière boundary and becoming part of the Grand Trunk Railway in 1854. But Joly and his son, Henri-Gustave, continued throughout the 1850s to defend Quebec City's interests by promoting what became known as the North Shore Railway.[109]

Energetic as Joly's promotional efforts may have been, they failed to sustain the good relations that he had briefly established with the local community. Although he had supplied most of the lumber for the new church at the Rivière Bois Clair, the parish priest clashed with him over the issue of alms collectors in 1847,[110] and that same year, in his capacity as president of the Grand Jury, Joly reported that the countryside was plagued by thefts, murders, pillages, arson, and acts of violence that always went unpunished. Justices of the peace, he claimed, were feeble, timid, ignorant, and motivated by self-interest. To support his charges, he cited the case of an unknown vagrant who had died in the home of a local farmer and who, according to Joly, had been treated in an inhumane manner by the doctor, the curé, and the captain of militia.[111] Joly appears to have been suggesting that outsiders such as himself were mistrusted by the Canadians, a theme dealt with a century later in Germaine Guèvremont's classic rural Quebec novel *Le Survenant*. The increasingly alienated Joly was clearly in the habit of unburdening himself to his mother, who wrote in 1846 that she could resign herself to never seeing him again if only she could believe he were happy and contented, but "la maladie, les mécontentes, les soucis et les peines de tout genres te poursuivent."[112]

Joly crossed the Atlantic with Julie-Christine and their daughter for an extended visit in the fall of 1847,[113] but relations did not improve with the people of Lotbinière. The following year his seigneurial agent clashed with the municipal council over the construction of a road in the seigneury, arguing that it would injure the seigneur's logging business.[114] Due partially, no doubt, to his authoritarianism, and partially to his alien national and religious status, Joly suffered the indignity in 1852 of the removal and smashing of the seigneurial pew. An official inquiry failed to uncover the identity of the culprits, and following Joly's complaints to the bishop, the *fabrique* passed a motion condemning the action. But it also moved that since seigneurs no longer had the right to such a distinction in churches (which was clearly not the case), the pew would not be replaced. Furthermore, the curé was authorized to hire a lawyer to support this motion, if necessary. At the bishop's urging, however, a subsequent meeting disavowed, by a vote of seventeen to nine, the second and third resolutions and voted to replace the seigneurial pew at the *fabrique*'s expense. Three years later, after the seigneurial system and all associated honorary rights had been legally abolished, the same body was quick to pass a motion stating that the contested pew should be removed, but the Joly family was still refusing to relinquish it formally in 1907, though they did grant the use of it to the curé and his successors.[115]

Meanwhile, before going to Paris, Joly had reportedly left instructions for a large manor house to be built near the gristmill on the Rivière du Chêne, which was the economic centre of the seigneury. Even though there had been a manor as early as 1677, the Joly family had apparently been occupying a modest house owned by one of the censitaires. Joly disapproved, however, of the new manor's low-lying location when he returned home, and in 1851 he built another one in Ste Croix, just beyond the eastern boundary of the Lotbinière seigneury, on the elevated site known as Pointe Platon. Joly had built a wharf at this site, as noted previously, but the house was clearly an extravagant expenditure; between 1850 and 1853 Julie-Christine borrowed £4,200 in four separate instalments from the Portneuf seigneur, Edward Hale.[116] In choosing this site the Jolys were conforming to the current bourgeois Parisian penchant for building country houses with attractive views and health-giving properties such as sunlight, moving water, and fresh breezes.[117] Now restored as a historic site, Maple House conforms to the pictur-esque neoclassical style that characterized a number of the villas then being constructed on the outskirts of Quebec City.[118] It was painted light grey rather than white to blend in more with the surrounding environ-ment,[119] and its numerous front-facing windows and two-level wrap-around verandas trimmed with lacy frieze adorned with maple leaves (for which the house was named) offered a commanding view of the St Lawrence as well as a close connection with the large garden, with its lawn, meandering stream, pond, shrubbery, and flowering perennials. Like the landed estates of Britain, then, Maple House looked out on a carefully designed picturesque view that symbolized the naturalness of noble property.[120]

Physical attractiveness and healthful advantages aside, the choice of a building site beyond the border of the seigneury was a strong indi-cator that, in contrast to the resident seigneurs examined by historian Benoît Grenier, Joly had little interest in cultivating close relations with the censitaires.[121] There would be ongoing friction concerning the loca-tion of the new parish church, with the seigneur wanting it close to the new manor and with the curé and bishop preferring a site that was more accessible to the majority of the parishioners. Grenier identifies the Jolys as resident seigneurs as of 1850,[122] but it is not clear how much time they spent each year in Lotbinière. Joly travelled extensively, they depended on a seigneurial agent, and the manor house appears to have been designed for summer residence only, a practice then becoming popular with the bourgeoisie as well as seigneurs.[123]

Without a detailed examination of the seigneurial management of Lotbinière, it is impossible to judge the degree to which the landhold-ing system was oppressive on the one hand or utilitarian on the other, to use Grenier's contrasting terms. Grenier suggests that the seigneurs who lived on their seigneuries (never more than 39 percent of the total) did play an active role in their development and that the censitaires – led by local notables such as the notary, captain of militia, and village merchant – did not tolerate failure to provide services such as a prop-erly functioning gristmill. In short, Grenier argues, the seigneuries with resident seigneurs were neither the idyllic communities with paternal-istic lords of the manor and deferential peasants that romantic memoir-ists such as Philippe Aubert de Gaspé and Robert de Roquebrune have described nor the increasingly oppressive and conflict-ridden societies depicted in the more recent Marxist-influenced studies of Louise Dechêne, Allan Greer, and others.[124]

As for Lotbinière, Pierre-Gustave Joly's continued promotion of local economic development failed to earn the gratitude of his censitaires.[125] In 1854 he became involved with the company formed to build and operate the steamboat that would connect Lotbinière with Quebec City,[126] but that did not prevent the local circulation of a petition that claimed the seigneurial system was "un obstacle à l'industrie du peuple, à l'avancement du pays, et au développement de ses ressources," one that forced the youth of the province to emigrate to the United States. In particular, the petitioners complained that the "droit de retrait est un grief insupportable" and that the "droit de banalité paralyse l'industrie canadienne." They also claimed that some seigneurs charged an extra fee for land grants, so that the *cens et rentes* had risen from two sols per arpent to as much as twenty sols, though they were not referring to Lotbinière in particular. Rather than compulsory commutation, which it claimed would be ruinous without explaining why, the petition advocated the reduction of rents to their original level and voluntary commutation on the part of the censitaires. How this approach would end the mill site monopoly that the petition claimed was suppressing industrial development was not made clear.[127]

Contrary to Grenier's model, tensions between seigneur and censitaires actually increased in Lotbinière after the seigneur became more visible and more active. Grenier does suggest, however, that such tensions were more typical of seigneuries owned by members of the nobility than those owned by commoners, who tended to intermarry with the local population.[128] Joly may not have been from a noble family, but he had married into one and he was also a foreign Protestant, so the social chasm between him and the censitaires was even wider than in the case of the old Canadian nobility. But even as a nonresident for extended periods of time, Joly – representing his wife and, later, his son – was more of a utilitarian improver than he was a parasitical *rentier*. In contrast to the seigneurs of Sainte-Anne de la Pérade and Beauharnois, for example, he did not hold land back from settlement in anticipation of commutation to freehold tenure.[129] He also took steps to ensure that the seigneury was well managed by a succession of resident Swiss agents during his extended absences. In 1847, for example, Joly drafted instructions that "rien ne doit se passer dans mes chantiers, et peu de choses dans ma seigneurie, sans que vous en ayez connaissance." He added that not only should everything that needed doing be done "promptement et *desuite*," but also the agent should foresee and prepare for everything that would need doing, keeping Joly informed of all his activities. Above all, he was to execute all of Joly's orders "*à la lettre*."[130]

Lotbinière is clearly an example of how the seigneurial system was not as incompatible with capitalist production as historians of rural Quebec once assumed.[131] Like his contemporary Barthélemy Joliette, who established the sawmill village of L'Industrie, Pierre-Gustave Joly was a "seigneur entrepreneur," to use historian Jean-Claude Robert's term.[132] Furthermore, unlike the seigneur of L'Isle Verte Louis Bertrand who felt compelled to enter into a partnership with timber magnates Price and Caldwell in order to lessen his financial risk, Joly injected considerable capital into the local economy from across the Atlantic.[133] Although Joliette and Bertrand lived in their villages, however, Joly's ambitions were more focused on the wider world, and he was ultimately less interested in commerce and industry than in science and technology. His Middle Eastern travel journal is more preoccupied with innovations than with antiquities, he claimed to be able to effect cures through electromagnetism, and he won honourable mention at the New York Industry of the Nations exhibition of 1853 for his vegetable fibre prepared from milkweed (*asclepias Canadensis*).[134] In 1845 his mother had written in jest that a Paris museum owner wished him to acquire "une des Montagnes Rocheuses, un ours de tes Forêts ou au moins un Jambon, un pied mignon d'Entilope ou une chevelure de Huron," and in 1860 and 1861 he investigated the possibility of introducing yaks to Canada as well as furnishing plants and animals to Paris's newly established Jardin d'acclimatation, which supplied him with Algerian melon seeds.[135] In December 1861 he was appointed Quebec delegate of the Société impériale zoologique d'acclimatation.[136]

Conclusion

Although he inherited his business sense and political liberalism from his father, Henri-Gustave Joly's social identity and status were bestowed by his mother's side of the family, a family that had been at or near the peak of the ruling elite since the early days of New France. It was only after Julie-Christine Chartier de Lotbinière married a Protestant foreigner, however, that Lotbinière was effectively exploited as a source of capital and, as we shall see, only when their eldest son

Henri-Gustave took over its ownership that it became a base for political power. As Christian Dessureault has pointed out, assessments of the post-Conquest seigneurial system have been strongly influenced by political ideology, with neo-nationalist liberals arguing that it was not incompatible with modernization, anti-nationalist liberals claiming that it perpetuated an Ancien-Regime 'mentalité' and hindered the development of capitalism, and Marxists stressing the exploitation of the peasant families.[137] The preceding chapter includes evidence that might support each of these conflicting interpretations, but the fact remains that it and the chapters that follow support Daniel Salée's judgment that Quebec historians have been too quick to assume that "the appearance of capitalistic productive forces and the extension of the market economy immediately tolled the bell of the traditional social order."[138]

Michel-Eustache-Gaspard-Alain Chartier de Lotbinière, grandfather of Henri-Gustave Joly. Bibliothèque et Archives nationales du Québec, P1000, S4, D83, PC63–2.

Julie-Christine Chartier de Lotbinière around the time of her
marriage. Bibliothèque et Archives nationales du Québec,
P1000, S4, D83, PJ10–1.

Pierre-Gustave Joly as a young man. Domaine Joly de Lotbinière Collection.

Portage gristmill and dam built by Pierre-Gustave Joly. Domaine Joly de Lotbinière Collection.

Pointe Platon by Henri-Gustave Joly de Lotbinière. There are people on the dock awaiting the approaching steamboat. Domaine Joly de Lotbinière Collection.

Chapter Two

Family Man

Henri-Gustave Joly corresponded regularly with widely scattered relatives, responding to pleas for assistance in some cases and inviting even those in France to serve as godparents for his children.[1] He also appears to have had a close relationship with his mother and father, if not with his sister and brother, though most of his youth was spent apart from his parental family while he attended school in Paris. Both Joly's siblings as well as his mother came into conflict with his rather strict and restless father, but he enjoyed warm and affectionate ties with his own wife and children, sons as well as daughters.[2] The eldest son became Joly's business partner, and in keeping with the family heritage and Joly's imperialist sympathies, the other two became British military engineers. Not all the four daughters had happy marriages, but they did marry into the same tight social network, and they did maintain a close bond with Joly throughout his life.

Parental Family Relations

It appears that Joly's parents had become estranged by 1861, when his mother gave him full possession of the Lotbinière estate.[3] His father, responding to pleas from his own aged mother, finally returned to Paris in 1865, where he died a few months later.[4] Julie-Christine was not left in financial need, however, for her marriage contract had stipulated that in lieu of dower she would receive a £200 annuity after her husband's death. As the only surviving son, Henri-Gustave assumed this obligation[5] and also made annual payments to his sister Amélie, who had separated from the rather irresponsible British officer Henry George Savage several years after their marriage in 1855. Amélie would spend her last years in France with her only daughter, who followed the example of her Bingham first cousins by marrying into the French nobility.[6]

Edmond, the younger brother of Henri-Gustave and Amélie, had been killed as a young man after following a career path that conformed to the more traditional aristocratic pattern of libertine masculinity. Upon completing his education at the Quebec Seminary and in Paris, Edmond-Gustave joined the Thirty-Second British Infantry in India in 1850, at which time he made it clear to his mother that he was anxious to prove himself: "In a few months I will be sent to a campaign; combat, glory, honour, that is what I aspire to. Happy times, Oh! Approach. But if instead of this beautiful future it is the contrary. If instead of advances in combat, I retreat; instead of glory, shame; instead of honours, cowardice. But no, given the exaltation I feel, simply in thinking of it, I cannot conduct myself thus. Impossible." ("Dans quelques mois je vais être envoyé dans une campagne; combat, gloire, honneur, voilà à quoi j'aspire. Temps heureux, Oh! Approche. Mais au lieu de ce bel avenir si c'était tout le contraire. Si au lieu d'avances au combat; je reculais; au lieu de la gloire la honte, au lieu des honneurs; la lâcheté. Mais non, à l'exaltation que j'éprouve, seulement en y pensant je ne peux pas me conduire ainsi. Impossible.")[7]

The impetuous Edmond-Gustave had a troubled relationship with his father, who was rather belatedly proud enough of him to submit a posthumous entry to Morgan's *Dictionary of Canadian Biography*. According to this account, Edmond had found no chance to distinguish himself during the relatively peaceful early 1850s, apart from a few skirmishes with hostile frontier tribes.[8] Pierre-Gustave did describe one adventure, however, that illustrates Edmond's desire to impress him. Coming upon a high monument popularly believed to have been erected by Alexander the Great over the bones of his warhorse, Bucephalus, Edmond emulated his father's colonialist exploits by scaling the monument with ropes and dropping inside the opening, only to find nothing of interest. Soon afterward, while he was galloping across the countryside, he suddenly came to a ravine so wide that his horse failed to survive the jump. Having already angered the local tribesmen with his lack of respect toward the monument, Edmond symbolically appropriated the Bucephalus legend by having his horse's body dropped through the hole at its apex.[9]

Although it has been assumed that no French Canadian fought in the Crimean War,[10] Edmond Joly was an exception (despite being only one-quarter French Canadian by blood). On his way home to enjoy a two-year leave in 1855, he decided to serve as a volunteer with the Buffs and later with the Connaught Rangers during the siege of Sebastopol. His goal in volunteering for service there, he claimed, was to gain the promotion he felt he deserved after his active service in India and to regain the respect of his father. Edmond wrote from Aden in 1855 that his father had accused him of being "un menteur, un voleur presque, et pour finir un lâche!!" – adding that he would soon be in the place that he was accused of avoiding, perhaps joining the hundreds of soldiers who were dying daily.[11] A few days later from Alexandria, Edmond addressed Pierre-Gustave: "And you, my dear father, adieu; may you soon change your opinion about me in learning one day that to my beautiful phrases and promises I can add action, and may you one day regret having accused me of dishonouring your name." ("Et toi, mon cher père adieu; puisses-tu bientôt avoir changé d'opinion à mon égard en apprenant un jour qu'à mes belles phrases et promesses j'y puis ajouter l'action, et puisses-tu un jour regretter de m'avoir accusé de déshonorer ton nom.")[12] Edmond was soon in the trenches of Balaclava, complaining that one had to be a noble or have very high connections to be promoted in the British army and stating that he was determined to have the commanding officers take notice of him.[13] He survived nearly two months on the Crimean front, but a fever caused him to miss the major battle at Sebastopol and therefore a chance for promotion.

From France, Edmond's aunt – who had commented earlier about how he had been led astray by his wealthy young friends – wrote that she hoped he would be a consolation to his father: "La vie dure qu'il a menée a mûri son jugement et ses sentimens sont excellents. S'il y a encore un peu de légerité [sic] à craindre, c'est un défaut qui se corrige avec l'âge." ("The hard life that he has led has ripened his judgement and his feelings are excellent. If there is still a little lightness to fear, it's a fault that will correct itself with age.")[14] But the charming young lieutenant had become a popular figure in Paris society, being chosen by the empress on one occasion to dance a cotillion and indulging in flirtations with high-placed married women at court before returning to India to join his regiment in 1857.[15] The so-called Indian Mutiny broke out before Edmond-Gustave reached the subcontinent,[16] but his late arrival only spurred him to make a heroic, indeed foolhardy, 700-mile cross-country journey by himself from Calcutta through the rebellious countryside. His journal describes in detail how, after former governor general of

British North America Lord Elgin had refused to grant him permission to proceed on his dangerous mission, he had managed to reach the detachment at Allahabad that was to join General Henry Havelock at Cawnpore. This was where the wives and children of soldiers in Edmond's Thirty-Second Regiment had been massacred, but his luck ran out in the street fight that followed the siege laid by the remaining officers of his regiment at Lucknow.[17] Despite the fact that this operation gripped the British popular imagination, the young Joly failed to gain the fame that he was seeking, for his heroic death at the age of twenty-five appears to have gone largely unnoticed in his home province.[18]

Bourgeois as the Joly side of the family may have been, it also appears to have had a military tradition, for as noted in chapter 1, Pierre-Gustave's uncle, Fehr de Brunner, was a retired lieutenant colonel when he became the seigneury's estate manager. Furthermore, Pierre-Gustave Joly was himself appointed major in the First Battalion of Lotbinière County in 1830.[19] If the Joly de Lotbinière family was at all typical, then, it would appear that the military ethos of the French-Canadian nobility did not dissolve as quickly as historian Roch Legault has assumed.[20] Henri-Gustave may have been a sharp contrast to his younger brother in that he conformed to the more conventional Victorian-era model of family-centred masculinity, but he supported British imperialism, and as we shall see, two of his sons attended the Royal Military College, and two of his daughters married British military officers. Finally, in keeping with his own military bearing, Henri-Gustave enjoyed playing the role of rugged outdoorsman when, as seigneur, he strapped on his snowshoes to inspect his forests and to supervise the dangerous spring log drives.

Growing up in Paris, Henri-Gustave Joly did not feel the oppressive weight of his father's expectations and demands to the same degree as his younger brother, Edmond. He did, however, spend a good deal of time with his paternal grandmother and aunt while attending the recently established Keller Institute, the first Protestant school in France since the revocation of the Edict of Nantes in 1685. His report cards from 1842 to 1849 were issued by the Collège royal Saint-Louis, which became the Lycée Monge in 1848 and was affiliated with the Université de France. Joly was apparently a good but not outstanding student, generally receiving seconds in history, Latin, German, English, Greek, and philosophy.[21]

In the first surviving letter home, apparently written in 1846 when he was seventeen years old, Joly thanked his father for sending him on a very pleasurable voyage to Geneva with his cousin, where they had narrowly missed a major riot. He also enclosed the first part of his travel journal, thereby following Pierre-Gustave's example of recording his observations while sight-seeing.[22] In forwarding an inventory of his expenses, which greatly exceeded the limit set by his father, Henri-Gustave's aunt noted that this list did not include the small gifts he had purchased for his mother and sister or the great many cigars he had smoked, a habit he shared with his father.[23] Although he had brought 200 cigars back to Paris, Henri-Gustave had promised his aunt that he would smoke only on Sundays, a somewhat surprising statement given their Calvinist beliefs. He was now attending Madame Keller's three weekly soirées, speaking only English at one and only German at another and discussing religion at the third. There was also the opportunity to flirt with the young women of the Keller family and to enjoy Madame Keller's tea and cakes. The aim, according to Madame Keller, was to create a stronger bond with the students and to habituate them "un peu au monde." The young Joly admitted that he was only fifteenth in his class at this point, but his aunt explained that he had just started and that more effort would be made to improve his mathematics.[24] Henri-Gustave reported, himself, the same year that he had come fifth in German, second in history, and second in Latin. To demonstrate his manliness to his father, he added that he was now being given difficult horses to ride and that he enjoyed being on a mount "qui ne se fâche pas quand on lui donne un coup de cravache." Furthermore, he hoped to report in his next letter that he was going to the cold baths.[25]

Joly appears to have flourished socially if not academically in Paris, his grandmother writing on one occasion that he was "gai comme un oiseau en Liberté."[26] Although the Jolys were members of Paris's Reformed Church, it is rather doubtful that young Henri-Gustave was "profoundly affected by an austere and inflexible religious climate," as historian Marcel Hamelin assumed.[27] He attended the theatre in Paris and also took painting lessons long enough to become a skilled water colourist,[28] and the letters of his grandmother and other French relatives do not reflect the obsession with spiritual matters that one would expect of strict Protestants. When he married the Anglican Margaretta Josepha (known as Lucy) Gowen in 1856, Joly's eighty-seven-year-old grandmother wrote from Paris that he appeared to love his new wife so much that she loved her as well, "de tout mon coeur."[29]

After receiving his bachelor of letters degree from the Université de France in 1849,[30] Henri-Gustave returned home to article in law, passing

the bar exam in 1855.[31] He had begun assuming ownership of the seigneury in stages as early as 1851, but he still reported property-related
activities to his father, also relying on him to back up his orders.[32] With
the lumber industry recovering, and with the generous indemnity from
the seigneurial commutation (examined in chapter 3), the Jolys were in
a good position to sell their property and return to Europe, but perhaps
partly because of Henri-Gustave's return and marriage, and partly out
of grief for Edmond, Julie-Christine decided to remain at home. She
refused to bow to her husband's wishes, granting the former seigneury
to Henri-Gustave instead in 1860.[33]

Not surprisingly, Henri-Gustave was devoted to his mother, and out
of respect for her religious affiliation, he asked the local priest to say 100
low masses after her death in 1887.[34] Also, because her death marked
the end of the Chartier de Lotbinière line, Joly took steps soon afterward
to have "de Lotbinière" added to his family name.[35] In congratulating
him on the Legislative Council's unanimous vote in favour of the petition, Judge J.B. Caron expressed his pleasure that "un des fiers noms
de notre ancienne mère-patrie" would be carried on.[36] Pierre-Gustave
had occasionally appropriated the suffix himself, but Henri-Gustave
objected when his eldest son's mother-in-law ordered greeting cards
for her daughter that dropped the name Joly. He wrote that they could
not stop people from calling them simply de Lotbinière, "but it would
be a want of delicacy and self respect to assume it."[37] This was not only
a legal matter to Henri-Gustave, then, but also a recognition that family
inheritance was considered to pass largely through the male line.[38]

The Domestic Circle

Although Henri-Gustave Joly's correspondence with his father was
invariably respectful, he did defy Pierre-Gustave's wishes in marrying Lucy Gowen. The objection was presumably not based on Henri-
Gustave's conversion to his new wife's Church of England (though he
was still listed as a Calvinist in the 1871 dominion census), for the elder
Joly had himself been recorded as an Anglican when his son Edmond
was baptized in Montreal.[39] And Pierre-Gustave was certainly no religious bigot, for one of his closest friends was a Jesuit, and his daughter
was raised in the Catholic faith.[40] But it appears that Joly disapproved
of Lucy's family, even though her father, Hammond Gowen, was a
prominent merchant whom his contemporary Philippe-Joseph Aubert
de Gaspé referred to as "one of the oldest most respected citizens of

Quebec."[41] It is perhaps telling, however, that Pierre-Gustave Joly had no close ties with English Canadians.

Henri-Gustave may have avoided courting young Catholic women, given that the tensions between his parents were doubtless exacerbated by their religious differences, and elite French-Canadian parents may have disapproved of him as a match for their daughters during that era of ultramontane ascendancy. In any case, his marriage to Lucy was clearly a love match, which was the norm for the seigneurial nobility.[42] Their first child, Julia Josepha, was born less than two years after their marriage, and when their son, Edmond Gustave, followed a year later, Joly wrote to his father:

> Il est énorme ... & a une voix d'un développement extraordinaire. Quand à sa physionomie, ne le dit pas à maman, mais je crois qu'il ressemble à Voltaire, ou à son père quand il est né; c'est à dire qu'il n'est pas beau, pour le moment, mais nous le trouvons charmant. Lucy est bien mieux que je n'espérais, mais très faible, comme de raison. Elle a beaucoup plus souffert que la première fois, avant la naissance de l'enfant; j'espère que tout se compensera, & qu'elle souffrira moins après.[43]

> (He is enormous ... & has an extraordinarily developed voice. As for his physiognomy, don't tell maman, but I believe that he resembles Voltaire, or his father when he was born; that is to say, he is not handsome, for the moment, but we find him charming. Lucy is much better than I had hoped, but very weak, as to be expected. She suffered much more than the first time, before the birth of the child; I hope that in compensation she will suffer less afterward.)

It is not known whether members of the old French-Canadian elite generally continued to have large families in the Victorian era when the urban bourgeoisie were beginning to practice birth control, but it is certainly striking that there were a total of eleven recorded Joly births and at least one miscarriage, though only seven offspring survived early childhood.

Although neither his mother nor his sister Amélie had happy marriages, as we have seen, Joly remained devoted to his wife throughout their many years together. A resident of Charlottetown later recalled to Joly that when he and Lucy visited Prince Edward Island in 1869, thirteen years after their wedding, he was struck "by the kind attention and devotion evinced by you towards her ... as you carefully assisted

her over the fences and other intervening obstacles as we strolled along
the River bank. Until better informed, I came to the conclusion that you
were a newly married couple enjoying your honey moon."[44]

One of their few separations was in 1879, when the dismissal of the
lieutenant governor took Joly to London in an attempt to save his government. Lucy was apparently about to deliver another baby, for she
wrote to tell her husband "just three words which I know will comfort
you. I am all right. It came on the very day you left, you can imagine my
gratitude & thankfulness to God, you know how I dreaded it, & how I
kept awake at night thinking of the last agony when little Justine was
born." Lucy added that she felt "it" was an answer to prayer and that
they "must both much more earnestly tell everything to God in prayer.
How long the time will be for us both, but we are one in everything &
your anxieties are mine, dear one and it is such a comfort to feel all is
well."[45] Lucy, who was forty-two years old by this time, must have been
referring to a miscarriage, for the letter she wrote four days later makes
no mention of an infant, noting instead that everyone was astonished
that she did not go to London with her husband. Furthermore, Justine,
born four years earlier, is their last child to appear in the church records. She had died of diphtheria at the age of two and a half, only a
week after Joly's administration was returned in the 1878 election. The
fact that Justine had been predeceased by two young brothers in 1875
suggests that the later-born children had less immunity to childhood
diseases than their older siblings.[46]

Despite her apparent pregnancy, the reason Lucy gave for not accompanying her husband to London was financial, for she wrote, "I
am sorry I did not take what I have in the bank and go to be near you
my own one. I know you will miss me (if you are not too busy) at any
rate I miss my dear bright loving pet always so good, and thoughtful
and generous, and kind. I don't think any other couple are as happy
together as we are, do you?" Lucy also reminded her husband to purchase some shirts and socks for himself and their nineteen-year-old
son, Edmond, who had accompanied him, adding,

> As you do not like pillaging nor defrauding the revenue, I shall only ask
> you to bring me a couple of pairs of black silk stockings. They are $3.00 a
> pair in Quebec & not good at that, & Julia wants a black satin parasol lined
> with pale blue and white lace edge, now don't forget stockings and gloves
> for me and parasol for Julia. I think of you darling so much, and I hope
> when you come back you will find me better than I was to you, and more

ready to cheer and help you darling, sometimes I am so selfish and don't
do my duty in that respect.

The following page, which is either a postscript or the end of a different
letter, is in a considerably less obsequious voice: "I want you to bring
me a dozen pairs of kid gloves, dark shades, six pairs of sixes and 6
pairs of 6 ¾. Now don't forget. I do not ask for much."[47]
Even though the separation of goods specified in the marriage contract ensured that Henri-Gustave would have complete legal control
over the seigneurie,[48] Lucy was clearly not entirely sheltered from the
family business concerns. In the first of her aforementioned letters, she
added the news from the estate manager that "the booms are across
the river, news was sent to the men to throw in their logs, no damage
done by the ice, & every thing going on prosperously." She continued,
"There was a letter from your mother yesterday asking for three hundred dollars so I had to write a note to Mr Stevenson of the Bank, asking
him to give Fred that money and I will write & send it to her today. I was
also obliged to give $8.00 for hay, & pay for Edmond's singing lessons –
I will keep a strict account of every extra."[49] It is clear, however, that
Lucy was playing the role of messenger more than that of manager and
that she was under Henri-Gustave's close supervision even in domestic matters. Nowhere was this more evident than when their daughter
Ethel was married, for it was Henri-Gustave who handled the financial
details with the florist, as well as the dressmaker in England.[50] Indeed,
recent scholarship suggests that companionate marriage, or what historian Bettina Bradbury refers to as companionate patriarchy, often led
the husband to be more assertive rather than less so.[51]
But Lucy's role was certainly not inconsequential, for as the new
wealth based on commerce and industry threatened to overwhelm the
social dominance of the gentry, female social rituals such as formal calls
and leaving cards served to maintain the class boundary.[52] Thus, after
his election as member of Parliament in 1896 Joly wrote to son Edmond,
"We have two nice moderate size rooms, bedroom and dressing room
where we sit and write when at leisure. Mama receives her innumerable guests in the large reception room, and every afternoon about 4:30
we start on our pilgrimage to return visits."[53] Lucy also reinforced her
husband's status by organizing women's Shakespeare clubs in the cities
they inhabited, and by becoming the honorary president of the National
Council of Women during her years in British Columbia.[54] Finally, social deference was encouraged by her charitable activities in Lotbinière.

In 1890, for example, Joly referred to sewing machines that Lucy had donated to two local women, adding that they "bless you, in their gratitude, day and night."[55] Six years later he wrote to Edmond that his mother was "too good for us, there is no one like a mother. She is so much better than I am and makes me ashamed of myself."[56]

Lucy died in 1904, while Joly was serving as lieutenant governor of British Columbia. In her diary, Susan Crease, who was a frequent visitor in Victoria, recorded how Joly remained devoted to his wife despite her increasing irritability. An entry written shortly before Lucy's death notes that she had been unusually talkative but had made mistakes, adding: "Poor Sir Henri's face a study – such grief when out of sight (of her) such courage when in."[57] Had Lucy not predeceased Joly, she would have been left with a comfortable inheritance, for the will he drafted in 1899 bequeathed her $2,000 a year on the understanding that she would forfeit the $600 a year she was receiving as an annuity. The will noted that she had inherited houses in Quebec City and the sum of $10,000 from her father and that this amount was to be repaid to her from Joly's life insurance policy. The ever-cautious Joly urged that his wife invest the money in Dominion securities, "without allowing herself to be tempted by higher rates of interest." In addition, Lucy owned the silver plate, French inlaid furniture, Indian carpets, and other furnishings of the Pointe Platon manor house that marked the genteel social status of the family. She was to have the life enjoyment of the manor, including gardens, orchard, and buildings, with their eldest son, Edmond, acting as executor, paying the taxes, and keeping all in good order and repair. Joly's paternalism was also reflected in his instructions that, given the "load and responsibility" that management of the farm would entail, Edmond would "assume it, at once." He hoped, however, that Lucy would "continue to take the same pleasure and interest in it as by the past and still give valuable supervision and advice for which Edmond will, I feel certain, be grateful." He also added, "Edmond knows what his mother will require, and I trust him to spare her all trouble, such as a woman alone is certain to be more or less exposed to. I earnestly hope that she and our dear children, whenever they can come to her, will spend many more happy summers together at Pointe Platon." If Lucy preferred to spend her summers somewhere else, however, Edmond was to occupy the house in her absence.

Reflecting the traditional inheritance system for seigneuries as well as the status that title to a former seigneury still bestowed after the turn of the twentieth century, Joly bequeathed most of the landed estate to his eldest son, Edmond, who had been helping to manage it for a number of years.[58] The relatively equal inheritances of the other six off-spring, however, would represent a considerable burden to the estate. The youngest son, Gustave, and the three younger daughters would each receive $400 per year, and the second son, Alain, would receive $1,000 a year. Alain would also inherit the domaine property, including the mill, and the eldest daughter, Julia, to whom dowry payments of $400 had fallen behind, was to be paid the $1,900 now owing, in addi-tion to receiving the cottage on the hill with its surrounding grounds. Joly's life insurance policy would soon be worth $42,000, but from it Edmond's wife was to be repaid the $7,400 that had been borrowed from her, and there were three additional debts totalling $10,000, plus the $40,000 Joly owed his sister in France by virtue of his mother's will. Joly left no money to more distant relatives, but to Edmond as executor he "recommended" his uncle Hammond Gowen and his Alléon cous-ins in Paris.[59] Somewhat surprisingly, there is no reference to religion, and no bequests were left to the Anglican Church, but the large plaque and the stained glass window dedicated to Joly and his wife on either side of the entrance to the Quebec Cathedral suggest that a separate endowment was made.

In contrast to his own experience, none of Joly's offspring experi-enced youthful exile from the bosom of the parental family. The third son, also named Henri-Gustave, attended Bishop's College, a private school in Lennoxville, but at least three others appear to have been enrolled in Catholic institutions in Quebec City.[60] Despite Joly's busy work schedule as a lawyer, lumberman, and politician, he was clearly an intimate father rather than the absent or tyrannical figure stressed by earlier historians of the Victorian family.[61] A letter written by Joly's nine-year-old daughter Ethel while he was visiting London as Quebec premier in 1879 reflects the closeness of the family circle as well as the curiosity of a child about the world beyond that circle: "had you a nice voyage to England, were you sick and how did Edmond get a long? have you seen Colonel Strange? Maggie and Tilly [daughters Marga-retha and Mathilda] send you their love. was Edmond sick going a cross? we have had fine wehether. is their any snow in England? when do you think you will come home. Mama is going to take out her little carrage to morrow wont that be nice."[62]

This is the same image that emerges in the semi-fictional narrative by Joly's granddaughter, Hazel Boswell. Written for a juvenile audience from the perspective of Boswell's mother, Julia, as a fourteen-year-old,

Town House, Country House obviously must be approached with a critical eye.[63] There is no hint, for example, that the Jolys were Protestants, and a central figure is Oncle Édouard, who is clearly modelled on the adventuresome Uncle Edmond, who had been dead fifteen years in 1872, when the story begins.[64] Despite such liberties, however, Boswell's narrative was clearly based largely on stories she heard from her mother, and it therefore provides an intimate, if romanticized, glimpse of the family when the children were still young.

As in the sentimental late-nineteenth-century memoir of Robert La Roque de Roquebrune, household servants are central figures in *Town House, Country House*, and they include a curmudgeonly Irish nursery maid, a housemaid, a coachman, and the cook, Beau-Charles, described as a handsome rogue who tests Joly's patience because of his drinking bouts.[65] There are only two Irish maids and a single French-Canadian servant listed in the 1871 census, the period when Boswell's narrative is set, but in the 1881 census Joly's status as recent premier is reflected by a household staff consisting of a French-Canadian coachman, two housemaids (one French-Canadian and one Irish), an Irish pantry maid, and two cooks (one French-Canadian and one Irish).[66] The four-storey house facing the Quebec Citadel became increasingly crowded, for Joly's mother, three daughters, two sons, daughter-in-law, and infant grandson were all living there in 1886.[67] By 1891, however, there were only two daughters remaining at home, and there were no servants listed in the household census. The Jolys had taken a city apartment by this time, so any serving staff most likely would have been living elsewhere, but as we see in the next chapter, the family lumber business was also then in crisis, with the bank refusing to advance money to finance the year's operations.[68]

Boswell's storybook suggests that the Jolys formed the close bonds to servants that were characteristic of the traditional gentry household,[69] but this may have been a romantic fiction, for household servants are rarely mentioned in the Joly family correspondence. They lived in a separate building during the summers at Pointe Platon, and much more common are references to the estate manager (whose family appears in *Town House, Country House*) and a few other men who worked on the farm and in the woods, and who benefited from Joly's patronage in times of crisis and need.[70]

Even while living in distant locales, Joly maintained a close watch over developments in Lotbinière through frequent correspondence with son Edmond, who became his law partner in addition to helping supervise the lumber business. According to the parish historian, Edmond was of "un caractère charmant et d'une bienveillance extrême."[71] He lacked his father's conciliatory manner in dealing with the people of the seigneury, as discussed in chapter 3, but his letters show no trace of impatience with Henri-Gustave's propensity for offering paternal advice, even in matters related to his own family after he married Lucy Campbell, the daughter of a Quebec City notary.[72] A month after the marriage, Joly advised Edmond that "quand un jeune homme se marie il faut que sa belle mère soit bien féroce ... ; dans tous les cas, c'est ton devoir de faire toute en ton pouvoir pour concilier la mère de Lucy."[73] If Edmond's relationship with his mother-in-law was somewhat tense, Joly clearly had a close relationship with his daughter-in-law, even buying her a bicycle at a time when they were still a novelty for women.[74]

By 1888 Edmond and his family were spending part of their summers in their own small house close to the manor at Pointe Platon,[75] and father and son obviously took pleasure in each other's company. Joly wrote in March 1886, for example, that he was delighted that Edmond enjoyed snowshoeing, "comme tu dis cela te fait autant de bien, *au moins, moralement* que *physiquement*."[76] As Christmas approached in 1889, he wrote that he was looking forward to some long walks with his son during the holidays.[77] The following year, without informing Edmond, Joly asked "Mr Irvine" (presumably George Irvine, the prominent Quebec City lawyer and Liberal politician) to take Edmond as a law partner, but nothing appears to have come of the initiative.[78] Their own practice was evidently not flourishing, but Joly was optimistic in the spring of 1890, writing, "Pas de nouveaux clients mais nos vieux amis commencent à s'intéresser à nous, et me parlent de questions légales ce qui est bon signe."[79] Edmond took advantage of the lack of law business that summer, as well as others, to vacation with his family at Bic on the lower St Lawrence, where his wife's parents owned a property. There he indulged in his passion for fly fishing while his father managed their business affairs in Quebec City and kept an eye on the farm operations at Pointe Platon.[80]

Joly maintained control of the lumber business during the years when he was in Ottawa as a member of Parliament, but Edmond was finally given more responsibility after his father became lieutenant governor of British Columbia. Edmond continued, however, to defer to his father's judgement even in matters of his own family. In 1906, for example, he asked to have his son, Alain, remain at Bishop's University after his first year because he was not yet capable of passing the College of Physicians and Surgeons exam to study medicine at McGill. Edmond added, "I hope that you will not think Alain deficient, either in energy or good will. The poor lad works as hard and earnestly as he possibly can and I know that later on when once he is a medico that he will be a credit to us all."[81] There is no hint in their correspondence, however, that Joly was lacking in respect towards his oldest son. In the fall of 1896 he advised Edmond to accept the medal he was being offered for saving a drowning person, adding that fathers were prouder of their sons' honours than of their own.[82] Not only would Edmond never experience the adventures of his brothers or even most of his sisters, as we shall see, but he also would not have long to exercise his independence after his father's death in 1908, for he died suddenly only three years later at the relatively young age of fifty-two.

Joly's younger two sons were much less under his influence once they became military officers, but they maintained a correspondence with him throughout his life, and he certainly played a role in launching their careers. After Alain graduated from the Royal Military College (RMC) with a first class certificate and had practiced as a mechanical engineer for two years, his father asked the Conservative minister of militia, Adolphe Caron, to help ensure that he was accepted into the Royal Engineers.[83] Joly also reminded the commanding officer at the college that Alain's uncle had been killed at Lucknow with Havelock "and would doubtless have disposed the Military Authorities to look with favor on my son's application; it may still help him now."[84] And Joly's decision to collect funds for the families of the Quebec troops sent to fight Riel certainly could not have hurt his son's chances. After Alain received the coveted position, apparently the only member of his class to do so, Caron wrote that he had not ceased to press his case and he offered to intervene with Generals Wolseley and Middleton, as well.[85] Finally, revealing how close-knit the Quebec politicians' community was, despite party differences, Joly's long-time Conservative rival, Adolphe Chapleau, wrote to him the following fall that he had not had time to visit Alain while in England, but had been informed that "il est très estimé et apprécié par ses Supérieurs et par ses compagnons de sa bonne conduite et ses Excellentes qualités."[86]

Alain continued to confide in his father, complaining in late 1886 about how his future father-in-law, Colonel Campbell of Kingston, was hindering the organization of the wedding. Colonel Campbell was not opposed to the marriage of his daughter, Marion Helen (known as Cerise), to the young Joly, writing that – with his military pay and allowance from his father – Alain would have about £400 a year, which was "rather more than I commenced married life on." But Alain was about to leave for England, where the wedding was to take place, and there was a strong possibility that he would be sent to India in early February. Alain was very concerned, therefore, that the arrival in England of Cerise and her father in mid-January would not allow her sufficient time to make the elaborate preparations required for the ceremony, and he asked that either they take the first vessel in January or Cerise be placed in charge of the ship's captain and then stay with her aunt. Complaining to his father that Colonel Campbell's "real motive is one of pure selfishness" and that he was "putting aside our happiness and comfort for his," Alain concluded with the request, "I don't ask you to write to the Col only keep your eye on him and if the chance occurs put in a word for prompt action on his part, and not this half hearted delaying policy he has adopted."[87]

Joly did intervene with Colonel Campbell, and a grateful Cerise wrote to him, "If trying to be a good wife to Alain will in any way repay you, be sure that I will do my best."[88] Alain was stationed in Kashmir between 1892 and 1900 and in Bangalore in 1901, when his father expressed the hope that he would be transferred to a more salubrious outpost.[89] After serving ten years in India, where he was granted high honours for his pioneering advances in hydroelectric development,[90] Alain applied for an inspectorate in England. However, he was back in Kashmir a year later, in 1905, having earned the rank of major.[91] He directed a major project that provided electricity to the Punjab and assumed responsibility during World War I for supplying water to the Allied forces in Gallipoli and Mesopotamia.[92] Alain retired to England in 1921, dying there in 1944 at the age of eighty-one.

The military adventures of Henri-Gustave Joly's brother, Edmond-Gustave, clearly played an important role in the family lore, for the story about burying his horse in the tomb erected by Alexander the Great is repeated in *Town House, Country House*.[93] It is not entirely surprising, then, that the third son, affectionately known as Gus (who appears as the "already philosophical" Henri in *Town House, Country House*), followed his brother Alain to RMC. After the Christmas break in 1887, Gus wrote affectionately to his parents, "This letter is being written in my small sanctum, and I am back again as if nothing had happened, but I do not feel that way. I cannot forget those lovely holidays, you have no idea what a change it is from our life here and I can tell you it has done me good, and I have made up my mind to render a better account of myself in my next exams, you will see that I was very badly beaten in the last, only coming third. I never have done so badly before, however it won't happen again."[94] Young Gustave was true to his word, for he won the governor general's gold medal when he graduated at the head of his class the following year, and Joly was congratulated for his son's accomplishment: "You have now in your own family the roots of all knowledge. Edmond the Classical, Alain the practical and Gustave the Mathematician."[95]

As they had done for Alain, Colonel E. Panet and Adolphe Caron took steps to ensure that Gustave was accepted into the Royal Engineers.[96] Before leaving for England in November 1888, with forty-six pounds of maple sugar packed in his baggage, Gustave spent some time at Pointe Platon. There he took long walks with his father, who was helping him improve his French by correcting his translations of English passages, a task that Gus admitted required "much patience" because "languages is not my forte."[97] By Christmas, Gustave was feeling homesick. He wrote to his brother Edmond that English "fellows" were as described by Alain, not as friendly or as jolly as the Canadians: "I have a feeling that at the end of my two years I will know them about as well as now." Furthermore, he had not enjoyed the Royal Engineers' dance: "I was introduced to a lot of girls, there were some fine looking, and all beautifully dressed, but almost without exception very heavy to dance with – and no animation, no bright, lively, and pretty."[98]

Like his brother Alain, Gustave would soon be on his way to more exotic locales. Much to his disappointment, he was first sent to Gibraltar, but in 1892 he was assigned to Gilgit in what is now northeast Pakistan to improve communications in that mountainous region.[99] There he won the approval of his commanding officer, who reported two years later that "the admirable services he has rendered us would be a resumé of nearly all the bridging, wood, irrigation and extension of cultivation work which has carried on in this district from August 1892 to October 1894. If I may be considered qualified to offer such opinion, I should say that Lieutenant de Lotbiniere is a model Royal Engineer Officer."[100] In a lengthy letter to his father in September 1894, Gustave reported that he had recently returned from a memorable trip to Gurais, deep in the Himalayas, and would be coming home on a year's leave, but not before spending four months in Kashmir as the replacement for the commanding engineer of that province. He was enthusiastic about the opportunities for "improving the country," adding that "of course there are objections, chiefly the obstacles put in one's way by native officials, and the wholesale corruption of subordinates in a native state is very discouraging, but in time I have no doubt this state of affairs may change for the better."[101] By January he was in the railway centre of Ambala, 200 miles north of Delhi.[102]

Gustave moved a good deal during his military career, and 1896 found him in the "disagreeable" Yemeni port of Aden.[103] The following year Joly suggested that Edmond should write to cheer him up, as he himself had done twice the previous week, adding, "Tell him about your trip here, your expeditions in the woods, etc."[104] But Gustave would soon have little time for melancholy because he was back in India in the fall of 1897, stationed at the British military headquarters of Rawalpindi. This was a period of unrest among the local tribes, and Gustave's regiment was involved in the fighting, giving Joly considerable reason for worry about his youngest son.[105] He survived, however, to participate in the South African War. In 1901 he was instructing the natives on growing crops near British military posts, and in areas less exposed to Boer attack, because of the fear of food shortages.[106] By 1907 he was back in Kashmir, where he met the Earl of Minto, who was the viceroy and governor general of India as well as past governor general of Canada. Lady Minto wrote to Joly that she and her husband had enjoyed "seeing all his wonderful electrical works on the road to Srinagar. You must feel very proud of all he has already achieved and there are such endless possibilities in that wonderful country. I hope ere long he will have the joy of seeing the railway on which he has set his heart a fait accompli."[107] Like Alain, Gustave eventually retired to England, where he died at the advanced age of ninety-one in 1960.

There is little mention of the four daughters' accomplishments in the Joly correspondence, one exception being an acquaintance who wrote in 1889, "I hear your daughters have been distinguishing themselves at some Amateur theatricals – give them my kind regards and say I hope there was not such a disorderly person present as there happened to be when I saw them in Tableaux Vivant!"[108] The girls were clearly being educated to reinforce the cultural status of their future husbands, and the fact that all four married engineers, two of whom were military men, indicates how strong the role of family connections was in their courtships. The family correspondence suggests, nevertheless, that Joly's sons-in-law found it difficult to measure up to him in the eyes of his daughters, with whom he had close relationships.[109]

Certainly, the marriage of Margaretha Anna (referred to as Maggie in the family correspondence and as the "temperamental" Mic in *Town*

House, Country House) was not a happy one, and the situation was exacerbated by the fact that her husband, Herbert Colborne Nanton, was
stationed in remote parts of India. In a letter to Joly in 1894, Gustave
wrote that his sister Maggie had accompanied him partway on his
trip to Gurais in the Himalayas and that she was thinking of visiting
Canada with him. Gustave added,

> Putting everything else aside but the question of her health I think it very
> desirable. I do not think there is much chance of her getting really well in
> this country, and even in Canada it won't be easy unless everyone is re-
> ally and honestly affectionate and good to her. Her spirits are what must
> be kept up. I fancy it will do her little good if she went home, and anyone
> should make her think she had done wrong and been unkind to her hus-
> band in any way. In my opinion neither one nor the other are very fond
> of the other, and I know Herbert is anxious for her to have a trip home, he
> wrote and told me so. Maggie will do her best (such as it is, & I am sure he
> will do the same, such as it is) but I cannot help thinking it would be easier
> for Maggie at all events if she feels she can occasionally come back to you
> all on the old footing, let bygones be bygones.

There was clearly no question of a divorce, for Gustave added that they
"get on very well if let alone, and they both are quite ready to make the
best of it. Alain last summer tried to bring them more together but as he
admitted to me, he made a mess of it, and I am quite sure he did more
harm than good."[110]

Maggie appears not to have accompanied Gustave to Canada, however, for her husband wrote the following summer, in July 1895, "I'm
afraid even now Maggie hasn't quite got over the indigestion. It is terribly hard on her and I hoped she would be well long before leaving India again." Herbert Nanton was posted at Dargai, which was clearly no
place for an upper-class non-native woman. Apart from the rebellious-
ness of the local populace, the heat was "simply awful" according to
Nanton, with the temperature reaching 104 degrees even in their mud
huts.[111] Nanton's mother wrote to Joly in the spring of 1896 that she
had received a long letter from Nanton deploring his inability to have
his wife with him, but saying that he had obtained leave for her to pay
him a week's visit. Mrs Nanton added, "Between ourselves, I think it
a very wise thing that ladies are not permitted to remain up there," for
Herbert had to be guarded by a small escort of cavalry while travelling.
He had indicated that his work would likely be completed by the end

of June, which was just as well for him because hostilities were about to intensify, and the British forces would suffer heavy losses at Dargai Heights in 1897.[112] How the marriage resolved itself is not clear, but Maggie moved in with her father in Victoria after her mother's death in 1904,[113] and despite the earlier concerns about her health, she reached the ripe old age of ninety-four, dying in England in 1949.

Although John Tosh claims that the anxiety that characterized Victorian middle-class fathers in Britain was "in nearly every case, focussed on sons, not the daughters,"[114] this was clearly not the case for Joly, even in relation to Matilda, known as Tilly and described as the "sensible one" in Boswell's fictional memoir. Two years younger than Maggie, Matilda married only a few months after her sister to a civil engineer from Cornwall, Ontario, named Henry Smith Greenwood.[115] Joly was not fond of this son-in-law, suggesting to Edmond in 1897 that because of Greenwood's jealousy, he should not take young men to Pointe Platon when his mother was absent. Joly added,

> It is very unfortunate that Harry Greenwood should be such a disappointed man. He belongs to the class of those who have such a high opinion of their merits that their life is spent in complaints of the injustice of mankind, and of course such a feeling of wrong makes them and all those depending upon them miserable. I don't know if he has impregnated Tilly with the same feeling, but she certainly is one of the dissatisfied ones, and I fear that instead of giving courage to her husband, her continual complaints, comparing her fate with that of her sisters, must tend more & more to crush him down. Anyhow, we must not make matters worse for her by letting him think that his wife is surrounded with young men and leading a gay life, while he is plodding along at his work.[116]

Perhaps Greenwood was envious of the more adventuresome careers of his military brothers-in-law, for he and Matilda were in South Africa in 1903 when she died of pneumonia at the early age of thirty-six.[117]

Joly's paternalistic concern for his daughters was even more marked in the case of the youngest, Ethel Blanche. Harry Strange commented in 1889 that he had heard that they "all bow down and worship her,"[118] and Ethel certainly appears to have been pampered. In December 1889, when she was nineteen and visiting friends in Montreal, for example, the very busy Joly took the train from Quebec City in order to accompany her home.[119] The following summer he wrote a rather remarkable

letter on her behalf to the smitten English officer Captain Dudley
Acland Mills:

> Ethel has shown me your letter. You ask her to answer yes or no, and
> *tho she is decided to answer no,* I understand that she should shrink
> from giving what would appear such a brutal answer, to a letter like
> yours. It was a great relief to her when I offered to write in her stead ...
> You who, at thirty, think it perfectly right to give your love to an ideal that,
> within three months, it has assumed the form of three different women,
> will you deny to a girl of twenty, the right of keeping her heart for her own
> ideal? You say that if she is not already engaged you will not give her up.
> I earnestly hope that you will give her up and spare her the pain (if she
> is compelled by you to answer once more) of answering with one single
> word "no."

Joly closed by admitting that his letter might seem harsh and wrote,
"But, look around you, you will find other families where the children
love their parents, and where both children and parents humbly try to
do their duty to God and to one another."[120]

Mills was presumably being transferred out of Canada, but his ar-
dour did not cool, and Ethel (though described as "impulsive" in *Town
House, Country House*) was still vacillating about his proposal four years
later, in 1894. From India, her brother Gustave had written to her, "We
four from Maggie downward are of a sentimental nature and I fancy
wish to be children always." He added to his father that Ethel "has always devoted herself to girls and not to men friends and fears the leap."
She may have been spooked by the troubled marriage of her older sister, and Gustave admitted, "There are unhappy marriages which appear to me to fall heavily on the women, who have not the work to do
that men have, to keep them occupied and interested." But he added,
"I really think Ethel is a girl that will adapt herself happily to the change
of circumstances and life this must entail, and I have therefore written
more strongly than I would have done otherwise ... I do trust that Ethel
will come to a right understanding and at bottom I know she is a good
girl and wants to do her duty."[121]

Ethel did "do her duty" by Mills, spending the following winter on
an estate in North Cornwall with her future in-laws even though she
was in poor health and her betrothed was in Boston, from where he
wrote frequent letters to his now supportive future father-in-law.[122]
Ethel had been accompanied on the voyage by her older sister, Julia,

and Julia's family, and Joly wrote concerning a violent storm that they experienced: "Poor little Hazel [the future author of *Town House, Country House*] was in my mind all the time; so nervous and excitable, she must have suffered more than the others; I suppose Olive laughed and little Hugh wandered; as for you, you are familiar with the perils of the deep."[123] The parsimonious Joly did admonish Ethel to "be saving, and only get useful things; really it is not my fault if our children have got extravagant ideas, nor mama's either about money matters."[124]

But Ethel obviously made a good impression because her future mother-in-law wrote in January 1895, "It would be our fault, not hers if we did not love her." The wish was to "marry up Ethel and Dudley as soon as the Doctors permit,"[125] but it was most likely Mrs Mills's health that caused the delay, for she was slowly dying. Joly asked Ethel in February 1895 if she would "have the heart" to return home with her brother Gus and sister Maggie, leaving "Mr Mills in a moment when your presence and sympathy would be so precious to him." To make his position even clearer, Joly added, "They have received you like a daughter. Will you not have to stand by them? I know it will be a great sacrifice, perhaps more than you can make, alone, but pray God and he will guide and help you."[126] To add to this pressure, Ethel's mother wrote the following month: "Even if you find it hard dear child, do what is right, and it brings its own happiness. You are your father's daughter and must live as he has done. You have always had a noble example in him."[127] After the much-delayed wedding finally took place nearly a year later, Ethel settled with her husband in his home county of Cornwall,[128] and – aside from lengthy visits to Quebec – she presumably spent the rest of her life in England, for that is where she died at the age of sixty-five in 1935.

As Protestants, Joly's daughters did not have the option available to their patrician Taschereau cousins of choosing a vocation by entering a convent.[129] And the fact that four of them married engineers, the profession of two of their brothers, suggests that they socialized within a rather limited circle as members of Quebec City's Protestant elite. The eldest daughter, Julia (the romantic Julie in *Town House, Country House*), would continue to do so, for she was the only one to remain in Quebec throughout her life. She married the civil engineer St George Boswell in 1881, and they were summering in a small house at Pointe Platon three years later when Joly wrote that he and others had spent a good part of the day there planting spruce trees, tidying up the surroundings, cording wood, and cutting some brush to improve the view.[130] By this time,

having decided to resign his provincial seat, Joly had placed his Quebec house on the market and moved his family to Pointe Platon, where
he devoted his full attention to the seigneury's lumber business.[131] His
friend Colonel Thomas Bland Strange approved of the decision and remarked, "It will be a little dull for your girls, but then they are educated
now, and no place where you and they are will ever be dull."[132] Strange
was right as far as the married Julia was concerned, in any case, for Joly
reported a year later that she and her daughter Hazel "sont enchantées
d'être ici, un autre hiver."[133]

Joly also took an active interest in his grandchildren, writing in reference to Julia's infant son, "Poor little Hugh, I am so concerned about
that twist in his legs. I hope dear Julia will follow the Doctor's advice,
and get those boots at once for him; the dear little man, he is really
heavier than any child I have ever seen, but we must not neglect that
and allow him to become a cripple for life."[134] When Julia and her husband went to England with three of their children and Ethel during the
winter of 1894–5, they rather surprisingly left an infant in the care of
her grandparents. Assuming the role of playful grandfather, Joly wrote,
"At first the baby screamed if we offered to touch her, but now she
comes to us willingly. I have rigged up a little tramway, and, when
my time to nurse her comes as it does after dinner, I put her in her
little carriage and by an ingenious combination of ropes, send her flying through the big archway between the dining room and the office ...
the whole depth of the house. She delights in the operation, and never
tires of it, neither do I. Mama finds it a very lazy dodge."[135] When Julia
and family returned home in April, Joly wrote, "We had the pleasure of
handing over to them the dear little baby in the best of health."[136] Julia
was certainly devoted to her father, for after his election to Ottawa in
1896, she wrote that she prayed for him every day and added, "I think,
nay I *know*, that you understand the perplexity and worry of finding
myself cut off from you this summer."[137]

The Jolys had soon tired of the rural isolation during the winter, for
Henri-Gustave reported in January 1889 that the Pointe Platon house
was closed because the family was in town.[138] With most of their offspring out of the nest by this time, they rented a city apartment during
the winters until 1895, when the anticipated visit of Gus and Maggie,
as well as Ethel and her fiancé, caused them to take a house in order to
give "la chère petite maman ... la satisfaction d'avoir encore une fois
son ménage et sa maison comme dans le bon temps passé."[139] But even
if less time was spent each year at Pointe Platon than in the city, it was

in the Lotbinière manor that the family formed its closest bonds. The exterior of the house may have symbolized the naturalness of noble property, as we saw in the previous chapter, but the interior provided a warm and nurturing space for the growing family. Perhaps the best example is the dining room, which was a relatively new innovation at the time the Lotbinière manor was built. According to John R. Gillis, dining rooms "ritually constructed a sense of togetherness,"[140] so it was presumably no accident that the one in Maple House was the only room in the house that had the walls and ceiling panelled completely in wood, a yellow-tinted butternut that still lends the room a warm intimate air. And at time when in the United States comfortable parlours or sitting rooms were replacing the more formal drawing room and bringing family activities back to the front of the house,[141] Henri-Gustave's large family transformed their relatively small drawing room into a space comfortable enough to occupy in the evenings. Notable as well is the fact that most of the upstairs space was divided into three large front rooms whose partitions could be removed to improve air circulation and increase light, while also heightening the sense of intimacy among the children who slept there. As described in *Town House, Country House*, Maple House was an idyllic summer residence where the father could form stronger bonds and exercise greater influence over his wife and children than was possible in the city with its many distractions. And when Joly felt the need for solitude, he could retreat to the library on the main floor (expanded as a study in 1889–90) or to the small laboratory nearby, where, like his father before him, he was able to indulge his passion for scientific experiments.[142]

Conclusion

Historians of gender and the family until recently associated what they referred to as the cult of domesticity with the rise of industrial capitalism. They argued that the middle-class home was increasingly viewed as the male breadwinner's haven from the pressures and anxieties of the market at a time when the public sphere was becoming more remote and formal.[143] Leonore Davidoff and Catherine Hall shifted attention from the economic transition to the rise of evangelical religion, and still more recently, John Gillis has pointed to the rise of secularism and individualism, stating that the Victorian middle classes began to attribute "qualities that previously had been associated with divine or communal archetypes" to those with whom they lived.[144] But

Henri-Gustave Joly was not alienated from the public sphere, nor was he either an evangelical or a secular individualist. And even if his close ties to his wife and children were a hallmark of the English middle class in the later Victorian era, that relationship did not reflect the decline in paternal deference that Tosh feels was a corollary.[145] Indeed, it was quite compatible with Joly's patrician paternalism. Relatively little is known about aristocratic Victorian masculinity, but the dichotomy between a new bourgeois manliness attuned to the market and a less domesticated genteel manliness grounded in land ownership has broken down in recent studies.[146] And just as family historians now insist that the division between the home and the outside world is largely an artificial construct and that the family was not simply a dependent variable in the process of modernization,[147] so we shall see that Joly's paternalism and frugality were characteristics that marked not only his gender identity and family life but his public career as well.

Edmond-Gustave Joly in British army officer's uniform with a medal that presumably reflects his participation in the Crimean War. His stiff stance and defiant gaze reflect a sense of insecurity that would drive him to a heroic early death in India. Domaine Joly de Lotbinière Collection.

Amélie Savage, née Joly, whose unhappy marriage ended after the birth of her first child. This daughter married into the French nobility. Bibliothèque et Archives nationales du Québec, P98, S44, P1.

Family portrait, including the seven children who survived to adulthood.
Note the emphasis on intimacy, the fact that the eyes of the daughters (all
but the defiant youngest one) are modestly fixed on books while the sons
strike manly poses and form a protective circle around their mother, and the
attachment of one daughter to her relaxed and contemplative father in the
foreground of the photograph. Domaine Joly de Lotbinière Collection.

With its face towards the Citadel, the four-storey Gowen house (the tallest
building in this recent photograph) was occupied by the extended family of
Henri-Gustave and Lucy Joly de Lotbiniere after the death of her parents.
Domaine Joly de Lotbinière Collection, photograph by Marielle Sylvain.

East view of the ivy-covered manor house and formal gardens at Pointe
Platon, 1904. Domaine Joly de Lotbinière Collection.

Family gathering at Pointe Platon. Moving from the left upper corner in
a clockwise direction are Henry Greenwood, Sir Henri-Gustave, Dudley
Mills, author Hazel Boswell, Hazel's mother Julia, the Greenwood and
Mills grandchildren, and their uncle Edmond-Gustave. It is perhaps
telling that the sons-in-law appear to be vying for Henri-Gustave's
attention while his son, Edmond, is relaxing with their children.
Domaine Joly de Lotbinière Collection.

Chapter Three

Seigneur and Lumberman

In a pamphlet published during the 1878 election, Guillaume Amyot asked why his Lotbinière opponent Henri-Gustave Joly had failed to facilitate colonization in his own county, charging that his refusal to grant lands "aux enfants du peuple" was forcing them to migrate to the United States. In Amyot's decided opinion, the abolition of the seigneurial system in 1854 had not ended Joly's obligation to develop his ancestral estate.[1] Amyot was referring in particular to the large tract that Joly's father had set aside as a timber reserve, low-lying land that was actually of little agricultural value. But politically motivated though this criticism of Joly was, it does raise questions about how he managed the former seigneury of Lotbinière. Did he continue to think of himself as the paternalistic seigneur with certain obligations to the local community, or did he introduce a highly restrictive sales policy on the land that he now owned in fee simple? And what about the attitude of the former censitaires? Did the elimination of seigneurial rents on their lots, along with the abolition of their feudal obligations, mean that they began to see the seigneur as irrelevant, or that the resentment many of them had felt in earlier years was now a thing of the past? Albert Soboul has suggested that this was not the case in parts of post-revolutionary France where feudal rents were simply transformed into constituted rents, but, according to one study, the average former censitaire in Lower Canada (formally known as Canada East after 1841), ended up paying only one-third to one-half what he had before.[2] Another reason for resentment might have been the fact that succeeding generations would have to pay the market price for any uncleared lots the seigneur decided to sell, but in Lotbinière, as in the rest of the seigneurial zone, there was little arable wild land left by mid-century. Resentment concerning the monopolization of land in Canada East was therefore directed largely towards the absentee proprietors of the freehold townships.[3]

Given the nature of our sources, it is easier to assess Joly's attitude than that of the farming families who lived in Lotbinière, but we shall see that his paternalism did ensure that a certain sense of popular loyalty persisted in the community, though obviously not a loyalty that was entirely divorced from the economic dominance Joly exercised over the rural population. In the second section of this chapter we examine how, by following his father's policy of what was essentially an early example of sustained yield forestry, Joly ensured a dependable long-term source of employment for farmers on the marginal land of Lotbinière. Joly clearly benefited from having a dependent local source of labour, but he was not simply a rentier, for he did have to pay careful attention to his lumber business in order to provide his growing family with the advantages that their elite social status demanded.

Seigneur

In 1851, a year after the seigneurial manor was constructed, and on the eve of his twenty-second birthday, Henri-Gustave Joly was granted title to the seigneurial domaine and the mills, though without the right to sell or mortgage any part of the property.[4] With railway construction and industrial development promising an economic revolution in Canada East, seigneurial tenure was becoming increasingly anachronistic as an impediment to waterpower development, land speculation and capitalist accumulation. Presumably fearing that the upcoming abolition of seigneurial tenure would limit the amount of ungranted land they could claim as their own (a fear that ultimately proved to be unfounded), Joly's parents granted him 3,000 arpents (1,200 hectares) as a censitaire in 1853.[5] They used the same basic contract (with the same conditions) that the ordinary censitaires were required to sign, but this was obviously a formality. It would appear that Joly was being groomed to take over management of the entire seigneury, whose ownership he assumed in 1860. His father continued for a time to manage the family lumber business, but he also had commercial connections in France as well as business interests in the United States, where he had investments in the stock market and in copper mines.[6]

The attempt in 1852 to reform the seigneurial system by limiting certain seigneurial privileges and placing a ceiling on the *cens et rentes* had been rejected by English-speaking commercial interests who objected that this would perpetuate a system that interfered with commerce and industry by removing the incentive of censitaires to commute to freehold tenure. With the seigneurial commutation bill passed two years later, in December 1854, land became a commodity, subject to speculative investment and with no legal impediments to the construction of mills. Nor were seigneurs the losers, for they were compensated by the government for the loss of their feudal privileges, and the *cens et rentes* paid by the former censitaires simply became annual constituted rents, albeit rents that could be paid off in a single lump sum.[7]

A commission was appointed to determine the amount each seigneur was to be compensated and to fix the constituted rent for each former censitaire. For Lotbinière the commission reported that the *cens et rentes* of 300 of the lots had been reduced to four cents per arpent eight years earlier, in 1849. As a result, the total of the annual constituted rents of the 1,019 lots was calculated at £212 ($848), or an average of only 4.2 shillings (84 cents) per lot, a small sum compared to the price of freehold land in the neighbouring Eastern Townships.[8] In addition, the indemnity for the loss of the *lods et ventes* (sales taxes) was determined to be £61 17s. per year for the agricultural lots and £16 10s. for the building lots, which was less than the amount estimated when Julie-Christine first claimed the seigneury (as we saw in chapter 1) and certainly a very small sum when compared to the amounts reported for the seigneuries in the Montreal district.[9] Nothing was allowed for other seigneurial privileges, including the loss of the gristmill monopoly. The commissioner's reasoning was that income from the mills would remain as high as ever, but the Jolys challenged this decision, and in 1861 the Court of Revision added £135 ($540) as damages for the loss of the gristmill monopoly, even though it was becoming less valuable as farmers moved from grain to potato and dairy production.[10] Furthermore, the Lotbinière seigneurs had taken possession of the best mill sites, and when a local farmer did erect a gristmill on the Bois Clair River in 1859, Pierre-Gustave Joly sued him successfully for building a dam on his property. Joly later offered to settle with the farmer for 25 percent of the mill's annual production but then agreed to sell the mill lot to him for $1,200.[11] The fact remains, however, that the Joly family continued to own and operate the two gristmills into the 1940s.[12]

With a total annual indemnity of £213 ($852), plus the constituted rents of £212, the Jolys collected the tidy sum of £425 ($1,700) a year, not including the profits from their mills. (As we shall see, their farm operated at a loss.) Although lot holders could choose to pay off their constituted rents in a lump sum, few chose to do so despite the fact that, based on average annual rent of only eighty-four cents per lot, the amount would not have been high.[13] It presumably would have been in the seigneur's financial interest to receive the capital rather than the 6 percent per year because of the costs involved in collecting the rents, particularly when they were in arrears, as they often were throughout Quebec. Certainly, when the former seigneurs were given the opportunity in 1859 to claim the capital of their indemnity for loss of feudal rights, minus 25 percent, the Jolys took advantage of this option, thereby claiming $15,669, though the government did not complete its payments until 1875.[14] But the annual collection of the rent in the fall of the year may well have carried enough symbolic weight as the last remaining vestige of seigneurial homage that the Jolys and their counterparts were not eager to see it end.[15]

As far as the Jolys' economic interests were concerned, the most important feature of the 1854 bill was the amendment imposed by the Legislative Council that granted absolute ownership of all ungranted land to the former seigneurs.[16] Even if most of this land had little agricultural value, seigneurs had not enjoyed the legal right to cut trees on unconceded land,[17] as the protests against Pierre-Gustave had indicated. When added to the 1,200 hectares that had been granted to Henri-Gustave and the 43,300 hectares previously converted to freehold tenure, this amendment ensured a lasting supply of raw material for the Joly family's lumber business. In short, the Jolys were now the absolute owners of a very sizeable property, one that the municipal assessor valued at £200,000 ($800,000) in 1857.[18] The municipal and school taxes were the only fly in the ointment for the former seigneurs, for they were informed that same year that whereas seigneurial property had been taxed at only one-quarter of its assessment value, upon being commuted to freehold it would be subject to the full rate.[19] The Jolys' total annual tax bill is unknown, but in 1870 they were billed for $9,244 by the school corporation of only one parish.[20]

Benoît Grenier has observed how remarkable it is that an event as important as the abolition of seigneurial tenure in 1854 has been largely forgotten in the public memory of Quebec.[21] The main reason for the lack of commemoration, clearly, is that this was not the result of a groundswell of popular protest or revolution, such initiatives having been quashed with the rebellions. For most of the former censitaires, in fact, the change in tenure failed to result in a substantial improvement in living conditions. They no longer had to pay a tax or mutation fine when they sold their land, and they might have a little more choice in where to grind their grain, but the great majority of them continued to pay an annual rent equivalent to the *cens et rentes*, small as that might be. One indicator of the local poverty is the fact that the average assessed value of all the properties in the parish of St Édouard was only $767 in 1887, a year in which land in the timber reserve of Joly township was valued at $4.50 an arpent, the equivalent of $270 for only sixty essentially unarable arpents (twenty-four hectares).[22] Even though some families owned more than one property,[23] the value per acre was clearly very low. As late as 1906 the Jolys' rent collector announced that he was attempting a new method by which he would visit each parish on a fixed date when debtors would come to him because there was no task "plus triste" than having to go from door to door. In fact, there was still a "bureau seigneurial" in Leclercville in 1947, though the rents were paid as taxes to the local municipalities after 1940.[24]

A significant disadvantage for the former censitaires was that they would now have to purchase undeveloped land at the market price, and the former seigneurs now had the legal right to hold it back from settlement until prices increased. There may not have been much arable wild land remaining in Lotbinière by mid-century, but at least one conflict can probably be attributed to the change in the tenure system. In 1861 two brothers defied Pierre-Gustave Joly's orders to vacate the lot they were occupying next to that of their father without permission. The Beaudets may have been trying to assert the censitaire's traditional right to claim land, but despite their repeated declaration that they were willing to face imprisonment rather than give in, commitment to jail did persuade them to sign a statement agreeing to vacate the lot. They refused, however, to accept the seigneurial agent's conciliatory offer to let them pay off their legal charge by cutting logs for the Jolys the following winter.[25]

Abolished in a formal sense, the dependency relations of the seigneurial system were slow to die, at least in Lotbinière. In contrast to the English-speaking seigneur of Beauharnois, who exacted full payment within a short period of time for his lands converted to freehold, Henri-Gustave Joly claimed in 1890 that whenever he sold a lot to a local farmer, he collected only the interest on the purchase price.[26] In fact, an undated memoir outlining sales conditions states that purchasers were not to pay the principal on their lots until the mortgage on the Lotbinière seigneury was discharged, but were to pay 5 percent per year (that is, a constituted rent) instead.[27] Although this policy was obviously beneficial to the farmers in one respect, it also ensured that they would remain bound to Joly for an indefinite period.[28] Another sales condition was that the lot in question could not be mortgaged or sold without Joly's permission. This condition was obviously enforced, for when a widow requested permission to sell a bush lot that her husband had purchased from Joly, Edmond sent his father a detailed list of the mortgages that were on the property of the person who wished to purchase the lot. In short, the Jolys would not be satisfied with a simple transfer of their mortgage to a third party; they had to feel confident that the third party already owned property that was not mortgaged for more than it was worth.[29]

Serge Courville speculates that commutation had little impact in general because by that time economic changes were driven by "big capital and urban requirements,"[30] but in the case of the Jolys the new tenure system provided increased financial security and tied them to Lotbinière more tightly than ever. There was now nothing to prevent them from selling their undeveloped land in one or more large sections on the open market and either spending the capital by living in luxury or investing it in other enterprises; instead, they increased their investment in the local lumber business, and descendants continued to play the role of seigneur until the estate was finally acquired by the provincial government in 1967. In response to an unsolicited offer to purchase the former seigneury in 1888, Henri-Gustave Joly replied that he had sold a number of lots to residents of Lotbinière "to enable them to settle their children near them, or provide them with firewood when they have none left on their farms, but I have never thought of parting with the seignory."[31]

One of the reasons for not selling the estate was that Joly clearly enjoyed acting as a father figure to the people of Lotbinière.[32] To take one example, he supported the independent free school opened in 1861 by his own father for the children of the sawmill employees,[33] asking the Department of Public Instruction in 1889 to send it a series of small books on design because the students "ont un goût naturel, qui ne demande qu'à être développé." The boys could learn how to improve the design of the furniture that they were making, and some of the girls exhibited "un certain talent artistique dans leurs ouvrages." The reply was that the department had no books of this nature,[34] but it was more helpful in 1894, when Joly expressed his thanks for a collection of maps. Further reflecting his interest in practical education, he added that he would mount them on cloth himself, "ayant fait mon apprentissage dans cette branche d'industrie."[35] Joly was also concerned that "les rêgles les plus élementaires de l'hygiène" were ignored in the country-side, and he advised the Council of Public Instruction that these rules should be taught in school.[36]

Joly's sense of paternalism towards the people of Lotbinière is also illustrated by his attempt in February 1887 to intervene on behalf of two local men arrested for distilling whiskey. In response, the inspector of inland revenue, James M. LeMoine, who was a well-known writer of romantic local history, wrote that he could not intervene – "tout dé-sireux que je sois de vous êtes agréable" – because his officers had been threatened with violence.[37] Joly replied, in turn, that only one of the men was guilty of such threats and that this man had been unaware that his still could be legally seized. Joly promised not to interfere fur-ther, but after stating, "Vous etes trop juste pour refuser de faire ce que je viens vous demander de faire," he added that he had informed the minister of justice that the general opinion "dans nos campagnes" was that one could distil liquor for one's own use. In short, even though seigneurial courts had been discontinued after the Conquest, and Joly could not – as a practicing lawyer – serve as a justice of the peace, he could still exercise the prerogative of mercy by leaving LeMoine with little choice but to comply with his wishes.[38] He would not be quite so compromising about illicit distilleries after becoming minister of inter-nal revenue in the Laurier government nine years later.

On another occasion, Joly responded positively to the curé's plea for lumber to enable a local indigent to finish building his house.[39] He also acted on his own initiative in certain cases, as when he gave his old black fur coat to a fifteen-year-old boy who, despite suffering from in-flammatory rheumatism, had to take charge of his family's farm after the death of his father.[40] Several years later, Joly provided an annual grant of $50 to enable a young man to attend a Montreal institution for the hearing- and speech-impaired.[41] He also asked Edmond in 1903 to give $20 to "poor Romuald Bourré, a man who has always supported me faithfully in our election struggles and who has been very unfortu-nate. I would like to help him."[42]

In addition to such individual acts of charity, supplemented by those of his wife, Joly sometimes acted as a local mediator, as in 1887 in the case of a road dispute between two municipal councils. The grateful curé wrote, "Je suis bien persuadé que sans vous, l'affaire au-rait été loin."[43] Although membership in the local municipal council would have been beneath his social status, Joly was able to exercise influence through his highly trusted estate manager, Fritz Parrot, who was mayor of Leclercville by 1888.[44] This did not prevent the treasurer of the local school commission from complaining to Joly that same year that he had neither paid his school taxes nor responded to letters during the previous two years.[45] Joly was more careful to provide material support to the local Catholic church, making annual donations to the Soeurs du Bon Pasteur, who operated a school in Lotbinière, as well as donating a 48-arpent lot for use by the curé of St Édouard.[46] In later years Joly would also donate a woodlot to each of the parishes of St Édouard and Ste Emmélie.[47] The curé of the latter parish complained in 1888 that Joly's new estate manager was charging him rent for a lot that his predecessor had allowed him to use free of charge, but relations with the parish priest clearly remained cordial, given that Joly was invited to the blessing of the new church bells the following year.[48]

The degree to which the local inhabitants remained deferential to the Joly family is difficult to judge, but a presumably fictional incident described in *Town House, Country House* suggests that harmonious class relations were part of the family lore. Upon the sinking of a crowded paddle wheeler after the boat hit a timber raft in the St Lawrence, Joly is described as taking command of the situation, and his children are the first to disembark, as if their right to do so was simply assumed.[49] Much the same picture emerges from a petition presented on behalf of the women of Lotbinière parish in 1878, for it referred to the respect felt towards Joly and declared, "L'attention marquée, que vous avez toujours manifestée à notre égard est un titre à ajouter, non pas à votre gloire et à l'admiration que vous avez toujours inspirées, mais à l'amour et à la reconnaissance d'une population qui gardera de vous un souvenir ineffaçable." ("The marked attention that you have always manifested towards us is a title to add, not to your glory and the admiration that you have always inspired, but to the love and recognition of a population that will keep an indelible memory of you.")[50]

But this was an election year, and the petition was unsigned, so it may have been written for political purposes. Certainly, despite Joly's paternalism, his former censitaires were not always respectful of his authority. In 1885 one of the few English-speaking settlers informed him that 600 to 800 loads of tamarack had recently been drawn off the "continuation" (meaning the timber reserve known as Joly township) by residents of his seigneury, with eight to ten men working in "bees." The informant added that "they make a brag of it now, and say that you have let them off so far and won't do anything to them." As a result, "it will come hard for us to pay for the Land when you sell it."[51]

Joly's paternalism itself became a bone of contention in 1897 when he was informed that a number of the local residents to whom he had several years earlier sold land in the Lucieville area had cut trees in the sections of their properties reserved as woodlots.[52] Having become very concerned that the Quebec countryside was being depleted of firewood (as discussed in chapter 7), Joly had drafted sales contracts that specified that the only wood that could be cut for sale beyond the front thirty arpents was red spruce and wild cherry. He had also sold smaller parcels exclusively as firewood lots with the similar restriction against clearing, burning branches, or selling any wood from them except for the few trees suitable for planks or square timber, should there be any.[53] His initial impulse in 1897 was to sue two farmers for the $100 fine specified in the sales contracts, adding that it was in the general interest "as well as our own" to make an example of them. He also accepted Edmond's advice to print and distribute a warning to the community in question, but this backfired when he learned that there were actually fourteen "trespassers." Joly fretted to his son that if the warnings were already distributed, there was no choice but to sue all fourteen individuals, "or we would lose all our authority on these people, and I have always avoided threatening them when not fully decided to carry on the threat."[54]

Fritz Parrot, the estate manager, was sympathetic to the settlers, agreeing with them that the reserved land was not in the best place because it was arable and close to the royal road and noting that they were quite willing to respect such a reserve at the opposite end of their lots. Edmond disagreed, arguing that the reserve was located where it would best protect the family's domaine land from forest fire, but it appears likely that some sort of settlement was reached out of court.[55] The issue emerged again eight years later, however, when Joly wrote to a local farmer that he would visit his lot at the first opportunity, warning that if the allegations were true, "ne soyez pas surpris si je me trouve forcé de prendre les procédures contre vous telles que pourvues par votre contrat." The 1897 circular was distributed once again in January 1906, with the added reminder that "il est absolument nécessaire que les conditions de cette clause soient rigoureusement observées, non seulement dans mon intérêt, mais aussi dans celui de vos voisins et de la vôtre."[56] Remarkable as it may seem, Joly's grandson was still enforcing that clause in 1945.[57]

As a leading proponent of agricultural improvement, Joly operated a farm on the seigneury that was clearly meant to serve as more of a model for the local habitants than as a source of income. He was proud, for example, of the homespun made from the wool of his sheep, donating such a suit to Premier Mercier in 1891, and he was complimented by the Duke of Argyle in 1906 for his barn's "arrangement to let all the refuse descend into the lowest part for carting out."[58] Yet the cost of labour meant that expenditures outweighed income by an average of $1,508 a year between 1898 and 1904. The sales figures did not include the value of the pork and hay furnished to the logging crew – or the pork, chickens, potatoes, eggs, butter, cream, and milk supplied to the manor house as well as the families of Edmond and Julia, totalling $930 in value in 1902 – but the deficit in the farm accounts was still significant.[59]

Proud though he was of his family's seigneurial status, Joly was liberal and pragmatic enough to realize that Quebec was far from being feudal France or even contemporary England. In a lengthy letter to an improving English landlord in 1895, Joly wrote,

Speaking broadly, where you have three Distinct classes, landlords, farmers and farm labourers, we have only one, composed of the owners of the soil, which they cultivate themselves. There are so few farm labourers here that they do not constitute a separate class. Every man owns his own land, and with wise management can live comfortably and bring up a large family with no anxiety for his old age, nor for the future of his numerous boys. They can purchase good lands for a mere song, a couple of shillings an acre with long terms of payment, and tho' the opening of such lands is hard work, cutting down the forest, removing the stumps, etc. wherever they have been wise enough to settle on good arable land, perseverance and steadiness are ultimately rewarded.

The chief problem, Joly added, was that not all the country people in Quebec were wise enough to turn their advantages to a good end:

The fact that they are their own masters and that life is so easy with them, leads many to carelessness and extravagance. Many run into debt to the country store keepers, mortgage their lands and then leave for the U.S. where they obtain high wages in the factories, some save their money to free their land from encumbrance and return to us wiser and better men, but alas too many waste their earnings, become fixtures in the factory and never return to their old home.[60]

Even though Joly's letter erased the seigneurs as a distinct class in the Quebec countryside, he clearly shared much of the anti-modern perspective of romantic English-language writers who viewed the French-Canadian habitant as a link to an earlier less materialist and less superficial era. Joly was actually considered to be an authority by journalists such as C.H. Farnham, who published a *Harper's* article on the subject in 1883; H.A. Kennedy, who had been writing articles on "Jean-Baptiste" and his language for London's *Contemporary Review*; and Eleanor McNaughton, who wrote an article titled "A Habitant Woman" in 1896. In a letter to Joly, McNaughton stated that she had described her subject as having the qualities he had recognized as typical, particularly the women's "simple faith and goodness and the courage to plod through hard work without complaining."[61] The last words of the will Joly drafted in 1899 enjoined his son Edmond "not to abandon our workmen and employees, when accident or old age force them to rest," and trusting that he would "live happily" among "our country people ... as my father and I have done, for so many years."[62] Wrong though he was in claiming that his father had enjoyed a good relationship with the local farmers, Joly clearly epitomized historian Brian Young's observation that "while the merchant or manufacturer might presume to operate in a realm of individual interest, of freedom of contract, and of the autonomy of the factory walls, patricians understood their complete interdependence with the local, the producer, the *censitaire*, the tenant."[63]

But feudal traditions were becoming increasingly anachronistic, and Edmond clearly lacked the patience of his father. When a logger he employed to cut 10,000 railway ties in 1898 signed a separate contract with Price and Company, Edmond exploded: "Maintenant, cher monsieur, je désire que vous fassiez bien attention à ce que j'ai à vous dire ... Je vous défends d'accepter un seul centin de Mr Price. Vous travaillez non pour le compte de Mr Price mais pour celui de mon père et Mr Price n'a pas le droit de vous donner aucun ordre ni de vous offrir un centin de plus que le prix dont je suis convenu avec vous et que vous avez accepté."[64] And when a local farmer cut and sold a thirty-five-foot spruce tree on the domaine, rather than taking a smaller balsam or hemlock for his own use as he had requested, Edmond demanded that he pay the price he had received, adding that he would never be allowed to cut another branch on the Joly property: "J'avais pleine confiance en vous et je n'aurais jamais cru que vous auriez abusé de ma confiance comme vous venez de le faire."[65] But Edmond did intervene on behalf of one of his men whose horse had been killed by a locomotive at the Joly siding, writing to the general manager of the Intercolonial Railway that "his loss is a very serious matter for him" and that "the Engine drivers, from what I have been told, are very careless about whistling at crossings."[66] He also hesitated to resort to the courts in case of trespass, choosing instead to invoke threats and moral authority, as in 1903 when he asked the curé of St Édouard to intervene with parishioners who were chopping down his elm trees for the bark, presumably for medicinal uses.[67] Edmond may have been less paternalistic in outlook and approach than his father, but he clearly still thought of himself as the seigneur of Lotbinière half a century after seigneurial tenure had been abolished.

Lumberman

A much more important source of income than land rents for the Jolys was their lumber business. As we have seen, Pierre-Gustave Joly built two new sawmills in the early 1830s, and local inhabitants worked in the forest for him each winter thereafter. Despite the onset of an international financial crisis in 1857,[68] the senior Joly contracted with thirty "entrepreneurs" that year to supply him with 17,500 logs. Sixteen of these contracts were for only 200 logs each, and there were only five contracts specifying 1,000 logs or more, so there was clearly an agriforestry economy in Lotbinière, as in the township zones north and south of the St Lawrence valley.[69] Even though provincial wood exports declined by 44 percent in 1858, Pierre-Gustave Joly increased production to 25,400 logs that year, having agreed to supply 45,000 to 55,000 spruce deals (a term used for softwoods between two and four inches thick and nine and eleven inches wide) to Charles E. Levey of Quebec.[70] In order to keep up with this demand, he had a large new waterdriven sawmill built on the Rivière du Chêne, one with forty-two saws measuring four feet four inches across, in addition to sixteen sevenfoot saws, at the sizeable cost over-run of $16,500.[71] Even though the economy had not recovered by June 1860, Joly's mill was producing as many as 1,140 deals per day. The 1861 census reported a capital investment of $50,000, an employment force of eighty men earning $1,500 per month, and the processing of 36,000 logs valued at $6,000 to produce 100,000 spruce boards and 45,000 pine boards.[72]

Although most of the lumber went to the United States, Joly also tested the French market, sending a load of spruce boards to Nantes in 1861.[73] The Nantes firm was able to sell the lumber at the relatively high price (considering the depressed market) of 12,029 francs (approximately $5,000), but the freight costs reduced Joly's return to only 2,024 francs ($843). The French firm concluded that the only wood worth shipping across the Atlantic would be oak and elm.[74] With the American demand for lumber still in decline in 1861, Joly also began to cut firewood (1,000 cords for the winter of 1861–2), presumably for the Quebec City market.[75] The demand for lumber rebounded as the Civil War progressed, however, for Joly was approached by a number of merchants wishing to purchase his deals, including in one case all the red spruce on hand from 1860 and 1861.[76] The 23,650 pine and spruce logs Joly issued contracts for in the fall of 1862 and the 23,500 of the same two years later were only slightly less than the number for 1858, the year before the new mill was built.[77]

Whereas Pierre-Gustave Joly had dealt with a number of different agents or brokers each year, Henri-Gustave left the marketing to two Quebec City firms: Bennett and Company, which dealt largely with merchants in Whitehall, New York; and John Burstall and Company, which supplied the British market.[78] Henri-Gustave's correspondence makes little reference to the lumber business during the 1860s and 1870s, but production appears to have been on the upswing for a time because in 1865 he contracted with the operators of thirty-five *chantiers* (the term used for the team of loggers associated with a specific timber 'shanty') to cut 33,250 logs, one-third pine and two-thirds white spruce.[79] Although Joly was a prominent advocate of agricultural improvement, and he did report operating a small flax processing mill for the local farmers in 1871, he was evidently not troubled by the common complaint that woods work led to the neglect of farms.[80] By 1881 Joly was purchasing logs from the large G.B. Hall firm of Montmorency, which owned land adjacent to Lotbinière, but it appears that most of his raw material continued to come from his own timber reserve.[81]

In the meantime, production in 1871 had remained stable, according to the census of that year. The mill work force had dropped from the eighty men reported a decade earlier to forty-five in summer and twenty-five in winter receiving a total of $10,500 in wages, but the number of logs processed remained the same, at 36,000, again mostly spruce. The value of the finished product, however, had increased from $36,000 to $42,000.[82] With 1874 came an international economic crisis, with the result that production was lower in 1881 than a decade earlier.[83] Finally, in 1884, Joly was forced to transfer his life insurance policy of $40,000 to the Quebec Bank as security for the arrears of the previous year, which amounted to $23,000. He assured the bank that his tenants and those who had purchased land from him owed about $10,000 and that he had issued stern warnings that they "must make earnest effort to pay next year." Should he not be able to make a significant reduction in his debt within a year, he would give the bank a mortgage on the seigneury. The encumbrance of $46,666 on the seigneury, for payment of rents to members of his family, was light, Joly claimed, in comparison to its total worth. In conclusion, he asked the bank to advance another $13,000 by the following spring, obviously to fund his lumber operations and to renew his outstanding notes, a request that the bank rapidly complied with.[84]

Joly was clearly having difficulty collecting debts, for as of 1885 his miller on the Bois Clair River was behind by four payments, amounting to $430. Another concern was that the machinery of the main mill at the mouth of the Rivière du Chêne was beginning to wear out. Although a railway crossed the southern part of the seigneury, the rivers and streams that carried the logs in the spring drained northward, so Joly continued to operate the water-driven sawmill located close to the St Lawrence. As a result, he had to continue shipping his timber by sailing vessels to Quebec City, where it was loaded onto wharves before being sent to the American market. In 1883 the sawmill and mill site of twenty-nine arpents in the village of Leclercville were assessed at only $18,205, much less than the original cost of construction.[85] During the summer of 1885 Joly informed his son Edmond, who was now also involved in the business, of a fourth interruption in the operation of the mill, this one very serious. A 2,000-pound flywheel had broken, bringing production to a halt at a time when the water would soon be too low to operate the machinery. The foreman had gone to Montreal for a replacement, but the same model could not be found, and the least difference "pourrait tout gâter." Rather than venting his frustration, however, Joly concluded, "Il faut de la philosophie, en ce monde, et il y a 26 ans que ce fly-wheel fait son devoir."[86]

The repair having been made, another setback occurred in early October when the schooners loaded with the Jolys' lumber encountered strong headwinds and had to return to Pointe Platon. Joly claimed that he was trying to find other schooners because these ones were "ensorcelées" (bewitched).[87] Enough boats had been found by mid-month, but the mill's capacity continued to be sharply reduced by the shortage of water.[88] Finally, in the first week of November, Joly could report that the mill was going very well; they were loading two large boats and were expecting their schooners to arrive with the first northeasterly.[89]

Well into the age of steam, then, Joly's lumber business was dependent on wind and water power – and therefore on the vagaries of the weather – even though the logging of the Rivière du Chêne watershed was markedly reducing its summer flow.

Fortunately for Joly, the economic contraction had ended by 1885, and in addition to hiring his own crew, he was able to contract with thirty-five of the local farmers that fall to cut 24,400 logs.[90] This was at the high end of what was being produced in the 1830s and 1840s, as we saw in chapter 1. The fact that Joly reported 64,870 logs the following spring, which he claimed was nearly 6,000 more than the previous year, suggests either that he had signed more contracts or, perhaps more likely, that he was purchasing from other suppliers. He wrote to Edmond that this was a lot more wood than he had wanted, but he would not regret it if the mill could process it all.[91] The river was already dangerously low by mid-May, but sixty-eight boatloads of deals were shipped between May 14 and November 17, 1886, with an additional one being lost to shipwreck.[92]

The surviving accounts for that year provide a detailed view of the Jolys' production. They delivered 11,325 pine deals varying from under nine feet to twelve feet in length, but their main commodity was spruce deals, of which they shipped a total of 105,692. With the 563 pine culls and 8,067 spruce culls, the total production was 125,647 spruce and pine deals, all but a few of which were of three-inch thickness. The sales prices are not recorded, but expenses included $8,393 for the contractors' six "collages," presumably meaning the money paid for cutting the logs, plus $1,711 paid to the foreman of the Jolys' own *chantier*. In addition, $186 was paid to the cullers, and the expenses for the timber drive totalled $1,218, including $66 for 720 pounds of pork. The expenses for sawmill wages, piling the deals on the wharf, and so on totalled $17,032, and miscellaneous costs such as deliveries and mill repairs amounted to $488, resulting in a total expenditure of $29,094.[93] Clearly, then, the Jolys' lumber business injected a significant amount of capital into the local economy.

The year 1886 was obviously a profitable one for the business because the Jolys were able to repay the Quebec Bank $7,500 in advance notes the following January, thereby reducing their mill account to $4,500. Because they were considered to be good customers, the bank offered to make the usual advances "from time to time as required, in proportion to the number of logs delivered on the Bank of the river, ... and in this connection your *own* statement of the number so delivered will suffice."[94] The bank manager also wrote that the directors would be amenable to a "special and exceptional advance" in anticipation of the sale of real estate or from other sources.[95]

But the winter of 1886–7 proved to be a much more challenging one for logging operations, for Joly wrote in late January that the "entrepreneurs" were abandoning their *chantiers*, presumably because of heavy snow. He sympathized because they would not earn much that year but added that he would not allow a single one to leave. In addition, he was sending a large horse of his own to one of the *chantiers* in order to help increase production.[96] To take advantage of the promising market conditions, Joly decided to purchase a substantial amount of pine timber the following September.[97] This proved to be a good gamble, for Burstall and Company contracted for the year's entire production two months later, and conditions in the woods were greatly improved over the previous winter.[98]

Joly refused, however, to sell hemlock bark until he could find a market for its timber.[99] Being no longer involved in politics, he had more time to devote to the forest conservation movement, as we shall see in chapter 7, and he did not approve of the wastage of wood caused by the tanning industry's demand for hemlock bark to produce tannin.[100] His patience was rewarded the following year when a company from Whitehall, New York, offered to take his hemlock, in addition to his one-inch spruce sidings, but this did not prevent trespassers from cutting ninety-two of his hemlock trees for their bark in August 1888.[101]

At this point Joly's lumber business was challenged less by the supply of raw material than by the seasonal fluctuations in the flow of water to his mill. On October 9, 1887, for example, his manager worried that there was only enough water for one saw and that he might have to shut it down as well. Heavy frosts a few days later forced the manager to wake the men up at midnight in order to saw as much as possible before the river was frozen over for the season.[102] During the first week of November several thousand logs were stuck in the ice, and Joly was worried about saving them, though a break in the weather granted the required reprieve.[103] The other major worry was the ebbing tide that left only a few days to load the large amount of lumber onto boats before the winter set in.[104] This must have been a time-consuming process, for more than sixty boats were loaded in the fall.[105]

The weather cooperated fully in the spring of 1888, when as many as 3,000 logs a week were processed by the mill due to the high water.[106] Possibly reflecting his concern that the local supply of firewood should not be exhausted, Joly turned down a request that year by the Association des colons des Laurentides to sell it 10,000 cords of fire-wood for the Montreal market.[107] The following spring his contractor informed him that "the news from England keeps good, and it looks as if the year 1889 will be a good one for Lumbermen."[108] A lack of water threatened to make the log drive "a long and expensive one," but the weather turned wet enough to keep the mill operating throughout the summer and fall.[109] Although high marine insurance rates diminished the attractiveness of the English market, demand in the United States remained strong.[110]

Money was presumably becoming scarce, however, for in 1890 Joly placed fifty-five lots on the Rivière du Chêne on the market, selling thirty-five within short order, and he also began to seize land from de-linquent debtors.[111] Still vigorous at the age of sixty, he had spent part of the winter keeping a close eye on operations in the woods. He reported to Edmond that the interminable log drive had taken twenty-nine days, as compared with fifteen the previous year and ten the year before that, but the weather compensated by again providing plenty of rain to op-erate the mill throughout the summer.[112]

Unfortunately, the international market was entering a recession, and the manager of the Quebec Bank advised Joly in November 1890 that the directors had advised against logging operations that winter. Any advances would therefore be small in comparison to former years: "In the meantime they would like to know the amount you have still to get from sales of this year's cut." This rather belated notice placed Joly in a bind; he replied that he had signed logging contracts the previ-ous week, and the men had begun work. He had sold all the previous year's production but was still owed $1,535 by his regular customers in Whitehall.[113] To the bank's request for a detailed account of his claims and liabilities, Joly responded that he owed his sister $40,000 as her share of the family inheritance, on which he paid an annual interest of 6 percent. He also owed $4,600 to her daughter, $7,400 to his daughter-in-law, $400 per year to one of his daughters by her marriage contract, and $7,200 to a Mrs Wurtele to pay off an old mortgage on the Hale estate. The total liability was $70,666, but the interest had always been paid regularly, and the debt was secured on the seigneury as well as other property at Pointe Platon and Rivière du Chêne.

On the credit side, the life insurance policy the bank held was now worth $46,000. In addition, the seigneury contained about 100,000 acres, for which he could get $5 an acre because "the farmers want the land very badly for firewood, of which they have scarcely any left, and for settling their children near them." As a sort of postscript Joly mentioned still owing half the $1,200 his mother had left to charitable institutions, $802 to his lumber brokers on the previous year's account, and approximately $1,200 in taxes and other sundry accounts, but these amounts due were more than offset by the seigneurial rents and arrears, plus his lumbering operations for the year showed a balance of $12,602 to the good. Joly therefore hoped that the bank would advance the requested sum of $17,500 in spite of the gloomy market prospects.[114]

The directors were not to be persuaded, however, and they refused to advance Joly any money whatsoever, though they did assure him that they would not pressure him to repay his debt, so that he would have time to remove his relatives' mortgages on part of the seigneury.[115] Those mortgages were therefore preventing Joly from raising money on the security of his land. How he managed to finance the year's operations is not clear, but the American market rebounded in 1891, and he was dealing with the Bank of Montreal by 1893.[116] In the spring of that year Joly wrote to Edmond from Chicago, where he was helping to supervise the province's forest exhibit at the World's Fair, that even though the water might still be too low for the spring drive, he had confidence that the dam on the Rivière aux Cèdres would offer a big advantage over the situation in previous years. He even hoped that they would be able to drive down the old pine logs that had been lying for a long time at the head of the river.[117] In the fall of 1893 Joly contracted for more logs than he had the previous year, despite the fact that Britain and the United States were entering another short recession.[118] He must have been able to sell most of the lumber the following spring, for the saws operated without stop throughout the summer and early fall, and he contracted for the same number of logs in the fall of 1894. The only disappointment he expressed was that the weight of their red spruce had limited the amount that could be shipped, but his manager did find a good local market for it. Joly was clearly in an optimistic mood when he wrote to Edmond in October 1894, for early frosts had frozen the swamps, enabling the loggers to get an early start, and the habitants had been paying their corvées, which presumably meant work in lieu of rents since all traditional servitudes owed to the seigneur had been abolished in 1854. Joly may well have found it symbolic, then, that with the evening sunset, "le ciel était comme de l'or et le Fleuve aussi."[119]

There is less correspondence concerning the lumber business during the next several years, but more trees than usual were cut in the winter of 1894–5, and with approximately 56,000 logs to saw in 1896, the business clearly remained almost as active as ever.[120] A shortage of water that summer, however, meant that the Jolys were not able to pay all their notes in time, and Edmond wrote that the $8,000 per year that his father would receive as his ministerial salary in Ottawa would be "a welcome addition to your strained budget and relieve the dear family Minister of Finance from some of his worries."[121] That same fall, Joly was pleased to learn that lumber prices were increasing, but he instructed Edmond to reach the best bargain possible in selling railway ties to timber magnate Herbert Price, for "nous aurons besoin de tout l'argent que nous pourrons nous procurer cet hiver."[122] He also wrote that they would have to lower the prices of the remaining lots in Lucieville in order to raise enough money to pay the notes coming due on the Banks of Montreal and Quebec.[123] Joly had no intention of profiting from his position as Minister of Internal Revenue, however, writing that if the Burstalls asked to buy hemlock for a government wharf, he would be forced not to sell because of the conflict of interest that the sale would entail.[124] Finally, in April, he was relieved to learn that all their lumber had been sold on the American market.[125] His only concern now was the log drive, especially on the Huron River, where the number of logs would be double that of the previous year and where their own men would not be involved. Joly asked Edmond to go there himself, not so much to supervise as to give the workers courage. Undoubtedly more useful in that respect was the man whom Edmond was instructed to take with him because he was said to have shown much bravery and talent on the Rivière aux Cèdres.[126]

The business was still on a firm footing in the fall of 1897, when Joly was able to pay the bank advance for the year, leaving only $2,000 in arrears from the previous year.[127] He also recommenced the annual dowry payment of $400 a year to daughter Julia, which had fallen behind by five years.[128] A new concern, however, was the sparks from the Intercolonial Railway (ICR) locomotives, which were setting fires along the newly laid tracks that crossed the rear of the seigneury.[129] The Jolys insisted during the winter of 1898–9 that all bark removed from the railway ties cut on their land be burned, and they hired men to suppress small fires along the railway line during the following dry summer, when they also asked that the railway section men burn or remove "the hay, leaves, etc." that they had left on both sides of the track. These precautions were evidently effective because there is no mention of serious losses to fire, though Edmond continued to complain to the ICR about defective smokestack screens during the next several years. He claimed in June 1903, for example, that his men had extinguished five fires on one day alone, but not before one of them had caused $71.59 in damages.[130] Fortunately for the Jolys, lumber prices were increasing sharply by the fall of 1899, enabling them to pay off their long-standing debt of $7,000 to the Quebec Bank.[131] The following year Edmond and his wife took advantage of the situation to embark on a six-month holiday in Europe, and in 1901 they spent the two summer months visiting his parents in the lieutenant governor's residence in Victoria.[132]

Although they created a fire hazard, the construction of two railway lines across Lotbinière in the late 1890s had allowed the Jolys to diversify their production, for one historian has calculated that from the late 1870s to the end of the century railways consumed 20 to 25 percent of the "annual timber product" in the United States.[133] In 1900 the King Brothers paid the Jolys $790 for tamarack and hemlock ties used in building the Lotbinière and Megantic Railway and $2.25 a cord for 800 cords of tamarack firewood.[134] The Jolys also offered Herbert Price 3,131 feet of square hemlock, having sold him 10,000 railway ties a year earlier. A Quebec City tanner had begun purchasing their hemlock bark, and they placed 500 cords on the market for the spring of 1902.[135] Edmond had finally assumed the management responsibilities when his father moved to Victoria in 1900, and he was clearly an astute businessman. In December 1900, for example, he persuaded the Intercolonial Railway to grant reduced freight rates on square timber and bark from the Rivière du Chêne on the grounds that his father owned 100 square miles of "well wooded forest land, which naturally will give a great deal of freight to the I.C.R."[136] He also asked the local station agent to keep a careful account of the number of cars loaded at the Joly siding because the railway had agreed to pay him $2 each.[137] Diversifying further, Edmond installed a shingle mill in 1902 that would produce 15,000 to 20,000 shingles a day.[138]

But the manufacture of saw logs was still the heart of the business, for the Jolys paid off $14,456 in advances from Bennett and Company in 1901.[139] Edmond's installation of a new circular saw the following year caused production to increase from 500 to 700 logs a day, with the same number of hands. His obviously pleased father observed, "C'est une preuve frappante de progrès qui doit faire ouvrir les yeux à un vieil antédiluvien comme moi."[140] Market conditions clearly warranted expansion, for Joly wrote in the fall that it took his breath away to see the prices now offered in comparison to a few years earlier: "In my father's time we got less for our *first* spruce, than we are going to receive for our *fourths*, and the pine at $17.00 per 1000 ft B.M. which is, I think, equivalent to $46.75 p. 100 standard deals is a good price." But the ever-cautious Joly was less interested in making windfall profits than in achieving independence from creditors. He added, "With such bright prospects of good returns for next summer, we must earnestly strive to economize more than ever, doing only at Platon and everywhere what is *strictly necessary*, and watching every cent. What a joy it would be, if, by next fall, we had laid by enough, out of our profits, to dispense with further advances for the winter's operations. – Then think of the year after next, our actually beginning to lay by, for the future, instead of borrowing."[141]

Fulfilment of this dream had to be postponed, however, for the log drive of the following year was a failure.[142] Joly wrote to Edmond in November, "Dear mama has often asked me to take her money from the Savings Bank to help us – Now dear Edmond, I solemnly warn you against touching one cent of her money, so patiently laid by, by her, for so many years. God knows how useful it may be for her. It is sacred money."[143] The money would not, in fact, be needed by Lucy Joly, for she died the following year, but Edmond was at least able to sell $2,541 in hemlock bark during the winter of 1903–4.[144] Also, although his father had been urging him to lead the campaign against the export of raw logs and especially pulpwood (as discussed in chapter 7), Edmond had some pulp trees cut the same winter. As always, Joly avoided criticizing his son, simply stating that he was "very glad that it is not to be taken as a precedent, but only under exceptional circumstances, and to utilize the trees that are falling on the ground, for the want of support after the removal of so much hemlock."[145]

The drive was obviously successful the following year, for Edmond reported that he expected to have 120,000 logs, which was double the usual amount. He had signed a contract with a mill operator from a neighbouring parish to build a steam sawmill near the Intercolonial Railway that would process as many as 15,000 hardwood logs per year. The contractor would operate the mill at a predetermined price for each log, but the Jolys had the right to purchase it from him whenever they so desired.[146] In his report to his father, Edmond also mentioned 4,000 ash logs, plus 350 to 400 cords of firewood from the tops and buttings, which, he wrote, "will give us a nice little return and will help considerably to pay the cost of our steam installation."[147] In addition, he had for sale 3,500 railway ties at thirty-five cents each and 750 cords of bark at six dollars a cord.[148]

When Joly retired as lieutenant governor and returned to Quebec, he resumed control of the lumber business for a time, despite his failing health. The contractors had cut enough trees by early December 1906 to request that the "collage" take place a month early,[149] but heavy snow and a coating of ice in January caused some of them to ask if they could abandon the woods without filling their quotas. They were told by the cullers to do their best because the Jolys had not opened their own *chantier* that year in order to give them employment. One "entrepreneur" was warned that if he did not recommence operations, he would not be paid for the 2,000 logs he had piled in the woods. Only 41,739 logs had been culled as of January 21, but there were still nine *chantiers* to go, and estate manager Parrot felt that they could get 120,000 of the 130,000 logs contracted for, if the Jolys were severe.[150] Fortune was on their side, for snow levels soon dropped, and Parrot was able to report only ten days later that all but two or three entrepreneurs would be able to fulfil their contracts. By early February, he had become worried that there would be too many logs for the mill to process.[151]

The fact that the family lumber business was on solid footing by the end of Joly's life was due largely to his careful management in what tended to be a volatile economy. His strategy could not have been more different from that of John Caldwell, seigneur of nearby Lauzon, as described by the local historian, Joseph-Edmond Roy, in 1894:

La forêt fut donc mise en coupe, et ce fut une coupe fantastique, extravagante, une véritable ronde de sabbat. Une armée de travailleurs pénétra jusqu'aux points les plus reculés de cette région. Torrents, rapides, précipices, rochers abrupts, aucun obstacle ne les effraya. Une grande partie de la jeunesse vaillante de la seigneurie s'enrôla dans ce régiment de coupeurs, de scieurs, d'équarisseurs, de charretiers. Les premiers défricheurs sur les bords du lac Etchemin, à plus de dix huit lieues du fleuve, trouvaient encore, il y a trente ans, des traces de son terrible passage. Sur des milles et des milles de distance, on ne pouvait plus voir un seul arbre de pin. Tout avait été battu, jété à la rivière, trainé au fleuve, scié par les machines de Caldwell.[152]

(Cutting thus began in the forest, and it was a fantastic and extravagant cut, a veritable ring of Sabbath. An army of workers penetrated to the furthest points of the region. Torrents, rapids, precipices, steep cliffs, no obstacle frightened them. A great part of the valiant youth of the seigneury enrolled in this regiment of choppers, of sawyers, of squarers, of carters. The first settlers on the banks of the Etchemin, at more than eighteen leagues

from the river [St Lawrence], still found, thirty years ago, traces of this terrible passage. For miles and miles, one could not see a single pine tree. All
had been cut, thrown in the rivers, dragged to the St Lawrence, sawed by
Caldwell's machines.)

Joly's business approach was not only to ensure that his supply
of raw material would not be exhausted, or his financial investment
overextended, but also to rely on the same contractors responsible
for the same *chantiers* year after year. An example of how carefully
he and his son managed their woods was their rejection in 1898 of
a request to make cordwood of the tops of the trees that had been
cut for railway ties. Edmond informed the interested party that his
father allowed only logging and railway tie contractors to work in
their forests. He explained that there had been so many abuses in the
past that they preferred to lose some wood rather than run the risk of
greater losses.[153] The following year, Joly went as far as to refuse the
$82.32 forwarded by the ICR for timber it had cut on his land. Speak-
ing for his father, Edmond explained that he was "naturally anxious
to protect his property from depredation" and that he expected the
railway authorities to instruct their subordinates "not to fell timber
except where absolutely necessary to secure the safety of the road and
the telegraph wires." He also expected to receive "a strict and correct
account of all timber which you may find it absolutely necessary to
fell."[154]

It is quite possible that the Lotbinière forest would not have been able
to sustain the increased harvest of logs for lumber in later years, but the
demand for pulpwood was presumably a boon for the Joly family, as
it was for owners of woodlots throughout the province. Henri-Gustave
had been reluctant to enter this market, for he was a very cautious businessman who chose to manage his forests carefully in order to supply
his mill for the long term instead of cutting young trees or marketing
raw logs that would deplete his natural resource as well as further
reduce the flow of water to his mill. Rather than risk bankruptcy by
investing in steam technology, Joly had faced the annual anxiety of
whether the fall rains would suffice to operate the sawmill long enough
to process all his logs. Only when he was in British Columbia, and the
economy was on a dependable upswing, did his son take the initiative
of selling pulpwood as well as acquiring a supplementary steam mill
(though at the financial risk of its operator), thereby significantly increasing their annual output.

Joly's business conservatism was, in part, a reflection of his shortage of capital, for he had to approach the banks for each winter's operating expenses. This was also the practice for large-scale lumber firms such as C.S. Clark and Company,[155] but Joly's inherited financial obligation to his sister meant that when the market went into a downswing, it was very difficult for him to raise capital despite his credit worthiness.[156] Even if he had had access to sufficient capital to add value to their lumber by manufacturing products such as doors and windows, Joly's political career did not leave him enough time to become a true entrepreneur. And by temperament as well as necessity, he scrupulously avoided risking money in such speculative schemes as his father had been involved in. Henri-Gustave invested in Colonel Strange's ill-fated western ranch, probably because Strange was a close friend,[157] but to take only two examples from 1889, he refused that year to become involved in the construction of the Lotbinière and Megantic Railway, even though it would run near the western border of his landed property, or to purchase three lots in the Lake Megantic area that were purported to be rich in gold.[158] In the final analysis, given that the Joly lumber operations did not produce much surplus investment capital and that they had a mutual dependency on a local population whose farms were too marginal to allow for much market production, this case study supports Salée's argument that seigneurial manufactures were little more than "technical inroads with limited societal impact" as far as Quebec's transition to the capitalist mode of production is concerned.[159]

Conclusion

In an unidentified and undated news clipping in the Joly de Lotbinière papers, written under the mistaken assumption that Joly was to enter the Senate, the author stated,

> Dans les relations d'affaires, M. Joly a fait preuve du même patriotisme et du même désintéressement qui lui avaient merité de nombreuses sympathies dans l'enceinte parlementaire. Élevé au milieu des avantages que procurent la fortune et le prestige d'une famille issue de la vieille noblesse française, jamais l'égoïsme ou l'ambition n'ont trouvé place dans son coeur. Pour lui, les richesses sont un moyen de faire le bien de ses compatriotes et le bonheur de son pays. Il a illustré ce noble sentiment par son dévouement à la cause de l'agriculture pratique et au développement de l'industrie manufacturière. Le comté de Lotbinière, qui en ressent les

bienfaits incalculables, est unanime à rendre hommage à son mérite, et au nom de *seigneur Joly*, comme l'appellent les compagnards, la satisfaction se peint sur toutes les figures.[160]

(In his business relations, Mr Joly has demonstrated the same patriotism and even disinterest that merited him numerous sympathies within parliamentary circles. Raised amidst advantages associated with the wealth and prestige of a family from the old French nobility, never did egoism or ambition find a place in his heart. For him, riches are a means to benefit his compatriots and the fortunes of his country. He has illustrated this noble sentiment by his devotion to the cause of practical agriculture and the development of industrial manufacturing. The county of Lotbinière, which has gained from this devotion incalculable benefits, is unanimous in rendering homage to his merit, and at the name of *seigneur Joly*, as the compagnards call him, satisfaction is painted on every face.)

The sycophantic tone aside, such statements support Grenier's suggestion that if the seigneurs had been truly resented, 1854 would have brought a greater rupture in their social dominance.[161] But the fact remains that – despite relief from the seigneurial mill privileges, taxes on property sales, the annual corvée, and some lesser obligations – subordination to the former seigneurs did not disappear overnight. In some respects, it intensified because former seigneurs now had absolute title over the former seigneury's ungranted land and could therefore impose strict conditions on the sons of local farmers who wished to settle in the area. Furthermore, few of the former censitaires had the incentive or the wherewithal to pay off their constituted rents, and as far as Lotbinière was concerned, local inhabitants were more likely than ever to work in the Joly *chantiers*, thereby becoming semi-proletarianized. The sawmill and wharf also employed a sizeable number of men, and by 1876 there were nearly a hundred occupied lots in the village of Leclercville at the mouth of the Rivière du Chêne, in addition to the seventeen that were inhabited by the mill's employees.[162] But much of Lotbinière's capitalist production continued to be based on lingering pre-capitalist social bonds and obligations, for it did not challenge the dominance of the "seigneur" and it perpetuated habitant ties to the land. The case of Lotbinière reveals, therefore, that the agri-forestry system and what Gérard Bouchard has referred to as the social and economic "co-integration" between capital and the family-based rural economy were not limited to Quebec's colonization zones.[163]

By patronizing the same local contractors year after year, the Jolys did help foster the development of a small rural capitalist group within the seigneurie, and there were two sizeable foundries and finishing shops in the parish of Lotbinière by 1871, as well as a grist mill that out-produced that of the Jolys. There were also fourteen brick manufacturers, six saw mills, two carding mills, two fulling mills, and two grist mills in the parishes of St. Jean and Ste. Emmélie, but all on a very small scale,[164] so there was certainly no challenge to the community's ongoing economic subordination to the "seigneur" in an era of rising liberal individualism. Although E.P. Thompson warned that one must be wary of the word "paternalism" because "it is a description of social relations as seen from above,"[165] the fact remains that the careful exploitation of the Lotbinière forest resource provided income and long-term security for families who would not have been able to survive for long on their farms had the forest reserve been sold to an outside lumber firm. From a Marxist perspective such encouragement to remain on marginal farms "helped to perpetuate a system that entailed endless toil and poverty on the treadmill of the agro-forestry economy,"[166] but the option of joining the ranks of the urban factory workers clearly had little appeal for those who chose not to abandon their Lotbinière farms.

Not enough work has been done on rural industry in Quebec for us to judge how typical the Jolys' enterprise was, aside from its unusual longevity, a record that can be attributed in part to the well-connected family's access to bank loans (circumscribed as that access may have been) at a time when these were not generally available to rural entrepreneurs.[167] Henri-Gustave's business conservatism was clearly another factor during the difficult economic climate of the later nineteenth century. It could be argued that his approach to business represented a synthesis of his father's entrepreneurial outlook and the aristocratic ethos of his mother's family. That ethos was reflected in Henri-Gustave's insistence on reserving the seigneurial pew, perhaps to help compensate for the fact that, as Protestants, he and his family were unable to participate in Roman Catholic ceremonies in which they normally would have played an honorary role, thereby solidifying seigneurial hegemony.[168] He was also careful to provide the local curés with building materials and other assistance, when requested. The Joly de Lotbinières' social position did not permit them to socialize on a regular basis with the local notables, and they usually did not live in the seigneurial manor during the winter, but they did play the role of community benefactors with such initiatives as the establishment of a local agricultural society as well as the acquisition of government funds for local improvements, not to mention individual acts of charity. In short, a system of dependency – both coercive and benevolent – existed in Lotbinière that, as we shall see in the next chapter, helped to make Joly virtually unbeatable in elections even as a Protestant and a Liberal during an era of ultramontane ascendancy.

Henri-Gustave and Edmond-Gustave Joly de Lotbinière. Note the account book in Edmond's hand, symbolizing the fact that he had assumed management of the seigneury by this time. In wearing a quasi-military suit, Edmond is advertising his manliness as well as his authority.
Domaine Joly de Lotbinière Collection.

Seigneurial office, Leclercville. The picturesque design of this building, built ca 1850, conforms to that of the manor house at Pointe Platon. Domaine Joly de Lotbinière Collection.

Embarcations à Saint-Jean-de-Deschaillons, watercolour on paper by Henri-Gustave Joly de Lotbinière, 1882. Joly lacked his father's interest in photography, but he had studied painting as a student in Paris, and eleven of his St Lawrence River scenes painted in 1882 and 1883 are to be found in the Musée national des beaux-arts du Québec in Quebec City. Romantic as this painting is, Joly depended on such schooners for the delivery of his lumber deals to the wharves of Quebec City. Collection Musée national des beaux-arts du Québec, accession no. 1945.70, photographer Denis Legendre.

Sawmill workers' houses and lumber at Leclercville. Domaine Joly de Lotbinière Collection.

Chapter Four

Liberal Deputy

Although Pierre-Gustave Joly was a friend of Papineau and Lamennais and a champion of liberal causes – as we saw in chapter 1 – he was too tied to his property and business interests to be a true radical. He complained in a letter from Paris in 1848, for example, that no one dared express sympathy for King Louis-Philippe, who had been forced to abdicate, and that one of his nephews had been dragged in the mud simply for asking why lanterns were being broken in the streets.[1] It is rather doubtful, then, that the young Henri-Gustave was caught up as a university student in the radical tide that swept over Europe that year. Certainly, he would be a moderate liberal throughout his political career, which began with his election to the Legislative Assembly in 1861. Joly was a champion of fiscal prudence, honest government, and agricultural reform – which were then signature Liberal tenets – and his reform initiatives also reflected his patrician sense of responsibility as well as distaste for the materialist values and ruthless business practices of the bourgeoisie.

Pre-Confederation Politics

Pierre-Gustave Joly had declined the invitation to run in Lower Canada's 1830 election, claiming that he was unfamiliar with Canadian laws,[2] and his subsequent unpopularity as a seigneur undoubtedly precluded further offers. When he attempted to attract recruits to a volunteer militia company during the U.S. Civil War's Trent Crisis in 1862,[3] his seigneurial agent assured him, "Vous ne frapperez pas à une seule porte sans que vous y trouviez un ou des soldats qui seront heureux de prendre place dans les rangs de Votre Compagnie," but this proved to be far from the case even with the strong support of the local curé.[4] Joly had recently returned from New York, where he had been speculating on the stock market as well as in gold, and a far-fetched rumour was circulated that he had made a transaction to sell each volunteer to the Union army for £10.[5] The following spring, in what was clearly a ritualistic act of humiliation, his horses were "maltraités" by persons unknown.[6] He ultimately had to be content to see Henri-Gustave become captain of the local militia battalion that same year, in 1863.[7]

Clearly unelectable himself, Pierre-Gustave had pushed his son to contest the Lotbinière seat in the Province of Canada's Legislative Assembly as early as 1851, only a year after Henri-Gustave had returned to Canada and while he was still articling in a law firm. When the *Journal de Québec* counselled the censitaires of the four seigneurs who were running for office in the Quebec district that they should not feel obliged to vote for them, the senior Joly wrote to the editor that he should offer the same advice to those who were in debt to the fifty to sixty lawyers who currently sat in the Assembly.[8] After the election Pierre-Gustave informed his old friend Louis-Joseph Papineau that Henri-Gustave had been on the point of success despite the opposition of all the clergy and the "anti-rentiers," with seven parishes supporting him, but he was soundly defeated in the eighth after some 100 Irishmen took violent possession of the pole: "depuis ce moment ce n'a plus été que violence et illégalité."[9] The winning candidate in the three-way race was the Liberal incumbent, Joseph Laurin, who probably had the support of the Irish voters because he was a champion of Quebec City's ship labourers, though he would be defeated by the Irish vote in 1854.[10]

Laurin had mocked the young Joly as more suited for the role of dance instructor than that of politician,[11] and Joly did not contest the seat in 1854 or 1858, but he did run again in 1861. Claiming to be an independent, Joly defeated a rival with the Irish name of Mullen by a vote of 797 to 356. His father's reconciliation with the parish priest proved useful,[12] for Joly polled a remarkable 416 votes to Mullen's 1 in the parish of St Louis, which covered the same area as the seigneury of Lotbinière; 145 to 1 in neighbouring St Jean; and 123 to 30 in the county's chef-lieu of Ste Croix. In two more distant parishes he lost by a substantial margin, and in a third the vote was tied. Mullen was disadvantaged by the smaller voter turnout in the parishes that favoured him. For example, whereas 417 of the 476 men on the voters' list for St Louis registered their votes, only 143 of the 307 on the St Apollinaire list did so. Of those 143, 134 voted for Mullen. In addition, Mullen was obviously handicapped by the fact that the three parishes with large Irish populations – St Giles, St Sylvestre, and Ste Agathe – were barred from voting, as they would be in the following two elections, because of their refusal to have their properties assessed for municipal taxation. In fact, St Sylvestre alone had registered 2,255 of the county's 4,933 votes in the preceding election, even though it had scarcely 300 qualified electors. Irish Catholics, in their attempt to ensure the return of John O'Farrell, the Quebec City lawyer who had successfully defended members of their community two years earlier in the famous Corrigan murder case, had registered not only many of the local dead but also famous names such as George Washington, Napoleon, and Julius Caesar. All but twenty-one apparently voted for O'Farrell. It was clearly to Joly's advantage, then, that the Irish had become effectively disenfranchised.[13]

To help ensure that his politician son would have favourable press, Pierre-Gustave Joly joined five others in purchasing Le Canadien in 1862, paying £225 for his single share.[14] By this time the reform opposition to the ministry of John A. Macdonald and George-Étienne Cartier, which had won the election with a reduced majority in Lower Canada, was divided between the Parti rouge followers of Antoine-Aimé Dorion, allied with George Brown, and the less radical faction led by Louis-Victor Sicotte, allied with John Sandfield Macdonald. Given that the Brownites had opposed Upper Canada's contribution to the seigneurial indemnity fund of $3,250,000, an issue that affected Joly personally, it is perhaps not surprising that he supported Sicotte.[15] Upon the defeat of the Liberal-Conservative administration's militia bill in 1862, John Sandfield Macdonald became the new premier, with Sicotte as his Lower Canadian lieutenant. But some of Sicotte's followers (known as Violettes because they blended Conservative blue and Liberal red), returned to Cartier's camp in May of the following year, bringing the government down. Sandfield Macdonald, Brown, and Dorion agreed to combine forces in the ensuing election, which they won despite Cartier's substantial majority in Lower Canada.[16]

Henri-Gustave Joly, who had been re-elected by acclamation, was now in Dorion's camp, for he later explained that he feared the possibility that Sicotte would arrive at an agreement with Cartier and John A. Macdonald, thereby bringing back to power "the very men whom he had taught his followers to regard as inimical to the best interests of the country."[17] Joly did not echo his outspoken father's public call for independence from Great Britain (albeit with one of Queen Victoria's sons as head of a hereditary Canadian monarchy), as the surest way to avoid attack by the belligerent Northern forces during the U.S. Civil War.[18] But like his father, he did reject the Rouge label that he claimed "was applied to the Lower Canadian Reformers, with an eye to injuring them in the eyes of the people."[19]

Opposing Confederation

After a series of combinations had failed to establish a stable government, George Brown, John A. Macdonald, and George-Étienne Cartier established the Great Coalition to pursue the federal union of the British North American colonies or, failing that, the reorganization of the Province of Canada along federal lines. Brown invited A.A. Dorion, L.H. Holton, and Joly to join the committee to investigate the constitutional problems, but Dorion refused, and Holton rejected its conclusion favouring a federal system, either limited to the two Canadas or including all the British North American provinces.[20] Whether Joly took part is not clear, but it appears unlikely. In any case, like all the Lower Canadian Liberals, he would play no role in the Charlottetown and Quebec Conferences, and he would take a firm stance against Confederation when the Quebec Resolutions were presented to the legislature in February 1865.

English-Canadian historians of Confederation have generally described it as an inevitable yet visionary response to the crises of the early 1860s, and viewed its opponents as provincial-minded defeatists.[21] Perhaps not surprisingly, then, they have paid little attention to Joly's carefully reasoned and somewhat unique arguments.[22] But the fact remains that the deputy for Lotbinière spoke in the provincial legislature for an entire day on February 20, 1865, and his speech was considered important enough to be distributed in pamphlet form.[23] Much like his more senior colleagues in the Rouge opposition, Joly attacked Confederation on three basic fronts. He argued that confederacies (a term he used, rather than federations) had historically fostered tribalism and political unrest – witness the American Civil War that was raging at the time; that the supposed benefits of Confederation could be achieved more economically in other ways; and that the proposed constitution would threaten the cultural survival of French Canada. Standard fare as these themes were for the French-speaking anti-Confederationists, Joly's speech was distinctive in its erudition, with copious references to political philosophy and history, and in its argument that the scheme should be opposed because it would weaken the connection with Britain.

Beginning with his first major point, Joly cited Lord Brougham's dic-
tum that federalism created "mutual estrangement, and even hostility
between the different parts of the same nation." Taking the conservative position that "history is the statesman's safest guide," Joly charged
that his opponents had "based all their arguments on the future; they
have tried to prophecy [sic], but for them the history of the past is a
dead letter."[24] He then referred to Macaulay's description of the feeble
Dutch government and disintegrating Central American Confederacy
and to his argument that the Swiss Confederacy survived only because
France, Prussia, and Austria had a common interest in keeping it "as a
neutral and independent state."[25]

Concerning the inherent weakness of confederacies, Joly stated that
historically most had failed due to their lack of homogeneity: "The
strongest bond of union among the citizens of a state is a community
of language and religion. We have neither in common." What Joly referred to as "knowledge" might serve as a mitigating factor, but if the
people of the United States were not educated enough to prevent civil
war, what chance would a British North American confederation have?
When criticized for referring only to republican confederations in his
historical analysis, Joly replied that he had "made no mention of mo-
narchial confederations, because none have ever existed, and none can
exist. The principle of the monarchy is that the power resides in one
person; the principle of confederation is that it resides in all members
of the confederation."[26]

As for the touted benefits of Confederation – increased trade with
the Maritime provinces, coordinated military defence, and a greater
role in international decisions – Joly claimed that they were all over-
stated. He supported the removal of trade barriers with the Maritime
provinces, but he also argued that if they were purchasing Canadian
flour from the Americans, it was because the Americans could transport it more cheaply. Confederation would not change that. Concerning defence, railway access to an ice-free port north of the American
border would obviously be desirable, but this could be built without a
political union.[27] Joly also ridiculed the idea of conjoined colonial forces
defending against an American invasion, pointing out that the Americans would likely attack on multiple fronts, as they had during the War
of 1812. Although opponents of Confederation were accused of being
annexationists, Joly expressed concern that a factionalized and strife-
ridden union would attract the attention of the United States, "which
for a long time has looked on our provinces with a covetous eye."[28]

Canadians might even welcome absorption into the American union once the added administrative costs of Confederation had fomented general unrest by increasing the tax burden, he argued. In proportion to the ratio of their population in the new country, central Canadians would have to contribute three-quarters of the cost of the intercolonial railway, as compared with less than half under the 1863 arrangement. Canadians would also be burdened with the cost of fortifications in the North West at a time when their customs revenue would be decreasing to appease the Atlantic provinces.

To those who supported a strong central government, Joly replied,

> We already possess ... a central power stronger than any power which you can create, and to which we submit without complaint, because it is perfectly compatible with the existence of local powers – I mean the power of England. It is exercised by men who live too far from us to hearken to the bickering of race or of party, or to be mixed up with them in any way. But if that central power was wielded by men taken from among ourselves, men who have taken part in our quarrels and animosities, and who would make use of it to give effect to the views of their party, it would become unsupportable.[29]

Pursuing his third major point, the harmful effect that Confederation would have on French-Canadian cultural survival, Joly charged that – in order to "prolong the ephemeral existence of his administration for a few months" – Attorney General Cartier had "sacrificed, without a scruple" his "precious trust" as "the chief of the French-Canadian nationality."[30] Referring to John A. Macdonald's insistence that there would be no amendment of the terms, Joly accused Cartier's Bleus of taking less care in entering Confederation than they would in buying a horse. He predicted that the anglophones of Lower Canada would convince their counterparts elsewhere in the country to impose a uniform system of provincial governments, one that would soon be dispensed with as a "perfectly useless" expense. Joly also reminded his audience that the historical proponents of British North American confederation had been men such as Lord Durham, whose aim had been French-Canadian assimilation.[31] He clearly saw no contradiction, then, between British imperialism and French-Canadian nationalism.

In his concluding remarks, Joly painted a rosy picture of French-Canadian progress since the British Conquest, as well as French-English relations in Canada East. Now numbering a million people, the

French-Canadian population was increasing rapidly as new townships were opened "in every direction." In fact, the Eastern Townships, originally settled by anglophones, was "slowly giving way to the French-Canadians." Rather than conflict resulting, there was "a friendly rivalry between the two races, a struggle of labor and energy; contact with our fellow-countrymen of English origin has at last opened our eyes; we have at last comprehended that in order to succeed, not only labor is needed, but well-directed and skilled labor, and we profit by their example and by the experience they have acquired in the old countries of Europe." As a result, French Canadians now held "a distinguished position in the commerce of the country," having established savings banks and "one of the finest lines of steamboats in America." In addition to rapid steamboat communication between cities and small towns on the St Lawrence River, railways ensured "that we now measure by hours the duration of a journey which formerly we measured by days." French Canadians also owned foundries and factories, and boasted "a literature peculiarly our own," as well as "several excellent colleges, and an university in which all the sciences may be studied under excellent professors. Our young men learn in the military schools how to defend their country." In short, Joly argued, "We possess all the elements of a nationality,"[32]

Now, however, French Canadians were being told that their aspirations were nothing but dreams: "Il faut briser l'ouvrage d'un siècle! Il faut renoncer à notre nationalité, en adopter une nouvelle, plus grande et plus belle, nous dit-on, que la nôtre; mais ce ne sera plus la nôtre."[33] Cartier had declared that Lower Canada would be the sun of Confederation, but a more fitting symbol for the new country would be the rainbow: "By the endless variety of its tints the rainbow will give an excellent idea of the diversity of races, religions, sentiments and interests of the different parts of the Confederation. By its slender and elongate form, the rainbow would afford a perfect representation of the geographical configuration of the Confederation. By its lack of consistence – an image without substance – the rainbow would represent aptly the solidity of our Confederation."[34]

Emotional as some of his language was, Joly had avoided the rhetoric of Rouge members such as Joseph Perrault, who accused English Canadians in general – and the followers of George Brown in particular – of aiming "to destroy the influence and liberties of the French race" in Canada.[35] But Solicitor General Hector-Louis Langevin was completely wrong in accusing Joly of appealing to the religious and nationalist prejudices of the English-speaking minority in Lower Canada.[36] Instead, he had ended his speech with a reminder to his "fellow-countrymen ... of the precious inheritance confided to their keeping – an inheritance sanctified by blood of their fathers, and which it is their duty to hand down to their children as unimpaired as they received it."[37]

In his opposition to Confederation, Joly was a closer adherent to classical liberal values such as free trade and low taxes than were those who supported it. But his opposition to the centralization of government was not primarily for fiscal reasons, as Andrew Smith suggests was the case for Liberals in Lower Canada,[38] nor did he point to Grand Trunk machinations or criticize Confederation as a socialist threat. In fact, as we shall see, he would support provincial ownership of the North Shore railway, he eventually accepted the need for protective tariffs, and he favoured other government initiatives such as school reform and forest conservation measures. Joly's main case against Confederation was not based on liberal political ideology so much as on the conviction that it would prove to be unstable and that it would threaten French-Canadian cultural survival. Finally, Joly's social conservatism made him temperamentally opposed to radical change and prompted him to envision the imperial Crown as the ideal supra-provincial power, one strong enough to hold the colonies together, while distant enough to prevent that strength from becoming a burden.[39]

Opposition Leader

Ged Martin argues that one reason the anti-Confederation movement did not leave a legacy of bitterness was that critics such as Antoine-Aimé Dorion and Joseph Howe soon reconciled themselves to the new regime by assuming prominent roles within it.[40] Perhaps a more important reason was that French-speaking Quebecers considered Confederation to be a separation at least as much as a union.[41] The Rouges initially remained split on the issue, but Joly was quick to declare that he did not wish to "drag the *rouge* party around like a ball and chain."[42] Elected to the Quebec Assembly by acclamation in 1867, even though the broader Quebec City region went strongly Conservative as usual, Joly announced his acceptance of "le grand plan national de la Confédération" and his eagerness to work towards its "perfectionnement."[43] In the House of Commons, where he also sat due to the double mandate, and where he was also returned without a contest, Joly declared that even though he had opposed Confederation, "the die was now cast ... If the Union were destroyed it would jeopardize all that was British in Canada."[44] This would appear to have been a rather abrupt shift from the arguments in his anti-Confederation speech, but Joly was consistent in that he remained committed to the British tie and the constitutional status quo throughout his career.

Joly would have a low profile in Ottawa, where most of the senior Rouges had opted to sit, and in May 1868 he was even ordered into the custody of the sergeant-at-arms for failing to appear on the day appointed for the swearing in of a committee he was supposed to chair. He had left the city, however, and the matter was dropped.[45] Joly's efforts were largely spent in Quebec City, where he quickly assumed a leading role as government critic and where, despite his relatively youthful age of thirty-eight, he was one of the most experienced members as well as one of the few who were not Conservatives.[46] Halfway through the second provincial session, Joly announced that because a loyal opposition was necessary to the functioning of constitutional government, he now considered himself to be an opposition member.[47] In fact, a small caucus of Liberals had elected him to assume the role of opposition leader. Montreal's *L'Evénement* declared, "L'opposition naissante ne pouvait se donner un chef plus honorable, d'un caractère plus loyal et plus sympathique. M. Joly est un excellent orateur parlementaire; sa parole est claire, précise et, quand il le veut, éloquente."[48] Quebec's federal Liberal deputies also approved of the choice of Joly, for they forwarded a resolution to him two years later, in 1871, thanking him for his "direction à la fois ferme, digne & modérée" and asking him to remain provincial leader.[49]

An obvious handicap for Joly was that the ultramontane campaign reached its peak in 1871, the year that the *Programme catholique* instructed Church members as to what qualified a candidate for their support. Marcel Hamelin states, however, that the contests were very localized in the ensuing provincial election, sometimes more personal than political.[50] The Liberals made slight gains, claiming approximately twenty seats, but the ultramontane challenge on the eve of the ensuing federal election prompted some young Liberal party members to adopt a moderate program under the new name of *Parti national*. Among the measures they supported were provincial autonomy; tariff protection; the secret ballot; education reform; measures to encourage colonization within Quebec rather than western expansion; abolition of the double mandate, the Legislative Council, and the provincial police; and reduction of the number of cabinet ministers and public servants, including school inspectors. Joly supported the movement, presiding over the public meeting in Quebec City in March 1872, where he stressed the need for commercial independence and protection of home industries, a notable switch from his earlier defence of free trade. The party did not survive long, but Joly declared in 1876 that he had not abandoned its policies, and he continued to support tariffs on all American goods except raw materials needed for Canadian manufactures even after the Liberals had adopted reciprocity with the United States.[51]

Apart from this brief experiment, Joly would always identify himself as a Liberal, but he was also very careful not to alienate the Catholic clergy. Whereas the Quebec Liberal members of Parliament Lucius Huntington and Alexander Galt were sounding the alarm bells in response to what they felt was the Catholic Church's threat to civil liberties, Joly warned that the Protestant Defence Alliance, established in 1875, could precipitate a religious war.[52] Joly also protested when the Liberal candidate for the 1876 federal by-election in Charlevoix, P.A. Tremblay, publicized confidential letters from two Quebec-area priests who had been critical of his Conservative opponent, Hector-Louis Langevin. Though he did not accept *Le Canadien*'s statement that Tremblay had falsified these letters, Joly pointed out that the Liberals could not continue to complain about clerical interference at the same time that they themselves were bringing the Catholic Church into politics.[53] This did not prevent Tremblay from challenging Langevin's victory in the courts on the grounds that the curés of Charlevoix had used "influence indue" against him, a path-breaking case that he won in the Supreme Court of Canada.[54]

By keeping his distance from this case, Joly won the approval of priests such as the Reverend Auclair, who wrote to him in 1877 that he had known Joly's father, who was characterized by his "droiture d'esprit, sa noblesse de sentiments et aussi sa générosité proverbiale chaque fois que se présentait l'occasion d'encourager une bonne oeuvre." From father to son, Auclair added, "la belle nature de l'un s'est photographié dans le beau caractère de l'autre."[55] Joly's political security in Lotbinière clearly depended on maintaining good relations with the local curés, but he was also particularly sensitive to issues that threatened to divide Quebec along religious and cultural lines. His main target initially was the tough-minded and ambitious Joseph Cauchon, who was embittered by the fact that his opposition to the guarantees promised for the Protestant school system by Langevin and Cartier had cost him the premiership. In 1868 Joly accused Cauchon of writing a newspaper article that criticized the disproportionate number of English-speaking members on the Permanent Committee for Private Bills. When Cauchon rather perversely opposed the motion that would add two French Canadians to the committee, arguing that proper notice had not been given, Joly dropped his normally gentlemanly pose to declare that Cauchon "had lost his power and his influence, and would never in his life regain it by fomenting, as he has done and was still doing, dissensions among the people of the Province."[56]

But generally, rather than drawing attention to such divisive issues, Joly avoided them, with the result that the opposition was somewhat hamstrung when it came to important matters such as immigration and education. Joly appears to have left the former issue almost entirely to his oppositionist colleagues,[57] and he remained remarkably silent about the first critical issue faced by the provincial administration – namely, how it would respond to the same minority schools issue that had cost Cauchon the premiership. In fact, there is no evidence to suggest that Joly played a role in the events that ultimately led to a Protestant victory, with school taxes paid by corporations divided according to population regardless of denomination, but taxes on private property owned by Protestants going entirely to the Protestant school commissions.[58] In the Assembly, Joly confined himself to praising the school reforms proposed by Premier P.J.O. Chauveau, stating that his long experience as minister responsible for education guaranteed that "les efforts qui seront faits pour développer l'intelligence de la jeune génération seront dans le sens le plus libéral et en conformité des besoins croissants du pays."[59] When Chauveau's bill was presented, Joly supported it without reservation and with little comment.[60] To go further on this controversial issue would have been to risk alienating his Catholic constituents and to jeopardize his self-assumed role of mediator between the two communities as well.

Joly was liberal enough, however, to challenge the deficiencies in the Catholic education system. The father of two engineers, though they never worked in Quebec, Joly declared in 1874 that it was absolutely essential to establish schools that would train engineers, mechanics, and geometricians. Quebec had constructed more than fifteen railway lines, but it was impossible to find a French Canadian who could render more than menial service: "Il est pénible de voir que dans notre province, l'éducation pratique est entièrement sacrifiée à l'éducation classique; nous avons un trop grand nombre de collèges où la jeunesse vient se bourrer de grec et latin, ce qui fait que toutes les professions libérales sont encombrées."[61] In his reply to the speech from the throne in 1876, Joly deprecated the state of primary schooling in Quebec and argued that teacher salaries should be increased significantly. In his words, it was all very well to build railways, "mais il faut avant tout propager l'éducation et alors, dans les campagnes les plus reculées, on comprendra l'utilité des voies ferrées."[62]

Bruce Curtis has argued that inspectors were an essential component of the liberal state's education project,[63] but Joly was not a supporter of such state intervention, at least at the expense of teachers' salaries. During the 1876 session he spoke against the government motion to increase the budget for school inspectors, arguing that the public was hostile to them and that teachers should have priority because many were leaving the profession due to low salaries. In fact, when he became premier, Joly would attempt to abolish the inspectorate. Meanwhile, the government simply took refuge in the fact that the request for more money for the inspectors had come from the newly established Council of Public Instruction, which reflected the wishes of the bishops.[64]

As with the controversial school tax issue of 1868, Joly had remained notably silent on the Boucherville ministry's replacement in 1875 of the Ministry of Public Instruction with a semi-independent council that gave the Protestant minority and the Catholic Church essential control over a school system divided along confessional lines. This was certainly a retrogressive step from the perspective of the liberal values that Joly professed, but the hierarchy of his own Anglican Church supported a separate Protestant school system, and Joly obviously did not wish to alienate the Catholic clergy at a time when ultramontanism was reaching the peak of its political influence. In fact, he was not alone in his silence, for his Liberal colleagues and the Liberal press followed his example.[65] Joly's main focus during his years as the leader of the political opposition in Quebec was on the less culturally sensitive issues of the double mandate, political corruption, fiscal management, economic development, and forest conservation. The first four issues are examined in the remainder of this chapter, and the last – which was Joly's most enduring preoccupation – is discussed in chapter 7.

Given that the double mandate reflected the subordinate position of the provincial governments, Joly found himself in a somewhat awkward position as a member of Parliament (MP) as well as a member of the Legislative Assembly (MLA). He declared himself in favour of abolishing the double mandate in early 1869, stating that his constituents had selected him for the provincial legislature only because they had been caught off-guard by the need to return two representatives. In Joly's words, he had come to realize that the double mandate was "préjudiciable aux intérêts de la province de Québec et à la liberté du pays" because federal cabinet ministers were exercising a good deal of influence in the Quebec Assembly. Given that the powers of the provincial and federal governments were not clearly separated, there would inevitably be a clash of interests between Quebec and Ottawa.[66]

The provincial opposition again introduced a bill to abolish the double mandate late in 1870, but the government responded by making it a ministerial issue, on the grounds that it would deprive Quebec voters of a fundamental right.[67] Two weeks later, after having laid the blame for Quebec's defeat in the pre-Confederation debt matter (to be discussed later in the chapter) at the feet of its federal cabinet ministers, Joly introduced a bill that would end the double mandate only for members of the federal cabinet.[68] The government again defeated it, and in the following session Joly complained that with the double mandate, the current system was little more than a legislative union. He noted, for example, that the premier had been forced as a government supporter in Ottawa to vote in favour of a tariff on coal, flour, and salt that was not in Quebec's interest.[69] The 1871 provincial election saw seventeen candidates elected who also had seats in Ottawa,[70] but finally, in late 1872, Joly succeeded in getting the provincial government to put his motion to abolish the double mandate to a free vote. By this time, the thinly populated provinces of Manitoba and British Columbia were the only ones besides Quebec still adhering to the double mandate, but Premier Chauveau insisted that abolishing it would deprive the Assembly of its best men, those who the people had indicated were most capable of representing them: "On veut ainsi enfreindre les libertés du peuple." Chauveau and other Conservatives also drew on the nationalist card, arguing that abolition would weaken French-Canadian influence in Ottawa.[71] The bill nevertheless passed its third reading in the Assembly with a majority of nine, having attracted a number of Conservative votes, but it was rejected by the Legislative Council, which included a number of federal deputies.[72]

In his reply to the speech from the throne in December 1873, Joly criticized the fact that no mention was made of the double mandate. The new premier, Gédéon Ouimet, replied that the reason was that it had virtually been abolished by federal legislation, but Joly later complained that Quebec MLAs could still sit in the federal Senate.[73] The Liberals subsequently introduced a bill to rectify this situation, a bill that the premier opposed while declaring it an open vote, which allowed it to pass, though not without being amended by the Legislative Council.[74] When the federal election took place in 1874, Joly opted to retain his provincial seat. His decision offered the federal Conservatives a good opportunity to take Lotbinière, for Joly wrote to a local notable named Levasseur in January that he had arrived in Ste Croix the previous night to regulate difficulties that threatened to divide the party and cost the election. Joly requested that Levasseur join in ensuring Henri Bernier's election, adding, "Je n'ai pas d'ambition personnelle; je sacrifie mon avenir politique pour remplir mon devoir en restant ici, dans la Législature locale." In return, Joly wrote, he was asking his friends to send a man to Ottawa who belonged to the same party.[75]

Joly's plea was successful, and the following year, when the Liberals were in power in Ottawa, they attempted to entice him to join their ministry. Senator Hector Fabre, who was editor of *L'Événement*, wrote to Prime Minister Mackenzie that Joly was the most popular man in the district, and his selection would "give us great prestige, which we lack just now." Another good reason for choosing Joly was that his removal from the provincial scene would enable his colleagues to pursue "some combination to upset the Conservative ministry" – namely, a coalition with dissident members of that party. (Although he was far from being a radical, Joly consistently opposed any union with Conservatives.) Fabre felt that Wilfrid Laurier would also be a good choice, but some objections had been made to his nomination, and "as his day is sure to come, he can afford to wait."[76] Joly himself urged Alexander Mackenzie to appoint Laurier instead because he was not prepared to abandon his friends in Quebec after their recent electoral defeat. He added, however, that he continued to think the party leaders had made a mistake in asking him to remain in Quebec when the double mandate ended. "The Province of Quebec will never consent to have a Protestant for a Premier," he wrote, "and I am not ready to say, looking on the matter from the point of view of the majority, that they are quite wrong." He had recently offered "to withdraw altogether from public life" because he felt he was "a stumbling block in their road to success," but his colleagues would apparently not hear of it.[77]

The prime minister chose the controversial Joseph Cauchon instead of Joly or Laurier, even though Fabre had warned that Cauchon was a political liability because he had alienated the English-speaking voters during the previous election, which had been marked by considerable violence. Mackenzie explained to Joly that he did this because Cauchon had been put forward by the French-speaking members "on almost every occasion" during the previous two sessions – "it seriously embarrasses me now," he explained.[78] Fabre felt that Cauchon would give way to Joly if offered the lieutenant governorship, but putting his own career advancement aside, Joly came out firmly against the choice of Cauchon for that position. He informed Mackenzie that the Liberals in the provincial Assembly were unanimously opposed to Cauchon and that they felt they had the right to be consulted in such a decision. Cauchon was passed over as lieutenant governor, but rather than acceding to the provincial deputies' recommendation of Maurice Laframboise, Mackenzie rather inexplicably chose the Rouge standard bearer Luc Letellier de Saint-Just.[79]

In January 1877 Letellier transmitted Mackenzie's second offer of a federal cabinet position to Joly, including a seat in the Senate. The assumption was clearly that he would replace Cauchon as chief Quebec spokesman. The ever-upright Joly replied that his old enemy should be treated fairly by the party that had accepted his services, and Letellier reported to the prime minister that once that was done, Joly would certainly move to Ottawa.[80] Joly had made it clear, however, that he would never serve in the same government as Cauchon because he considered Cauchon's appointment to the cabinet to be a flagrant contradiction of Liberal principles. Even though Mackenzie assured him that the obstacle would disappear within a few months, Joly declined his invitation.[81] Although Joly had little reason to assume that his political prospects in Quebec would significantly improve, a year later he would be premier.

Government corruption was not a major theme in the beginning years of Quebec's history as a province, but Joly had charged in 1871 that Cauchon's provincial seat should be declared vacant because he was receiving a government subsidy as owner of the Beauport Asylum.[82] Cauchon argued that the asylum actually belonged to two doctors who worked there, but the permanent committee on privileges and elections, which included Joly, finally recommended in December 1872 that his seat be vacated.[83] Under pressure from the government, Cauchon resigned before a vote could be taken in the Assembly.[84] Joly was not prepared to let the government off quite so easily, however, and he moved that a special committee be appointed to investigate the renewal of the asylum's contract, which had been granted eighteen months before it was due to expire and without consultation of the Assembly. He charged that Cauchon was being rewarded for contributions made to the Conservatives' election coffers, but Premier Chauveau denied knowing that Cauchon was the true owner of the asylum, and Joly's motion was defeated by the governing majority.[85]

The hasty return of Cauchon by acclamation in the following by-election provided Joly with one more opportunity to embarrass the government, for Cauchon's opponent had been disqualified by the electoral commissioner. Suggesting that the commissioner had been bribed, Joly moved that he be brought before the House to explain himself. When his motives for attacking Cauchon were questioned, Joly declared that if individuals who held government contracts were allowed to sit in the Assembly, the body would become no different than the corrupted legislatures of the United States, "un ring d'hommes sans principe et sans honneur qui déshonoreront et pilleront la province."[86]

Two years later, in 1874, Joly was again on the offensive in the much more politically damaging Tanneries scandal, invoking the honour of "les anciens Canadiens" and the Conservative Party itself in a speech that lasted four hours. The complex and protracted Tanneries affair can be summarized briefly as a case in which the government traded a parcel of land in an area of Montreal known as the Tanneries for a larger but considerably less valuable one on the outskirts of the city for the purpose of building two new hospitals.[87] It was soon discovered that the man who had brokered the deal had paid $50,000 to the Montreal MLA and cabinet member Louis Archambault and $65,000 to Arthur Dansereau, editor of the pro-government La Minerve and close friend of prominent Conservative politician J.A. Chapleau. As a result, three cabinet members – George Irvine, J.G. Robertson, and the pro-ultramontane J.J. Ross, who self-identified as a French Canadian – resigned from office, bringing to an end the second Conservative ministry since the 1871 election.

Some of the leading provincial Liberals demanded that Prime Minister Mackenzie instruct Lieutenant Governor Caron to appoint Joly as the new premier, arguing that lieutenant governors were effectively federal functionaries. How Joly felt about this line of argument is not known, but it certainly contradicted his stance on provincial rights. In any case, the Liberals were barely a third of the MLAs, and Cauchon's proposal for a union of the parties went nowhere. As a result, Ouimet was replaced by C.E. Boucher de Boucherville, whom the Montreal Witness labelled a "lay Jesuit."[88] Boucherville was chosen by the Conservatives largely because of the hope that his reputation for honesty and integrity would be sufficient to overcome the stigma of the Tanneries scandal. In the estimation of historian John Saywell, "his political position was based on a tradition of seigniorial eminence and leadership – a kind of North American *noblesse oblige* – and in a sense he stood aloof from the baser activities of the politicians."[89] Much the same could be said of the equally patrician Joly.

Having declared that the new ministry was established only to "effacer les traces de cette infâme transaction des Tanneries," Joly presented a motion of non-confidence as soon as the speech from the throne had been read. Referring to the Pacific Scandal in Ottawa, he claimed that while visiting France the previous summer, he had been embarrassed to learn that Canada was known there only for its government corruption. Now one of the provinces of this vast empire could boast of having its own scandal.[90] To ward off further criticism, the new government appointed a bipartisan commission of inquiry, including Joly and another Liberal among its five members, but this did not prevent the Liberal leader from arguing that legal steps should be taken immediately to annul the Tanneries contract. His non-confidence motion subsequently attracted twenty-five votes, considerably more than the number of Liberals in the legislature.[91] The issue would continue to dominate the session until late February 1875, when the committee report was passed condemning the transaction and recommending that it be cancelled.[92]

When the government lost the ensuing court case against the owners, Joly demanded a copy of the amended declaration provided to the government's lawyers, thereby implying that it had purposely bungled the case. He also vigorously rejected the claims by Ouimet and Chapleau that their innocence had been proven, pointing out that they had not been on trial.[93] Joly continued to focus on the Tanneries and Pacific scandals during the provincial election that took place in June 1875. One of his first acts was to challenge Boucherville to a public debate anywhere in the province. According to historian Robert Rumilly, not to accept such an invitation would be to incur mortal shame, but one never challenged a sitting premier. In any case, in subsequent acts of one-upmanship, Boucherville chose Joly's constituency of Lotbinière, and Joly in turn selected the chef-lieu of Sainte-Croix, which was reportedly the centre of the county's Conservative strength. The debate, which took place immediately after the Sunday Mass, became the major event of the election, with ten candidates taking part and six steamers from Quebec and surrounding counties carrying between 1,400 and 3,000 people to the festive occasion.[94]

In a two-hour discourse, Joly focused largely on the Tanneries scandal, charging that the Boucherville ministry was simply keeping the perpetrators' seats warm. He was supported by the still more eloquent Wilfrid Laurier and L.H. Fréchette. According to Rumilly, Boucherville wrapped himself in his overcoat as if it were a toga and attacked the treatment of Quebec and Louis Riel by the Liberal government in Ottawa, but he was not a talented speaker. Fortunately for him, Chapleau's passionate plea for French-Canadian unity in the face of increasing anglophone domination carried the day. In Rumilly's words, "si les orateurs précédents s'étaient fait admirer pour leur belle tenue, pour l'élégance ou la vigueur de leur style, lui [Chapleau] s'était mis en communion avec l'âme de ses auditeurs."[95] The debate foreshadowed the election result, for the Conservatives were returned with as strong a majority as ever, in large part because of the Catholic Church's interference and because they were able to divert voters' attention towards the unpopular Liberal government in Ottawa.[96] Joly's own majority in Lotbinière was reduced to a mere 149 votes.[97]

Debates concerning political scandals absorbed a lot of time in the Assembly during the unstable 1870s,[98] but Marcel Hamelin's authoritative study states that the burning issue was how to staunch the flow of French Canadians to the New England mill towns, a flow that threatened to weaken Quebec's weight in the House of Commons. The principal remedies recommended were industrialization, agricultural improvement, colonization, and railway construction. Contrary to historian Michel Brunet, Hamelin argues that "agriculturisme" was not the dominant ideology even though most assumed (and not only in Quebec) that agriculture was the basis of a healthy society. Hamelin admits that the provincial government subsidized wooden railways as a means of facilitating colonization, funded colonization societies that were promoting settlement in marginal areas, and envisioned factories largely as a means of increasing markets for agricultural production, but he adds that few deputies echoed the clerico-nationalists' claim that industrialization and urbanization would lead to the moral and physical decay of the "race." Furthermore, as good nineteenth-century economic liberals, they could hardly be expected to support a direct role for the state in the industrialization of the province.[99]

As a seigneur and representative of a rural constituency, Joly's philosophical inclination was certainly towards a rural-based society, as reflected by his hesitation to abandon free trade at a time when, according to Hamelin, support for tariff protection was unanimous in the Quebec legislature. Joly argued in 1871 that the country's internal market was too small to support industrialization and that producers of raw materials in Canada would secure a much larger market through reciprocity with the United States.[100] He did begin to support protective tariffs the following year, as we have seen, and he later took a strong stand against the export of raw logs, but Joly's chief economic preoccupation was with agricultural improvement. He had, for example, founded an agricultural society in Lotbinière County in 1863 and remained its president and moving spirit until the mid-1890s.[101] Daniel Samson argues that in Nova Scotia these societies were essentially state agencies whose mandate went far beyond economic issues to promote "the proper conduct upon which the broader society should be governed." Given Joly's pejorative comments about the Cape Breton Highlanders during his Maritime provinces' tour of 1869, he clearly would have agreed with the Nova Scotia improvers that the "ancient habits of the ignorant Highlanders and their like would be broken by emulation, not the civilizing force of the market."[102] Not surprisingly, then, the Chauveau government's attempt in 1868 to reduce the annual subsidy to agricultural societies from $800 to $600 was one economizing measure that Joly did not support.

Despite not being a Bleu, Joly was appointed head of the province's twenty-one-member Council of Agriculture when it was established in 1869, a body he belonged to for two decades. The council's duties were to organize a provincial agricultural and industrial exhibition every two or three years, guide agricultural societies, establish model farms, and encourage agricultural education. It effectively assumed the role of the government as far as agriculture was concerned between 1871 and 1875, but it was criticized repeatedly as ineffective by the leading agricultural expert in the province, Édouard-A. Barnard. Although English-born, "Edward" Barnard was an ultramontane nationalist who opposed the council's promotion of imported British breeding stock over the Canadian horses and cattle.[103]

Joly and Barnard saw eye to eye, however, when it came to the sugar beet industry that was being promoted by entrepreneurs from Europe in the early to mid-1870s. Quebec farmers were looking for new markets after trade reciprocity with the United States ended in 1866, and, like the other politicians Hamelin identifies as "apôtres de l'industrialisation," Joly tended to favour industries that were linked to agriculture and forest resources.[104] In 1874, for example, he sponsored a bill to establish the Industrial and Agricultural Company of Lotbinière.[105] Joly's view, as expressed several times in the House of Commons, was that the state of the industrial classes in England "must make us hesitate before trying to make Canada a manufacturing country," but the sugar beet industry would not introduce the same evils because production would be by farmers, themselves.[106] In 1875 Joly congratulated the Quebec government for providing a $5,000 annual subsidy for five years towards the establishment of a sugar beet factory, but reflecting his fiscal prudence, he did urge caution in meeting the Belgian company's demand that it be raised to $7,000 a year for ten years. Joly's suggestion was that the company be required to invest $100,000 in the project before having access to the government grant. Two weeks later, however, he uncharacteristically threw all caution to the wind by supporting the government motion for the $70,000 subsidy. Unfortunately, the climate and the inexperience of Quebec farmers would prevent the industry from gaining a secure foothold in the province.[107] But tobacco was still grown in Quebec, and as a means of forcing reluctant manufacturers to purchase it, Joly declared in 1876 that he supported a protective tariff against American imports as well as tax relief on Canadian production.[108]

Meanwhile, given that colonization was the most popular issue in the Legislative Assembly during the early 1870s, Joly was surprisingly reserved about the Church-inspired movement. In keeping with his concern about government profligacy, in fact, he was initially critical of the Conservative administration's haste in devoting large sums to the promotion of agriculture and colonization. But this was obviously a politically untenable position, and Joly publicly withdrew his criticism of the government's agricultural policies at the beginning of the third session in November 1869, congratulating it on its support of Church-affiliated colonization societies as well as its encouragement of wooden railways, "l'agent le plus puissant de colonisation."[109] Joly's stance presumably helps to explain his appointment to the Council of Agriculture that same year, as noted previously, but he made it clear during the following session that he felt the best way to assist colonization and prevent emigration to the United States would be to concentrate on building major roads and railways rather than devoting funds to smaller routes, as the government was doing for patronage purposes.[110]

Joly's main criticism of government railway policy was that it was too extravagant. He clearly believed that his main role as opposition spokesman was to act as financial watchdog, and he accused the government of financial recklessness over and over again.[111] Thus, when a coalition of deputies forced the cabinet to restore the MLAs' $600 indemnity, which had been reduced to a $450 maximum, Joly objected that it was important to demonstrate that they placed the interests of agriculture and colonization first and foremost.[112] In 1869 and 1870 he attacked the provincial treasurer Christopher Dunkin for financial irresponsibility with regard to the construction of the lieutenant governor's residence and other public buildings.[113] Joly was also vehement in his opposition to a provincial police force, arguing somewhat speciously that it would effectively be a militia or army and thereby would infringe on federal responsibility to maintain order and good government. Joly claimed, as well, that the government had not explained why the municipal police forces were inadequate, particularly when mayors and magistrates had the power to call out the militia to suppress riots and other major disturbances.[114] In fact, Montreal declined to participate when a provincial force was established in 1870, and the force was effectively dissolved in 1877 because the Quebec City council refused to increase its financial support.[115]

When the government introduced a bill to impose a new round of liquor license fees, Joly responded by advocating that expenses be lowered instead, beginning with a reduction in the number of cabinet ministers as well as a decrease in salaries to the same level as those in Ontario. Chapleau, who was skilled at avoiding substantive issues by engaging in personal attacks, characterized Joly's leadership of the opposition as "marquée au coin de l'ignorance de toutes les traditions parlementaires." He charged that Joly, who did not hesitate to support subsidies for companies that he directed, was like the faithless dog that barked after the danger had passed, and he argued that his opponent's stand against new license fees would profit only drunkards and tavern keepers.[116]

Joly continued to harp on the government's wasteful spending policies in the following sessions, but he was especially concerned about the negotiations with Ontario concerning the pre-Confederation debt of the province of Canada.[117] The Quebec Conference on confederation had decided that the federal government would assume a debt of up to $25 per person for each of the provinces, amounting to $62.5 million for the former province of Canada, but the province's debt had been considerably more than this. To determine how the shared assets and debts would be divided, the BNA Act had provided for an arbitration panel of three, one member chosen by Quebec, one by Ontario, and one by Ottawa. Ontario offered to share the debt either by calculating how much had been incurred for projects in each section of the former province or by basing the share on the respective populations of the two sections in 1861. Either method would result in Quebec assuming approximately 44 percent of the debt, or close to $4.7 million, but Quebec insisted that the dissolution of the union should place the two provinces where they had been fiscally when the union was formed, and Upper Canada's debt had been approximately $5,825,000 as compared to Lower Canada's slight surplus. By this calculation, which assumed that Lower Canada did not benefit in any way from the canal construction that funnelled Upper Canadian wheat through Montreal, Ontario would assume 78 percent of the debt, leaving Quebec with only slightly more than a $2 million deficit. When both the Ontario and the federal commissioners indicated that they would support Ontario's position, the Quebec commissioner, Judge Charles Dewey Day, resigned in protest.[118]

Joly subsequently blamed the Quebec government for failing to demand adequate time to appoint a new member of the arbitration commission, but Premier Chauveau simply replied that his government no longer recognized the commission's legitimacy.[119] When the arbitration report was officially tabled by the two remaining members in September, assigning Quebec nearly half the debt, the Quebec government expressed its outrage, but Joly attacked the ministry for incompetence and the Quebec cabinet ministers in Ottawa for failing to defend their province. Joly argued that Lower Canada had saved Upper Canada from bankruptcy at the time of union in 1841 and that the $1.2 million Lower Canada had contributed to the construction of the St Lawrence canals should be credited to Quebec because this expenditure was exclusively for the benefit of Upper Canada, which had prospered at Lower Canada's expense.[120] Joly then introduced a resolution expressing regret that the federal government had not intervened in the case as well as the hope that it would refuse to recognize the decision. A milder government motion was passed instead, simply stating that a mistake prejudicial to Quebec had been made and asking for redress.[121]

Joly returned to the same issue nearly a year later, criticizing the Quebec government's threat to have the case referred to the Judicial Committee of the Privy Council. In Joly's view, this tactic would only cause further delays, and there was a risk that the Judicial Committee might rule against Quebec on a technicality. He warned that the annual interest charges on the debt would consume approximately 17 percent of the provincial budget and possibly necessitate the introduction of direct taxes. Despite his strongly partisan stand, Joly was not willing to go as far as his political ally Félix-Gabriel Marchand, who stated that this case was an example of what the anti-Confederationists had been predicting. Instead, Joly chastised Cauchon for suggesting that the matter could break up the country. Finally, in 1873, the federal government assumed the entire Province of Canada debt and compensated the other provinces accordingly. This decision would allow the Quebec government to develop a much more ambitious railway policy.[122]

The provincial government had been keen to extend the province's railway network to the neglected north shore since 1869, and it was convinced that wooden rails would be an economical means of opening the backcountry to colonization. Even though he had no land on the north shore, Joly himself became the leading force behind the proposed link between Quebec City and Gosford township in northern Portneuf County, which lay directly across the river from Lotbinière. Joly denied that his role as president of the company placed him in a conflict of interest as a member of the legislature, given that the company was not asking for a government subsidy, but this would not be the case for long.[123] When the directors did resolve to request a land grant in 1871, Joly attempted to resign as president, arguing that an opposition MLA would not be in a good position to approach the government and that he did not want to compromise his position as opposition leader. He was convinced to remain in the chair for the sake of the company, but six months later, when the government offered a grant of 10,000 arpents per mile of construction in order to extend the line to Lac Saint-Jean, Joly informed the other directors that his services were no longer crucial to success.[124] He later claimed in the Assembly, however, that he was no longer involved in the company because he felt the extension to Lac Saint-Jean would be too costly (wooden rails had proven impracticable by 1873) to offer any hope of earning a profit.[125] Joly may well have been sincere in the latter statement, but he clearly also wished to be free to criticize the government's railway policy.[126] In fact, even though the subsidy caused the railway's shares to shoot up in value, Joly was scrupulous enough to divest himself of those he owned at the same devalued price they had declined to before the subsidy was announced.[127] By doing so, he was conforming to a much higher ethical standard than that adhered to by the vast majority of politicians during his era.

As the economy entered a recessionary cycle, the provincial government became increasingly involved in extending the north shore railway network, and during the 1874–5 session Joly frequently complained of incompetence and secrecy, citing in particular the granting of funds to railways that had not been assessed by a government engineer.[128] With railway construction at a standstill and the companies virtually bankrupt by late 1875, despite the provincial government's expenditure of over a million dollars that year, the government finally announced that it was taking over the North Shore Railway and Montreal Colonization Railway to create the Quebec, Montreal, Ottawa, and Occidental (QMOO) Railway that would, as the name suggested, link Quebec City with Ottawa.[129] Joly, in response, blamed the government for allowing the North Shore company to fail and sarcastically congratulated the premier for seizing the opportunity to lose as much money on railways as had the federal government. In addition to questioning whether it was a good idea to sacrifice support for all other railways to the QMOO, Joly raised concerns about the possibility of a direct tax.[130] He later also argued that the federal government should provide a subsidy for what would become a major link in the transcontinental railway, a suggestion that the provincial government rejected out of hand because the Liberals were in power in Ottawa.[131]

Having repeatedly warned that the government's extravagant spending would result in direct taxation, Joly spoke against the assessment on financial transactions that was introduced in 1878 after the government had been forced to negotiate yet another emergency loan, this time for $400,000.[132] He also opposed the government bill to force the municipalities to meet their obligations, arguing that by threatening to take recalcitrant municipalities "by the throat," as Attorney General Angers had put it, the government was effectively shooting itself in the foot because capitalists "would assuredly refuse to have anything to do with bonds exacted by such means from the municipalities."[133] Finally, Joly opposed what he referred to as additional subsidies for railway construction in late February 1878, but which the government referred to as emergency loans.[134] As we will see in the next chapter, the government's financial difficulties, along with the hostility of the municipalities that were forced to contribute to the railway at a time of financial crisis, would provide the recently appointed lieutenant governor, Letellier de Saint-Just, with the excuse needed to bring his Liberal allies into office.

Conclusion

Joly was a moderate in politics, but he was also a man of principle who advocated certain causes with passion. Having opposed Confederation largely because he felt that it would be unstable and would lead

to the inevitable centralization of power to the detriment of the French-
Canadian minority, he remained a champion of provincial rights. Joly
was also a consistent opponent of corruption and waste and therefore
a supporter of small, accountable government. Sympathetic as he may
have been to the French-Canadian colonization movement, the fact that
he never became a leading proponent was due in part to his concern
that much of the government expenditure was being squandered. Although his lumber business relied on the labour of marginal farmers on
his own seigneury, Joly was no doubt also aware that the poor soil and
the lack of access to markets in the colonization zones were not condu-
cive to the scientific agriculture that he so strongly favoured.

Joly's reformist tendencies trumped his fiscally conservative ones in
the case of the Beauport Asylum, which he felt the government should
purchase because it would be motivated to heal people rather confine
them as long as possible for financial reasons. He also stated in 1875
that he opposed the system of placing "lunatics" on a farm rather than
under the care of psychiatrists.[135] There was no conflict between this
liberal-minded stance and Joly's paternalist instincts, but he was also
democratic enough to advocate the secret ballot as well as single-day
elections, to oppose the $2,000 property qualification for electoral can-
didacy, and to favour extending the franchise beyond property holders.
Joly's elitism was manifested instead in his off-hand suggestion that
there be an intellectual qualification for voting, noting that in China – a
country that had preceded the West in becoming civilized – it was intelligence alone that was honoured.[136] Contradictory as some of Joly's
policies may seem, then, they make sense from the perspective of someone influenced by the liberal circles his father had moved in and whose
privileged class status gave him a sense of social responsibility.

Henri-Gustave Joly in his younger years. Bibliothèque et Archives nationales du Québec, P1000, S4, D83, PJ11–1.

LE DEFI!

"The Challenge. A Modern Version of 'Roland and Olivier'" by Henri Julien. The McCord Museum's copy of this political cartoon appeared in an unnamed English-language newspaper on 12 June 1875. Several days later it reappeared as "Le Défi" in *L'Opinion Publique* 6, no. 24 (17 June 1875). Olivier de Vienne was a fictional knight in the French epic *La Chanson de Roland* who is commonly seen as recklessly courageous. Henri-Gustave Joly appears here as Olivier, throwing his glove at the feet of Premier Boucher de Boucherville as a challenge to engage in a debate on the hustings during the 1875 election. Contemporary readers would have been quite aware that both men were members of the seigneurial elite. The public debate, which attracted as many as 3,000 spectators, was the major event of the election. McCord Museum, M992X.5.84.

Chapter Five

Quebec Premier

If the first seventeen years of Joly's political career were rather uniform insofar as he spent them firmly ensconced within a weak parliamentary opposition, the following seven years were much more eventful. Following a brief tumultuous period as provincial premier, he would find himself back in the role of opposition leader before resigning that position in 1883 and giving up his seat in 1885. During these years, Joly was faced with hard political choices, choices that forced him to clarify some of the ambiguities in his liberal ideology, particularly when it came to the role that government should play. Although he had been a persistent critic of Conservative government expenditures on the railway, for example, as premier he would ensure that the North Shore line was completed despite the deepening recession. And he would become a vociferous critic of the succeeding Conservative administration's sale of the same railway to private interests. Despite the politically motivated inconsistencies, however, Joly would remain true to his obsession with political honesty and fiscal prudence, an obsession that ensured a short life for his government, as well as his ultimate replacement by a more opportunistic Liberal leader.

Premier

Having been engaged in political battles against the Conservatives and the Church since 1850, newly appointed Lieutenant Governor Letellier de Saint-Just wasted little time before challenging the financially strapped Boucherville administration.[1] Because of his fear that Letellier would provide the Liberals with ammunition to attack ministerial policy, Boucherville tended to flout constitutional practice by withholding information about government decisions. Finally, in late February 1878, the lieutenant governor demanded a report concerning the bills aimed at coercing municipalities and imposing taxes on certain legal transactions. Rather than reserve the offending bills for the federal government, a week later he dismissed Boucherville as premier, declaring that his municipal coercion bill represented an arbitrary and unjust infringement of the executive on the judiciary and that his railway policy would lead to ruin. When Boucherville refused to name a successor, Letellier called upon Joly as leader of the opposition to form the Executive Council.[2]

In the words of one historian, the coup d'état produced the effect of "une bombe."[3] Not only were the Conservatives shocked, but Prime Minister Mackenzie and Wilfrid Laurier in Ottawa also felt that Letellier had overstepped his authority.[4] Nor have historians been sympathetic,[5] and the question arises as to whether Joly was instrumental in the coup. Letellier had been in close contact with him ever since assuming the lieutenant governorship, but it seems unlikely that the seasoned veteran would have taken directions from the younger Joly.[6] Furthermore, given that Letellier gave Boucherville the opportunity to name another Conservative as his successor, it is possible that Letellier hoped to forge the union between the moderate Bleus and the Liberals that Chapleau had recently been considering and that Joly never would have consented to.[7]

The question remains as to how a Liberal who had consistently advocated greater provincial autonomy could justify the interference of a federally appointed official in the affairs of the provincial administration, much less his dismissal of that administration without a vote of non-confidence in the Legislative Assembly. Given his strong sense of duty, Joly may have simply felt obliged to step into the breach after the lieutenant governor went too far in his contest of wills with Boucherville, but the years in opposition with no electoral victory in close sight also must have tempted the Liberals to grasp at this rather fortuitous opportunity to seize power. Furthermore, Joly was clearly convinced that the Conservatives were corrupt and incompetent and that the province was in a serious crisis. Partisan feelings had obviously risen to a fever pitch when the normally temperate Joly refused to apologize in the Assembly for stating in the heat of debate that the government was threatening to use "la force brutale" to push its measures through the legislature. After being censured by the speaker, Joly had been fêted in Quebec City by a banquet of 200 people.[8]

The Liberals could not govern without a majority in the Assembly, and in the ensuing March election they did their best to bury the constitutional issue by focusing on Conservative corruption and the threat of higher taxes. A Liberal election flyer printed in Joly's name declared that the Boucherville government had opened the door to taxes that had, until then, been happily unknown to the "habitants de notre province."[9] Another Liberal brochure claimed that there had been a conspiracy among the ministers and their friends to share the spoils. Millions of acres of the best timber land had been secretly delivered "aux favoris, aux entrepreneurs d'élections, aux organisateurs de la violence, aux oppresseurs de la liberté électorale." Railways had become engines of speculation and corruption, and Attorney General Guillaume Amyot had threatened to introduce an act that would enable the government to seize, without trial, the property of councillors representing any municipality that refused to pay the capital and interest on their debentures. All hope would have been lost had Providence not given to the province of Quebec "un homme énergique" (namely Letellier), capable of defending the interests of the people "foulés aux pieds."[10]

In a paradoxical reversal of political ideologies, however, it was the Conservatives who were in a position to criticize the Liberals for infringing on popular rights. In challenging Joly for the Lotbinière seat for the second time, Amyot published a lengthy pamphlet declaring that the grievances outlined in Papineau's Ninety-Two Resolutions against the oligarchy of the time had disappeared under the beneficent influence of the popularly elected Conservative government: "Béni soit le jour où cette constitution britannique nous a été octroyée, et malheur, mille fois malheur, au premier traitre qui y portera une main sacrilège!" ("Blessed be the day when we were granted this British constitution, and misfortune, a thousand times misfortune, to the first traitor who lays a sacrilegious hand on it.")[11]

Although Prime Minister Mackenzie offered little more than his moral support to assist Joly in the election,[12] Amyot identified the provincial Liberals with all the unpopular measures passed by the government in Ottawa. These included the removal of the military college from Quebec, the refusal to provide railway subsidies, and the introduction of a Supreme Court that would cost the taxpayers $75,000, increase Liberal patronage, and provide the Protestant majority with the opportunity to overrule provincial courts that had a Catholic majority.[13] Amyot also took advantage of Liberal vulnerability on the religious issue, though he did not go as far as Israël Tarte's Le Canadien, which

attacked Joly as a foreigner, or the *Journal des Trois-Rivières*, which declared that a "suisse d'origine, étranger de naissance, huguenot en religion" was a strange "chef" for a French Catholic population.[14] The first
page of Amyot's pamphlet did, however, repeat the inaccurate Conservative charge that George Brown was the instigator of Letellier's "coup
d'état" and did ask, "Who has voted to deprive the Sisters of Charity of
their liberty of commerce? Who has asked for the abolition of our national processions?" The first point referred to Joly's opposition to the
bill that would recognize the right of the Montreal religious order, and
by implication all others in the province, to "exercer certaines industries." Joly's position, like that of other Liberals and Montreal's English-
speaking business community, had been that this bill would represent
a dangerous precedent by giving tax-free corporations a competitive
advantage over privately owned businesses.[15] As for his second point,
Amyot declared that the disorder caused by the "orangiste" parades
was not sufficient reason to abandon "la fête de la patrie," adding, "Canadiens, votre drapeau a droit de se dérouler publiquement, au vent de
la liberté, sur le sol du Canada, arrosé du sang de nos pères, et malheur
à celui qui voudra l'enfermer dans l'étui du déshonneur." ("Canadiens,
your flag has the right to unfurl publicly, to the wind of liberty, on the
soil of Canada, drenched with the blood of our fathers, and misfortune
to he who would cast dishonour upon it.")[16] In fact, even though Joly
had suggested in the wake of Montreal's Orange riot of July 12, 1877,
that patriotic societies should refrain from holding processions "in order to prevent the effusion of blood, and that the greater good of all
races and opinions might be attained," he had voted with the minority
against the bill to suppress "les processions de parti" in Montreal.[17]

Amyot also appended an extract from *Le Canadien*, purportedly written by several local electors, accusing Joly of fomenting a religious war
because he had not repudiated the Montreal *Witness* for champion-
ing the apostate Chiniquy, Lucius Seth Huntington for his Argenteuil
speech of 1875 warning of the threat posed by the rise of ultramontanism, or the subsequent formation of the Protestant Defence Alliance
(PDA).[18] Joly tended to avoid religious controversy, but the charge
concerning the PDA, at least, was untrue, as we saw in the previous
chapter. In a second "letter" to the electors of Lotbinière, Amyot again
did his best to embarrass Joly by translating excerpts from the *Witness*
such as one complaining of the thousands of dollars spent to repatriate
French Canadians from New England to the Eastern Townships in order to curtail English-speaking colonization in the region.[19]

It is difficult to know how effective this nationalist appeal was, though a few priests did interfere against Liberal candidates, including against Joly himself in the case of at least one parish.[20] But Church hostility had been tempered by the recent visit of the papal delegate, Monseigneur Conroy, when rising Liberal star Wilfrid Laurier had delivered his famous speech distinguishing between his own party's moderate British liberalism and the radical liberalism of Europe.[21] And on the plus side for the Liberals, there appears to have been a Protestant backlash in their favour. One Conservative voter who switched sides was Edward Carter, the former deputy for Montreal Centre, who wrote to Joly that "the mode of attack adopted by certain Roman Catholic Journals, that you and your party should be crushed because you (the leader) was [sic] a Protestant, had [sic] completely changed my view."[22] Sherbrooke's former Conservative MP Alexander Galt also assured Joly that he would "rejoice" in his success." But even though he was very critical of the province's railway policy and had published attacks against the ultramontane threat to civil liberties, Galt refused to take a public stand, claiming that he no longer had political influence in the Eastern Townships.[23] Galt's successor as head of the British American Land Company, Richard W. Heneker, also offered his best wishes but claimed that he was too busy to become involved in the election.[24] Finally, the fact that most of the Liberal gains were made in the broader Quebec City district, which was largely French-speaking, tends to contradict historian Pierre Trépanier's statement about the key role played in the election by a Protestant switch to the Liberals.[25]

The Liberal anti-tax message was clearly heard by many French-Canadian voters, who were presumably not reassured by Amyot's reminder that the taxes imposed by Boucherville would have been for a two-year period only and would have had little impact on farmers, amounting to only fifteen cents on transactions over $200.[26] In fact, the chief spokesman of the former Boucherville government in the Assembly, Auguste-Réal Angers, was defeated by the twenty-six-year-old Charles Langelier in the solidly French-speaking riding of Montmorency, a riding that had long been a Conservative stronghold.[27] In Lotbinière, Joly defeated Amyot by 336 votes,[28] and even though the final tally of seats appears to have resulted in a Conservative majority of one, party affiliations were loose enough to allow the Liberals to hang onto power once the independent Conservative, Arthur Turcotte of Trois-Rivières, agreed to become Speaker. The future of the Joly administration would depend largely on Turcotte's vote,[29] but this did not prevent the Liberals from holding a victory parade in the streets of Quebec. *Le Courrier du Canada* complained that "red was everywhere. There were red flags, the men were dressed in red outfits, and wagons, along with their horses and their drivers were coloured red ... These must be the types of processions that the Liberals will give to the people to make them forget their more traditional, national ones."[30]

Rather than making the challenge of premiership easier by avoiding firm commitments, Joly was resolved to balance the budget without increasing taxes and to bring the municipalities into line without resorting to force.[31] He thereby accepted an almost impossible challenge that ultimately ensured that his administration would be a short-lived one. Aside from announcing the abolition of the railway commission, the district magistrates' courts, the provincial police, and the Legislative Council, he also called for a reduction in the salaries of the deputies, ministers, and the House speaker.[32] The Conservative-dominated Legislative Council rejected the bill that would have brought its existence to an end, as one would expect, but also the bill that would have enabled the government to divert money from the consolidated fund to railway expenses and other measures.[33] Although the government failed to adopt any major legislation, Joly managed to avoid defeat in the Assembly during a six-week session in which the opposition took advantage of every opportunity to bring him down.[34] His goal was quite likely to hang on until economic conditions improved and to go into another election after loosening the purse strings, but the defeat of the Liberal government in Ottawa in September 1878 presented yet another serious challenge.

The federal ballots had hardly been counted when Quebec's Conservatives began to demand the dismissal of Lieutenant Governor Letellier. Prime Minister Macdonald was in an awkward position. He depended on Quebec support in the House of Commons, yet Governor General Lorne had warned him that such a dismissal would be an unwarranted intervention in provincial affairs, given that Quebec voters had not censured Letellier's dismissal of the Boucherville ministry in the ensuing provincial election. Furthermore, the constitution stated that lieutenant governors were appointed by the governor general in council, but served during the pleasure of the governor general, suggesting that he alone had the authority of dismissal. Macdonald nevertheless informed Lord Lorne in late March 1879 that his government had decided to dismiss Letellier. When the governor general expressed his disapproval, Macdonald suggested that he refer the matter to the secretary of state for the colonies.[35]

While the Quebec Conservatives were railing against the governor general's refusal to cooperate, Joly's cabinet protested against Macdonald's decision as an infringement on provincial autonomy. The constitutional debate then shifted across the Atlantic as Macdonald sent two of his men, Hector Langevin and J.J.C. Abbott, to defend the federal government's case. Joly himself went on behalf of Letellier, though when he reached Halifax, he was informed that the colonial secretary, Sir Michael Hicks Beach, had indicated his presence was neither required nor desired. Arguing that the case should be decided by the Judicial Committee of the Privy Council, Joly used his political and social contacts to meet a number of dignitaries, such as Lord Carnarvon, Lord Dufferin, and the Duke of Manchester. He even managed to win audiences with Gladstone and Hicks Beach. The prime minister was sympathetic, but the colonial secretary made it clear that he considered the lieutenant governor to be simply a functionary of the federal government. If the government wished to dismiss him for wearing a black tie when ordered to wear a blue one, it could do so.[36]

Meanwhile, the Joly government had been successful in negotiating a railway loan of nearly $3 million on the New York market, and it would manage to squeeze additional sums from the foot-dragging municipalities. As commissioner of agriculture and public works, Joly had assumed direct responsibility for the railway, and he pushed construction throughout the winter of 1878–9, going so far as to inspect the lines himself on snowshoes. Despite his administration's straitened financial circumstances, Joly saw the construction of the Quebec, Montreal, Ottawa, and Occidental (QMOO) Railway through to completion and even managed to find some money for several south shore lines. He also called on the Montreal Volunteer Force, B Battery from St Helen's Island, the 65th Rifles, the 6th Fusiliers, and the Montreal Garrison Artillery to take possession of the western section of the railway from the recalcitrant contractor.[37] In short, Joly demonstrated remarkable energy in his role as railway commissioner in the face of formidable financial and political obstacles.

The Joly administration's efforts were rewarded with four by-election victories in the summer of 1879, including two in former Conservative ridings.[38] It was the Conservatives' turn to accuse the government of jeopardizing the province's future with its extravagant railway expenditures, particularly through building an expensive spur line in Trois-Rivières as a reward for the local Conservative deputy agreeing to become House speaker. Joly was also attacked for initiating construction of the railway bridge in Hull without consulting the Assembly.[39] When this tactic failed to bring the administration down, the Conservative newspaper publisher Israël Tarte raised the cry of corruption. He claimed that the government had charged Joly's brother-in-law, Hammond Gowen, only $5,000 for a $17,000 mortgage on a farm at Notre-Dame-des-Anges, near Quebec City. A bipartisan committee of inquiry cleared Joly when it reported in August 1879 that the farm was probably not worth more than $5,000 at the time the mortgage was sold and that the premier had been absent when the transaction took place. At worst, the government had made an error in not waiting until the value of the property increased.[40]

Not to be discouraged, the opposition proceeded with accusations related to contracts for the École normale Jacques Cartier, but to little effect.[41] More serious was the charge by the Legislative Council that there were irregularities in the contract that provided the patent holder of railway nutlocks (which ensured that rails remained joined together) with the highly inflated price of $50 a mile for installation on the QMOO. A later inquiry reported that Liberal MLA Charles Langelier had received a kickback of a couple thousand dollars to spend in three by-elections. But the contract had been signed without Joly's approval while he was in London, and his government had been dismissed long before the inquiry took place in 1885.[42]

Meanwhile, the Liberal government continued to argue that Ottawa did not have the right to dismiss a lieutenant governor because he represented the Queen, not as a federal officer but as chief of the provincial executive. But it would be 1892 before Joly's argument was vindicated by the Judicial Committee of the Privy Council decision that provincial governments were sovereign within their own sphere, with the result that the Crown was effectively federalized.[43] Meanwhile, on July 3, 1879, the colonial secretary sent a dispatch to the governor general stating that a lieutenant governor held the power to dismiss his ministers but was directly responsible to the governor general for any action he took. And the governor general had to follow the advice of his ministers. Macdonald, who had been facing a revolt from his Quebec MPs, dismissed Letellier three weeks later. Théodore Robitaille, one of those restive MPs, was appointed in Letellier's place.[44]

Facing an obstructionist Legislative Council and hampered by a significant budget deficit, the Liberal government was increasingly weakened by regional and ethnic rivalries within the party.[45] Joly was forced to back down on his plan to lease the QMOO as well as his policies for abolishing the Legislative Council and regulating the municipal loan fund. He also felt compelled to introduce retrogressive social legislation in order to lower expenditures. For example, even though public costs for care of the mentally ill were much lower than in Ontario, due to the role of religious orders in Quebec,[46] a bill was passed declaring that institutionalization of a mentally unfit person at the state's expense would require a written statement by a friend or guardian that he or she could not provide for that person's needs. And even though Joly consistently opposed private asylums, arguing that Beauport was a "manufacture d'aliénés" and therefore more expensive than a publicly run institution, he introduced a bill declaring that "imbeciles" and "idiots" were not to be the state's responsibility unless they represented a public danger or scandal.[47]

More consistent with Joly's earlier positions, the government also declared that as an economic measure it would introduce a bill to eliminate the position of school inspector. When this move was strongly opposed by both the Protestant and the Catholic committees of the Council of Public Instruction, neither of which had been consulted, Joly announced that they would be permitted to manage their affairs as best they could on a reduced budget, though the government would ask that unqualified inspectors not be employed.[48] As the Anglican Bishop of Quebec pointed out, the government was thereby relinquishing effective control over the school system.[49] Another bill was aimed at abolishing the government's school textbook repository, though teachers protested that this service had lowered the cost of books and also ensured that semi-literate school commissioners were not duped into purchasing poor-quality texts. The upper house rejected this bill, which Joly clearly saw as a cost-saving measure rather than a beneficial reform. He did introduce more progressive bills, including one that would disallow senators from sitting in the Legislative Council, and another that would protect indebted farmers from the seizure of two oxen and a cart or labourers from the seizure of more than half their salaries. But these bills were also scuttled by the Legislative Council, as were Joly's painstaking efforts to reach a negotiated settlement with the municipalities.[50]

Finally, on August 28, in the wake of bloody confrontations between Quebec City's French-Canadian and Irish ship labourers,[51] the upper house suspended its vote on the budget. Although its English-speaking Conservative members refused to play this partisan game, the majority in the Legislative Council voted for the motion declaring that the Joly ministry had been fiscally irresponsible and that it no longer enjoyed enough confidence in the Legislative Assembly to govern effectively. Joly instructed the lieutenant governor to inform the upper house that his government had not lost a vote of confidence and that the recent by-elections proved that his administration was increasingly supported by public opinion, but Robitaille's response was that this message would not restore harmony between the two branches of the legislature.[52] Calling the Legislative Council's bluff, the Liberals passed a motion adjourning the session for two months, thereby stalling public works as well as leaving civil servants without salaries and charitable institutions without operating funds. On September 11 the upper house passed a motion condemning the adjournment for damaging the public credit, declaring that this step by the Liberal administration was "une nouvelle preuve de leur incurie et une admission de leur impuissance à administrer efficacement les affaires de cette province."[53]

As a way out of the impasse, Letellier and other leading Liberals recommended a coalition with the moderate Chapleau wing of the Conservatives on condition that the Legislative Council be reformed. But Joly chose, instead, to organize a series of province-wide assemblies in order to demonstrate to the upper house that his government enjoyed the public's support. The Conservatives struck back with a page from the Liberal playbook by distributing a handbill that praised the Legislative Council for removing the key to the public coffer from ministers who were pillaging it to give money to their relatives, friends, and contractors who had donated funds to their election. In short, the upper house had acted as "un bon père de famille qui, voyant son fils faire des dépenses extravagantes, ne lui donne plus d'argent."[54] Determined to answer such charges even in hostile territory such as the Conservative stronghold of Joliette, where he was strongly advised not to appear, Joly made arrangements with his local opponents "pour assurer une libre discussion aux deux parties."[55] Meanwhile, the lieutenant governor remained impervious and uncooperative, interfering in purely administrative matters and refusing to sign orders-in-council or the special warrants needed to pay expenses connected with the operation of the QMOO.[56] After the two-month recess had ended, Joly's position was weaker than ever, due in large part to the Conservatives' use of bribes to attract to their camp corruptible Liberal deputies, including one cabinet minister. While Langevin dispensed patronage liberally from Ottawa, François-Xavier Cimon contributed generously to the Conservatives in repayment for having been awarded the contract for the new legislature buildings in 1876, and railway contractor Louis-Adélard

Sénécal distributed largesse for future considerations – namely, a major role in the QMOO.[57]

Rather than negotiate with the opposition, Joly continued to take a hard line, declaring that the Legislative Council had revealed itself to be not only an expensive luxury but even a dangerous and revolutionary body. When his motion reaffirming the subsidies that had been ratified in the Legislative Assembly two months earlier was defeated by the same body by a vote of thirty-five to twenty-nine, Joly requested its dissolution in order to allow the people to pronounce on the constitutional issue.[58] But Chapleau threatened to resign his seat in Ottawa if the federal government did not prevent the lieutenant governor from granting this request. Robitaille therefore replied to Joly that it was unreasonable to request two dissolutions in two months (thereby confusing the recent adjournment with a dissolution) and declared that it was not in the public interest to hold an election so soon after the previous one. Following Letellier's example, Robitaille pronounced that the principal goal of restoring harmony between the two branches of the legislature could be achieved without another election, simply by changing the composition of the provincial cabinet. Joly had no choice but to resign, and the Liberals returned to the opposition benches for seven long years.[59]

Les froides régions de l'opposition

With the opening of the spring session in 1880, Joly demanded to know what the new government had offered its members who had abandoned the Liberal Party, but he promised that the opposition would not adopt the obstructionist tactics that it had recently been subjected to. Rather, he and his colleagues would support "ce qui sera bon, essayant d'améliorer ce qui sera défecteux, et nous opposant seulement à ce qui sera radicalement mauvais." ("what would be good, trying to improve what would be defective, and opposing only what would be radically bad.") Premier Chapleau, who was Joly's next-door neighbour according to the 1881 manuscript census, welcomed Joly back to "les froides régions de l'opposition, où il parait évidemment plus à l'aise, et où, une fois de plus, il brille par cette amabilité et cette courtoisie qui le distinguent et le caractérisent à un si haut degré." ("the cold regions of the opposition, where he appears evidently more at ease, and where, once more, he shines by that amiability and that courtesy that distinguishes him and that characterizes him to such a high degree.")[60] There was an element of truth to Chapleau's backhanded compliment, one that would make the Liberals increasingly restive under Joly's gentlemanly direction.

In the meantime, Joly objected to the appointment of Sénécal as head of the province's railway, claiming that it was obviously a political pay-off. He did, however, signal his approval of the government's announced policies on the development of mineral resources and the manufacture of beet sugar, stating that every means possible should be taken not to fall behind the other provinces "dans la lutte d'avancement et de progrès."[61] In this vein, Joly and fellow Liberals opposed the bill presented in July 1880 that would grant mineral rights to all landowners, arguing that it would prevent the development of future mining operations.[62] This was a quiet session, however, one in which the demoralized opposition members presented few serious challenges to the government that had displaced them without even holding an election.

Joly was more combative in the session that took place a year later, in the spring of 1881, charging in his reply to the speech from the throne that the government had sacrificed provincial autonomy in the interests of political vengeance when it demanded the head of Letellier de Saint-Just, a man whom posterity would remember as having been truly dedicated to his country.[63] Joly also observed that the Conservatives had followed the route outlined by his own government (including the controversial Trois-Rivières loop line) in completing the QMOO to Ottawa, after having used the Legislative Council to delay completion of the railway by a year when in opposition.[64] Noting that they were entering a critical period because of the debt incurred in building the railway, Joly served notice that the people would not accept direct taxation, which he feared was on the horizon.[65]

During the ensuing session, Joly was able to score some strong political points in relation to the newly established Crédit foncier Franco-canadien, which had been given a provincial monopoly as a mortgage-based provider of loans.[66] After complaining that it had announced an interest rate of 6 percent, instead of the promised 5 percent, Joly declared that the government had given the company a fifty-year monopoly to drain thousands of dollars to France. Furthermore, the premier, the provincial secretary, and two other deputies had accepted salaried positions with the company, placing them in a direct conflict of interest, especially given that Chapleau had lobbied in Ottawa against the chartering of a competing company. Chapleau's rather uninspired respose was that he and his colleagues were not on the company payroll, though it might choose to pay them a stipend. Chapleau also denied a newspaper report that he and some of his colleagues had accepted bribes from the company, but Joly persisted in demanding to know whether anyone had accepted any money, whatsoever. The committee he headed to investigate the issue found that only one MLA had accepted the $14,000 bribe offered by the company,[67] but it remained a political liability for the Conservative government. In financial straits by 1882, the credit company requested permission to raise its interest rate yet again, giving Joly the opportunity to remind government members that he had warned against their involvement in the enterprise for the very reason that if it failed, the province's credit rating in France would suffer.[68] The Paris-educated Joly also probed indirectly at old anti-French resentments when he described how the Crédit foncier Franco-canadien investors must have cried with joy in learning that "malgré l'abandon dans lequel la France nous a laissés, dans la lutte suprême, sans aide, sans armes, sans argent, combattant jusqu'au dernier soupir pour défendre le drapeau de France, que notre coeur est toujours français et que, tout en demeurant fidèles à l'Angleterre, nous aimons toujours la France." ("despite France's abandonment of us in the supreme struggle, without aid, without arms, without money, fighting until the last breath to defend the flag of France, that our heart is always French, and that, while remaining faithful to England, we always love France.") Unfortunately, Joly added, the model that the current government had chosen to follow was not Montcalm, Frontenac, or Lévis, but the notorious Bigot.[69]

Chapleau finally called an election in December 1881 and ran largely on the promise to solve the problem of the railway by selling it for $8 million, which was $5 million less than it had cost the government to build. In response to Chapleau's argument that the government had been willing to pay a $5 million subsidy towards construction costs, a Liberal election pamphlet argued that having taken the financial risks, the government should not allow a private company to reap the profits. If properly managed, the railway's revenue would soon exceed $400,000 annually, or the equivalent of the 5 percent interest on the $8 million for which Chapleau was willing to sacrifice the railway. Outlining Sénécal's history of corruption before taking over management of the QMOO, the pamphlet promised that a Liberal government would abolish the Legislative Council, purify the civil service, and address "the DEPLORABLE STATE OF EDUCATION" in the province.[70]

The result, however, was that the Conservatives won fifty-three of the sixty-five seats with Sénécal's generous financial assistance. Joly took his seat by acclamation, but the only strong support for the Liberals came from the English-speaking population, leading Chapleau's mouthpiece, *La Minerve*, to accuse the opposition newspapers of organizing a crusade against the French Canadians.[71] Sénécal received his reward when the eastern branch of the QMOO went to him and the Conservative contractor, Thomas McGreevy, following the sale of the Montreal-Ottawa branch to the Canadian Pacific Railway (CPR) in February 1882. Complaining that the negotiations had taken place in secret, Joly charged that Sir Hugh Allan and others had been willing to purchase the entire line – and for a higher price.[72] All were aware, Joly added, that breaking the line into two sections would make Montreal the terminus of the transcontinental railway and jeopardize the development of Quebec City and the other north shore communities. It was now the Conservative government's turn to be torn by internal disunity, for the provincial treasurer and minister of agriculture both resigned in protest against the railway sale, and the ultramontane wing – which would soon be known pejoratively as the Castors – launched an attack on Chapleau from the Legislative Council.[73]

Ever the gentleman, however, Joly offered to delay the debate on the ratification of the sale to the CPR until Chapleau, suffering from attacks of bronchitis and "irritated nerves," had recovered sufficiently to allow him to return to his seat. When the acting house leader announced that the premier would be back within a week, Joly suggested delaying the debate several more days in order to hasten his recovery by not applying undue pressure on him.[74] Instead of pushing for an extended debate in the Assembly, in fact, Joly called for a commission of inquiry into the railway sale.[75] When the inquiry was denied, Joly apologetically declared that it was his duty to make remarks that might seem severe; his intention was not to wound his adversaries, but rather to open their eyes to the fact that they were selling the province to "railway rings." Referring to the charge that his party was launching a personal vendetta against Sénécal, Joly declared that it was not a single individual that he was attacking, but the system symbolized by that individual, for Sénécal was Canada's Boss Tweed. As for the accusation that the Liberals were stirring up popular agitation in speaking at public protest meetings, Joly stated that at the beginning of each speech, he reminded the members of his audience that they were exercising their constitutional rights, but that he would condemn any attempt to intervene in the deliberations of the Assembly. Joly also supported the right of the Legislative Council, with its ultramontane Conservative

majority, to oppose the sale. He argued that this was an entirely different matter than refusing to vote for the subsidies his government had
passed and that the Conservatives could hardly support the continued
existence of a body that would serve merely as a rubber stamp for government bills.[76] A frustrated Chapleau, no longer grateful for the role
the Legislative Councillors had played in bringing him to office, later
wrote to Macdonald that "if Joly had not been an ass, he would have
had a splendid opportunity of crushing forever that disgusting clique
of religious pickpockets, the pest of all governments. But Joly will die
what he was born, a good natured fool."[77]

Chapleau was referring to Joly's opposition to a party coalition that
would have spelled the end of the Legislative Council. Joly had consistently held to this position, having announced as early as 1875 that
the day Chapleau crossed the House to the Liberal side would be the
day he left politics.[78] Some Liberal MLAs, notably the ambitious young
member for Saint-Hyacinthe, Honoré Mercier, were more flexible. Mercier had been flirting with Chapleau for some time,[79] but by March 1882
it was Joly and the Castors who appeared to be making public advances
to each other because of their common opposition to the government's
railway policy.[80] Joly denied such rumours in the Assembly, however,
declaring that as the leader of a party that had been soundly defeated
in the previous election, he would not even consider intriguing with
Conservative malcontents in an attempt to return to office.[81]

Meanwhile, Mercier and Chapleau continued their behind-the-
scenes negotiations, for the latter was determined to destroy the influence of the Castors before accepting Macdonald's invitation to move
to Ottawa. In December 1882, the Liberal organ *L'Électeur* argued that
although coalitions generally resulted from two parties sacrificing their
principles for the sake of power, there was no fundamental difference
between the moderate majorities of the Liberals and Conservatives:
"M. Chapleau et son groupe sont aussi libéraux que M. Mercier en ce
qui concerne les réformes à opérer, dans le sens démocratique, dans nos
lois électorales, dans nos lois d'éducation, dans nos lois civiles, dans
l'organisation du service public. M. Mercier est aussi conservateur que
M. Chapleau en ce qui touche aux grands principes sociaux et religieux,
aux rapports entre l'Eglise et l'Etat."[82] ("Mr Chapleau and his group
are as liberal as is Mr Mercier in relation to democratic reforms of our
electoral laws, our educations laws, our civil laws, in the organization
of our public service. Mr Mercier is as conservative as Mr Chapleau on
what relates to grand social and religious principals, on the relations

between Church and State.") Despite his opposition to the coalition negotiations, Joly wrote to the radical Honoré Beaugrand of *La Patrie* in January 1883, asking him not to attack Mercier for having supported the idea, which failed to come to fruition. In a somewhat dispirited tone, Joly claimed that although he was resigned to wait for the day when the people would open their eyes and recognize their true friends, he could not blame those who did not have the same confidence in the future.[83]

Joly was about to make way for Mercier as party leader, but in the meantime, his strong moral stand against the bill that would institute the "Grande loterie nationale de Québec" revealed how his Protestant values could conflict with those of the Catholic majority. The declared purpose of the lottery was to help fund the construction and repair of churches, as well as religious and educational institutions, and the expansion of colonization, but much of the emphasis was placed on the last goal. To the argument that lotteries for charitable purposes had been legal since 1869, Joly replied that the difference with this bill was that it would sanction cash prizes and therefore appeal to cupidity. People who purchased a ticket to win a pair of slippers too small for their feet, or a child's toy, or a bouquet of wax flowers, or a watch that did not tell time were giving away their money rather than gambling. Joly added that in a country as young and vigorous as Canada, every man of heart could earn his living or aspire to wealth and attain it "au travail courageux et persévérant." The government, however, was indicating that there was a quicker and less tiring way to make a fortune, one that depended on the throw of a dice or the spin of a wheel. Finally, he argued, experience elsewhere in the world proved that legalized lotteries were a social plague. As a fellow Protestant, Solicitor General W.W. Lynch agreed with Joly, but the bill's sponsor simply replied that the lottery had an important national purpose, that the principle was the same whether the prize was in cash or in kind, and that the organizers included priests such as Curé Labelle, the well-known proponent of northern colonization and driving force behind the proposal. The bill passed quickly in the Assembly, only to be rejected by the upper house with its high proportion of ultramontane Conservatives, who resented Labelle's attempts to unite Chapleau and Mercier within a single party.[84]

Joly also took a principled stand against the government's proposal to raise the salaries of MLAs and cabinet members. Perhaps sensing that Chapleau was attempting to mollify disgruntled backbenchers, he argued that even if this move was now affordable because of the sale of the railway, this was a shameful way to mark the sacrifice of "notre grande entreprise nationale, ce chemin de fer qui devait faire la fortune et la prospérité de la province."[85] For the same reason, Joly opposed the proposal to erect a new legislative building, projected to cost $150,000, arguing that it could wait until the government was able to pay off its debt without increasing taxes, as it was now doing. Also, while noting that the Liberals respected the Crown, Joly objected to the $7,000 budgeted for the stables of Spencer Wood, noting that the expenses of the lieutenant governor's residence were increasing each year. Questioning, as well, the need for an agent in France with a salary of $2,500 a year, Joly concluded as a good patrician, "On veut vivre maintenant de la politique et par la politique. On semble oublier qu'on entre dans la politique pour servir son pays et non pour y vivre des revenus qu'elle peut rapporter." ("We live now for politics and by politics. We seem to forget that we enter political life to serve our country and not to live from the revenues that it can bring.")[86]

Increasingly demoralized by the political venality and corruption of the province, as well as by the pettiness of inter-party intrigues and the political liability of being a Protestant, Joly was now delaying his resignation as party leader only because the Liberals from Montreal and Quebec City supported different successors.[87] Though from the latter city, Joly appears to have willingly made way for Mercier, Montreal's choice, when the transfer took place prior to the opening of the 1883 session. He explained to Goldwin Smith in Toronto that "matters in the province were getting from bad to worse, every day aggravated the complaints. I think it was right before attempting another assault to try the experiment of disburdening ourselves from such loads as might have hampered us hitherto; religious prejudice against us, mode of warfare not adapted to the occasion, etc." Joly was clearly recalling attacks such as the one by the Conservative press against his participation in the parade to honour Bishop Laval, as well as admitting that many Liberals were looking for a more fiery leader.[88] He insisted, however, that the change of leadership "entailed no abandonment of of [sic] what we had always contended for," and he objected to Smith's suggestion in the *Bystander* that his resignation was an indication that French Canadians were not temperamentally suited to elective institutions. But his statement that they were "not trained to self Government," being misled by "those who cannot account for them satisfactorily" (presumably meaning their priests), did reflect his paternalism as well as his disgust with politics.[89] Joly remained cagey with Smith, however, evading his repeated requests to publish his opinions on the Quebec situation in his periodical.[90]

Discouraged though he may have been with provincial politics, Joly still refused Laurier's invitation to run for federal office in Lévis,[91] and he showed no signs of flagging interest during the next two years in the Assembly, where his interventions were as numerous and as pointed as ever. In his swan song as retiring Liberal leader, he supported Mercier's demand that the government seek better terms for Quebec,[92] and later in the session he returned to his favourite theme of government financial irresponsibility and the possibility that if the government were forced to resort to direct taxation, the people might lose their horror of sacrificing provincial autonomy. Joly was particularly critical of the decision to appoint a three-man commission to recommend reforms of the civil service. Complaining of the commission's cost and of the government's decision to raise public servants' salaries by a total of $37,000 before the report was even tabled, he reminded the house that his administration had reduced expenditures by combining positions in the face of numerous demands for patronage posts. He made no mention of the premier's announcement that, like Ottawa, Quebec would introduce civil-service exams and appoint an auditor general, for Joly's rather outdated and impractical message was simply that the government should exercise the self-discipline that would make such innovations unnecessary.[93]

When Chapleau's successor as premier, J.A. Mousseau, resigned, and yet another ministry opened the 1884 session, this one with a stronger Castor presence led by J.J. Ross, Joly sarcastically suggested that the Conservatives might consider resorting to alphabetical order as a means of simplifying the process. The aim, he argued, was to avoid responsibility for their actions, but "le grand coupable c'est le parti conservateur qui gouverne, quel que soit ceux qui dirigent les affaires en son nom." ("culpable foremost was the governing Conservative Party, no matter who was directing affairs in its name.") Referring once again to the crippling debt, Joly argued that by constantly going cap in hand to Ottawa, the provincial government was lowering Quebec's esteem in the eyes of the rest of the country.[94] Outside the Assembly, he opposed the Quebec government's demand that in return for supporting the contribution of an additional $22.5 million to complete the CPR, the province should receive a "bribe" – namely, an increased federal subsidy, a bridge at Quebec City, reimbursement for the North Shore Railway costs, and so on. Even though it was rumoured that the Great Eastern running through the county of Lotbinière would receive some of the largesse, Joly wrote, "Let the Government bring out the measure manfully on its own merits & stand or fall by the result. If it is wrong no amount of bribing of the Provinces will make it right."[95]

Despite his private criticism of Mercier's ongoing with flirtation with first one and then the other wing of the Conservative Party, Joly resisted invitations to switch to the federal scene, writing to Lotbinière's MP when he offered to step aside in the next election, "La Providence m'a fixé ici, j'y reste sans me plaindre, espérant que malgré tous les obstacles mon travail ne sera pas complètement perdu." (Providence has fixed me here, I remain without complaint, hoping that despite all obstacles my work will not be completely lost.")[96] By late April Joly was becoming increasingly critical of federal interference in areas of provincial jurisdiction, particularly with respect to railways and the issuing of licenses to stores, hotels, and other businesses. The Conservatives, in turn, defended the constitution and the federal government, arguing that tariffs on all railway lines, local or not, had to be as uniform as possible and that dual government control would be ineffective. As for licenses, they pointed out, Prime Minister Macdonald had long held that provinces had the authority to raise money from them, but not to regulate license holders.[97] Joly, in reply, argued that the interprovincial agreement of 1865 had been unilaterally, and therefore illegally, altered before being submitted for Britain's approval in the case of railways as well as the issuing of licenses. The Quebec Conference agreement had stated that railways to be built within only one province could be declared *in advance* to be of national interest, but the BNA Act allowed the federal government to make such a declaration *after* a province had built such a line. As a result, Quebec was losing control of the railways it had made such heavy sacrifices to subsidize. Joly received no support from the provincial government, however, which argued that the Quebec Resolutions adopted by the provincial legislatures on the eve of Confederation had no legal status before being enacted by the imperial parliament.[98]

It was also Joly who launched a major attack on the government in late May when he demanded a full-scale inquiry into Sénécal's admission under oath that he had provided between $500 and $600 towards the election of the Conservative candidate for Verchères in the 1881 provincial election. Sénécal, who had been superintendent of the QMOO at the time, also suggested that he had provided similar sums in other counties. Joly charged that the current government was trying to limit the political damage by restricting the terms of inquiry to the financial accounts of the QMOO rather than examining its sale the following

year to Sénécal and his associates. Pointing out that the difference between the two political parties in the 1881 election had been only 5,000
to 6,000 votes, despite the Conservative landslide in terms of seats, Joly
questioned the legitimacy of the government.[99]

At the opening of the 1885 session, Joly complained about the lack of
progress being made by the one-man judicial inquiry into the railway
issue.[100] That issue became somewhat irrelevant, however, when Prime
Minister Macdonald succumbed to pressure from his Quebec deputies
and provided a large subsidy to the CPR in order for it to purchase
the Montreal-Quebec branch of the QMOO.[101] In the meantime, Joly
criticized the government's announcement that it would increase expenditures to promote colonization, claiming that it should first reduce
its crippling debt.[102] To Joly, colonization was a code word for more
railways, and he had opposed the granting of more money to the Lac
St Jean line the previous year.[103] He also ridiculed the creation of the
new ministry of railways at a time when the province no longer had
any significant rail lines under its authority.[104]

Pointing to the disunity in the Conservative ranks in a lengthy
speech delivered on April 14, Joly declared that the Liberal opposition
was united and that it had confidence in its leader: "Nous admirons son
courage pour combattre en faveur des intérêts de la province."[105] Ironically, six days later he voted against his party's resolution calling on
the Assembly to issue a statement that blamed the federal government
for causing the Northwest Rebellion. Refusing to explain this dramatic
action,[106] Joly had cast his last vote in Quebec's Legislative Assembly.

Conclusion

Henri-Gustave Joly's political ally Charles Langelier wrote of him that
"issu d'une de nos familles canadiennes-françaises les plus distinguées,
d'un caractère absolument audessus de soupçon, il possédait tout ce
qui était nécessaire pour inspirer au public le respect et la confiance."
("born into one of our most distinguished French-Canadian families, of
unimpeachable character, he possessed all that was necessary to inspire
public respect and confidence.")[107] But others were more critical, for
Mercier claimed that his colleague lacked "de sens pratique et dédaigne
les intrigues légitimes."[108] Another Liberal, Senator Raoul Dandurand,
claimed that Joly was "peu combatif," and Rumilly judged that he was
"même un peu naïf."[109] These statements do not necessarily contradict Langelier, for they too reflect Joly's image as a patrician above the

common fray. As Trépanier notes, however, Joly's courtesy did not prevent him from being an accomplice of the opportunistic Letellier, nor did he lack either energy or tenacity.[110] It was no mean feat to complete the North Shore Railway during a period of economic recession and in the face of formidable political obstacles.

Otherwise, the Joly government's list of accomplishments was admittedly not very impressive. Given that he had handicapped himself by exploiting the public's atavistic fear of direct taxes at a time when significant government deficits were virtually out of the question, Joly had little choice but to reduce expenses by making cuts in areas such as the legal, educational, and mental health systems. He even defended some of these measures on political grounds, stating, for example, that the police had served as Conservative tools during elections. And although he ultimately bowed to pressure from the Council of Public Instruction concerning school inspectors, he did cut the education budget and declare that the current inspectors had done little but collect their salaries and meddle in politics.[111] Neither fiscal retrenchment nor the elimination of such agencies of state coercion was incompatible with liberalism in the strictest sense, but given his commitment to public education, Joly was surprisingly quiet about school reform. This was the issue that Mercier stressed to win support from the Rouge element in his campaign for party leadership,[112] but compulsory schooling was simply too sensitive politically to be championed by a Protestant who wished to maintain Catholic support. In fact, Mercier himself failed to deliver on this promise when he became premier.[113]

On the more positive side, Joly did support legislation that would improve working conditions for labourers. In 1876 he spoke in favour of the Liberal motion that would enable the government to compensate subcontractors and railway construction workers when the main contractor did not complete the work and was therefore ineligible for the government subsidy.[114] As premier, he abolished the law declaring that an employer's sworn testimony concerning employment conditions for domestics or servants was inviolable in case of a salary dispute.[115] And when back in opposition, he presented a bill that would make employers legally responsible for any injury or death of a worker caused by the negligence of the employer or an overseer. Citing the report of an American expert that three-quarters of all workplace accidents were preventable, Joly argued that during the previous twenty-five years mechanization had increased the danger of the workplace and that some employers were slow to install safety devices. He claimed that he himself had prevented many accidents in his mills by taking such precautions. Joly's bill also stated that no prior agreement between employer and employee could negate the employee's right to seek compensation. Although he acknowledged that the law already declared that a negligent employer must compensate an injured worker, Joly pointed out that it was very difficult to obtain a conviction under current regulations. Railway companies, for example, invariably blamed accidents on the carelessness of their employees.[116] When the Conservative government introduced legislation in 1884 that would prohibit factory work for boys under the age of twelve and girls under fourteen, Joly was pleased to declare, "Il n'y a pas de législation qui fasse plus d'honneur au gouvernement que celle-là."[117]

Joly also spoke out against a bill that would allow municipalities to charge vagabonds a fee for their imprisonment. Stating that he sympathized with the honest municipal taxpayers who had to pay the costs of keeping these individuals in jail, Joly nevertheless insisted that a criminal could be justly punished with a fine or imprisonment, but not both.[118] In short, as noted in the previous chapter, Joly's fiscal prudence did not always win out over his sense of justice. His liberal values and paternalist instincts were clearly compatible with a limited protective role for the state, but they also prevented his social reform initiatives from being bold enough to establish for him a reputation as a friend of the working man. It would be endeavours of a different kind that would gain him national stature after he resigned from the provincial legislature in April 1885.

The Hon. Luc Letellier de St-Just (lieutenant governor of Quebec) and the Hon. Henri-Gustave Joly de Lotbinière (premier of Quebec). Library and Archives Canada, Mikan no. 3415421.

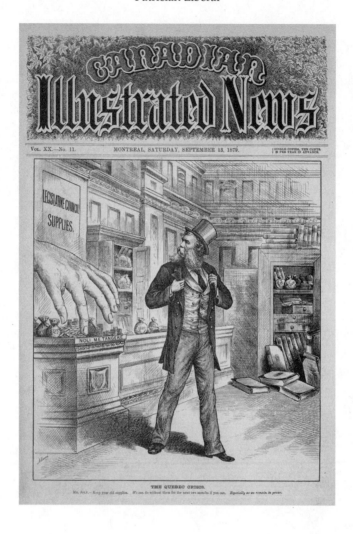

"The Quebec Crisis," by A. Leroux, in *Canadian Illustrated News* 20, no. 11 (13 Sept. 1879): 161. In this cartoon Premier Joly is saying to the Legislative Council, "Keep your old supplies. WE can do without them for the next two months if you can. Especially as we remain in power." Library and Archives Canada, Canadian Illustrated News: Images in the news: 1869–1883, record 35PA-026577.

Chapter Six

Promoter of National Unity

Upon resigning from the Quebec legislature, Joly's plan was to retreat to Lotbinière, concentrate on operating the family lumber business, and restrict his public service to the promotion of agricultural improvement and the North American forest conservation campaign. But the English-speaking minority of the province relied on Joly to intervene with the Mercier government on its behalf, and as the crisis in national unity deepened, he grew increasingly concerned about the backlash in English Canada against the Quebec government's nationalist policies. Despite his imperialist sympathies, therefore, Joly refused all pleas to support the imperial federation movement on the grounds that it would stir up more divisions in the country. Finally, with his strong sense of noblesse oblige, Joly decided to help mend the rift between French and English Canada, defending Mercier's management of the Jesuits' estates question and then speaking out on behalf of the Catholic minority in the Manitoba schools' issue.

The Riel Crisis

Joly was not inexorably opposed to civil disobedience, for in 1876 he donated to the defence fund for the Acadians arrested following the Caraquet Riots that had erupted in protest against New Brunswick's compulsory taxes for non-sectarian schools.[1] He had even expressed sympathy for Riel, declaring during the 1875 election that he did not consider the killing of Thomas Scott to be a murder, "but a very grave mistake." Furthermore, he argued, "the action of the Conservative Government at Ottawa had driven the people of the North West territories well nigh to madness."[2] To establish a provisional government prior to the transfer of authority to Canada in 1870 was one thing, however; to lead a rebellion against the Dominion government was quite another, particularly to someone of Joly's patrician status and military connections. He was a friend of Colonel Thomas Bland Strange, as already noted, and Strange kept him informed of his actions as head of a western field force raised to help quell the 1885 uprising.[3] Furthermore, Joly's son, Alain, was about to graduate from the Royal Military College in Kingston. In fact, as we saw in chapter 2, Joly had asked the minister of militia, Adolphe Caron, to ease Alain's way into the Royal Engineers.[4] Joly may even have shared some of what historian Gillian Poulter refers to as the widespread belief that the rebellion "furnished an opportunity to temper the developing sense of Canadian nationality in the forge of war and to prove that Canada had entered the ranks of modern, progressive nations."[5] Certainly, he helped raise funds for the Quebec volunteer force organized by his former rival for the Lotbinière seat, Colonel Guillaume Amyot. And, when the uprising was crushed and Joly was invited to a meeting to deliberate on how to provide the Métis prisoners with the means to defend themselves, he simply replied, "Je n'ai pas la moindre sympathie pour Riel; il a déchaîné les Indiens."[6]

Joly was in a difficult position, then, when Riel was executed and the notables of St Louis de Lotbinière invited him to a public meeting to protest the failure of the federal government to intervene. The meeting was to follow a mass sung for the repose of Riel's soul, and Joly replied that his decision not to attend was not due to religious prejudice, for he had gone to the funerals of Judge Caron, the Honourable Letellier, and other public men. Nor was it for lack of respect for the memory of Riel, for the courage he had shown at the moment of death gave him the right to the respect of all. The reason he would not attend was that he did not approve of the movement then taking place to establish a nationalist party. Referring to the proposed resolution that such a party would ensure the respect for, and free enjoyment of, French-Canadian rights, Joly did not mince words: "Je suis d'opinion que les Canadiens français ont la libre jouissance de nos droits. S'ils n'en ont pas tiré un meilleur parti, ils ne doivent s'en prendre qu'à eux-mêmes." ("In my opinion the French Canadians have the free enjoyment of our rights. If they haven't taken more advantage of it, they have only themselves to blame.") He could not see how the formation of the *Parti national* could improve their situation, but he did fear that it would make that situation worse as well as compromise the future of Confederation.

Having been born and raised in France, Joly wrote, he had returned to Canada with a French heart after graduating from college, only to be astonished to hear his political adversaries declare in elections that he could not understand or share the innermost feelings of the French Canadians. He now recognized that they were right: "Je ne puis ni comprendre ni partager les sentiments manifestés aujourd'hui avec tant de force par la grande majorité des Canadiens français dans la Province et dans le Comté." ("I can neither understand nor share the sentiments manifested today with such force by the great majority of French Canadians in the province and in the county.") Joly concluded by stating that he was in too great a disagreement with his constituents not to step down and allow them to choose a representative in sympathy with their sentiments.[7]

Joly's statement represented a major embarrassment for the Liberals. The MP for Lotbinière, Dr Côme-Isaïe Rinfret, wrote to him that his resignation would deal a mortal blow to the party locally if it signified a disapproval of the political events that were unfolding. Appealing to Joly's sense of loyalty, Rinfret added that it would deeply sadden their friends who "jusqu'ici nous ont supporté de si grand coeur."[8] But Joly had a broader sense of loyalty, and he took steps to ensure that his response was read well beyond his constituency by sending an English translation to the *Montreal Witness*, in addition to asking Honoré Beaugrand to print it in his newspaper. To Beaugrand, Joly suggested that the new party was simply another of Mercier's attempts at a coalition and that the result would probably be the same as in the past, "c'est à dire que le Parti Libéral se fera exploiter une fois de plus."[9] This time, however, the Rouge element supported the coalition.[10]

Quebec's English-speaking deputies would obviously be marginalized by these developments, but the Liberal G.W. Stephens of Montreal nevertheless wrote to Joly, "I think your action was precipitate." Stephens argued that "the National Party cry will be dropped as soon as it has served its purpose" and that Riel's execution "is only an incident in a long chain of misgovernment which you condemn as well as I do." Adding that Joly's absence "will be an open wound," Stephens pleaded, "Cannot you close it and come back to us again?"[11] Dr Alexander Cameron of Huntingdon, who wrote that he had supported Joly's measures during eleven sessions, was less sanguine than Stephens, stating that his constituents did not support the new party but wondered, "Where will we be in the Assembly?"[12]

L'Électeur was inclined to be gracious about Joly's resignation, regretting in a somewhat condescending tone that the former party leader misunderstood the sense and importance of the nationalist movement, but complimenting him for his sense of honour.[13] Israël Tarte, editor of *Le Canadien*, was less forgiving, stating that Joly had waited two years to take revenge after being deposed as chief of the provincial Liberals.[14] Joly protested, in return, that far from feeling mistreated by the party, "je n'ai que de la reconnaissance envers lui."[15] At Joly's request, *L'Électeur* published his letter, but editor Ernest Pacaud wrote to him that he would have expressed more enthusiasm in his own explanatory note had he not feared annoying Mercier or intensifying the "coup terrible que votre résignation a porté au parti libéral."[16]

Pacaud was obviously referring to the federal Liberals, since the provincial party no longer existed, and he added that Joly's resignation had had a disastrous impact on the English-speaking Members of Parliament, few of whom sympathized with Riel. Laurier had the task of repairing the damage,[17] but he remained conciliatory towards Joly, writing that he agreed entirely with his statement to the voters of Lotbinière that French Canadians had all the rights they could desire. To establish a French-Canadian party, Laurier declared, "ne serait pas seulement un crime, ce serait une faute."[18] Writing from Toronto, J.D. Edgar also agreed with Joly's stance against the *Parti national* and declared that the Liberals did not wish to fight on the ground of Riel's execution. But he added that the Conservatives were interpreting Joly's resignation as a rebuke against Liberal leader Edward Blake's condemnation of the government's misdeeds in the Northwest. Edgar therefore asked Joly to write that "you are with us heart and soul" in endorsing Blake's speech on the Riel affair.[19] But Joly's resignation was not simply a reaction to Mercier's formation of a coalition with the Castors, and he was not willing to issue a clarification that might suggest any sympathy for Riel. He replied rather curtly to Edgar that he could not make his explanation for resigning any clearer, and he stuck to this vow of silence thereafter, explaining only that further comments would be turned against the Liberals by an administration that he had opposed for many years.[20] When invited to participate in the victory celebration of Lotbinière's new *Parti national* MLA in 1886, Joly declined, stating that he had not participated in the election and it would therefore not be fitting to join in the triumph.[21]

By this time Joly had moved his family to Pointe Platon, where he planned to devote his full attention to the seigneury's lumber business, even resigning as a member of the Anglican Cathedral Select Vestry.[22] Meanwhile, he refused an offer from Dr Cameron to run in his place in the largely English-speaking riding of Huntingdon[23] and also turned down a persistent offer to contest the Megantic seat, even though it was to the immediate south of Lotbinière and had a substantial English-speaking population. The sitting member, François Langelier, had alienated this population by defending Riel in court, but Joly clearly wanted to avoid identification with the English-speaking opponents of the rebel leader, fearing that he would thereby exacerbate tensions between French and English Canada. In response to the Megantic invitation, he explained that he had no wish to appeal to the English-speaking majority of the country to counteract the French-speaking majority of the province.[24] Joly further suggested that the English Protestants of Megantic who now mistrusted Langelier could take heart in the fact that, as mayor of Quebec, he had ensured the rights of the Salvation Army.[25]

Joly also explained to Laurier that he could not approve of the Liberals' exploitation of the Riel issue and that if he were to run in the election, he would have to say so publicly, which would only injure the party's chances of victory. He felt that the Liberals were playing with fire, one that with a sudden burst of wind could burn from one end of the country to the other. Finally, he concluded, it might be charged that if he had stronger sympathy for French Canadians' aspirations for a distinct nationality, he would judge the nationalist movement less severely, but "vous ne me ferez pas ce reproche, car vous devez avoir confiance dans l'avenir du Canada."[26]

Not willing to take no for an answer, Laurier again wrote that he agreed with Joly's Lotbinière speech and denied that he or the other Liberal spokesmen had appealed to national prejudices. He had accused the government of committing judicial murder but had not done so in the name of French-Canadian rights, nor had he appealed to French-Canadian prejudices. Rather, he had stated that the conduct of the government, from start to finish, was a violation of the rights possessed by all British subjects. In his view, the author of the rebellion was not Riel but the Canadian government, and the Métis leader had been conducted to the scaffold by the authors of this crime. Finally, Laurier argued that Joly's disagreement with his political friends on only one point should not deprive them of his services: "Nous libéraux, nous réclamons pour nous-mêmes, la liberté d'avoir chacun sa manière de voir sur toute question."[27]

In his brief reply, Joly stated that he ardently wished for Blake's victory, but he reminded Laurier that the Riel affair was *the* central issue in the election, adding that if Macdonald exploited it to arouse anti-French sentiment outside Quebec, it would split the country. Furthermore, Joly made it clear that Laurier had failed to grasp his antipathy towards Riel: "si vous connaissiez toute ma pensée, qui sait, si vous ne me mettriez pas au rang des *pendards*?" ("if you knew all my thoughts, who knows if you might not place me in the ranks of the *scoundrels*?") Finally, he wrote, he would have preferred to remain silent had he not felt obliged to explain why he believed his candidacy would render "un mauvais service à mes amis et au pays."[28] Joly did, however, break his public silence briefly by declaring that his disapproval of the Riel agitation should in no way be interpreted as approval of the Macdonald government, a statement that, according to one informant, was "cited & discussed *ad infinitum* by the newspapers."[29]

The Anglo-Protestant Minority and Imperial Federation

Joly's public appearances now became limited to non-political events such as agricultural exhibitions and forestry conventions.[30] He soon received pleas to intercede with Mercier from public servants who had been dismissed as a result of the new administration's patronage appointments, a feature of politics that Joly had always found distasteful. He could only reply that, not having taken part in the election, "it would not be very becoming on my part to ask for favors nor to interfere with their administration of public affairs."[31] Joly did, however, occasionally write in support of local residents for minor positions,[32] and Mercier appears to have relied on his advice concerning patronage matters in the Eastern Townships, where Joly was granted an honorary doctorate by Bishop's University in 1887.[33]

Also in 1887 Joly intervened on behalf of the aged G.F. Bowen, after he was dismissed as sheriff of Sherbrooke, by ensuring that he would be appointed district prothonotary. This appointment angered the leading Liberals of neighbouring Stanstead County, who made it clear to Mercier that Sherbrooke's Conservatives had held sway in the region far too long. Bowen was a member by marriage of the elite Hale family of Quebec City, however, and Joly replied that he had wished to repay the political debt owed to Bowen's nephew, Jack Hale, "le plus désinteressé de nos amis."[34] Another of Joly's rare interventions with Mercier was also on behalf of a member of the province's English-speaking elite, for

W. Selby Desbarats claimed that he had been persecuted as a government official because the provincial secretary was jealous of his social position. The premier simply replied that Desbarats had been accused of falsifying his accounts and that the inspector of government offices would conduct an impartial inquiry.[35]

Mercier continued to treat Joly with respect, however, appointing him to be one of Quebec's delegates to the Chicago exhibition of 1888, though Joly declined on the legitimate grounds that he had not been given sufficient notice.[36] He was also becoming increasingly concerned about the nationalism of the Mercier government, writing in early 1888 to one of the Anglo-Protestant deputies, Colonel William Rhodes,

> I honestly felt that your victory at Megantic would open the door for a reconciliation between the Protestant minority of the Province of Quebec and the Government. I felt confident that, in order to continue the work so happily begun the supporters of the Government and their Official Press would seek every opportunity to re-assure the Minority by proofs of their sympathy & goodwill. Unfortunately, there appears a growing disposition to do exactly the reverse. Not only all opportunities to wound the feelings of the Minority are eagerly seized, but, when opportunities do not arise naturally, they are forcibly created. It is enough to make me suspect that, after all, your opponents at Megantic were not far from the truth when they represented the Parti National as decidedly hostile to the English Protestant minority of the Province.[37]

To François Langelier, who had alienated the Catholic bishops by winning the famous *influence indue* case for the Liberal appellant, Joly wrote in confidence that he regretted the influence Mercier was allowing the Catholic clergy to exercise on the government. Noting the role that the Church had played in Liberal electoral defeats, Joly declared that its participation in politics was neither in the interest of the Catholic religion that he respected nor in the interest of the province. He added that he did not condemn his political friends for entering this pact, however, because they had the difficult choice between attaining power and the ostracism that they had endured for a generation.[38]

Joly also expressed concern to another correspondent that Mercier was turning towards commercial union, declaring, "Je ne désire pas que le Canada se mette complètement à la merci des Etats Unis. Qui protégera nos intérets? Nous ne pouvons pas nous attendre à ce que 60 millions d'Américains sacrifient leurs intérêts commerciaux à ceux

de 5 millions de Canadiens."[39] ("I don't wish Canada to place itself entirely at the mercy of the United States. Who will protect our interests?
We cannot expect 60 million Americans to sacrifice their commercial
interests to those of 5 million Canadians.") When asked by the editor
of Detroit's *Evening News* to comment on John Sherman's speech to the
U.S. Senate concerning annexation, Joly replied, "We feel that our system of Government compares favorably with yours. Your Republic can
no more dispense with one head than a monarchy, only in your case
the head changes every 4 years after a struggle which becomes every
time more & more dangerous." As for commercial or political union,
Joly wrote, they were virtually the same because one would lead to
the other, and Canadians' reaction to Sherman's speech had demonstrated that they did not favour annexation. In Joly's words, "annexation would bring an increase of wealth, but money is not everything in
this world." Still, Canadians needed to follow the American example
"and develop our resources which we have so far neglected."[40]

Joly's ideology was more compatible with another political current gaining strength at this time, the imperial federation movement,
and, given the lack of support for this movement among the French-
Canadian political elite,[41] he was certainly an attractive prospect for
its chief promoters. In fact, W.D. Lighthall's novel *The Young Seigneur*,
published in 1888, reflected how attracted English-Canadian imperi-
alists were to the romantic notion of the benevolent French-Canadian
seigneur.[42] Upon sending Joly an invitation to chair a YMCA meeting
on the subject in November 1888, R.R. Dobell claimed that he needed
someone who was "not a strict party man, but who is patriotic enough
to look beyond the petty boundaries of any section."[43] As we have seen,
Joly had defended the imperial connection in his anti-Confederation
speech, but largely because he felt it was more compatible with a decen-
tralized distribution of power in British North America. Furthermore,
his imperialist sympathies had been at a low ebb in 1870 when he made
a statement in favour of Canadian independence. Noting that Britain
was on the verge of declaring war with Russia, Joly had asked what
would happen if the United States decided to side with the latter country. Given that the last soldier had departed for England and that the
cannons of Quebec and Montreal had been melted down to sell as iron
to the Americans – and perhaps be used against Canada – Joly asked
how the government could pretend that England would rush to the
country's defence in case of danger. As the country was now considered "un fardeau onéreux" for England, the only loyalty that could now

exist was loyalty to Canada.[44] But Joly had clearly changed his views by the mid-1880s, for in his last speech as Liberal leader in 1883, he asked that the throne speech be modified to recognize Major Hébert, a Canadian soldier who had died while serving with the victorious British army in Egypt.[45]

Joly appears never to have written a detailed defence of British imperialism, nor is there any indication that he realized that the liberal imperialism "which tied together a theory of imperial legitimacy with the project of improvement" was in crisis, as Karuna Mantena argues.[46] After all, two of his sons were helping to develop India's economic infrastructure. But the fact remains that when Joly felt that his imperialist sympathies conflicted with his nationalism, he placed what he felt were the interests of Canada first. Thus, he rejected Dobell's invitation to chair the 1888 YMCA meeting on the grounds that public opinion, once stirred up, would be difficult to control: "A few months ago no one spoke of annexation in Canada, no political man, no Paper advocated it." Now, however, the press was "taking up the question in a way which shows how dangerous it is to startle the Public with the proposal of unexpected changes."[47] Like the Liberals prior to the 1887 federal election, the imperial federationists were reluctant to take no for an answer. Joly was listed as a supporter who was not able to attend the May 1889 meeting of the Imperial Federation League of Canada and (without his permission) as a council member at the special meeting of the following October.[48]

Joly had already expanded privately on his views in his lengthy commentary on his friend Major C.B. Mayne's paper promoting imperial federation. He objected particularly to the League's declaration that the choice for Canadians was either imperial federation or annexation. In Joly's words, "one of the warmest advocates of Imp. Fed.," Sir Rawson Rawson, had written of "the bonds of kinship and of mutual interest & sympathy" that were knitting Great Britain and her colonies more closely together. Yet the Canadian public was being told that radical change had become "a fatal necessity." In the absence of any explanation concerning the form that imperial federation would take, the imaginations of Canadians were "shrinking from the mysterious unknown," and their minds were dwelling "with less alarm on the other alternatives of Independence or Annexation." Joly was also concerned that in instigating this debate, the imperial federationists were "raising the hopes of our neighbours and awakening their ambitions at a time, of all other, when we ought to act with the greatest prudence

& unanimity." Reflecting his belief that stronger trade ties naturally led to stronger emotional bonds, Joly argued that the logical first steps were a commercial union between Great Britain and her colonies, the subsidization of a fast fleet of steamers that would carry the mail between England, Canada, and Australia, and the laying of a telegraph cable between British Columbia and Australia: "a community of interests would lead to mutual intercourse & closer friendship."[49]

Historian Colin Coates's statement that "no influential French Canadian joined the calls for Imperial unity" may be accurate in the strict political sense, then, but Joly did favour stronger ties with the empire.[50] Referring to the importance of having French-Canadian support, honorary secretary of the League J. Castell Hopkins asked for Joly's opinion as a "representative French Liberal" concerning "the gradual development of our political institutions from the present Colonial dependence into a position of Imperial equality ... a system of organized naval defence," and "perhaps a form of Commercial union." Joly replied not as a "French Liberal" but as a "Canadian," reiterating much the same concerns as he had in his letter to Colonel Mayne and stressing that the question of improving Canada's position in the empire was "most delicate," especially in Quebec.[51]

Not to be discouraged, Hopkins invited Joly to speak at the League's annual meeting in Hamilton, or at least to send an address that could be read at the meeting. Joly replied that although the issue had yet to be addressed in Quebec, the new complication of the Jesuits' Estates Bill meant that this would not be the proper time to discuss it. He also advised Hopkins to canvas "*representative* French Canadians, Sir Hector Langevin, Sir Adolphe Caron, Mr Chapleau, Mr Laurier and other leaders of both political parties who feel clearly the pulse of their people."[52] When the mercurial former ultramontane champion Israël Tarte announced his support for the Imperial Federation League, however, Joly remained unimpressed. After the annual meeting of January 1890 unanimously passed a motion endorsing Joly as the Quebec vice president, he replied by telegram that he regretted not having been notified in advance, given that he had made his views on the subject clear to Hopkins.[53]

Meanwhile, Joly's concern about the rift between French and English Canada had forced him out of his self-imposed exile from the political scene. He threw his support behind Colonel Rhodes in the Megantic by-election that followed the appointment of the aging mining and railway entrepreneur to the Mercier cabinet in December 1888.[54] Joly's own son,

Edmond, was caught off-guard, for he wrote to his father that everyone in Quebec City was asking how his personal letter of congratulations to Rhodes had ended up in the press, given that "it is well known that the combat in Megantic will be carried on mainly through the Riel martyrdom cry & the public know that you have no sympathy for that 'cri de guerre.'" But Joly chastised his son for not reading the letter carefully enough to realize that it was not private and for not telegraphing him "avant de porter une si grave accusation contre un homme honorable comme le Colonel Rhodes." Joly added that he had for a long time been awaiting the opportunity to put an end to the malaise that reigned in the province, "avant que la brêche qui tend à aliener les deux races & les deux religions ne devienne irréparable." Mercier's enemies were doing their best to undermine the peace and would succeed in doing so if a Protestant were not included in the cabinet by popular election. Joly even conceded that he now regretted shirking his duty to sacrifice himself by accepting the portfolio that had been offered him: "le Colonel Rhodes s'est sacrifié à ma place, c'est à moi à le supporter." If the government alone were to suffer, he would say that it deserved to do so, "mais la Province et, plus encore, la Puissance entière souffre, il est temps d'intervenir."[55] Joly exhibited an almost messianic fervour in a telegram of the same day: "The time has come for men of good will to put an end to uneasiness and divisions[.] I have waited long enough, now is the day."[56]

Joly appeared on the hustings in addition to entering into a debate in the pages of the ultra-Protestant Montreal *Witness* when correspondents complained that, in contrast to Joly, Rhodes had endorsed Mercier's Riel platform. Joly's rejoinder was that Rhodes' election "will heal a dangerous wound, kept open too long, and will restore peace and good will among us." He added that those who thought he had "set a good example in 1885 will not refuse to follow me now."[57] Rhodes did win the by-election, crediting Joly's intervention for "giving the County of Megantic to the Mercier government and enabling me to return to the rock City a triumphant old man, instead of an old Gentleman invited to remain at home."[58] Even though the sixty-seven-year-old Rhodes – once known as the "Great Northern Hunter" because of his many hunting exploits[59] – declared that he intended to leave participation in the debates to younger men, Joly continued to feel that his entry into Mercier's cabinet was a major step forward. Joly wrote Rhodes on New Year's Day, "You and I and more than one of our friends must have felt in our inmost hearts cheered by the thought that our work was real

Christmas work, striving to restore peace & good will among men."[60]
To Mercier he declared that he had never taken part in an election with
a stronger conviction "d'un devoir à remplir qu'à celle de Mégantic."[61]
To avoid the impression that he was expecting a political reward, Joly
rejected an appeal that he use his influence to obtain a government
posting for his own son-in-law.[62]

But Joly soon became disillusioned again when the Legislative Council rejected the bill drafted on behalf of McGill University and Bishop's
University to recognize their bachelor of arts degrees as qualification,
without further examination, for admission to study for the liberal
professions.[63] Although the bill was officially supported by the Mercier government, one of the cabinet ministers had voted against it on
the grounds that Laval University would be placed at a disadvantage.
Stung by this result, Joly wrote to David Ross, a Protestant cabinet member, "I really had some hopes of better times when Colonel Rhodes was
returned for Megantic. Instead of improving, matters are getting worse
every day."[64] Rhodes tried to reassure Joly that the question would be
better understood in the next session, as public attention was drawn to
it. In a letter to Principal William Dawson of McGill, however, Joly criticized Rhodes and Ross for allowing the vote to be an open one, stating
that "their turn had come to insist upon the unanimous support of their
Colleagues." He also made it clear that he expected them to take that
stand in the next session.[65]

Nearly a year later, Joly wrote to Ernest Pacaud, the editor of
L'Électeur, arguing that the BA Bill did not constitute a special concession to the Protestant institutions because Laval's objections had been
satisfied by an amendment that recognized its degrees as bachelor of
letters and bachelor of science. Opponents argued that the diplomas
of the Catholic colleges were also the equivalent of the BA from McGill
and Bishop's, but Joly's response was that even if the bill was for the
exclusive benefit of the religious minority, it would simply give that
minority the same privilege as the majority – namely, the privilege of
adhering to the system of education that it deemed best. If the majority
wished to force the Protestants to conform to the system applied in the
Catholic colleges (namely a qualifying examination), he asked, "où sont
les droits égaux de la minorité, en matière d'éducation?"[66] The letter
was somewhat superfluous as far as the fate of the bill was concerned,
however, for Pacaud had already informed Joly that Mercier had given
in to his wish; he would ensure that the bill passed the upper House,
which it did.[67]

The Jesuits' Estates Crisis

Mercier clearly had political reasons for placating the Protestant minority and particularly Joly, for the Jesuits' Estates question was about to explode with D'Alton McCarthy's resignation from Macdonald's cabinet, followed by his formation of the Equal Rights Association.[68] True to his belief in mutual toleration, Joly spoke out against the agitation aroused by Mercier's bill, which not only provided a monetary settlement for the land the Jesuits had once owned but also invited the Pope to advise on the fund's distribution within the Catholic Church. Writing to the Montreal *Witness* in January 1890, Joly lamented the fact that "men who, for so many years have lived together in confidence and fellowship, notwithstanding differences of origins & religious creed, are now growing suspicious of one another and gradually getting estranged." He pleaded that "every effort must be made to preserve the old feeling of mutual trust and forbearance which has made us Canadians, English and French, Roman Catholics and Protestants live happily side by side, in peace in days when there is so little peace in the world."

Despite blaming Mercier's Riel agitation for resulting in a dangerous counter-agitation, Joly argued that "neither the execution of Riel, on the one side, nor the Jesuits' Estates Bill, on the other, appear to justify the appeals made, from both sides, to the religious and national feelings of the two component parts of our Canadian Nationality." He expressed strong doubts that the "real nature" of the Jesuits' Estates bill was understood by those who condemned it and insisted that the $400,000 to be paid by the government was not an endowment but a very modest settlement of a long-standing and legitimate claim. The property had not been confiscated but vested in the Crown by virtue of the law of escheat after the Jesuit order had been suppressed by the Pope in 1773, and this had not taken place until its last Canadian member had died. Joly was splitting hairs, for the fact remained that the British government had been moving towards abolition of the Jesuit order and confiscation of its property (as had taken place in France, Spain, and other Catholic jurisdictions) even before the papal suppression, and the government had chosen not to place the Jesuit properties in the hands of the local bishops, as the Pope had decreed. The restitution claim clearly rested on moral more than legal grounds, but Joly also declared that if he had been in the legislature and the Pope's name had not been mentioned in the bill, he would have insisted on its inclusion because a legal contract required the approval of the head of any corporation that was party to it. He simply passed over what the Protestants mostly objected to, the Pope's involvement in the distribution of the fund.[69]

Joly received a number of letters in response, all sympathetic to him but most of them critical of Mercier's bill. He was stung, however, by Goldwin Smith's suggestion in the *Bystander* that he had been motivated by a desire to maintain party cohesion. In response, Joly pointed to his letter on the BA Bill as evidence that he would not sacrifice the Protestant minority. Smith replied, "No protestation on your part is needed to convince me that you follow the course which you consider best for the country," but he still felt that national unity was "growing more hopeless every day."[70]

Joly was clearly not motivated by political ambition, for when he was invited in June 1890 to be the Liberal candidate for Quebec West, he declined without explanation.[71] But he did accept Mercier's invitation in January 1891 to serve in his place as commissioner of agriculture and public works during the four to five months Mercier planned to spend in Europe. The premier added that Joly would have use of his seal to execute his orders and that he could join the cabinet meeting any time he had a matter to be decided, for the ministers would be "enchantés de vous recevoir et de prendre votre avis."[72] Three months later Mercier thanked Joly for the report he had produced, adding that the only part he had changed concerned the control of agricultural schools by seminaries or colleges of priests, a system in which he had no confidence because their primary aim was to provide a classical education "à l'ancienne façon." Rather ironically, Mercier was writing from Rome.[73] But his alliance with the ultramontanes was clearly wearing thin, for Mercier also followed the policy that Joly had long championed of having the state take direct responsibility for the medical supervision of the mentally ill, a step that alienated his ultramontane supporters and helped lead to his defeat in the next election.[74]

In the meantime, Mercier assured Joly that he would never forget the services he was rendering him: "ma plume est impuissante à vous le dire."[75] Joly's duties with the provincial government prevented him from participating in the federal election of March 1891, but Laurier did inform him in September that there would probably be a vacancy in Beauce where he would easily be returned in the by-election.[76] By this time, however, Joly was contemplating a return to provincial politics. Mercier asked him, on short notice in September, to be his representative at a Montreal meeting, and when Joly sent him an "habillement" of "étoffe" (a suit of homespun clothing), the premier wrote that it would be a new link with his "ancien chef."[77] Joly's support was particularly valuable to Mercier at this time because of the Baie des Chaleurs Railway scandal. During the premier's absence in Europe, railway minister Ernest Pacaud had paid $175,000 to the railway contractor, who had then simply handed back $100,000 for Pacaud's use. Furthermore, Mercier had alienated the Catholic episcopacy by negotiating directly with the Vatican and filling the Council of Public Instruction with his supporters.[78]

Mercier hoped to remodel his cabinet by bringing in Joly and F.L. Béique, a radical Liberal who had become his personal secretary,[79] but he was dismissed as premier before this could take place. Laurier pressured Joly to take part in the ensuing election, assuring him that the Baie des Chaleurs transaction would be not only condemned but suppressed and arguing that reform of the provincial administration must come from the ranks of the Liberal Party. He also appealed to Joly's ego by stating that his return to political life would be the best assurance of "une prompte & efficace réforme dans notre malheureuse province."[80] Joly's sense of pride may have tempted him to return as the saviour of a party that had shunted him aside for the spoils of office, but the uncompromising moral principles that would have made his support so valuable at this juncture also prevented him from taking a step that would associate him in any way with the fallen government's tarnished image. He refused Laurier's request that he run as an independent Liberal, stating that each candidate would be bound to declare whether he felt Mercier or Boucherville would be the best premier. Although he admired Mercier's talent and energy, he felt that he had become a victim of the Liberal Party's adoption of the Conservative Party system, clearly meaning wastefulness and corruption.[81] Joly not only refused to take part in the election, he also rejected Laurier's request to make his negotiations with Mercier public, declaring that he would have been willing to work for the future, but he was not willing to defend the past.[82]

The disgraced Mercier had clearly been moving towards a reconciliation with the English-speaking minority. Asking for Joly's advice as to what Liberal Protestants should do in the upcoming election, J. Ward of Montreal noted that they were not blind to Mercier's mistakes but also could not ignore the fact that Protestants were "under many obligations to him, for instance instituting night schools, encouragement of better agriculture, giving the option to municipalities of establishing libraries & mechanics institutes, the passing into law the B.A. Bill, which Mr Hall could not have effected, but for the personal efforts of Mr Mercier, then the material and much needed help rendered so readily & willingly to our Protestant Hospital for the Insane." Ward even considered the Jesuits' Estates Bill, which set aside $60,000 for Protestant education, to be "a wise piece of policy."[83] Joly hesitated to give advice on the election, however, stating, "I feel bound to silence, for one word of explanation on my part would injure them and help their opponents." Joly was clearly torn between loyalty to the Liberals and a desire to condemn political corruption, for he added, "If I followed the dictates of my conscience, I would speak out loudly and I reproach myself bitterly for not doing so. You see that I am not fit to guide or endorse anyone, at this juncture."[84]

Joly acted as vice chairman of the Dominion Liberal Convention two years later, in 1893,[85] but otherwise remained aloof from politics in the early 1890s. He turned his attention instead to the organization of Quebec City's first winter carnival since the failed effort of 1883. Aimed at attracting American tourists in particular during the slow winter season, the carnival of February 1894 focused on winter sports such as curling, snowshoeing, and hockey. It also featured a costume ball open to the public, a Grand Ball for the social elite in honour of the governor general, and a storming of the ice palace, but it discouraged the public drunkenness and boisterous behaviour that had characterized the traditional pre-Lenten popular ritual. As honorary patron, Governor General Lord Aberdeen highlighted the crowd's self-control in his speech at the close of the event, thereby illustrating the fact that well-ordered recreation was now viewed as an essential means of alleviating the strains and pressures of modern urban life.[86]

Joly was well placed to act as honorary president for an event that, in the words of historian Frank Abbott, was largely "by, of, and for the small and medium-sized businessmen of the city whether French or English-speaking."[87] Particularly concerned with alleviating the growing tensions between French and English Canada, Lord Aberdeen thanked Joly for "the unique and notable reception accorded to us on our arrival," adding that the Queen would be "graciously interested and gratified" by the "success and éclat" of the carnival. This was particularly so "because the success has been so largely due to the activity of Her Majesty's French-Canadian subjects, whose loyalty is undoubtedly a source of pride and satisfaction to Her Majesty as it assuredly is also to the British people as a whole."[88] Lady Aberdeen confided in her journal, "M. de Lotbinière is the very dearest & cheeriest of old French seigneurs – he is the life of everything & keeps everybody up to the mark at the head of his 'boys' as he calls the snow-shoers. He is nearly seventy [he was actually sixty-five] but takes part in all that is going on, helping to pull up our sleigh, heading processions and well to the front in the attack on the ice fort." The two couples exchanged photographs and became fast friends from that point on.[89]

The financial success of the carnival led to a movement to draft Joly for mayor, with one newspaper editor declaring, "Nous croyons qu'il sera difficile de trouver un homme qui rallierait autant tous les citoyens et qui offrirait autant de garanties que vous."[90] ("We believe that it would be difficult to find a man who would so successfully rally all the citizens and who would offer as many guarantees as you.") Joly appears not to have been tempted, but he did agree to accompany Laurier on a tour of Ontario that was ostensibly aimed at combating the prejudices being stirred up by the Protestant Protective Association, which had risen from the ashes of the more moderate Equal Rights Association.[91] According to Lady Aberdeen, Joly had said to her and her husband that "the Protestants have & always have had more than their share of office & influence, that they in no way need to be protected & that he can give instance after instance to show how they have been treated with the greatest tolerance & liberality."[92] To assist Joly in his mission to convince Ontarians that Quebec was not under the thumb of Rome, Ernest Pacaud sent him issues of L'Électeur stating that Catholics recognized the Pope's jurisdiction in spiritual matters only and that their allegiance to the sovereign in temporal matters was absolute. Pacaud also included a copy of Mercier's speech in reply to the Equal Rights Association in which he marshalled statistics to demonstrate that the minority was fairly treated.[93]

Edward Blake pressed Joly to accept an invitation to attend a performance of Antigone at the University of Toronto, adding, "Other statesmen are asked, but I am requested to say what cannot be publicly or formally said of course, that you and Laurier are the two whose presence is most desired, as you are conceived to be the most academic of our public men and the best qualified to deal with and appreciate such an effort as is now being made."[94] Joly also planned to deliver a nonpartisan address on the French-English question, but he was informed that his task would be difficult because of the widely circulated attacks on the religious apostate Amédée Papineau by La Minerve. These attacks were considered to be particularly significant because the editor of La Minerve, Joseph Tassé, was a senator reputed to belong to the moderate wing of the Conservative Party.[95] Papineau, the eldest son of the famous Patriote leader, had married an American Protestant while in exile following the Rebellions, and he had apparently not been a practicing Catholic for many years. When he joined his beloved wife's Presbyterian Church shortly after her death, however, *La Minerve* accused him of throwing himself into the arms of the Swiss preachers in order to avoid his share of the assessment for construction of the parish's new Catholic church.[96] Controversies such as this may have made it more difficult for Joly to argue that Quebec's Catholic Church was tolerant towards Protestants, but they also reinforced his sense of mission to promote what he called "a truly national spirit." Because Toronto had "national societies of all kinds but no Canadian society," the decision was finally reached by his hosts in that city to have Joly's address sponsored by the Young Liberals.[97]

Joly also spoke in Kingston's city hall, where the president of the "reform association" asked him to "break through party rules and provide them with an independent address."[98] Declaring that his purpose was to dispel their prejudices against the people of Quebec, Joly admitted that the Protestant minority was not receiving its fair share of public appointments, but he added that neither was the Catholic minority in Ontario. Rather than being proof of hostility, this simply showed that majorities were generally greedy. In fact, Joly claimed, Quebec's Protestants were over-represented in the federal civil service because they belonged to the national majority. He also reminded his audience that five of the province's finance ministers had been Protestants. In response to the claims of the Protestant Protective Association, Joly insisted that the Quebec minority had no reason to complain and even suggested that the tithing system was the fairest way to remunerate the Catholic clergy. Reflecting his patrician status, Joly added that "what seemed to him the most beautiful feature of the system was to see the faithfulness and honesty with which the French-Canadian farmers paid their tithes." Whereas Ontario Protestants attributed the backwardness of French-Canadian farmers to the sacrifices they made for the building of churches, "no one would ever attribute any lack of success the Ontario farmer might have to his activity and liberality in behalf of his clergymen or churches."[99]

Joly was most likely making an oblique reference to the anti-tithing campaign of the rural Quebec newspaper editor Robert Sellar. Sellar's *Huntingdon Gleaner* had been arguing since the mid-1880s that the province's Protestant-owned farms were falling into the hands of French

Canadians because their priests were encouraging them to move into the Eastern Townships and other English-speaking areas simply because this would increase the Church's tax base.[100] Joly also claimed that any disadvantage the provincial minority had experienced in terms of the educational system had been removed by Mercier in 1890, when graduates of Protestant universities were given access to the liberal professions on the same basis as graduates from Catholic colleges (which was a misinterpretation of the issue, as discussed previously). Finally, he pointed out that the name and not the authority of the Pope was included in the Jesuits' Estates Bill and that his own Protestant affiliation had not prevented him from representing a Catholic constituency for a quarter of a century.[101]

Joly's speech reportedly made a deep impression on his audience, and a few weeks later Principal George Monro Grant of Queen's University offered him an honorary degree. Lord Aberdeen, who received the degree at the same time, wrote to Joly, "I sincerely hope that what you have said will do good. It surely must."[102] Joly replied that he thought he had done some good in Ontario and that the result in Quebec was more than he had hoped for. French Canadians had expressed considerable relief at the way in which his speeches had been received in the neighbouring province.[103] When Auguste Dupuis wrote that the county of L'Islet was very appreciative of Joly's efforts to convince Ontarians that "les Catholiques de la Province de Québec ne sont pas des misérables persécuteurs des Protestants, tels que certains journaux Conservateurs publiaient," Joly replied that the Quebec reaction to his campaign proved that he had not exaggerated when he spoke of the liberality and spirit of tolerance shared by the majority of French Canadians.[104] Though stating that Joly had "gone somewhat far in saying that the Protestants of this province have nothing to complain of," the *Montreal Daily Witness* approved strongly of his mission, comparing it to that of "Gordon hurrying alone across deserts to overcome the fanaticism and power of the Mahdi."[105]

In the fall of 1894, after Mercier's death, Joly was asked to resume leadership of the party, but he declined, writing to his son that he would have more enemies among his friends than among his enemies.[106] The role was filled by Félix-Gabriel Marchand, a friend since university days, and Joly delivered a powerful speech in his favour in Montreal during the 1897 election campaign, declaring that Marchand was the most honest man that he had met during his long career in politics.[107] After Marchand's victory, Joly advised him in terms of *realpolitik* that this was the moment to impose his views on the party, for those who had been elected expressly to support him were not in a position to make demands of him. In keeping with his own policies when premier, Joly then strongly counselled Marchand to introduce a policy of economy and retrenchment: "L'on se plaindra, l'on murmera, mais le peuple est avec vous." More specifically, he advised that the tax on inheritance not be abandoned (one more indication that Joly's liberalism was not entirely inspired by a commitment to individual property rights), that grants to charities and the so-called subsidies to agriculture and colonization be reduced, and that, once the books had been balanced, the focus be placed on improving the public school system. People claiming to have sacrificed for the Liberal Party would demand recompense, with interest, but Joly claimed that it was possible to resist such demands, even when accompanied by threats, without seriously offending those who made them if one applied the rule to everyone equally: "C'est bon pour les grammairiens de dire que l'exception confirme la règle. – L'exception tue la règle." ("It's fine for grammarians to state that the exception proves the rule. – The exception kills the rule.") When Marchand reported a budget surplus two years later, Joly congratulated him, writing, "Grâce à vous, nous allons être fiers de notre Province; pendant bien des années nous ne pouvions pas en dire autant." ("Thanks to you, we are going to be proud of our province; for many years we could not say as much.")[108]

The Manitoba Schools' Question

In the meantime, Laurier had written to Joly in 1894 that he was pleased with his decision not to resume the provincial Liberal leadership, adding that he had long hoped that Joly would return to the Ottawa scene where he would find a field of action "plus digne de vous, & sur lequel vous pourriez rendre au parti & au pays d'inappréciables services." He asked that Joly become a candidate in Portneuf where there would be a Liberal vacancy, appealing to his sense of duty by stating that the high esteem in which he was now held throughout the country would greatly facilitate the Liberal transition to office, should they win the next election. Laurier's letter ended, "Ne dites pas non, je vous en prie."[109]

Joly had obviously decided to throw his hat in the ring by the following February when he wrote to the editor of the *Montreal Witness* that he no longer supported a protective tariff because the experiment had failed in its aim of stimulating manufacturing. He now advocated moderate tariff that would "enable us to meet not the extravagant expenditure of the past years, but such *reasonable expenditure* as will be found *strictly necessary* and nothing more." If economical government had been a Joly trademark, another was political integrity, and he declared his opposition to the collection of election funds "under the false pretence of meeting *legitimate election expenses*" but in fact "to obtain the support of voters when an appeal to their reason & their patriotism ought to be sufficient; they serve as an excuse for the most gigantic frauds and they tend to destroy that feeling of honor & honesty which ought to be our guide in public as well as in private affairs."[110]

Joly had already written a letter to the *Witness* expressing his views on the troublesome Manitoba Schools Question. Although a school that could provide the same religious and secular education to all Canadian children would be "a perfect school," he argued, everyone realized that this was not possible. Protestants as well as Catholics opposed a purely secular education, with the result that Manitoba's "neutral" schools provided religious exercises that were sanctioned by the elected trustees. In short, Joly argued, the minority was expected to bow to the will of the majority.[111] Admittedly, Roman Catholic children need not be present during these exercises, "but if you abolish separate schools in order that your children should all be educated together, whatever their religious creed may be, and taught to look upon one another as if there was nothing to keep them apart," he wrote, "does it not strike you forcibly that the daily withdrawal of a number of children during prayers will defeat your purpose, and draw the division line between them more distinctly than ever?"[112] Three months later, in February 1895, Joly wrote to the editor of the *Manitoba Free Press* that he was certain that "very few among the Protestant majority are aware of the great injustice committed towards the minority; if they knew of it, they would protest against it at once."[113]

The following May Joly arranged for a meeting between Laurier and Bishop Langevin of St Boniface, who was planning to visit Ottawa in order to lobby for remedial legislation. Joly informed Langevin of the pastoral letter issued by the Anglican bishops in support of religious instruction in schools, adding that the Presbyterians had taken a similar position. It was on this basis, Joly wrote, that he asked his fellow Protestants to be just enough to recognize for Roman Catholics the right to give "cette instruction comme, dans leur conscience, ils considèrent qu'elle doit être donnée." Joly was concerned, however, about the statement by Manitoba's attorney general, Clifford Sifton, to the effect that the Catholic schools "ne forment que des ignorants." He asked the bishop if Manitoba did not have school inspectors as well as annual school reports. Even if there were abuses in the administrative system, Joly added, this was not an excuse to abolish separate schools. Finally, he urged the undiplomatic Langevin not to take an inflexible stance, suggesting, "On devrait commencer par se mettre à la place de ceux dont les opinions diffèrent des nôtres et se faire un devoir de considérer la question à leur point de vue, aussi bien qu'au nôtre." ("We must start be putting ourselves in the position of those whose opinions differ from ours and make it a duty to consider the question from their point of view, as well as from ours.")[114]

Tellingly enough, Joly refused the same month an invitation to attend a convention of French-speaking Protestants from Quebec and the United States that was to be hosted by Amédée Papineau in his seigneurial manor at Montebello. Papineau, who claimed that Joly's grandmother had attempted to convert Papineau's father during the family's Paris exile, wrote that he realized Joly could very probably not attend because he would be running for election in a Catholic constituency.[115] In his reply, however, Joly went further, stating that he would not have attended in any case because the aim of the convention could only be to propagate Protestant propaganda, and he had never approved of the efforts to detach French Canadians from their religion. In a country such as Canada, where Protestants and Catholics of French and English descent were destined to live together as a single people, it was necessary to work towards the same goal as much as possible, "mais sans chercher à imposer une uniformité que la Providence nous a refusée." Religious toleration was essential if Canadians were to live in peace, and Joly concluded by stating that he admired the fidelity with which French Canadians observed their faith, "et je ne crains pas de dire qu'ils nous donne l'exemple sous ce rapport."[116] Joly was not unaware of the difficulties faced by less elite members of the small French-speaking Protestant minority, however, for he had recently asked an English-speaking boot and shoe manufacturer to take one into his employ, only to be informed that because of the persecution Protestants faced in the factory, "they have been glad to seek employment elsewhere on the very first opportunity."[117]

A few days later, Joly was informed by the colonial secretary that the Queen had directed that on her birthday he be appointed to the Most Distinguished Order of St Michael and St George.[118] This, David Cannadine notes, was "the pre-eminent order of chivalry for those who

governed, administered and had gone to settle in the British Empire."
Joly's appointment to the second of the three ranks, that of Knight Commander (KCMG), was particularly notable, as it was generally reserved
for governors, albeit of second-class colonies.[119] Joly was clearly being
recognized as the chief mediator between French and English Canada,
for Lady Aberdeen had already expressed her pleasure that he would
be "re-entering Dominion politics for the sake of the country."[120] The
fact that her husband had put Joly's name forward for a knighthood at
this time certainly improved his electoral prospects. A widely circulated
petition had invited Joly to run in Portneuf, and he had accepted under
the same condition that he had applied in Lotbinière – namely, that he
would not spend a cent of his own money on the campaign.[121] In short,
he would handicap himself by refusing to resort to the bribery and
election-day treating that was standard practice at the time.[122] L'Électeur
predicted, however, that with Oliver Mowat as his Ontario deputy and
Joly as his Quebec deputy, Laurier would sweep the country.[123]

Prior to the election writ being dropped, Joly was appointed to head
the jury that would select the artist to design Champlain's monument, an
otherwise all-Catholic French-speaking body that had to placate ultramontanes as well as wealthy Protestant donors.[124] He was also involved
once again in the Quebec Carnival, and Lady Aberdeen expressed her
great disappointment that she and her husband could not, as they had
planned, attend because of the possibility that an election would have to
be called at any time.[125] She asked, however, that Joly "run up here for a
day or two as soon as possible. Your counsel & your experience just now
would be very valuable." Reflecting her active role in political matters,
Lady Aberdeen expressed the hope that Joly would avoid Tuesday, when
she had to be in Montreal, and concluded with the postscript, "Do you
not think a compromise on this horrible question is still just possible –
even at the eleventh hour. That is what we want you to think over & to
help in."[126] More diplomatically sensitive than the partisan wife of the
governor general, Joly replied that his sudden appearance in Ottawa as
a known member of Laurier's party might "lead to comments which it
would be better to avoid when affairs are already so badly mixed up."

As for his thoughts on a compromise, Joly wrote, "I would consider
that my life has been of some use, could I help, in the slightest degree,
in restoring peace and good will." He added: "it is not the Manitoba
School question which is on its trial with the Protestant majority, but
the Roman Catholic religion itself." Protestants, by definition, should
be tolerant of other religious views, Joly wrote, but many were as

bigoted as the extreme Catholics. The Protestants' assumption that, left to themselves, Catholic laymen would accept the current arrangement reflected their failure to understand that it was "of the very essence of the R. Catholic religion, that the Clergy should lead the people in matters in which their religious interests are concerned, such especially as the bringing up and educating of their children." On the other hand, Joly also blamed the Catholic clergy for their lack of "moderation & wisdom" in the current situation. He pointed in particular to the Bishop of Nicolet, who had stated publicly that when in Rome he had attempted to induce the ecclesiastical authorities to influence the Privy Council in favour of the Catholic minority. According to Joly, "it is from that moment that we can date the universal uprising of the fierce denunciations of the Orangist body."[127]

Although Joly argued that the Liberals must strive to obtain for the Catholic minority in Manitoba the same rights as the Protestant minority in Quebec, he had accepted Laurier's strategy of denouncing the remedial bill as a threat to provincial rights that should be avoided if at all possible.[128] Even at the cost of winning the Portneuf seat, Joly declared, he would refuse to support any measure that would result in the federal government "trying to enforce their mandate at the point of the bayonet." If the Catholic clergy insisted upon such a measure, he added, they would have to oppose him.[129] When editor J.S. Willison asked Joly to submit a brief statement of his view of the question to the Toronto *Globe*, Joly replied that Laurier had already articulated it.[130]

That position was still evolving, however, as reflected in Laurier's speech in the St Roch district of his own riding of Quebec East. Introduced by Joly, who declared that the Manitoba minority had the right to demand not "une demie justice comme l'on a prétendu vouloir lui donner, mais une justice complète, pleine et entière," Laurier committed himself to remedial legislation if his attempts at negotiating a settlement proved unsuccessful.[131] Liberal candidates who had not sat in the previous legislature and voted against the government bill could therefore pledge that they would conform to the demands of the episcopal *mandement* that asked Catholics to vote only for those who would promise to support a remedial bill, should it prove necessary.[132] Joly clearly made such a commitment, for Portneuf's retiring Liberal MP, Arthur Delisle, wrote that he had stayed out of the campaign because he felt that his vote on the schools' question would make him a liability.[133] Perhaps he had received a letter from Archbishop Bégin similar to the one sent on April 29 to Dr Rinfret, the Liberal MP for Lotbinière.

Bégin chastised Rinfret for voting against the remedial bill, declaring that he knew by heart all the arguments of those opposed to the remedial bill, "and I have not yet succeeded in convincing myself that you are not completely wrong."[134]

Rinfret still won the Lotbinière seat by a substantial majority, but the Liberals were not as strong in Portneuf. Whereas Lotbinière had returned Rinfret by acclamation in the previous election, Delisle had won in Portneuf against L.H. Stafford, Joly's current opponent, by only 150 votes.[135] Furthermore, Joly was an outsider who refused to spend his own money on the campaign and who was not inclined to accept assistance from Tarte, the chief provincial organizer. Finally, Liberal promises did not prevent Vicar General Marois of Quebec from instructing a Portneuf curé that it would be a mortal sin for Catholics to vote for a Liberal. According to the pro-Conservative Quebec *Chronicle*, however, only two priests had directed their parishioners to vote for Stafford, and "the fact that they have been rebuked for taking sides at all, shows that the Church is not opposing Sir H. Joly de Lotbinière as some would have the public believe."[136]

The following day the newspaper printed in translation Archbishop Bégin's June 5 letter to Joly stating, "I neither approve of, nor repudiate, the candidates who are soliciting the votes of the electors; it is not my duty. I cannot, however, extract from the candidates less than the joint mandement of the Bishops, the expression of their will on the Manitoba School question calls for. By adhering formally and solemnly to this document, you cannot be ostracized by the Catholic electors, or considered unworthy of their suffrages."[137] On June 12 the archbishop wrote to the Portneuf curés concerning Joly, "On devra s'abstenir de dire aux gens que c'est un péché mortal de voter pour lui." ("One must abstain from telling the people that it is a mortal sin to vote for him.") According to *L'Électeur*, this missive was read aloud from the door of almost every church.[138] As a result, Lady Aberdeen wrote, Joly's supporters left after Mass rejoicing, "On ne pêche plus, on ne pêche plus!"[139]

While the election campaign was still in progress, Joly attempted to work out a compromise solution that would appease the bishops while avoiding remedial legislation, but Bégin wrote from his confirmation tour on June 15 that his proposal was "fort élastique et fort précaire," especially when dealing with a provincial government that was "absolument hostile" towards separate Catholic schools. Bégin argued that the inevitable result of this "conciliation" would be to lessen "les droits incontestables de la minorité manitobaine." And to make his stand perfectly clear, he added that the only way to ensure that the constitution was respected "d'une manière stable" was to pass a federal remedial law.[140]

Historians such as K.M. McLaughlin and Arthur Silver argue that French-speaking Quebecers did not feel they were sacrificing the Manitoba minority to provincial rights in 1896. Given the publicity that Archbishop Bégin's correspondence with Joly received, however, Catholics in the Quebec City area, if not beyond, would have been quite aware that their church felt otherwise.[141] The fact was that the possibility of having a French-Canadian prime minister was a powerful incentive to vote Liberal, and Joly was clearly a good campaigner. Lady Aberdeen confided to her diary that "the dear old man is behaving so well under this trial & is entering into all the labours of the election like a boy."[142] He must have been aware that he faced a stiff challenge even though his opponent was an anglophone, for the final result was a Liberal majority of only thirty-six votes.[143]

Conclusion

The question remains as to how Joly, as a spokesman for minority rights, could justify to himself his opposition to a remedial bill that would reinstate the constitutionally guaranteed Catholic schools of Manitoba. Aside from the fact that he was a lifelong supporter of provincial rights, and that the Liberals were committed to such a bill as a last resort, the most plausible explanation lies with his deep concern that national unity was in peril. Joly was painfully aware of the visceral antipathy to the Catholic Church in Protestant Ontario, as in the other English-speaking provinces.[144] Bookended by the Riel Rebellion and the Manitoba Schools Question, with the Jesuits' Estates Question linking the two crises, this period saw the division between English-speaking Canada and French-speaking Quebec reach an unprecedented intensity. Although Oliver Mowat was considered indispensable to the Liberal victory, he was unable to prevent Ontario from returning another substantial Conservative majority in 1896, due in part to the fact that a considerable number of Conservative candidates opposed their own party's official policy on remedial legislation.[145] One might conclude, therefore, that Joly's 1894 tour of Ontario had made very little impact, but the fact remains that his reassuring message about Quebec's Catholic Church was well received, at least among the urban middle class towards whom it was primarily directed. Although it would be hard not to conclude that the Manitoba minority paid a steep price, the country could put its decade of political crisis behind it as it entered the boom years of the Laurier era.

Chapter Seven

Forest Conservationist

If political involvement was a public duty that Joly sometimes found distasteful, the promotion of forest conservation was one that he embraced wholeheartedly. Inspired by his scientifically oriented father, who had been invited in 1860 to write a series of articles on the Canadian forest industry for a French audience,[1] Joly developed an interest in silviculture and forest conservation at an early age. He managed the family's large forest reserve in a practical and responsible manner, as we have seen, and he was a persistent critic of the government's short-sighted forest policy. Furthermore, his retirement from provincial politics in 1885 provided him the time to focus on a conservation movement that was entering its early organizational phase due to the growing concerns of leading lumbermen that the forest resources of the United States and Canada were becoming exhausted.[2] As a lumber producer who was familiar with forest practices in Europe,[3] as well as a former premier with strong political connections throughout the country, Joly was well placed to become a prominent spokesman for the Canadian forest conservation movement. Despite his antipathy to an expansionist government bureaucracy, conservation was one area where the paternalist Joly felt that the state should play an active role, including education of the province's youth through the school system.

Forest Policy Critic

It was as an elected deputy in the 1860s that Joly first began to criticize the lax regulation of the timber leases on the province's Crown lands, though he expressed more concern in the legislature about the low monetary returns for the province than about how the forests were exploited. In contrast to the United States, the fact that the Canadian square timber industry had played such a crucial role for the mother country during the Napoleonic Wars meant that Crown lands were not sold outright, except for agricultural purposes. The Lower Canadian government first began to demand that licences be purchased to cut timber on Crown lands in 1824, with fees based on the number of trees that were cut during the year in question. After 1832 the commissioner of Crown lands was to specify the area that each licence would cover as well as the amount of wood that was to be harvested. Regulations were tightened in 1842, when the maximum timber limit was fixed at 100 square miles, and the lessee was obliged to cut a minimum of 5,000 cubic feet per square mile (366 cubic metres per square kilometre), paying a quarter of the fees in advance. In 1846 an effort was made to favour small entrepreneurs by reducing the size of the timber limits, but the regulation prohibiting individuals from holding contiguous limits was dropped. Furthermore, even though licences expired after a year, they now became renewable as well as transferable. The ensuing glut of the market resulted in minimum cuts being reduced to only 500 cubic feet (36.6 cubic metres) or twenty logs per square mile (2.6 square kilometres) in the larger limits. As a result, a small number of large-scale entrepreneurs quickly gained effective control of the Crown forests.[4]

Despite the efforts of Alexander Campbell as commissioner of Crown lands to introduce "sustained yield" forestry by a system of harvest rotation, there were no other significant reforms prior to Confederation.[5] As a first-term MLA, however, Joly did have a bill passed in 1865 that would set aside 5 to 10 percent of the land in each township as a forest reserve. Richard Judd argues that there was a strong tradition of protecting such commons in northern New England and that they reflected a popular moral assumption that was the basis of the American conservation movement,[6] but this was not the case in Lower Canada, where there was no tradition of local government to institute such commons. It seems quite clear that Joly's initiative was, instead, French-inspired. Lamenting that the colonization movement was depleting the more distant sources of firewood, the *Montreal Witness* noted approvingly in 1862 that in France no one could cut trees without authorization by the district supervisor of forests, and many parishes owned reserved forest lands as communal property with strict cutting restrictions.[7] As a sometime correspondent of the *Witness*, Joly may well have penned this article, but opponents of his bill objected, rather paradoxically, that the proposed law would deprive settlers of firewood, and it soon became a dead letter.[8]

Crown lands became a provincial responsibility with Confederation, and upon Joly's request, the Quebec government appointed a permanent forest committee in 1867 to regulate the cutting of wood on Crown lands and to provide for forest conservation. Joly later claimed that the reforms he had suggested in 1868 as president of this committee had reappeared the following year in the report of the commissioner of Crown lands, who failed to credit his source. Joly's first recommendation, based on his own experience, was that the pillaging of merchantable wood on Crown land be prevented by surveillance during the winter, when tracks in the snow were readily visible. To the objection that some logging sites were located far in the interior, Joly's response was that surveillance would be even easier in thinly populated areas. His advice was followed in 1873, when Quebec became the first province to appoint staff to inspect logging operations that were in progress.[9] Joly's second recommendation was to prevent the wastage of hemlock for its bark, used mostly by American tanneries, by imposing a tariff on its export. Neglecting to explain how the provincial government could impose an export tariff, Joly complained that the government had failed to take action in order to appease two MLAs from the Eastern Townships, the source of most of the hemlock. He conceded, however, that the administration had conformed to a limited degree to his third recommendation, which was to divide the Crown lands into two categories, those fit for cultivation and those fit only for lumber. The fourth and most important recommendation, in Joly's opinion, was that cutting permits be limited to a fixed number of years – ten or fifteen, for example – and that the holders of these permits be required to exploit them judiciously, reasonably, and actively. Conformity could be ensured, Joly felt, by requiring the construction of roads and other improvements. The government subsequently did impose a limit of eleven years, though permits would be repeatedly renewed. Joly's fifth recommendation was that fees on knees and other wood used for ship construction be removed. He argued that these charges had contributed greatly to the decline of the shipbuilding industry,[10] but in the age of steam and iron vessels, he was fighting a lost cause. He would not mention this recommendation again, but most of the others would resurface repeatedly in the ensuing years.

Joly soon became critical of the system that was allowing Crown timber leases to fall into the hands of a small number of large-scale merchants with minimal returns to the state. The Price family, for example, had accumulated 3,983 square miles (10,316 square kilometres) of forest concessions, of which 2,500 (6,475) were in the Saguenay–Lac-Saint-Jean region, and G.B. Hall had 3,370 square miles (8,728 square kilometres), of which more than 2,000 (5,180) were in the Mauricie region.[11] Despite his social and business connections with these members of the Quebec City elite, Joly complained in 1871 and again in 1872 that timber merchants were acquiring permits from the Crown and selling them at much higher prices, thereby depriving the province of revenues it should be collecting. The solution, in his opinion, was to follow Ontario's example by establishing a competitive sales system rather than awarding timber licences behind closed doors. In Joly's words, "le gouvernement a consenti à laisser arracher de la manière la plus illégale du monde les perles, les joyaux les plus riches de la Province de Québec. Nous ne les reverrons plus. Ils sont à jamais perdus." ("the government has allowed to be uprooted, in the most highly illegal manner imaginable, the pearls, the most valuable jewels of the province of Quebec.")[12]

The response of the commissioner of Crown lands was that the timber companies would simply collude with each other at auctions in order to keep the ground rents low and that returns from the Quebec forests were lower than those in Ontario because the former were further away from railways. He also stated that expansive leases had brought large payments to the Quebec coffers and that leasing timber limits to respectable merchants was the best means of preserving forests because they had a vested interest in avoiding forest fires and preventing the wastage of wood.[13] With even some of the ministerial newspapers demanding reform, however, the government finally terminated all private transactions in 1874, though most of the commercially viable limits had been granted by that time.[14]

Upon the resignation of the commissioner of Crown lands as well as the premier the following year, the Conservative government presented a motion to appoint a permanent committee of woods and forests with fifteen members, including Joly.[15] Elzéar Gérin of Saint-Maurice, whose *Le Constitutionnel* had been devoting articles to forest conservation since 1868, claimed to be the first MLA to demand the auction system.[16] In becoming a supporter of the new ministry, however, he left Joly as the uncontested champion of forestry reform. Joly charged that the new ministry under Gédéon Ouimet had been formed in order to prevent an inquiry into the corruption of its predecessor, and he asked whether the woods and forests committee would have the authority to inquire into the past administration of the Crown lands or would instead become "a simple debating society." More specifically, he moved that the committee examine the charge that Hector Langevin had received a bribe of $4,000 for using his influence as a member of the Assembly to obtain limits for a speculator. In Joly's pointed words, "it was a cowardly act on the part of the Government to sit and quietly submit to these charges of having squandered the heritage of the country and having spent the sole sources of revenue in maintaining themselves in office and purchasing the support they relied upon."[17]

Rising to the government's defence, J.A. Chapleau expressed great indignation that the head of a party with so few elected members would hurl "une accusation de lâcheté aussi futile qu'audacieuse." He insisted that only a minister, and not a permanent committee of the House, had the constitutional authority to interfere in the administration of a department. Taking shelter behind the restructuring of the administration, he reminded Joly that a government could not reveal the secrets of its predecessors and that members of the new ministry who had served in the preceding one were not responsible for its acts. Finally, Chapleau rather pompously charged that Joly had accused "une classe de citoyens des plus respectables et des plus respectés, une classe de citoyens dont l'industrie est une des plus importantes et des plus nécessaires au pays." The lumber merchants, Chapleau claimed, had done more than any other group to develop the immense resources of the province and increase external commerce: "C'est elle qui donne le pain à des milliers de personnes qui resteraient sans ressources et dans la misère, si on paralysait l'industrie forestière." ("It's it that gives bread to thousands of people who would be without resources and in misery, if one paralyzed the forest industry." Ignoring the frequent conflicts between logging companies and colonists, Chapleau even proclaimed that "c'est elle qui, en beaucoup d'endroits, a porté dans nos forêts l'étendard de la colonisation." ("it's it that, in many places, has carried into our forests the flag of colonization.") Such valuable self-sacrificing citizens as the timber merchants, Chapleau concluded without irony, should have been treated much more generously by the leader of the opposition.[18]

Promoting Forest Conservation and Reforestation

It proved difficult, however, to dismiss Joly's attacks on the government as politically partisan when they were echoed by forestry specialists,[19] and in 1877 his lengthy report on the state of the forests in Canada submitted to the Dominion Council of Agriculture was published in the *Sessional Papers*. After presenting an overview of the country's forest resources, which was necessarily brief due to the lack of concrete information, Joly recommended a number of reforms that foreshadowed the American Progressives' support for more active state involvement in forest conservation. First, he stressed the threat of deforestation to future commerce and noted that the "great forest of Canada, *par excellence*" grew on the territory drained by the Ottawa, Saint Maurice, and Saguenay Rivers. In Joly's view, this northernmost frontier of commercial timber was threatened by overexploitation. If managed properly, there was still enough spruce and second-class pine to exceed local wants for generations to come, but the prime-quality pine had become rare or inaccessible with the result that there would soon be a sharp decline in timber exports. Joly also reiterated his concern about the shortage of firewood in the Quebec countryside, claiming that a foreign visitor would have the sense that he was travelling through some of the oldest parts of Europe.[20]

An even greater threat than overexploitation, in Joly's view, was forest fires because so little could be done in such a vast country to combat them, and reforestation on a large scale was not economically feasible. Aside from naturally caused fires that could not be prevented, Joly pointed to settlers, timber drives, hunters, and fishermen as the chief culprits. He recommended first that settlement be confined as much as possible to hardwood lands because they had superior soil, and fires there would not spread as rapidly as among conifers. Recognizing, however, that it was necessary to burn brush and branches when clearing land, Joly advised doing so as soon as they were cut rather than waiting for them to dry out. (The policy on his own land was to burn the branches and tree tops of the winter's operations before summer set in.)[21] Municipal councils, he argued, should be made responsible for enforcing fire regulations in settled areas, and wood rangers should do so elsewhere. As for the fires caused by abandoned campfires during the spring timber drives, Joly recommended that lumbermen who allowed their workers to be negligent should lose their licences. Men who lived by hunting were not a major problem, Joly felt, because the forest was their home, and game laws required that sport hunting take place in the late fall, after the dry season had ended. But his report stressed that "*those who shoot in the woods, out of season, ought to be doubly punished, as they ruin the game and may be the cause of ruin to the forests.*" Fishermen were a greater danger because of the season when their activity took place, and Joly could only recommend that river-lease regulations be made more stringent, that the detailed stipulations concerning campfires legislated by Quebec in 1870 be adopted and enforced everywhere, and that forest rangers and fishery inspectors keep a watchful eye on the most popular fishing pools.[22]

Joly felt that those who cut timber illegally on Crown lands were a more manageable problem because they needed to build snow roads and use streams to get their logs out of the woods. As someone who had lost timber to trespassers on his own land, Joly advocated that they be treated as criminals, though the greatest punishment should be reserved for those who organized and directed their activities. Much more complex was the problem of overproduction. Based partly on his own experience, Joly painted a picture of lumbermen who could do little about it because they were dependent "on the will and caprice of others, from the obtaining of timber berths to work upon, the hiring of men, the supplying of provisions, the sending men, stores and horses hundreds of miles away, into the wilderness, down to the cutting, squaring, hauling, driving, booming, rafting, culling, loading and shipping," not to mention dealing with "the banks, the brokers, and the purchasers in England." But provincial governments could, without making themselves "open to the charge of undue interference with business," exercise more control over the Crown lands. In Quebec's case, for example, the timber dues would be open for revision in a year's time, so they could easily be raised. The volume of square timber, at approximately 25 million cubic feet,[23] was still one-eighth of the sawn lumber volume, and Joly reminded his readers that "those splendid beams, fit for giant's works, upon which we Canadians are wont to gaze with so much pride, and which have caused us to waste … so much valuable timber in squaring them, so much trouble in hauling, handling, stowing on board ship, are cut up, past recognition, as soon as they land." Why, Joly asked, should Canadians leave to others all the profit from processing the timber that they produced? Lumbermen might respond, "It pays us to make square timber, otherwise, we would not make it," but, Joly asked, "does it pay the country at large? What becomes of that fourth part of every tree that is lost, in the squaring? Does the lumberman pay for it? Does he pay for all the trees he fells and leaves to rot, on account of some defect which, in most cases, would not have unfitted them for making saw logs?"[24]

As for the even more wasteful practice of cutting hemlock for its bark, Joly reported that 10,000 acres of the best hemlock-producing land in the Eastern Townships had been stripped in 1868 to produce 23,000 barrels of bark extract for the American market. By 1876 exports had increased to 29,000 barrels, plus 43,000 cords of bark. Given that much of the hemlock grew on private land, Joly reiterated the suggestion he had made to the provincial government in 1868 – namely, the imposition of an export duty on hemlock bark and its extract. (As we saw in chapter 3, he refused to sell hemlock bark himself until he could find a market for the wood.) Joly also commended the Quebec government for imposing a twelve-inch-diameter minimum on the cutting of pine on Crown land. Furthermore, he suggested, the same minimum should be applied to other species and even increased to as much as eighteen inches for the rapidly disappearing pine. Finally, Joly noted that Quebec had the only society devoted to planting trees[25] and suggested that the federal government should encourage this practice in the Prairies, where fast-growing species such as poplars would provide shade and act as wind breaks, as well as serving as a supply of wood. Based on his own experiments, Joly argued that deciduous trees would generally be the best choice for Canada because of the value of their wood, the rapidity of their growth, the relative ease with which they could be transplanted, and their greater immunity to fire. Joly's report was a seminal one in that it would be cited in future publications and reach a broad audience, at least in the province of Quebec, by being reprinted in full in the *Gazette des Campagnes*.[26]

Having observed that much of the responsibility for forest conservation rested with provincial governments, Joly took the lead in the Quebec Assembly the following year, in 1878, when he noted that the province's lumber exports had declined from $20 million a few years earlier to only $8 million in the current year. Declaring that it had become necessary to apportion the annual cut in a manner that would ensure the province a regular and permanent revenue, Joly presented a motion that repeated most of the recommendations he had made in the federal report. To support his call for urgent action, he cited the report by Montreal lumberman James Little that warned of the dangers of fires and overcutting, though he did not repeat its rather alarmist claim that the province would soon have to import wood for its own consumption.[27] Joly believed that "for many years to come, the Province would have a sufficiency of ordinary timber, unless some much more disastrous fires should occur than had yet taken place." But he also cited the trade circular of Bell, Forsyth, and Company, as well as the *Timber Trades Journal of London*, to the effect that first-class timber was becoming scarce, adding that "everyone connected with the trade and with the sawing of timber, could bear witness to this fact," especially now that lumbermen had penetrated to the heads of rivers within the St Lawrence watershed.[28]

Joly was distracted by more pressing matters during his tenure as premier in 1878–9, but the following year he presented a paper titled "Forest Tree Culture" to the Montreal Horticultural Society. Although his government reports had recognized that reforestation was impracticable in the large and remote Crown timber berths, Joly was a strong advocate of planting trees in settled areas, arguing that they were "not only the most beautiful ornaments to a country and the most useful product of nature, giving fuel, timber, shade, shelter, retaining moisture and a protection against droughts, etc., etc., but, considering the question from a *strictly money-making* point of view, the culture of forest trees is perhaps *the best and safest investment* that can be made." Given that Quebecers had for generations "been brought up to look upon the forest as their natural enemy," Joly advocated that the state establish nurseries and large plantations to demonstrate "by practical results, that the culture of forest trees is within the reach of every one." He then went on to describe his own successful experiment with black walnut seed nuts, which he had acquired from the west in 1874, and to provide instructions on growing butternut, white oak, white elm, maple, ash, tamarack, Russian pine, and poplar. Joly concluded with the advice that "having no School of Forestry in Canada, we must educate ourselves; we have got books written on the subject by eminent and practical men, and we have got, always opened before our eyes, the great book of Nature."[29]

By this time the provincial government was becoming aware of the need for conservation, and Joly spoke in favour of its bill to reserve the pine on all public lands, including those already leased to timber companies.[30] The commissioner of Crown lands, E.J. Flynn, accepted Joly's amendment stating that colonists would not be allowed to use pine for building fences, but a month later he bowed to pressure from colonization proponents by introducing another amendment to allow settlers to cut pine once they had paid for the right to do so. Joly was not pleased, arguing that it would be next to impossible to collect levies on the pine cut by colonists and that the pine was worth more than the land itself at thirty to forty cents an acre.[31]

The Conservation Movement

The year 1882 was also the year that Joly began to move into a larger theatre by filling in temporarily for the president of the American Forestry

Congress during its meeting in Montreal.[32] The society's founding meeting had taken place only three months earlier in Cincinnati, at which time William Little, son of the aging James Little, had agreed to organize the Montreal meeting.[33] Joly's diplomatic skills were called into play in order to ensure that the Canadian lumbermen whom Little had invited could find common cause with the American delegates, who were mostly botanists, entomologists, and professors of agricultural science. After delivering an address that rendered homage to the pioneers of the movement and outlining his own experiences on his seigneury, Joly presented much the same paper he had recently delivered to the Montreal Horticultural Society. He also joined the committee that was to report on the forest fire problem, which recommended the setting aside of forest reserves, the banning of slash fires during certain times of the year, and the appointment of forest rangers to be paid from a special tax on woodlot owners.[34] Fires were a major threat to Joly's forest, as we saw in chapter 3, and in 1899 he served notice on the Canadian government, of which he was now a member, that he would hold it responsible for damages caused by sparks from Intercolonial Railway locomotives.[35] Joly's son Edmond reported to the Canadian Forestry Association meeting in 1903 that during dangerous weather they employed two gangs of men equipped with shovels, hoses, and buckets to patrol the six miles of their land crossed by Intercolonial tracks.[36] This was clearly a significant expense, for the Jolys paid four men a total of $1,500 in wages for fire protection in one year alone.[37]

Back in the legislature in 1883, Joly chided Premier Mousseau for stating at the Montreal conference that Quebec's forests would be able to provide the current supply of wood for another hundred years. Joly reminded him that the "chantiers de bucherons" had already reached the headwaters of the rivers that drained the province's forested regions.[38] Striking a non-partisan note, however, Joly stated that the interest displayed in the meeting's deliberations by Dr W.W. Lynch, the commissioner of Crown lands, gave him cause to hope that the government would take steps towards what everyone who studied the subject considered to be a good and sane policy. He recommended, particularly, that a part of the revenue from the Crown lands be set aside for protection of the forests. Lynch, in turn, praised Joly for his speech and noted that his appointment to an important committee of the Forestry Congress had brought honour to the province.[39] A month later Joly, who was still head of the Liberal opposition, also expressed satisfaction with the fact that Lynch had accepted his recommendations concerning the prevention of forest fires by appointing forest rangers to patrol limits, though he added that those who held sport fishing leases had yet to be held responsible for any fires they caused. Lynch, in turn, suggested that fishermen would not object to paying a small fee towards maintaining the service needed to protect fishing rights as well as rivers and lakes. Joly also had reason to be pleased by the fact that in 1883 Quebec became the first province to create forest reserves, though his colleague, Honoré Mercier, would abolish them in 1888 in response to pressure from the colonization movement.[40]

Meanwhile, having been named president of the newly established Forestry Association of the Province of Quebec in 1882, Joly became the first vice president of the American Forestry Congress at its St Paul, Minneapolis, meeting a year later.[41] Historians Gillis and Roach state that the latter association soon returned to being an entirely American body,[42] but nineteen of the 144 members were reported as Canadians at the 1886 meeting held in Boston, where Joly delivered an address on his cultivation of the black walnut.[43] He would remain involved in the American Forestry Congress throughout the remainder of his life. As for the Quebec association, its members were largely from the province's elite, and they were simply required to plant twenty-five trees a year on their properties, as well as submit reports on their progress.[44]

In an attempt to make a broader impact on public consciousness, Joly took steps in 1886 to have the American holiday of Arbor Day recognized in Quebec. Speaking in the provincial Assembly, Joly insisted that the proposal was not impractical, the proof being that millions of trees were being planted in the western states where there were few forests, as well as in Michigan, which produced much more lumber than all of Canada. He admitted that a proclamation by the lieutenant governor would not in itself result in the planting of millions of trees in Quebec, but he argued that it would help to shift public opinion by removing the prejudices inherited from the first colonists. It would portray the forest tree in a new light, "comme un ami, non plus comme un ennemi," and with the aid of the clergy and all men of "progress" and "education," the people would before long come to accept Arbor Day as one of their national institutions. Joly then stated that not only were good lots being sold at a sacrifice due to the lack of firewood, but additionally, deforestation was causing the drying up of streams followed by floods after each major rainfall. He pointed out that in France the planting of maritime pine had reclaimed land that had been smothered by advancing sand dunes. Despite expressing doubt that it would do much to change popular attitudes, Commissioner Flynn ensured that Joly's motion to institute Arbor Day was passed.[45]

Reflecting the regional differences in climate, May 7 was chosen for Arbor Day in the province's southwest and May 16 for the east. Schools were closed, and municipalities, religious organizations, and agricultural societies were invited to participate. The measurable impact proved to be limited, for most of the activity was centred on the beautification of urban public spaces,[46] but Joly had stated from the start that Arbor Day's chief contribution would be to change popular attitudes. He placed particular faith in the youth, making this the theme of the paper he delivered to the American Forestry Congress meeting in St Paul, Minnesota, in 1883. Joly argued that planting a tree was a valuable life lesson for a child, teaching "foresight, observation, patience, care for the smallest details and perseverance." Children were to be informed that it might take "twenty, thirty, forty years, or more" before a tree was big enough to cut down, but even if they moved away or died in the meantime, their work would not be lost: "if you do not profit by it others will, and you will have done more than many a grown up man has done – you will have left something useful behind you."[47]

The school program continued into the 1890s, with a circular printed by the Council of Public Instruction declaring that teachers were to instruct their students that trees would absorb "les émanations délétères qui s'exhalent du sol ou des habitations," as well as alter the climate.[48] Joly did not echo the alarmist rhetoric of American scientists and popular writers to the effect that civilisation itself was under threat of collapse,[49] but he did write to the Protestant committee of the Council of Public Instruction that because it was now recognized that forests influenced the climate and fertility of the land, it was time "to enlist the people of Canada, for the preservation of growing forest trees as well as the replacing of those which have been imprudently destroyed." The logical place to begin, he claimed, was with boys: "Wherever plantations are made, in our cities and villages and along the country roads, too often do we hear the complaint that boys injure the trees by pulling off branches, whenever they can reach them and damaging the bark. One must have planted a tree and watched it, growing steadily year after year, to understand the bitter disappointment with which it is, one day, discovered with some severe wound caused by a boy passing, thoughtlessly, without meaning mischief just for the pleasure of working off his superabundant activity by tearing off a branch." Made aware of the damage he had caused, the boy would feel shame, and "that feeling of protection and thoughtful consideration, once started within him, will not remain confined to inanimate trees." The council's response was to print Joly's letter and place it in the hands of inspectors for distribution in the schools.[50]

In an essay published in *La Revue nationale* the following year, in 1895, Joly conceded that relatively few trees had been planted on Arbor Day, but he argued from his paternalistic perspective that even the least reflective of individuals would be struck by the sight of the Queen's representative and "nos hommes les plus éminents" planting trees with their own hands. Schoolchildren looked forward to the holiday, but of still greater importance, some of them became attached to the trees they had planted, nurturing them from year to year, thereby learning the secret to success in life: "planter avec soin, cultiver avec persévérance."[51] Joly did not stress the impact of deforestation on the lumber industry, but he continued to worry about the increasingly critical shortage of firewood. Acknowledging that the transplanting of young trees from the forest was time-consuming and often unsuccessful and that commercial nursery stock was beyond the means of most farmers, Joly recommended that farmers create their own nurseries. He provided advice on when to plant seeds from a number of species, adding that in the case of maples, seedlings could simply be transplanted from the forest floor. Returning to one of his favourite themes, Joly added that farm children would, with a little encouragement, take pleasure in caring for the young trees: "Chez nous, les enfants, tout jeunes, s'amusaient, d'eux-mêmes, à semer des glands [acorns] et à voir pousser leurs petits chênes [oaks]."[52]

Joly had been supported at the local level by at least one priest, the curé of St Édouard de Lotbinière, who in 1885 published a poem in his honour in the ultramontane *La Vérité*. Striking a distinctly nationalist note, Abbé Gingras wrote:

Un profane étranger, de sa hache cruelle,
A mis en abattis mes plus chers souvenirs.

(A profane foreigner, with his cruel ax,
Chopped down my dearest memories.)

But Joly, "un citoyen de coeur," had come to the rescue and:

Son souffle fait partout renaître nos bocages,
Le pays se reboise et refait ses joyaux![53]

(His breath renews everywhere our woodlands,
The country reforests itself and remakes its jewels!)

By this time Joly was clearly becoming the leading spokesman for forest conservation in Canada. In addition to writing a number of booklets, he assisted Jean-Charles Chapais with the publication of his *Guide illustré du sylviculteur canadien* (1883), which was translated into English and reprinted several times. He also spoke about the benefits of forest conservation and reforestation at various horticultural and agricultural society meetings, as well as at the forestry convention in Kingston in 1888 and the Natural History Society meeting at McGill University in 1889.[54] That same year, in an apparent attempt to placate the forest conservationists after abolishing the reserves, Mercier appointed a commission to visit places in the province where the two members would be most likely to gain practical information for a report on scientific forestry. The professed aim was close to Joly's heart, for it was to encourage farmers to preserve some of their timber on woodlots. One of the commissioners, M.W. Kirwan, editor of Montreal's *True Witness*, wrote to Joly, "[We are] reading the best writers in French and English but we value a personal interview with you more than all our reading for we are satisfied that, with your experience, you will be able to place the subject before us in its most practical light and in such a way that we can present it to the public in its most attractive and truthful form."[55]

Despite the flattery, Joly remained critical of Mercier's forest policy. When appointed to represent the province at the annual meeting of the American Forestry Congress held in Philadelphia in 1889, Joly reminded the commissioner of Crown lands that this body had passed a resolution calling for the suspension of forest land sales until it had been determined which areas should be conserved in the public interest.[56] That same year, in an article published in the *Annual Report of the Montreal Horticultural Society and Fruit-Grower's Association of the Province of Quebec*, Joly also criticized the government for forcing "every year, thousands of square miles of timber limits on the market in advance of the legitimate requirements of the trade, and with the unavoidable result of glutting the European market." He made it clear, however, that he was a conservationist and not a preservationist: "The aim of Forestry is not, as many believe, to preserve trees for ever, or until they decay and fall. Quite the reverse, it is to select and cut down every tree ripe for the axe, making room for the young growth, and thereby insuring a continued reproduction and a steady growth."[57]

In 1890, after Joly came out of self-imposed political exile to support Colonel Rhodes in the Megantic by-election, a grateful Mercier agreed to host the annual meeting of the American Forestry Congress in Quebec City, with Joly as the chief organizer.[58] According to the account published by James MacPherson LeMoine in his *Maple Leaves*, the government placed rooms in the Parliament building at the disposal of the thirty-six delegates, seventeen of whom were from the province of Quebec, with another four coming from Ontario and the others coming from states as far away as Florida and Colorado. Joly presented a paper on the planting of trees on the Prairies, and on the third and final day he led an expedition to the historic Catholic shrine at Ste Anne de Beaupré. Joining the congress members were the governor of the Bahamas, approximately twenty members of the Paris Alpine Club, and a number of women. To add to the formal sense of ceremony back in Quebec City, Joly invited the wife of Bernhard Fernow, chief of the Forestry Division in Washington, DC, to plant a hickory tree from General Andrew Jackson's favourite grove in Nashville, Tennessee. Joly, himself, was given a piece of walnut from General Jackson's old log cabin home.[59]

Joly was next entrusted with preparation of the provincial forestry exhibit at the World's Fair in 1893,[60] as well as with lobbying to have a professional forester appointed for Canada. A.G. Lang, whom Joly and LeMoine supported, had been trained in the same German college as Fernow. Lang wrote from Scotland that he was "not at all unwilling to accept a humble post to begin with, trusting that my time will come when public opinion more fully appreciates the claims of Forestry,"[61] but five more years would elapse before the appointment of Elihu Stewart as Canada's first chief inspector of timber and forestry. Meanwhile, the persistent pressure applied by Joly and the province's lumbermen for forest reserves finally paid off in 1894 with the creation of the Laurentides and Mont Tremblant "national" parks.[62]

Although Joly's energies were increasingly devoted during the 1890s to preserving national unity and then to his portfolio in the federal government, he continued to give advice on how to transplant trees and manage private forests. Governor General Lord Aberdeen wrote in 1896 from his Coldstream Ranch in Vernon, British Columbia, for example, that he wished Joly could visit. "I would have 1000 questions to ask ... upon botanical and arboricultural matters," he wrote.[63] The previous year, the widow who had recently inherited the former seigneury of Beaurivage in Lotbinière County informed Joly that she depended on the revenue from the forest in order to pay taxes, keep roads open, and ensure that no wood was stolen. She added, however, that Joly's recent lecture "awoke me to a consciousness of my duty and I began making enquiries as soon as I came down here with the result that I am told in a few years there will be no wood." She had now forbidden the cutting of spruce, balsam, and cedar smaller than twelve inches at the base and was pleased that Joly had promised to offer more detailed advice.[64]

No pulpwood had been cut on Beaurivage or on Joly's land, but the pulp and paper industry had begun taking advantage of the province's plentiful supply of inferior grades of wood as lumber production went into decline. In a letter to *L'Électeur* in 1894 a concerned Joly conceded that pulp mills would serve a useful purpose near colonization zones by providing a market for small trees that were generally burned in the clearing process, "provided the lands thrown open to colonization by the government are really fit for agriculture." But he was adamantly opposed to the cutting of pulpwood on Crown lands: "By destroying the young trees, which in a few years would replace the mature wood fit for log making, one condemns a forest to a speedy death, just as a nation would be swept out of existence if every child that was born was done away with whilst in its infancy." If the pulp were manufactured in Canada, Joly argued, "it would be but half an evil," but most was being sold on the American market.[65] The proportion that was exported presumably declined as Quebec pulp and paper mills expanded, but Joly was still complaining in 1900 about the hundreds of thousands of cords sent to the United States.[66]

That same year Joly was appointed president of the newly established Canadian Forestry Association. He was probably too strong a supporter of provincial rights, however, to share the views of the Ottawa valley lumbermen who joined the association in the hope that the Laurier government would introduce the conservation measures that the governments of Ontario and Quebec had resisted. But the main goal of the association, which had been initiated by the federal inspector of timber and forestry Elihu Stewart, was to promote the cultivation of trees on that part of the western prairies that was still under federal control. And Joly would certainly have been sympathetic to the more scientific approach taken by the younger generation of foresters and bureaucrats who dominated the association, including their push for increased fire protection, control of pulpwood harvesting, more forest reserves, land classification, and forest management plans.[67]

Joly also encouraged his son Edmond to take up his mantle as a leading figure in the forest conservation movement. From Victoria in 1901 he instructed Edmond to join the Canadian Forestry Association as well as the American Forestry Congress and to attend their next annual meetings. Joly added, "You have, by this time, acquired a pretty good knowledge of forest tree culture, sowing, planting and transplanting, pruning roots and branches, and I would be proud to see you bring it out, as I have attempted to do and make a name for yourself, in such a useful and practical branch as forestry is for Canada." In retrospect, Joly claimed, his success in life was due more to forestry than to politics.[68] Edmond never emerged from the shadow of his father, though his biographical entry in *The Storied Province of Quebec* claims that he "made a study of Nature in her virginal purity and became one of the leading exponents of forest conservation, a subject upon which he was wont to make public lectures for the education of the masses in the value of the undeveloped resources that have been placed out of doors."[69] For Joly, if not for his son, it was not enough to support his family financially from his lumber business; the example provided to others by the responsible management of that business, in addition to his involvement in forest conservation, played an important role in sustaining the family's elite social status, a status that Edmond was being groomed to inherit and uphold.

In contrast to Frank Barnjum, who would pose as a conservationist because restrictions on exporting pulpwood from private woodlots meant lower costs to his Nova Scotia paper mill and higher prices for the trees on his Maine timberlands,[70] Joly's bottom line would not benefit from depressing the price for spruce, the reason being that his mills relied almost entirely on his own forest. Joly's conservationism was genuine, and he instructed his son to focus his address to the Canadian Forestry Association meeting in Ottawa on how the pulpwood industry would destroy Canadian forests "within a much shorter time than generally supposed." Edmond was further instructed to demonstrate with tree samples that "they take much longer to renew themselves than people believe." In short, Joly warned, "C'est un vrai suicide que nous commettons." He also asked Edmond to lobby for the prohibition of raw log exports. Pointing to "the good result of our B.C. legislation of last year ... compelling limit owners to manufacture their wood in the Province," Joly noted that another option was to do what Quebec had done in 1894, "but unfortunately had not the courage to stand by," namely, "put a prohibitory rate on Licenses for timber not manufactured in the Province. I think Ontario has done so and has stuck to it while poor Quebec!!?!!!!"[71]

Keeping the pressure on his son, an obviously anxious Joly wrote a week before the Ottawa meeting was to take place, "You can scarcely realize how much I look forward to your début, dear Edmond. I attach a great deal of importance to it and pray that it may be a success." He also instructed Edmond to call on Government House – "Minto takes a great interest in forestry" – and not to be afraid to make his address too long: "Tell them all you know."[72] Joly approved of the draft he received from his son a couple of weeks later, adding, "L'expérience que tu acquières dans nos bois sera aussi utile pour le pays que pour nous-mêmes."[73] Edmond's address did echo his father's long-standing concerns, focusing as it did on the minimum diameter that should be allowed for each species of tree before it could be harvested. He also added that even if forests could regenerate faster than he calculated, it was essential that a ban be placed on the export of pulpwood: "If nature has supplied us with a vast quantity of this valuable wood, infinitely more than we need, or may ever need, for our own use, by all means let us dispose of our surplus; but in doing so, let those who need it come to the province of Quebec to get it. Let them purchase their limits, erect their mills and manufacture the raw material here."[74]

Joly's official position as lieutenant governor may have prevented him from entering the fray publicly, but he continued to press Edmond to write articles that would point out that banning the export of the raw material "would be the means of giving work to their children at home instead of their having to go to the United States, and would keep the profits of manufacturing which are so much more considerable than the small profit of cutting down their trees for export." Joly added that limit holders should be on their side because it would secure a supply of spruce for their sawmills for a long time to come.[75] When he learned in December 1902 that the Liberal Quebec government had extended for seven years the current rate at which stumpage dues were set, Joly was incensed, despairing that his home province might well have thrown away the power to save its forests from total destruction. Edmond therefore had a duty to "denounce it firmly (without indulging in abuse) ... as a betrayal of the interest of the Province."[76] It was obviously too late to change the provincial regulation, but even as a supporter of provincial rights, Joly could only hope that public pressure would force the federal government to impose an export tariff on unmanufactured wood. He later admitted, however, that there was little use in pressing Laurier, who would not dare to alienate Quebec.[77]

Edmond played an active role in the 1903 meeting of the Canadian Forestry Association, which focused largely on the fire problem. He presented motions demanding that the number of fire wardens be increased on government lands, that all such lands not suitable for agriculture be declared forest lands in perpetuity, and that settlement on isolated lands be prohibited.[78] Edmond thus took a harder line against the colonization movement than his father had done, at least in his earlier years. The senior Joly remained more concerned about the pulp and paper industry, writing to Edmond in 1905 that if Canadians could at least "reap our fair share of the profits" by manufacturing the pulp at home, "it would not be a dead loss to us." By his calculations, a cord of pulp converted into unrefined paper would leave seventeen dollars in Canada; exported to the United States raw, it would scarcely leave three dollars – "and our people compelled to leave home and go the States, for work that we can give them here!!!"[79] Edmond had become sufficiently recognized in the Canadian Forestry Association by 1906 that he was asked to preside during Laurier's absences at the first forestry conference sponsored by the Canadian government, which was to include several hundred participants from all the provinces and territories of the Dominion.[80] After reading the newspaper account, Joly wrote to his son, "It makes me happy to see your name mentioned so honourably."[81] Again in 1908, only a few months before his father's death, Edmond warned the Canadian Forestry Convention about the evils of the pulp and paper industry, claiming that the American demand for young Canadian spruce and balsam was so high that "our forests are being sacrificed to the golden present."[82]

Returning to the theme of colonization, Edmond advised the government to follow his father's practice of requiring a perpetual wood reserve on each lot of land sold to a settler. Setting aside twenty acres of each hundred-acre lot would, Edmond claimed, provide the purchaser "with an inexhaustible supply of fuel and building material." Furthermore, "every new township instead of shortly becoming the treeless, parched desert our old settlements now are, would be covered with an ample supply of timber," thereby helping to maintain "the water powers with which a provident hand has so liberally endowed our favoured Province."[83] Left unexplained was how the government could enforce such a restriction on a large scale even if it were willing to risk alienating voters by threatening to do so.

The Liberal government took a more practical step, given that there was little arable wild land left in the province, by abolishing the

Department of Colonization in 1903. It attempted to placate the Liberal ultramontane Henri Bourassa and his nationalist followers, however, by appointing a colonization commission that same year. To represent the timber merchants on the commission, Premier Simon-Napoléon Parent chose George Washington Stephens of Montreal. But Stephens, an old friend of Joly, was too independent-minded to be the puppet of any special interest group. He wrote to Joly that he had been working alone on the commission and sent him a copy of a report that advocated restricting colonization to fertile areas, creating forest reserves, and giving limit holders a year to remove merchantable timber on lots claimed for settlement. Less palatable to the lumbermen were Stephens's recommendations that profits on the private sale of timber leaseholds be taxed and that stumpage dues be increased.

Joly clearly approved of these recommendations, and he was intrigued by the references to Sweden and Norway as models of sustainable forestry, but the recommendations were considered politically unacceptable, and Stephens had already resigned from the commission by the time he wrote his letter. He informed Joly that he had recommended Edmond as his replacement but that Parent had chosen instead a real estate expert named Brodie, a man "who knows about as much about Forestry and Colonization as a cat does about flying."[84] Given that Parent obviously favoured the forest companies, Joly could take some satisfaction in the decision of the provincial government to set aside 429,283 square kilometres as forest reserves between 1904 and 1908, as well as in the establishment of the province's first forest nursery in the latter year. Furthermore, Parent's successor, Lomer Gouin, followed Joly's advice when he sent two young men to Yale University's graduate program in the School of Forestry in order to establish a professional forestry service in Quebec.[85]

Like the forest conservationists of the Gilded Age in the United States, Joly was driven by a moral imperative, as illustrated by his faith that tree planting would ensure that youths became responsible citizens, but he did not share his American counterparts' suspicion of the state.[86] Despite his antipathy to socialism, Joly supported government ownership of the forest resource, and he would have agreed with the first chief of the United States Forest Service, Gifford Pinchot, that national prosperity "required a program of long-range, careful management that would put resource development on a thoroughly rational and efficient base."[87] Like Pinchot and the American Progressives of the early twentieth century, Joly may have conceived of forest conservation essentially as forest management – that is, the selective cutting of mature trees – but he had more than the long-term benefit to the forest industry in mind. As an economic nationalist Joly argued for the prohibition of raw log exports in order to promote manufacturing and employment. And one of his chief concerns was the conservation of firewood reserves for the use of farmers as well as city dwellers, reserves that would also benefit non-domesticated flora and fauna, though there is no evidence that Joly had this result in mind.

Natural History Enthusiast

Joly's conservationism was not entirely restricted to the forests, however, for he publicly supported the provincial government's policy, initiated in 1882, of leasing salmon fishing rivers to private clubs, often American in membership, on conservationist as well as fiscal grounds. His father had been a member of the Fish and Game Protection Club of Lower Canada, and his son Edmond became a founding member in 1893 of the very exclusive Triton fish and game club that controlled over 500 square miles (1,290 square kilometres) and 150 lakes east of the Batiscan River in the Mauricie region.[88] Joly himself showed relatively little interest in hunting and fishing, but he did not share Wilfrid Laurier's distaste for these sports,[89] and he criticized the provincial government's proposal in 1882 to impose a twenty-dollar tax on foreign hunters, arguing that they were the province's best publicity agents. If the tax did have to be levied, Joly added, these hunters should at least not be treated "comme des gens qui ruineront nos trésors sous le rapport de la chasse."[90]

Though far from having the ecological consciousness of Vermont's George Perkins Marsh or California's John Muir, Joly was certainly aware of the role that forests played in preventing floods and sustaining water supplies, as well as in reclaiming desert areas, and he also believed that they had an impact on moderating climate.[91] The water issue affected him personally, for as we saw in chapter 3, there was much worry each summer and fall that the Rivière du Chêne would drop too much in volume to allow the entire year's harvest of logs to be processed as lumber. Joly also claimed in 1904 that his family would never be able to live at Pointe Platon in the spring because the clearing of the land beyond their own eighteen-mile radius had resulted in major spring floods.[92] On a less immediately practical level, Joly had strongly supported the bill presented in 1885 to establish a botanical garden in

Montreal. Whereas other supporters dwelt on its pedagogical function, Joly declared that when men attempted on their own to discover the secrets of nature, their carefully accumulated knowledge was often lost when they died. The botanical garden would play an invaluable role in saving the province's forests from complete destruction.[93]

Joly may have had his father in mind and may have been thinking of his own experimental efforts with species that farmers could grow to supplement their agricultural production. Part of his black walnut plantation still survives as the most northerly one in North America.[94] A heavy, rot-resistant wood, black walnut is used in making boats, high-quality furniture, and veneer for cabinets, among other things. Having received his first seeds in 1874, Joly expanded his plantation to upwards of 11,000 trees in 1881 and 1882. He lost 300 saplings during the particularly hard winter of 1883, but each year he replaced those that died, proudly distributing seed nuts throughout Canada, the United States, and even Europe. He wrote in 1889 that the wood was sold for a dollar a cubic foot, nearly the price of mahogany, but because his trees were still not quite fourteen years old, he could not "yet assert that the success is complete."[95] Whether or not he or his heirs ever exploited the plantation commercially is not known, but black walnut and the other species Joly experimented with on a smaller scale were clearly too exotic and labour-intensive to be grown by either the province's farmers or its lumbermen.[96] And, despite Joly's claim that his particular interest in the black walnut stemmed from its high commercial value and fast growth,[97] it would have made more economic sense to replant the white pine that had been largely eradicated from his seigneury.

Joly's intellectual curiosity appears not to have extended to the latest theories of evolution, perhaps because they challenged his rather orthodox Anglicanism, but he was clearly motivated by scientific curiosity, and historian Doug Owram has suggested that Victorians adopted an empirical approach to scientific inquiry in order to avoid challenging basic religious doctrine.[98] One reflection of the period's natural history craze was the desire for public recognition that cultivation of an exotic species would bring.[99] But Joly also favoured deciduous trees for more practical reasons, writing in 1881 that "on a warm summer's day, the Desert of Sahara, with its lovely oasis, would be suggestive of coolness, compared with our country. No trees to shade the dusty roads, to shelter the panting cattle, to set off the neat white-washed houses; only far away, hidden nearly out of sight, the patch of small neglected timber which the farmer is compelled by our stern winters, to spare from the general slaughter."[100] Joly was not alone in making such an observation. J.G.A. Creighton's essay in *Picturesque Canada*, published a year later, complained that "the grand second growth of maples, birches and elms that succeeds the primaeval forest has been ruthlessly cut away, till the landscape in many districts, especially on the north shore, between Quebec and Montreal, is painfully bare in foreground, while the houses are exposed to the keen north wind and the cattle have no shelter from the sun and storm."[101]

Joly tried to ensure that woodlots would be preserved in Lotbinière, as we saw in chapter 3, and Creighton certainly would have been impressed by the Pointe Platon estate where the manorial property was landscaped in the approved English picturesque style, with exotic species such as Colorado spruce, Lombardy poplars, and Norwegian pine along the laneways and with shrubs and flowers such as hydrangeas, weigelas, and lilies on the borders of the carefully manicured lawn.[102] As Brian Young stresses in his study of the Taschereaus and the McCords, the fashioning of such a landscape reflects the fact that "high culture was a critical front in projecting the naturalness and the inevitability of inequality."[103] Young might have added, however, that patrician figures such as Joly felt it was their duty to set standards for others to emulate to the best of their abilities, engaging in beautification campaigns that extended well beyond their landed estates.

Conclusion

After he had moved to Victoria, Joly confided to his son Edmond on more than one occasion that working with the young trees he had planted was a welcome escape from political controversies.[104] Joly's conservation policies may have foreshadowed the American Progressives' utilitarianism, then, but the exotic tree species he introduced to the lieutenant governor's garden – including eucalyptus, almond, and Himalayan cedar – reflected a romantic fascination with natural history. His obituary in the Victoria *Colonist* claimed, somewhat fancifully, that to Joly "a tree was more than a growing piece of wood, to be cut down for timber or fuel, when needed, or allowed to remain for ornamental purposes. It was an example of creative work, than which nothing is more useful for the proper development of humanity. He saw in a tree a 'hiding of power.' It spoke to him of infinite possibilities. He realized far more fully than most men how completely the welfare of mankind and that of trees are interwoven."[105] Impractical or extravagant as some of Joly's tree-planting ideas and practices may have been, the fact remains that he was the only Quebec lumberman of the nineteenth century to manage a sizeable forest on a sustained-yield basis,[106] and he was the country's most prominent proponent of forest conservation when that movement was still in its infancy.

Chapter Eight

Laurier Cabinet Minister

Having long pressed Joly de Lotbinière to enter the federal arena, and having benefited from his national unity efforts during the Jesuits' Estates and Manitoba Schools controversies, Laurier clearly had to offer the veteran politician a position in the new government in 1896. *L'Électeur* predicted that he would become minister of agriculture,[1] but Joly was appointed instead to the junior portfolio of inland revenue, which initially fell under the authority of the ministry of trade and commerce. Joly appears to have been satisfied with his assignment, for he was clearly aware that Laurier had more ambitious young followers to appease, and in any case, the politically indispensable Israël Tarte was the only French Canadian appointed to a full-fledged ministry.[2] Joly's son Edmond wrote to him, "This honour has been conferred upon you without any seeking on your part. You choose a dignified course of conduct; you did not haunt Laurier's footsteps like many others who wished to make sure of their claims being recognized, but like Cincinnatus, the summons to the Capital found you, if not ploughing your land, doing the next best thing, getting your crop of hay in."[3] Rather than feeling beholden to Laurier for his appointment, then, Joly was free to manage his portfolio as he saw fit, and this would quickly lead to friction with other Liberals in the cabinet as well as the House of Commons.

The Patronage Issue

Laurier's decision to appoint such a well-known opponent of government waste and corruption to a significant patronage-dispensing post may appear somewhat curious. Joly had been criticized by Mercier for not being more partisan in making appointments while he was premier, and he had informed Premier Oliver Mowat of Ontario in 1882 that the subdivision of offices for the sake of patronage was "a great abuse" in Quebec, adding with a touch of black humour that at least they had not subdivided the sheriffs' offices, for "it would really be too hard on the poor fellows who have got to be hung."[4] But the fact remains that Joly's candidacy for election in 1896 had helped to refurbish the image of a party that had been disgraced by the Mercier regime, so what better post than one that was susceptible to abuse by a less scrupulous appointee? Laurier also may have wanted to clean up a department that, according to Joly, had been terribly neglected.

The task was daunting, for Joly did not even have a list of names for the more than 500 employees scattered across the country, and he admitted in the House of Commons that he had no experience in the complex and controversial issue of the western wheat standard.[5] He informed his son, however, that the only things that troubled him were the innumerable requests for positions and his inability to satisfy at least a few of them. Patronage demands from Quebec had reached "un tel point de férocité" that it was impossible for him to make recommendations except for individuals who had fought for the Liberal Party or who were strongly supported by Liberal chiefs in that province.[6] The president of the Portneuf reform association, for example, had made it clear that the local Liberals expected to share in the spoils of office: "Puisque nous avons contribué à porter notre parti au pouvoir, il n'est que juste, je crois, que nous ayions notre part de patronage." Having heard that of the 15,000 employees in Ottawa, none were from Portneuf, he asked that the son of a local resident be given a position in that city.[7] Another correspondent, upon hearing that an Irish Catholic would be dismissed from the Quebec City Custom House for taking an active part in the election, wrote that another Irish Catholic should take his place.[8] Joly's business acquaintances were no more reticent, and lumberman G.B. Hall soon submitted his choice for the city's Harbour Commissioner. In this case, Joly was quick to comply, but his task was not made any easier by his decision to consolidate a number of positions that had become vacant.[9] He reported in the spring of 1897 that he had reduced the number of employees in his Ottawa office from thirty to twenty-six, for an annual saving of $3,350, even while the revenue had increased from $6,504,000 to $8,041,096.[10]

This economizing measure only increased the pressure on Joly to replace employees deemed to be Conservative partisans. The practice had been resisted by Prime Minister Mackenzie, but when the Conservatives had returned to power in 1879, only seven of the sixty-seven weights-and-measures officers were retained from the Mackenzie era.[11] According to historian W.L. Morton it was the power to dispense patronage that gave a cabinet position "meaning and substance,"[12] but Joly set a new precedent by announcing in the House of Commons that if anyone had a complaint about an officer in his department, he would start by sending that complaint to the accused so that he could defend himself. Only if he were found guilty would he be dismissed. In fact, it was to avoid just such situations that Joly had forwarded a motion during his much earlier term in the House of Commons, in 1873, that would have disenfranchised civil servants.[13] And he had made the same recommendation four years later in the Quebec legislature, where he denied wishing to infringe on their rights as citizens but insisted that the measure was for their own protection.[14] Now he could only admit that it was "very difficult to define the exact limits within which a public officer can properly exercise his franchise as a citizen," while adding that he ought to have "the common sense to understand that a public official is not a servant of a party, but a servant of his country." After confessing that he had not consulted his colleagues before making the commitment to resist the spoils system, Joly was reminded by an opposition member that either the government was now bound by that commitment, or he would be obliged to resign from his post. Some of his colleagues were not pleased, Joly admitted to his son, "mais, dans l'intéret même de notre Parti (outre la question de justice) je tâcherai de tenir ferme, coûte que coûte."[15]

The informal rules of the Canadian patronage system dictated that the executive committee of a local constituency's party association vetted applications for government positions before forwarding them to the MP, and he in turn made his request to the cabinet minister responsible for the position in question. In his analysis of patronage distribution in John A. Macdonald's Kingston riding, Gordon Stewart found that "in no case in the correspondence was consideration given to the applicants' qualifications – the sole criterion was service to the party."[16] The civil service inquiry of 1908 also found that outside the home departments in Ottawa, "politics enter into every appointment and politicians on the spot interest themselves not only in the appointment but in the subsequent promotion of the officers." And nowhere was this more the case, the inquiry found, than in the portfolio of inland revenue, which suggests that there was a rapid return to standard practice after Joly resigned his position in 1900.[17]

Joly did not challenge the right of deputies to make recommendations, but his determination to resist, or at least limit, partisanship in
administering his office represented a significant challenge to a system that, according to Stewart, "was considered legitimate and nor-
mal" as late as 1911. For example, shortly after the 1896 election a party
organizer responded to Laurier's request to report on the patronage
requirements in the Quebec City area by writing that Joly would immediately have to replace Dr Fiset of St Sauveur with Dr Coté "pour faire
plaisir à nos jeunes amis de Québec," in addition to appointing Amédé
Gagnon of St Arsène as customs officer in Temiscouata County in place
of Philéas Dubé of Fraserville.[18] Joly was still being put strongly to the
test in November 1896 when he wrote to Edmond, "I am happy to have
lots of work, but my continual struggle ... to protect the officers of my
department against the demands of dismissal made by our friends is
hard to bear, and I think before long there will be a row and you can
foresee the result."[19] According to the disgruntled C.F. McIsaac, MP for
Antigonish, it was hard enough "for a representative to have to assume
the responsibility of becoming a prosecutor in every case but after having made the charges and having them placed on file to be told that
nothing will be done makes the situation simply intolerable." McIsaac
insisted that two local preventive officers "must go or I will have to go
myself."[20]

A few days later Joly confided to his son that the moment was approaching when he would have to decide between resigning and
dismissing a large number of his department's employees.[21] He now regretted his public promise, having had no idea how far the complaints
would reach. Joly was being advised to make inquiries and dismiss
only the guilty, but he felt certain that if all the officers who had been
mixed up in elections were dismissed, more than half his department
would have to go. He had dismissed a small number to set an example for the others, but this did not satisfy his colleagues.[22] In fact, Joly
informed Laurier on December 2 that if he gave in to even one such
request, he would not be able to refuse the thirty or forty others that
were pending, not to mention those that would follow in the future.[23]
Although Joly failed to mention it to his son, Governor General Aberdeen also was resisting official requests to dismiss civil servants simply
because they had taken part in the election against the Liberal Party.
He wrote in May 1897 that civil servants had a right to vote, and therefore "it would appear to be an infringement of the spirit of free institutions to punish independence of opinion or to encourage self seeking or

servility – provided always that such independence of opinion does not take the form of active opposition to the existing Government."[24] Joly had, in fact, agreed to serve notices to certain employees after meeting the prime minister the previous December, but only on condition that the accused be given a chance to defend themselves, as he had publicly promised.[25] He also requested that an order-in-council be passed authorizing him to make inquiries in each province, even though he had recently stated that the appointment of a commissioner to investigate accusations of participation in elections was reminiscent of the French Revolution: "Organize a tribunal to try people; the patriots are bound to find work for it, especially when condemnation is followed by confiscation."[26]

Joly also asked to be admitted to cabinet meetings in order to avoid similar conflicts in the future, and he made it clear that his motivation was not mercenary in nature by adding that he was perfectly satisfied with his current salary of $4,000.[27] He also continued to defend the employees of his department against demands for peremptory dismissal.[28] In two Quebec cases, the charges were simply that each of the officers had been seen in a carriage with the local Conservative candidate.[29] In another case, John A. Macdonell of Winnipeg charged, "Your loyalty to Conservative partisan officials is stronger than your loyalty to the Liberal Party and its representatives, of which I am one."[30] When Laurier himself asked that the assistant inspector of weights and measures in Ste Marie de Beauce be replaced with his own nominee, Joly replied that he would send his "Commissaire Enquêteur" once that officer had finished his inquiry in another parish. If the current inspector were found guilty, Joly wrote, Laurier's candidate would replace him, but he asked that all such appointments be conditional on passing the qualifying exam as soon as possible.[31] Joly reminded Laurier that the exam tested only the ability to read, write, and count, so it did not present a formidable hurdle.[32] In another case, however, Joly noted that the official in question was in charge of testing the alcohol content in a local vinegar factory, a position that required "certaines connaissances en chimie et une expérience que le premier venu ne peut pas posséder."[33] By June, Joly had dismissed eleven officers for political activities, and he confided to Edmond that his colleagues appeared willing to terminate their "règne de terreur."[34] Joly had survived this contest of wills with his principles intact, for eleven dismissals constituted a very small proportion of the 473 federal employees who lost their jobs after the 1896 election, 196 of them being fired for "offensive political partisanship."[35]

The price for this victory, Joly felt, was that it precluded him from supporting the applications of any of his friends or constituents for positions in other departments. But release from such obligations may actually have come as a relief to the scrupulous politician. Even though he had played an active role in the May provincial election, which had resulted in a Liberal victory, Joly refused to interfere in any way with provincial appointments.[36] There was also a personal price to pay, however, for there were rumours that year that Joly would be appointed lieutenant governor of Quebec, then of Ontario, and finally, of the North-West Territories, but he could hardly accept such a position when he himself had been waging a war on patronage.[37]

Joly had undoubtedly made himself unpopular in the Laurier cabinet, but this did not deter him from making it clear that he disapproved of his old enemy Tarte's more pragmatic approach towards building Liberal support in Quebec. He even refused to attend the opening of the new quay at Ste Croix in Lotbinière County because it was to be followed by a banquet in Tarte's honour. He also instructed Edmond not to join the excursion on the Drummond County Railway, which was owned by an influential Liberal supporter who was negotiating, through Tarte, to sell it to the government. In Joly's words, he was determined to be "strictly neutral on Tarte" until he felt Tarte deserved his sympathy.[38] That sympathy would certainly not be aroused by Tarte's outspoken opposition to the participation of Canadians in the Boer War, where Joly's youngest son, Gustave, was serving.[39] The irony was that Tarte too was accused by his suspicious Liberal colleagues of being too lenient with Conservative office-holders, albeit for political reasons rather than administrative or ethical ones.[40]

As already noted, Joly found a more compatible ally in his friend the governor general. In February 1898 Lord Aberdeen asked Joly to discuss his draft recommendations on civil service reform, recommendations that would warrant dismissal only for cause, as well as forbidding any participation by civil servants in future elections.[41] This was not a minor issue, for liberal reformers of Gilded Age America are said to have considered civil service reform to be a panacea for all the ills of the nation, and modernizers believed that the rationalization of the bureaucracy was the key to an efficient and progressive administration.[42] Although Joly's stance was certainly in line with the state formation process, however, he does not appear to have had in mind a reform as fundamental as that envisioned by Aberdeen or Britain's Northcote/ Trevelyan Report of 1854, which called for a civil service recruited by open competition, based on intellectual merit, and organized by a uniform system of grading. Canadian public service inquiries had recommended such a reform in 1868, 1877, 1881–2, and 1892, but Joly did not question the right of MPs to have preferential say in patronage appointments within their ridings, nor did he wish to adopt an American reform committee's proposal that civil servants be protected by law from arbitrary dismissal.[43]

As political scientist Ken Rasmussen points out, patronage was defended as a means of enhancing executive authority and political stability.[44] Joly certainly supported strong and stable government, yet his paternalistic sense of noblesse oblige as well as his conservative distaste for the American spoils system made him determined to protect his charges from dismissal without good cause.[45] Thus, in a paradoxical sense, Stewart's argument that the patronage system confirmed the power of the professional middle classes at a time when "there was no aristocratic or traditional landed class that still had an influence in public affairs" may help to explain why Joly, as a member of the latter class, refused to participate fully in the game. But there was a political cost during an era when most Canadians still lived in rural communities and when manufacturing had not yet reduced the heavy dependence on the government for jobs and contracts.[46] When the Liberals lost Lotbinière in the 1900 federal by-election, Joly took it personally as a reflection of his diminished prestige and influence in the county even though he was not a candidate, but rather than attempt to restore that influence through the distribution of patronage, he refused to play any further role in the constituency's politics.[47]

The Ministry of Internal Revenue

Joly was also determined as minister of internal revenue to resist pressures from the large tobacco producers to reduce tariffs on their raw product. Although opposition demands for a lower tariff on American tobacco, purportedly as a means of reducing smuggling, actually reflected the distaste of Canadian manufacturers for "le tabac canadien," Joly's agrarian sympathies led him to favour expansion of the home-grown product.[48] Similarly, Joly was not prepared to go so far as to prohibit the manufacture of ale or beer for family consumption, which shows that he was not beholden to the distilling industry.[49] Nevertheless, he had some reason to be concerned about the situation in Quebec, where fifty-five stills were discovered in 1896, as compared with only eighteen the previous year and only two in Ontario, seven in Nova Scotia, and none in the other provinces. According to Joly, people in the Quebec City area had become insane as a result of drinking this "poisonous" liquor. Rather than rely entirely on his revenue officers to deal with the situation, however, Joly asked each curé to draw the attention of his parishioners to the severity of the law and to explain that those engaged in illicit distilling sinned against religion, morality, and their own material interests.[50]

Whether or not he realized that alcohol prohibition would tend to increase bootlegging, Joly was a firm opponent of the state expanding its coercive influence in this manner. In an attempt to demonstrate the impossibility of enforcing prohibition, he went so far in 1898 as to humiliate publicly a wholesale merchant who was one of the movement's most outspoken supporters in Quebec City. He did so by producing at a prohibition meeting an invoice for three dozen bottles of beer that the merchant had supplied to one of his rural customers.[51] The following year Joly was attacked in the House of Commons for neglecting his office by campaigning against prohibition throughout the province.[52] Of course, total prohibition would cut into the revenues of the state, just as illicit distilling would, but Joly was probably more concerned about the Catholic Church's hostility to state intervention in the sphere of public morality, a position that was quite in keeping with his own paternalist instincts.[53]

Although Joly dedicated more funds to the pursuit of illicit liquor producers and distributors, perhaps to undercut the prohibition movement, he favoured divesting the central government of much of its responsibility for inspecting weights and measures. In his view, federal agents should increase the annual number of inspections of scales used at western grain elevators, Nova Scotia coal mines, and railway stations because the producers who had little or no choice but to rely on them had no means of determining their accuracy.[54] The same was true for consumers of gas and electricity. But Joly argued that the inspection of the far more numerous weigh scales used by local merchants should be left to municipalities, as in England, because customers could easily determine if they were being cheated and take their business elsewhere.[55]

Joly may have been cautious about expanding the state's coercive power, but he was obviously a promoter of efficiency and progress. During the 1898 session, having been elevated to the role of minister, he focused much of his attention on the passage of a bill that would standardize weights and measures, the most controversial item being how many pounds a bushel or a sack of potatoes must weigh. He also privately championed the twenty-four-hour clock as well as the metric system, noting in 1900 that the latter had been legalized in England and predicting that it would soon be made compulsory there as well as in the United States. Canada, therefore, had to ensure that it did not find itself out of step.[56]

Despite his advanced years, Joly was clearly an active and effective administrator, as well as one willing to challenge colleagues over what he considered to be issues of basic justice. One such issue was the Chinese head tax. Succumbing to pressure from British Columbia, Ottawa had imposed a fifty-dollar head tax on Chinese immigrants in 1886, but this had soon proved ineffective in slowing the influx, and the province had begun to demand a much more prohibitive $500 levy. Despite Laurier's promises in 1896 to bow to provincial will, his government continued to stall, concerned as it was that this would interfere with the expansion of Canadian trade with China.[57] Joly himself had played a role in the promotion of this trade in the fall of 1896 when he hosted the Chinese viceroy Li Hung-chang on the four-day central Canadian leg of his path-breaking North American tour. Joly met Li at Niagara Falls and left him at North Bay, unable to travel with him in his special train to British Columbia because the House was then in session. According to Joly, the highlight for Li was the Toronto Exhibition, where they spent an afternoon being entertained by trained elephants, high divers, horse races, and "ballets de danseuses plus ou moins costumées à l'Orientale, comme quelqu'un disait (skirt dance without the skirt)."[58] Li, in turn, was a sensation at the fair, where he was met by a deputation of dignitaries and the Queen's Own Regimental Band. After touring several buildings, Li was conducted to the grandstand platform, where he was introduced to more distinguished guests. Away from the throng of 100,000 people who jostled each other for a glimpse of one of the three greatest living men, according to the *Christian Guardian* (the others were Bismarck and Gladstone), Li and Joly engaged in a long conversation through an interpreter. Joly, whom Li showered with gifts, confided to his son that he had never spent a more interesting day. He had avoided speaking of the persecution by the labour associations of "ces pauvres petites fourmis [ants] qui travaillent humblement & fidèlement," but he had informed Li that the $500 head tax issue would not be raised during the current session.[59]

When the issue was nevertheless raised in the House of Commons, Joly was one of two eastern Liberals to criticize the attack against the

Chinese "race" voiced by the Liberal MP for Burrard in Vancouver, G.R. Maxwell.[60] He reminded the House that the Chinese were an ancient culture, that their opium habit had been forced on them by the British, and that their labour on the railways had opened British Columbia to development much earlier than otherwise would have been possible. Was it just, Joly asked, to discard the Chinese now that their labour was no longer considered essential? They were accused of coming to Canada to make money that they then spent at home, but was this not what Europeans did in China? The Chinese workers might only be "poor heathens," Joly declared, but "is it possible that where they are surrounded by churches and Christians, and such excellent examples as are presented by those who live around them, there is no chance of converting them? Then what is the use of sending missionaries all over the world to seek the heathen and to attempt to convert them in the wilder regions where they live?"[61]

In his attempt to dissuade his colleague from resigning when the draft bill was presented in October, Liberal MP David Mills concocted the somewhat illogical argument that – unlike the Riel affair, when Joly's resignation was "quite justifiable" – the Chinese question was "not a vital one to the country or its honor." Mills further argued, "To *maltreat* Chinamen is dishonorable but then nobody seriously proposed a *policy* of mal-treatment." Although he personally supported free trade in labour as well as goods, Mills added, many others believed in protection, and he did not "see *in principle* any distinction between excluding by high tariffs products of aliens and excluding the aliens themselves." Deplorable as might be "the selfish action of America-Australia (and Canada to some extent) as shown in their anti-Chinese legislation," Mills insisted that Joly's resignation "would not do near so much good as harm. It would show up for a moment the selfishness of the anti-Chinese policy but could hardly seriously affect action." Finally, appealing to Joly's ego, he concluded, "It would be far better that all the Chinese in Canada should go home than that you should leave Laurier. I've the greatest respect for tree planting and pond-clearing but the government of Canada is much more important."[62] Joly presumably did not back down, however, for the government did not increase the head tax, and he continued to take an interest in the issue while he remained in Ottawa.[63]

Joly's humanitarianism also extended to the famine sufferers in India, for he wrote to Lady Aberdeen that Canadians deserved to be reproached for not coming to their relief, especially given the fact that the

Indian crop failure "has operated in our favor by raising the price of our wheat." Joly suggested that the meeting of Lady Aberdeen's women's council would offer an excellent opportunity for her to appeal to Canadians "on behalf of their fellow subjects in India."[64]

The Canadian wheat boom alluded to by Joly had increased the need for inspectors in the Prairies, and Joly travelled west in 1898 in order to straighten out difficulties with the new law on the inspection of wheat, as well as to organize government services in the rapidly expanding towns of British Columbia's Kootenay region.[65] Joly had offered to cancel the trip if the prime minister felt that his pro-Chinese speech made him a political liability in the west coast province, but his mission was successful enough that Laurier asked him to become the province's lieutenant governor the following year. An uneasy truce may have been established over the patronage issue in Ottawa, but Joly had made the other cabinet ministers look corrupt in comparison,[66] and complaints about him did continue to surface from within the party. In May 1900, for example, provincial deputy Charles Langelier wrote to Laurier that Joly was allowing himself to be influenced by the Tories who surrounded him.[67]

Judging from his personal correspondence, Joly avoided political intrigues, and his record as cabinet minister appears to have been an admirable one. He could boast that, despite the sharp increase in the excise taxes, there had been a significant decline in illicit alcohol production and tobacco smuggling and that the expenses of his weights and measures department had decreased by $4,000 between the fiscal years of 1895–6 and 1899–1900, and the receipts had increased by $11,000.[68] During their annual probes into his expenditures, the Conservatives were able to embarrass Joly only about the acquisition of books such as *Burke's Peerage*, *The Canadian Men and Women of the Time* (which included a short sketch on his wife), and *Hart's Army List* for the departmental library.[69] The prime minister may, nevertheless, have felt that it was time to appoint a more pliant minister, and Joly himself may well have been tiring of the perennial debates about department expenditures, patronage appointments, and technical matters such as the standard size of the Nova Scotia apple barrel. Even at the age of seventy, however, he was not prepared to retire from the public sphere entirely, and he appears to have willingly accepted Laurier's request that he become lieutenant governor of British Columbia. The fact that the political crisis in that province ensured that the position would be no sinecure, as we shall see in the next chapter, probably appealed to his sense of duty.

Conclusion

In his book on the history of political patronage in Canada, journalist Jeffrey Simpson argues that Laurier was a successful prime minister because he "preferred to imitate the dubious morality of Sir John A. rather than the dismal rectitude of previous Liberal leaders, Alexander Mackenzie and Edward Blake."[70] Tellingly enough, Joly is completely ignored by Simpson and the academic scholars who have studied the patronage issue, perhaps because he did not fit the stereotype of a corrupt Quebec politician such as Tarte, who famously declared that elections were not won with prayers.[71] But if Simpson is right in stating that Mackenzie and Blake, as heirs of Upper Canada's "Clear Grit ethic," held "a more stunted vision of the nation" than did Macdonald or Laurier,[72] the same cannot be said of Joly. The Liberal MP for Lotbinière may have been an ardent supporter of provincial rights, but he had a more intimate knowledge of the country's two "solitudes" (to echo novelist Hugh MacLennan) than either of those prime ministers, as well as a greater sympathy for non-European immigrants. Impractical as his vision of a Liberal Party that took a firm stand on political honesty and integrity may have been, had the dominant Canadian parties done the same, there might have developed less cynicism and resentment in the general public towards this country's political system.

Chapter Nine

Lieutenant Governor of British Columbia

In her classic history of British Columbia, Margaret Ormsby states that "a terrible *malaise*" had the province's population in its grip in 1903, largely caused by the industrial dispute that had brought the operations of the Canadian Pacific Railway to a standstill and caused sailors in Victoria as well as longshoremen in Vancouver to wage sympathy strikes. The federal royal commission investigating the labour situation warned that society on the west coast was threatened with a breakdown in morality: "Business men had been dejected; English investors had indicated that they would transfer their money elsewhere; and even the Canadian Manufacturers' Association had threatened to withdraw its travellers from the province."[1] This labour unrest was considered to be symptomatic of a political system in crisis, one in which elected members of the legislature tended to ally themselves to whichever ministry could offer their constituency – and themselves as local investors – the most lucrative railway contract. The solution promoted in the province's major newspapers was for the provincial legislature to adopt the discipline of the federal party system. As lieutenant governor, Sir Henri-Gustave Joly de Lotbinière would be instrumental in putting such a system in place in 1903.

Appointment as Lieutenant Governor

It was because shifting political alliances had been making governments in British Columbia increasingly unstable that Prime Minister Laurier had, in 1900, appointed his trusted colleague to be the first (and ultimately, last) lieutenant governor to come from outside the province. The federal government's interest in the internal politics of the distant, thinly populated province was heightened by the fact that during the late 1890s central Canadian capital had finally begun forging the first strong transcontinental links to the west coast.[2] Joly's mission, in short, was to stabilize the state in order to restore the investor confidence that would ensure the continued growth of British Columbia as a satellite economy of central Canada. Joly can therefore be seen as an agent of what Ian McKay refers to as Canada's project of liberal order or rule,[3] though the acquisitive individualism that McKay sees as the basis of this liberal order was what threatened British Columbia with anarchy.

Lieutenant governors had an ambiguous status in the earlier years of Canada's history. Because they were not direct appointees of the Crown but of the federal government, they tended to be regarded by the governors general as subordinate officers.[4] But paradoxical as it may seem, even though the role of the country's governor general was increasingly symbolic (except when the administration lost the confidence of the House of Commons), the provinces' lieutenant governors could be quite interventionist for the very reason that they were appointed by federal authority. London's Judicial Committee of the Privy Council did find in 1892 that provincial governments were sovereign within their own sphere,[5] but we shall see that this did not prevent Laurier from advising the lieutenant governor of British Columbia on how to manage political issues. Not only did lieutenant governors still have considerable discretionary power in accepting or rejecting provincial legislation and appointments,[6] they continued to exercise the power to make and break governments in British Columbia, as they had earlier in Quebec. In fact, Laurier's first west coast appointee, Thomas R. McInnes, added to the instability of an already volatile political situation by high-handedly dismissing two administrations. Joly would act more patiently and diplomatically in exercising the same prerogative in 1903.

It was first rumoured that Joly de Lotbinière would be appointed lieutenant governor of British Columbia when the position became available in 1897,[7] but Liberal senator T.R. McInnes was chosen instead. Only when McInnes was dismissed in 1900 did Joly finally take up the position. As we saw in the preceding chapter, he may have felt some pressure to do so, given the whisperings that Quebec politicians were becoming increasingly impatient with his scrupulous handling of patronage,[8] but there is nothing in Joly's personal correspondence to suggest that he accepted the appointment begrudgingly. He had expressed interest in the west coast province's resources as early as 1878,[9] and the fact that the Ottawa timber entrepreneurs were beginning to turn their attention in that direction at the turn of the century may have intrigued him. Undoubtedly more important, however, was Joly's patrician sense of pride and duty, for the position would involve a considerable amount of pomp and ceremony, and he would be acting in the service of the country as a whole.

No one appears to have brought up the fact that Joly had roundly criticized the terms of union with British Columbia in 1871 as too generous,[10] but Laurier's choice of lieutenant governor did leave him open to attack from opposition newspapers such as the Hamilton *Spectator*. The newspaper declared that there were many good Liberals in British Columbia well qualified for the post, yet "Sir Wilfrid must needs send a French-man from Quebec to govern the British Canadians of the Pacific Province."[11] The standard practice had indeed been to consult the provincial party and even to delegate the selection of lieutenant governors to the provincial representatives in the federal cabinet, with the result that local residents had been chosen for British Columbia, as for eastern Canada, ever since Confederation.[12] What, then, had inclined Laurier to make what, on the surface, appeared to be a rather puzzling choice?

Joly may have been considered a political anachronism in his home province, after having served twenty-two years in the provincial legislature and eleven years in the House of Commons, but the prime minister was clearly not simply ridding his cabinet of a political liability, for he could simply have given Joly another appointment. Laurier actually had considerable faith in his old colleague's abilities. He explained in a private letter to a resident of New Westminster that the situation required "a man of national reputation and whose record for honesty, fairness and impartiality is well known. We found such a man in the person of Sir Henri Joly de Lotbinière. Sir Henri is a French Canadian of Huguenot descent and a protestant by faith. There is no more honest man living. I have great hopes that he will prove a great success."[13] Laurier might have added that, apart from his personal attributes, Joly had acquired a thorough knowledge of constitutional law while premier, and as we have seen, he had considerable experience in railway construction as well as the lumber industry, which happened to be the two main preoccupations of the British Columbia government.

In contrast to Ontario's *Spectator*, no British Columbia newspaper appears to have complained about Joly's cultural origins. More relevant was the fact that an easterner was being assigned to a western province that took considerable pride in its rapid development and that also felt some resentment towards what it perceived to be Ottawa's indifference. The Conservative *Victoria Daily Colonist*, despite praising Joly's credentials, objected to the principle of appointing an easterner, declaring that "if dissension in the Liberal ranks rendered it injudicious, from a party point of view, to select a supporter of the Laurier ministry, there are gentlemen in the Conservative party who are in every way available ... The people of this province are in all respects the equals of their fellow Canadians elsewhere, and, while they are always glad to see new-comers, would prefer that they should not arrive with federal commissions in their pockets." The *Colonist*'s sense of grievance was aggravated by the fact that Laurier did not take advantage of the opportunity to replace Joly in the federal cabinet with what would have been the first member from British Columbia.[14]

Liberal though it was, the Victoria *Times* agreed on the latter point, but it did not criticize Joly's appointment, claiming that he would ensure that "no pranks will be played; under him the province will re-enter on the constitutional path."[15] The Liberal Vancouver *World* was also diplomatic, declaring that "with the possible exception fo [sic] several well-known gentlemen in this province whose long and faithful service deserved recognition, a better man than Sir Henri Joly could not have been found for the position ... The people of British Columbia can look forward with some confidence to a regime which will serve to smooth away the angry passions that have been aroused, and will introduce here something of the grand old seigniorial hospitality which gave to Quebec, aforetime, a distinction all its own."[16] Even an organization known as the Provincial Rights Association of British Columbia declared that it fully approved of Joly's appointment, claiming that it was "a happy solution to the many perplexing problems which disturbed [the province] in the past and seriously menaced its future."[17]

Nor did the Conservative *Colonist* utter any further complaints after Joly arrived in the province. On June 29 the newspaper "extended a very cordial welcome," noting, "A reputation for a true conception of constitutional duty as well as for tastes and instincts of an elevated order has preceded him, and we feel every confidence that his career amongst us will more than justify the policy of Sir Wilfrid Laurier in selecting him for his new and responsible position."[18] Clearly, then, Joly's patrician status, with a knighthood that placed him in a direct and subordinate relation to the monarch, offered reassurance to the Anglophile elite of Victoria and Vancouver.[19]

When Joly arrived in Victoria on board the *Islander*, he was accompanied by the mayor and aldermen, a guard of honour from the Duke of Connaught's Own Rifles, and the regimental band. According to the *Colonist*, "a great throng had assembled at the outer wharf, and despite the rather unpleasant wind which blew from the West, making everyone turn up their coat collars, the wharf presented a handsome appearance, the brilliant uniforms of the officers of the army and navy ... contrasting pleasingly with the black frock-attired gentlemen representing the government, the bench, and the clergy." The carriage carrying the premier and the new lieutenant governor then made its way through "streets thronged with people" to the hotel where an informal reception was to take place. In short, Joly's arrival in the provincial capital is an illustration of imperialism as ornamentalism, defined by David Cannadine as "hierarchy made visible, immanent and actual."[20]

Referring to Joly's "charming ease and grace of manner," the *Colonist* concluded that he was "a fit occupant of the important post to which he has been assigned."[21] In addition to his knighthood and patrician background, Joly's fluency in English, his membership in the Church of England, and his public split with the Quebec Liberals over the Riel issue were all features that ensured Joly's warm embrace by Victoria's still very British social elite, as were his European education, patrician background, and self-identification as a seigneur at a time when the English-Canadian cultural elite was attracted by the romance of old Quebec as an antidote to materialism and Americanization.[22] Ideally suited as he was for the pomp and circumstance associated with the role of lieutenant governor, Joly also needed considerable skill and diplomacy to survive a five-year term with very little controversy during an era when the province's politics were exceptionally unstable and corrupt. Before examining how he managed this feat and the impact he had on British Columbia, we turn to a brief survey of the situation in that province prior to his appointment.

West Coast Prelude

By the time Joly replaced McInnes as lieutenant governor, British Columbia was being governed by its third administration in two years. A fully elected Legislative Assembly had been granted only with Confederation in 1871, and instead of adhering to party discipline, provincial politicians had formed unstable coalitions of local interests, with a major cleavage dividing Vancouver Island and the mainland.[23]

Following the depressed decade of the 1870s, with politics focused on forcing Ottawa to live up to its promise to build a transcontinental railway, the 1880s brought what Ormsby refers to as the "great potlatch," when immense acreages of Crown land were alienated to speculative railway ventures and other public works.[24] By the late 1890s, Martin Robin notes, public sentiment was turning against "the mounting public debt, extravagance, reckless favouritism, give-aways and kick-backs."[25]

Opposition forces, including a growing labour movement, found an articulate spokesman in 1898 with the election to the Legislative Assembly of the populist firebrand Joseph Martin, who had recently served as the controversial attorney general of Manitoba. After the votes were counted, so many newcomers had been elected that it was unclear whether Premier John Turner had enough supporters to remain in office. Without waiting for the recounts in twenty-nine contested seats, Lieutenant Governor McInnes dismissed the Turner government on dubious constitutional grounds. Martin was subsequently appointed attorney general in an administration headed by the Cache Creek cattle rancher Charles A. Semlin.[26] After Martin's erratic behaviour led to his dismissal from the cabinet, he led an attack against the government, accusing it of robbing public assets by granting 611,000 acres (247, 263 hectares) of coal-bearing land to a subsidiary of the CPR. Upon defeat in the House in January 1899, Semlin convinced some of the Conservative opposition members to accept portfolios in a reformed administration, but Lieutenant Governor McInnes insisted on immediate dismissal.[27] Fearing that McInnes would call on Martin to form the new ministry, federal secretary of state R.W. Scott wired him from Ottawa, stating that Semlin should be given more time to reconstruct, but the message arrived too late. McInnes had already turned to Martin, claiming that he was the strongest political figure in the province and the only leader who had not been given a chance to form a government.[28]

Although unable to find any supporters in the House, Martin defiantly created a cabinet of political non-entities and managed to delay an election for three months despite the fact that Laurier had urged McInnes to force an immediate dissolution. The day before the election did take place, the press announced that Martin had accepted $100,000 from J.J. Hill of the Great Northern Railway; as a result, only six or seven of the men who were returned to the Assembly could be counted on to support him. Laurier could finally feel fully justified in dismissing McInnes, for he had resisted earlier pressures to do so on the grounds that Ottawa would interfere only when the lieutenant governor's new advisers were not sustained by the people in the subsequent election.[29]

Although the Vancouver and Victoria Liberal associations defended McInnes,[30] Laurier argued that by choosing Martin as premier, McInnes had contributed to the political and economic instability of the province. Martin and McInnes had also been thorns in Laurier's side, for they repeatedly complained about what they felt was eastern indifference, an indifference reflected in particular by Sir Clifford Sifton's role as the sole western spokesman in the federal cabinet.[31] John Saywell notes as well that "these 'kickers' in British Columbia openly attacked the repeated disallowance of legislation designed to prevent Oriental immigration . . .; denounced the railway monopoly and the industrial monopoly that it supported . . .; complained of the tariff and the inequity of Dominion-Provincial financial relations; and criticized the operation of the federal administrative system in the west." In short, Martin and McInnes "were in a state of suspended rebellion against the Liberal party to which they nominally belonged."[32]

In protesting his dismissal, McInnes gave vent to those same sentiments in no uncertain terms when he wrote, "A Chinese chicken thief is accorded a fair trial by us, and is given a chance to speak in his own behalf. Is it going to be said that the people of British Columbia, or their elected representatives, have descended to the level of the nigger-roasting lynchers of the Southern States – and that against a pioneer of the province, who, for over a quarter of a century, has filled the highest representative positions in the country? If so, British Columbia is no fit home for a Briton now."[33] In turning to Joly, Laurier was clearly selecting not only someone who would rise above the internecine factionalism of west coast politics, but also someone who would bring a more pronounced degree of sophistication and decorum to the office of the Queen's representative.

Introducing Party Government

There is a certain irony in the fact that the constitutional precedent for McInnes's ouster by Laurier was set by Sir John A. Macdonald's dismissal in 1879 of Quebec's Letellier de Saint-Just despite the vociferous protests and appeals of none other than Henri-Gustave Joly as premier of that province. Being new to British Columbia, and having had his own premiership sabotaged by the obstructionist lieutenant governor who succeeded Letellier, Joly was unlikely to emulate McInnes's interventionist policies. As a Canadian nationalist and constitutional monarchist, he firmly believed that the lieutenant governor was considerably more than a figurehead, but he would have to work carefully and slowly behind the scenes while British Columbians continued to endure political instability during his first three years in office.

Serving as premier during much of this time was Joseph Martin's successor, the uncharismatic Vancouver Island coal baron James Dunsmuir, who was able to please neither his fellow mine owners nor organized labour at a time of economic decline in the industry. Beset by numerous railway promoters, Dunsmuir finally embraced his predecessor's ambitious policy of strengthening the rail links between the coast and the interior of the province. Although his administration was originally largely Conservative in composition, he had to rely on the support of Martin to pass the Railway Aid Act of 1901 because members of his own government opposed any challenge to the CPR monopoly. The upshot was the resignation of the minister of mines, Richard McBride, who then moved to replace Martin as the official leader of the opposition.[34]

Increasingly disillusioned with politics, Dunsmuir then tendered his resignation as premier. As a result, Laurier – who had recently been in the province with the royal tour of the Duke and Duchess of York – remained concerned about the province's political instability. Despite the fact that British Columbians were sensitive to federal interference in provincial affairs, and that Dunsmuir was a political opponent, Laurier asked Joly to refuse to accept the premier's resignation "in order to prevent another crisis and possibly another general election."[35] Joly had, in fact, already done so, informing Dunsmuir that he would have to remain at his post until a hostile vote of the province's representatives gave him the right to step down.[36] Dunsmuir's resignation was finally accepted at the end of 1902, when he was accused of corruption for negotiating to sell his Esquimalt and Nanaimo Railway to the Canadian Northern, whose extension from the interior of the province he had facilitated.[37]

Joly had written to his son Edmond in March 1902, "Avec notre système Parlementaire Anglais, il faut absolument la Discipline de partis. C'est un utopie que de rêver un gouvernement parlementaire stable, là où ceux qui le supportent refusent de prendre la responsabilité de ses actes." ("With our English parliamentary system, party discipline is absolutely necessary. Its utopian to dream of a stable parliamentary government in a place where those who support it refuse to take responsibility for its acts.") He added, however, "Mais c'est un terrain trop délicat pour un Lieutenant Gouverneur, & je m'arrête."[38] Obviously not convinced that the situation was yet ripe to press openly for a party-based government, Joly accepted Dunsmuir's recommendation in November that Colonel Edward G. Prior become the new premier. Prior was a former Conservative cabinet minister in Ottawa and the owner of a hardware and construction business who espoused the same pro-business policies as Dunsmuir. Furthermore, most of the same men remained in the cabinet,[39] but the railway activities that some of the ministers had engaged in during the Dunsmuir regime would return to haunt them.

It was discovered in May 1903 that certain of Dunsmuir's cabinet members had taken advantage of his temporary absence to pass an order-in-council reversing his cancellation of the grant of two oil- and coal-rich land blocks to the Columbia and Western Railway, a subsidiary of the CPR. Anticipating the judgment of the select committee inquiring into the situation, Premier Prior rather desperately dismissed both his commissioner of lands and works and his attorney general.[40] Joly quickly rescinded his promise to grant Prior a dissolution of the legislature, however, when it was disclosed that his company had submitted a successful bid to provide cable for a bridge on the Cariboo Road. The premier admitted that he had seen the competing bids, but he denied that he had passed the information on to his own company, while arguing that the public had benefited from the lower charge to the government purse. Prior further defended his company's right to submit a bid as equivalent to an attorney general having his law partner take charge "of looking after a private bill for anybody and lobbying it through the House."[41]

This was too much for Joly, who wrote to Prior that the views he expressed to justify his action "are so incompatible with, and so completely at variance with what I have always understood to be the true principles of Parliamentary Independence of Members and, above all, of Ministers of the Crown, that, while admitting that you must have honestly considered that you were doing no wrong, I am to my sincere regret unable to continue feeling that confidence in your judgement which would justify me in acting any longer on your advice."[42] Ignoring the counsel of Liberal newspapers such as the Vancouver *World*,[43] Joly called upon the leader of the opposition in the Assembly, Richard McBride. And even though McBride was a Conservative, Joly obviously advised him to select only individuals who belonged to the same federal party, just as the recent provincial Conservative convention had called for.[44]

Reflecting the sectional divisions within the province, the *Victoria Colonist* warned McBride, whom it had not forgiven for deserting Dunsmuir, that "if he plays fast and loose with the Conservative party, that party will drown him a thousand fathoms deep."[45] Even after McBride announced that he would form a strictly Conservative government, the *Colonist* declared that should the new premier wish "to show his loyalty" to the party, he must make it clear that "he does not pose as a leader, but merely as an expedient to facilitate an election upon party lines, and that he will leave it to the Conservative members elected to the next legislature to choose the leader of the party ... If that course is followed, the success of the party at the polls is practically certain. If it is not followed, the success of the party is doubtful in the extreme."[46]

Joly had chosen not only a Conservative to introduce party lines, then, but also a man whose potential for success was limited by the hostility of the Victoria-based Conservative elite, as well as by his failure to win the party leadership at the convention held in Revelstoke a year earlier. Risky as Joly's choice of McBride may have been, however, the fact is that he had little choice but to appoint a Conservative because the leader of the Liberal Party was still Joe Martin, whose reappointment was obviously out of the question. McBride had a strong claim because he was the opposition House leader, and Joly also must have felt some confidence in his skills at building consensus. After all, he too was the son of a Catholic mother and Protestant father. Finally, the lieutenant governor may have felt that McBride's relative youthfulness and inexperience would make him amenable to advice and pressure from an experienced mentor such as himself.[47] Joly confided to his own son, "Our Prime Minister is the youngest member in the House, and I think he is well disposed to do what is right. I treat him as if he were my son, so far as advice and encouragement can do it, and he trusts me."[48]

The Liberal Vancouver *World* accepted McBride's appointment with surprising equanimity, taking pride in the fact that he was the first native-born incumbent of the office and noting that he had "many admirable traits that are characteristic of the typical Westerner, and not the least of which is that of playing an open game consistently and well."[49] The Victoria *Times*, though it had quite naturally hoped Joly would choose a Liberal, admitted that he had adhered strictly to the constitution in choosing the leader of the parliamentary opposition.[50] Whereas the *World* was willing to accept a strictly Conservative cabinet, however, the *Times* was critical of McBride's decision to abandon his erstwhile Liberal allies by summoning only Conservatives to his ministry. The fact that the province was "to be blessed with the inestimable boon of a straight Conservative government" would be nothing new, the *Times* claimed – "We have had nothing else for a dozen or fifteen years, and we have obtained the reward we deserved. British Columbia is where she is to-day because of the firmness of her adherence to Conservative 'principles' as exemplified in the policy of a too long line of grafters."[51]

The formation of an all-Conservative government in British Columbia was not without controversy, then, but as Robin notes, the opening of new areas by the railways had balkanized the province, weakening the forces for political cohesion by increasing the power of mining and railway companies over individual MLAs. With the political spokesmen of the labour movement able to take advantage of the fluid situation in the legislature, it was hardly surprising that party lines and federal labels were favoured by leading Liberals as well as Conservatives in the province as a means of increasing parliamentary discipline and executive control.[52] From this perspective, it was entirely logical that Joly would set the particular interests of his own political party aside in order to facilitate the development of a province that promised to make a great contribution to the wealth of the country and its leading capitalists.

Counselling McBride

Joly quickly granted McBride the dissolution he had denied Prior, setting the stage for the first provincial election in British Columbia history to be fought under federal party labels. Even though the Liberals found themselves without a leader after the resignation of the demoralized Joe Martin, McBride managed to win by only a narrow majority due to the hostility of his old-guard Conservative critics on Vancouver Island and in the province's interior.[53] Once in office, he remained there for a remarkable twelve years, but he certainly did not achieve political stability overnight. Analysis of the votes for the first two sessions under McBride's premiership reveals that he obtained no more loyalty from his official supporters than had some of his predecessors and that there was a very high absentee rate.[54]

Given these circumstances, it is not surprising that, as Saywell notes, Lieutenant Governor Joly "pursued a policy of benevolent paternalism" towards McBride.[55] For example, soon after McBride became premier, Joly refused to sanction the appointment of John Houston as a member of his cabinet on the grounds that the Nelson MLA's rowdy conduct (which had not been exceptional in the provincial legislature) made him unfit to be a minister of the Crown. Instead of resenting this rather unusual intervention on the part of a lieutenant governor, it seems likely that McBride was more than willing to have Joly relieve him of a colleague he had felt obliged to put forward for political reasons.[56] Joly had also done McBride a political favour by allowing the provincial government to catch the opposition off-guard by holding the 1903 election on October 3 rather than October 31, as had been officially forecast when the legislature was dissolved in June.[57]

There are few surviving letters between Joly and McBride, in part because their offices were in the same building, though the fact that confidential letters between the two men in 1901 and 1905–1907 were later found in the basement of Victoria's Strathcona Hotel suggests that much of the intervening historical record has not been preserved. For the most part, Joly simply passed on the letters he received concerning public matters to the appropriate department head, but when individuals complained about actions taken by the government, McBride was careful to provide the lieutenant governor with detailed justifications.[58] The Premiers' Papers also reveal that Joly proffered strong advice on at least one railway issue in 1903 and that he made suggestions about how to approach Ottawa in connection with a federal government bill that British Columbia considered to be purely a provincial matter.[59]

Despite such examples, Joly's influence over McBride appears to have been largely informal in nature. He wrote to his son Edmond early in 1904, concerning the government's austerity measures, "I do my best to encourage them and do feel more hopeful for the future than I have ever felt since I came here."[60] Contemplating his retirement two years later, Joly told Edmond, "I am sad to leave B.C. our friends here, the daily work of my office, the responsibility of my position, as adviser to my advisers!!!!"[61] But the flow of his advice did not entirely end upon retirement, for Joly wrote to McBride in August 1906, "I am glad to see, by your letter, that your views and mine, exchanged so often between us, agree so well, on those questions with which the welfare of B.C. is so closely connected: preservation of our timber, manufacturing it here instead of exporting it to be manufactured abroad, agriculture, dairying, preserving your wild lands for *bonâ fide* settlers, not speculators, classifying them carefully, firm railway policy and firm resistance against the speculators and railway charter mongers, etc."[62] A year later, McBride wrote to Joly that he still felt that "an important part of my work is to account to you for what is going on."[63] The two principal issues during the last three years of Joly's tenure, and for many years thereafter, were the province's Crown forest policy and its relations with Ottawa. We will examine each in turn in an attempt to gain some insight into the impact that Joly had on the fashioning and implementation of provincial policy, as well as his effectiveness as a mediator between the two levels of government.

Crown Forest Policy

In 1901 Joly forwarded two resolutions of the Canadian Forestry Association executive branch – of which he was president – to the province's acting provincial secretary, noting that "the matters in question are of such vital importance to British Columbia, that they deserve the earnest consideration of the Government and of the Legislature."[64] Three years later, Joly asked the secretary of the Canadian Forestry Association to send him four dozen copies of its annual report, "which contains much useful information touching our forests and their preservation and management," so that he could distribute them to the members of the Legislative Assembly.[65] Aside from ensuring that the legislators were well informed about the latest conservationist ideas, Joly also forwarded to Ottawa unofficial documents requesting the establishment of a national park in the province, adding that it was in the urgent interest not only of the province but also of the entire dominion that one or more parks be set aside "where Game is still abundant."[66]

While Joly was lieutenant governor, however, the McBride government did not hesitate to take advantage of the rapidly growing Prairie market for lumber, placing the aim of generating revenue well ahead of any concerns about the long-term viability of the resource.[67] Joly was admittedly somewhat constrained by his official position. He wrote to his son in 1902, "La position que j'occupe m'empêche de prendre une part active à la lutte pour la protection de nos forêts contre les spéculateurs qui, ici, comme à Quebec et autre part, trouvent leur compte dans l'exportation de notre bois non manufacturé."[68] ("The position that I occupy prevents me from taking an active part in the struggle for the protection of our forests against speculators who, here, as in Quebec and elsewhere, benefit from the export of our unmanufactured wood.") But he had made his position clear shortly after arriving in Victoria, when he lamented in his address to the annual meeting of the British Columbia Board of Trade that thousands of young men were leaving Canada for the United States despite the fact that "nature has given us such bountiful materials by which we can give them the means of earning their living and keeping them here to raise their families." Fortunately, all logs taken from Crown lands in Ontario now had to be manufactured in that province, and Joly felt that Quebec would soon follow suit.[69] There can be little doubt, then, that Joly approved of the Dunsmuir administration's stipulation in 1901 that each holder of a pulpwood lease was legally required to operate a pulp mill with a capacity of one ton of pulp or half a ton of paper per day for every square mile leased.[70] Joly wrote to his son in the fall of that year, for example, that Dunsmuir's deputy minister of agriculture, J.R. Anderson, "is a great friend of mine, his devotion to Forestry being a strong bond of sympathy."[71] However, the question that remains is, how was the lieutenant governor's conservationist ethos reconciled with McBride's revenue-oriented policy?

Even though the Canadian principle of Crown retention of forest land was introduced to British Columbia with Confederation, the province did not begin to tackle the problem of treating forest land differently from agricultural land until 1887. The Land Act that was passed that year prohibited the sale of Crown land that was "chiefly valuable for timber." To further discourage lumbermen from buying land rather than leasing the cutting rights from the government, the price of first-class land was increased from $1.00 to $2.50 an acre the following year, in 1888. The new regulations also made a sharp distinction between leases and licenses, the former being designed for mill owners and the latter for small logging contractors who would pay an annual fee. The length of leases was set at thirty years, on provision that a suitable saw mill be constructed, and the term for licenses was set at one year, though they could be renewed. Given that license holders paid only half the annual rents and royalties that lease holders did, the main disadvantage for license holders was that they could hold only one license covering 1,000 acres (later reduced to 640 acres) for a maximum of five years, and the license was not transferable.[72]

By 1903 these terms had been modified somewhat to increase Crown revenue, but the major revision came in 1905, after which no more timber leases – only licenses – were to be granted. Logging companies had no reason to complain, however, for licenses were now renewable annually for a period of twenty-one years, they were now transferable, and there was no longer any limit to the number of licenses any individual interest might acquire. By making timber licenses into commodities, the McBride government had avoided the possibility that large numbers would be surrendered during market downturns, thereby lowering government revenue. The result was that from 1904 to 1907, the year timber prices started to collapse, the amount of land licensed in British Columbia multiplied by a factor of ten to approximately 9,600,000 acres, much of it quickly passing into the hands of American investors and lumbermen for use when their own stocks were depleted. Another result was that forest revenue increased from 17 percent of the provincial budget in 1905 to 41 percent in 1908.[73]

Retrogressive as the new system might appear to have been, the main reason for granting leases rather than licenses – which had been to promote the construction of saw mills – was somewhat redundant by 1905 because of the requirement imposed by the Dunsmuir government that all timber cut on Crown land had to be manufactured within the province.[74] Historian Stephen Gray argues that with the local lumber market already well supplied by lands in the Dominion railway belt, as well as by timberland that had been granted by the Crown in earlier years, the McBride administration had little choice but to license millions of acres at low prices if it wished to capture any significant immediate revenue from those lands.[75] There would subsequently be tremendous pressure on the government to allow the unrestricted export of saw logs from coastal districts, but the 1905 legislation did conform to the conservationist rhetoric of the lumbermen who insisted that long-term security of licenses was necessary to ensure responsible management of the forests.[76] Indeed, tenure stability and long-term fixed charges were seen by the government to be true conservation measures in the American Progressive tradition because they would stimulate efficient, large-scale industrial development.[77]

How direct a role Joly played in fashioning the forestry reforms introduced by the British Columbia government is difficult to say, but as we have seen, he had publicly advocated the manufacturing condition on pulpwood, which was imposed by Dunsmuir, and some of the reforms passed by McBride resembled those of Quebec, including the elimination of the requirement for a minimum annual cut, the twenty-one-year limit on timber licenses, and the hiring of government forest rangers and log scalers.[78] McBride made it clear that he had listened to the lieutenant governor's advice in drafting the reform legislation of 1905, and he wrote to Joly in the latter's retirement, "The people of

British Columbia will not forget the many good services you rendered them when Lieutenant Governor. In the splendid revenues which we are getting from our woods today, I can see the fruit of your timely advice to my colleagues and self."[79] From his manor house at Pointe Platon, Joly replied, "I feel a glow of pleasure at the good news of the financial result of your forestry policy, and earnestly hope that you will *persevere* in your determination to secure to your province the full and complete benefits & returns it is your duty to obtain from such an asset as Providence as [sic] placed in your hands, your forests, without any other work, on your part, than collecting your Dividends. You have *inherited* that wealth. Spend the *interest* wisely and take care of the *capital* for those who will come after you."[80] As we have seen, this was the credo that Joly lived by as far as his own estate was concerned, but it was unfortunately one piece of advice that McBride and his successors would fail to heed.

Federal-Provincial Relations

Any sense of gratitude McBride may have felt towards the Laurier administration for facilitating his rise to power was short-lived, for Victoria's long-standing sense of grievance against Ottawa only intensified during the early years of his regime. The two chief bones of contention were the federal government's continuing interference in British Columbia's attempts to limit Asian immigration and Victoria's persistent claim that it was not receiving as much federal transfer money as it was entitled to. Federal appointee and sympathetic to the Chinese though he was, Joly tended to support the province in both these causes. Perhaps it was natural that a former provincial premier would sympathize with the campaign to redress what is today termed the nation's "fiscal imbalance," but Joly's public defence of the Chinese had caused some concern in British Columbia when he was appointed lieutenant governor, a concern that some Conservatives had attempted to exploit for political purposes.

Shortly before Joly left for his posting in Victoria, the Hamilton *Spectator* proclaimed that he was "the sworn bosom friend and blood-brother of Li Hung Chang" and that "the sending of the champion of the moon-eyed lepers to govern them has made the British Columbians wild."[81] As already noted, the Ontario newspaper was wide of the mark in the latter respect, but prior to Joly's arrival in British Columbia, the Nelson *Tribune* did comment sardonically, "Sir Henri Joly, and his old friend

Li Hung Chang, are again dividing public attention between themselves, much as they did some years before, when Li allowed himself to be booked as an attraction for Toronto's big show, and Sir Henri was making his celebrated pro-Chinese speeches. Sir Henri is now speeding to Victoria, while Li Hung Chang jogs along on the road to Pekin, and the rest of the world stands waiting."[82] Finally, Sir Charles Hibbert Tupper – son of the former Conservative prime minister – referred to Joly as "the minister who sported the Chinese order of the Imperial Dragon." Joly quickly reassured Laurier, however, that he had never been offered such an honour, though "there may have been some talk of it at one time which misled the Parliamentary Guide." He added that he would not have accepted the order in any case because it "would have interfered with my freedom in dealing with the Chinese immigration question."[83]

It was presumably no accident that the same month Joly was appointed lieutenant governor, Laurier announced that the Chinese head tax would be increased to $100 and that a royal commission would investigate Chinese and Japanese immigration, but this failed to mollify the province's Liberals.[84] Although the Asian population was still only 11 percent of the provincial total, the number of Chinese and Japanese immigrants had been increasing dramatically, and there was growing concern among white workers about their impact on the labour market. The Japanese, who were concentrated in Vancouver, in the lower Fraser valley, and along the Skeena River, were considered more capable of assimilation, as well as being more protected by treaties between Britain and Japan. The Dunsmuir government had nevertheless passed an act (generally known as the Natal Act) requiring Japanese immigrants to pass a test demonstrating that they were proficient in a European language. Joly's opinion of this act is not known, but it was disallowed by Ottawa in 1901, as would be each reincarnation during the following ten years. In fact, the passage and disallowance of acts related to the employment of Chinese and Japanese workers became routine exercises during the years that Joly was lieutenant governor.[85]

However, even though McBride intensified the "fight Ottawa" rhetoric, his government did not develop a sustained attack on the immigration issue. Joly may well have been a moderating influence, and he certainly would have reminded McBride that Britain was backing Japan during the Russo-Japanese War of 1904–5.[86] Furthermore, the royal commission of 1901 had assisted in defusing the agitation against Asian immigration, as had the failure of such immigration to recover with the improving economic situation, largely because of the $500 Chinese head tax introduced by Laurier in 1903.[87] Reflecting his dependency on support from the two Socialist MLAs, McBride did introduce legislation in 1905 banning Asians from holding "positions of trust" in the mines, but only in 1907 did the issue of Asian immigration come to a head with the Vancouver riots.[88]

By that time Joly was enjoying his retirement in Quebec, but how had he reconciled his pro-Chinese position with the provincial government's attacks on Asian immigration and civil liberties? According to Senator William Templeman, who was the province's federal Liberal spokesman, Joly's sympathetic outlook had changed as a result of a visit to "some of the purlieus of Chinatown" in 1899.[89] Even if this visit did have an impact on him, the fact is that even in his 1896 speech Joly had suggested that gradual restriction of Chinese immigration might be necessary. Although he defended Chinese culture, Joly was clearly concerned that popular intolerance on the west coast, combined with the distinctive nature of Asian cultures, would impede or even prevent integration and assimilation into the province's "mainstream" society. He counselled McBride, however, to allow London or Ottawa to settle the Japanese question and cautioned that "Hindous" were British subjects "and, as such, cannot be treated as foreigners."[90]

Nor was Joly's concern about immigrant suitability limited to those of another skin colour. When a group of Doukhobors asked to settle in the province, advising that they did not recognize the authority of the state, an indignant Joly replied on his own authority, "Le Gouvernement, tout en étant prêt à recevoir avec plaisir les immigrants d'une classe désirable, refuse absolument d'entrer en negociation avec une classe d'emigrant [sic] qui débutent par déclarer qu'ils ne se conforment pas aux lois du pays."[91] ("The government, while being ready with pleasure to receive immigrants of a desirable class, refuses absolutely to enter into negotiation with a class of emigrants that sets out by declaring that it will not conform to the laws of the country.") To the premier, Joly fulminated, "They call themselves the Christian Community of Universal Brotherhood and they ignore the teaching of Christ when He said,:- 'Render unto Caesar, the things that are Caesar's And unto God the things that are God's.'"[92] In following a communal way of life while explicitly rejecting loyalty to the state, the Doukhobors had declared their intention to remain outside the mainstream society that Joly clearly felt Asians would contribute to if rapid growth of their numbers did not prevent assimilation.

As for the second major irritant between Victoria and Ottawa, Joly may have been a trusted colleague of the Canadian prime minister, but he had also been a provincial premier, and he strongly supported British Columbia's demand for better terms.[93] He wrote bluntly to Laurier in October 1901, after refusing to accept Dunsmuir's first resignation, that the premier's task "serait bien facile, si votre Gouvernement voulait accorder à cette Province la part de l'aide dont elle a plus besoin qu'aucune autre Province, et à laquelle, elle a droit, mais qui lui est refusée. Les résultats de ce refus sont facile à prévoir."[94] ("would be quite easy, if your Government would grant to this Province that share of the aid that it needs more than any other Province, and to which it has a right, but which is refused it.") To Laurier's rather annoyed request that he be more specific, Joly replied that it was a well-known fact that federal governments favoured provinces that were represented by the same political party. Joly added that he sympathized in particular with Dunsmuir's published report concerning financial relations, subsidies for railway development, the fisheries, and the uneven way the tax on Chinese immigrants was divided between the two governments. He closed by stating that the best means of attaching British Columbia to Canada and to the Liberal government would be to demonstrate that "malgré l'opposition que vous y rencontrez, elle peut compter que ses réclamations seront considérées par vous avec impartialité et jugées sur leur mérite."[95] ("despite the opposition that you encounter here, it [British Columbia] can rely on its claims being considered with impartiality and judged on their own merits.")

Joly adhered to the same position when McBride assumed office, for the province was in debt by over $13.5 million (with a deficit that year of over $1.5 million), the mining industry was in recession, and the banks were threatening not to carry the province any further. In advising McBride on how to extract better terms from Ottawa, Joly suggested a radical constitutional amendment that would follow the Australian system of returning to the provinces all moneys that were surplus to fixed expenditures by Ottawa. He also put forward an argument that would be stressed by McBride in future negotiations – namely, that "the great extent of the Province (which is much larger than any other in the Dominion) and the physical character of the Country, ... to a great extent accounts for the expenditure so far exceeding that of any other Province in proportion to population."[96] One could argue that Joly was only exacerbating federal-provincial tensions by proffering such advice, but he may well have helped to weaken the sense of western alienation by assuming the role of broker between Victoria and Ottawa.

Due to its program of strict economy and increased taxation and its unbridled approach to selling Crown land and timber licenses (examined earlier in the chapter), the McBride government was able to announce a small surplus for 1904–5. And fortunately for the government, the economy had begun to turn around, the boom being stimulated in part by the consolidation that was taking place in the mining, forest, and salmon-canning industries.[97] As a result, McBride was finally able to return to the old policy of promoting railway expansion in order to solidify his political support base, but that policy remained fraught with political dangers. The province's sale of land to the Grand Trunk Pacific on Kaien Island, where the railway's terminus of Prince Rupert was to be located, led to corruption charges by the Liberals and a divided commission of inquiry. The ever-scrupulous Joly had insisted on that inquiry, for he had forwarded to McBride a news clipping titled "To Hoodwink Lt.-Governor," to which he had added, "Of course, you will insist on having the Report of the Committee in time to lay it before the House, and get a vote from the House on the subject."[98] This was a reminder that the lieutenant governor still had the authority to dismiss a ministry that was tainted by corruption, but Joly would be gone before being faced with such a decision.

With his position as premier challenged from within his own party, McBride resorted to the well-tested diversionary tactic of intensifying his province's demand for better terms from Ottawa. He walked out of the 1906 federal-provincial conference in protest even though Ottawa had agreed to grant his province a special $100,000 subsidy per year for ten years, in addition to the substantial increase that all the provinces were to receive.[99] Joly was no longer in office to act as a restraining influence, but McBride did attempt to visit him at Pointe Platon after he made his theatrical exit. The premier spent a fruitless day in Portneuf trying to find someone who would ferry him across the stormy waters of the St Lawrence, and he later wrote to Joly, "Had it not been for the Fernie strike – which was then assuming alarming proportions and giving me a great deal of worry and anxiety – I should never have thought of leaving Quebec without first seeing you."[100]

McBride could take comfort in his mentor's communication that he approved of the position he had taken at the conference, though Joly did find fault with the proposal that the extra allowance be continued until the population of British Columbia reached two and a half million: "If we consider the ratio of increase in Provinces like Ontario and Quebec, which are so much better suited to profit by European immigration (which is the only one to be expected as long as B.C. keeps out Chinese and perhaps before long Japanese immigration) if we consider the said rate of increase, and even double or treble it for B.C. – how many years will it take before the Province reaches the two and a half million?"[101] This was a fair question given that the province's population was only 235,000 in 1911. In fact, when the population did reach the two and a half million mark in 1976, British Columbia had long ceased being a "have not" province. In the meantime, after returning from Ottawa to a hero's welcome, McBride called an election that saw his government returned with a comfortable majority.

It is less likely that Joly sharply influenced McBride's views on immigration and the federal-provincial fiscal arrangement than that he provided moral support as well as practical advice. It was perhaps simply coincidental that race relations deteriorated rapidly after Joly's retirement, and it was probably inevitable that McBride would adopt a less prudent economic policy that soon aggravated his relationship with Ottawa. But the fact remains that during Joly's term as lieutenant governor, complaints about Ottawa's high-handedness were relatively muted. From Ottawa's perspective, then, liberal order had been restored in a wider political sense than simply in the stabilization of the provincial administration.

Pageantry and Ceremony

Despite Joly's great popularity in British Columbia and his willingness to remain for another term, Laurier would not hear of it.[102] When the Anglican Bishop of the Columbia Diocese wrote in February 1905 that a petition begging for Joly's reappointment was about to be signed by a large number of people throughout the province and that "no appointment could possibly be made that would tend more to the moral and social good of British Columbia," Laurier replied testily: "Such a petition seems to be most unseemly. The office of Lieutenant-Governor is of such a character that I question the wisdom of putting it on the same rank as that of messengers, customs house officers and so on."[103] Perhaps Laurier's stance resulted from Senator Templeman's observation that Joly had "popularized himself with the Conservatives; the reverse with the Liberals who think they have been ostracized by him." The Jolys were certainly on close terms with the Crease family, pillars of the old colonial gentility, for Susan Crease's diary records regular visits to Government House, and Mrs Joly offered to send Susan's sister

Mary (who was prone to bouts of hysteria) to England for a vacation.[104] Rather than criticize Joly, however, Templeman noted that "few of our friends are in that circle," meaning that Joly could not be expected to socialize with the common middle class.[105]

Paradoxical as it may seem, Joly's widespread popularity as lieutenant governor reflected the fact that he was a member of the traditional elite rather than the nouveau riche, as in the case of his successor, former premier James Dunsmuir. Joly hosted with great success Governor General Minto and family in 1900, the Duke and Duchess of Cornwall and York (later King George and Queen Mary) in 1901, and Prince Arthur in 1905.[106] Historians such as William M. Kuhn have examined how during this period in England, ceremonies of monarchy were devised that reinforced class hierarchies as well as a sense of national community.[107] Similarly, Phillip Buckner argues that the Canadian royal tours served as national unifying forces in this era of imperial enthusiasm.[108] Not only did Joly play a leading role in such imperialist ceremonies, with their carefully ranked orders of precedence, but he was also a much-sought-after patron of dozens of public societies and events. As Bruce Curtis argues in his examination of Lord Durham's "political theatre," by mixing with the common people in this fashion, Joly was effectively strengthening relations of domination through their temporary denial.[109]

In *The English Constitution*, which Joly had doubtless read, Walter Bagehot wrote that English royalty "seems to order, but it never seems to struggle. It is commonly hidden like a mystery, and sometimes paraded like a pageant, but in neither case is it contentious."[110] The monarchy was particularly useful as a "visible symbol of unity" during Joly's term as lieutenant governor, when loyalty to party and therefore respect for the premier's office were still on shaky ground. As the Queen's local representative, Joly's official openings of fall exhibitions throughout the province provided especially important opportunities for disseminating the message of economic progress and for legitimizing the state.[111] Paradoxical as it may seem, Joly's presence at these rural fairs – no doubt wearing his plumed hat and sporting his badges of knighthood – must also have been reassuring to those who felt that, in Cannadine's words, the empire "was about land and agriculture and the countryside, and about the ideal, divinely sanctioned social order to which this gave rise."[112] Indeed, Laurier asked Joly to remain in office until September 1905 in order to open the dominion exhibition in New Westminster,[113] and he was still in Victoria in February 1906 when the prime minister asked him to carry on again until the fall, this time to open the provincial exhibition. Laurier added that Joly could even remain until the end of winter in 1907, as his friends had requested, but should resign immediately if he felt that there would be a dissolution of the legislature before the termination of the spring session, given that it would be advisable that his successor take on this responsibility. With his pride injured by Laurier's tone, and with his health in decline, Joly replied to the federal secretary of state that he did not foresee an early dissolution, but "considering his [Laurier's] last letter I think due him to ask to be replaced at once."[114]

Newspapers on both sides of the political divide praised Joly's urbanity, kindness, accessibility, and devotion to the interests of British Columbia.[115] In sending regrets that he could not attend his farewell dinner, Joly's old political rival Sir Charles Hibbert Tupper wrote, "I do not know of any of His Majesty's representatives who has so generally earned the respect & admiration of all classes of the district over which he carries on the King's Government, as yourself."[116] The mayor of Victoria wrote later in the year, "I must tell without any disloyalty to our present Lieutenant Governor [James Dunsmuir] that at times you have been sadly missed, especially during the visit of His Excellency the Governor General when your natural aptitude and easy presence would have made matters go off much less stiffly and awkwardly for some of us."[117]

When Joly died two years later, in November 1908, the Vancouver *World* observed that "for some five years he and Lady Joly dispensed a gracious and elegant hospitality at the capital. He came, it will be remembered at a time of political turmoil, when steadiness of purpose, knowledge of constitutional usages and great tact were absolutely indispensable. It is the best tribute to the success of his term of office that its conclusion was anticipated with a regret which caused the expression of a widespread wish that he should be continued here."[118] There had even been discussion of plans to transfer some of the trees Joly had planted at Government House to an avenue or park to be named in his honour, but they failed to be implemented, apparently for the want of a parks board to take on the responsibility.[119] Some of Joly's trees can still be found at the lieutenant governor's official residence, however, and the property is bounded on one side by Lotbinière Avenue.

Conclusion

No Canadian ministry has ever been dismissed by a governor general, but lieutenant governors have unseated premiers on five occasions,

three of those being in British Columbia between 1898 and 1903. Joly's
dismissal of Prior and appointment of McBride marked the last time
such a step would be taken not only in British Columbia but also in any
Canadian province.[120] Clearly, the key to government stability was the
party system that had been late to develop on the west coast, where
fixation on railway construction meant that even at the federal level
candidates had been hesitant to oppose the governing party.[121]

Robert McDonald argues, nonetheless, that 1903 was not a major
turning point in the province's political history, as generally assumed,
because "the shared interests and commonly held goals of the settler
community were a more important part of British Columbia's political
culture than was partisan attachment to the newly established provincial Liberal and Conservative parties."[122] While it may be true that liberalism formed the "common sense" foundation of British Columbia's
political culture, as McDonald argues, the fact remains that the party-
based patronage system was fundamental to the emergence of the stat-
ist type of government that has long been characteristic of Canada.[123]
Given that British Columbia was highly dependent on a fluctuating re-
source-based economy and sharply fragmented by its physical geography, the party system of government that was instituted in 1903 would
provide large-scale railway, mining, and logging companies with the
means to exercise more control over the state through the cabinet than
did a system in which they had to purchase the support of individual
politicians.

Just as the absence of community bonds ensured that the application
of civil law was considered perfectly compatible with liberal values on
the pre-Confederation gold rush frontier,[124] so did proponents of those
values see no contradiction in imposing a party discipline that would
subordinate local community pressures and demands to government
stability. An added bonus from the liberal perspective was that the Socialists would lose their influence once McBride was able to consolidate
his position, a development that Joly anticipated with some eagerness.
He wrote in the fall of 1906, "I take too much interest in British Columbia to be indifferent to her future. Let her be ruled by a Liberal or a
Conservative Government, as may be decided by the majority, but do
not let her fall in the hands of the Socialists. Stand up against Socialism,
whatever you and your party may risk in doing so."[125]

McKay does not include the implementation of the party system as
one of his seven "arresting moments" in the development of the "Canadian Liberal Revolution," but party discipline is a central feature of

the executive dominance that characterizes both levels of government in Canada.[126] From this perspective, Joly's mission contributed to what McKay refers to as the "liberalization" of the west (moment number four) and to what he suggests is the dominant underlying theme in Canadian history – namely, "the extensive projection of liberal rule across a large territory" in a process whereby liberal assumptions, particularly the sanctity of individual property rights, were "intensified and normalized within the dominion's subjects."[127] But it should be recalled that, in contrast to the United States, Canada's provincial governments continue to hold most of the country's forest land, and that the banning of raw log exports represented a strict limitation on the activities of timber licence holders. A major weakness of the liberal order concept as a framework for the history of Canada is that it fails to acknowledge the persistence of a paternalistic ethos that may have generally favoured capitalist expansion but that could also accommodate an interventionist state in the interests of social stability and even economic growth.

As for Joly's role in British Columbia, the province's historians have written as if the party governance system simply emerged automatically in 1903 out of the political chaos of that era.[128] Furthermore, McDonald has criticized McKay's implicit assumption that liberalism "advanced outward from a small part of central Canada to the nation as a whole,"[129] but the fact remains that the introduction and early nurturance of the party system required the skills of an experienced and capable public figure who was close to the central seat of power rather than identified with any of the province's rival interest groups. And Joly's patrician status was clearly also helpful in a provincial capital where, as Cannadine notes, "a highly Anglophile and self-consciously stratified society" had developed, and during an era when the British dominions "were presided over by governors who were by occupation mimetic monarchs."[130] McKay's liberal order framework pays little attention to the fostering of loyalty to sovereign and country, but by projecting a dignified non-partisan image as Queen Victoria's local representative at a time when Britain was at war in South Africa, Joly contributed to the popular legitimization of the state on the West coast, not only at the provincial level but at the national and imperial ones as well. Somewhat paradoxically, then, Joly de Lotbinière's patrician background made him an ideal agent for the implementation of a less personal and paternalist (and therefore more liberal and efficient) political system, one that facilitated capitalist expansion during the era that McKay sees as the apex of the liberal project.[131]

Joly in Chinatown, by Rostap in the *Toronto Evening Telegram*, 23 June 1900.
A dapper Joly de Lotbinière, with his shining knighthood medal on his chest,
and racially stereotyped Chinese celebrants in Toronto's Chinatown. Note
the link between Joly's cigar and the exploding firecrackers at his feet, a clear
reference to the danger he is unknowingly flirting with. The occasion was
Joly's chaperoning of the Chinese viceroy, Li Hung-Chang, while he passed
through Canada, but this visit took place in 1896. That the cartoon appeared in
June 1900 means it could only have been a critical comment on
Joly's appointment as lieutenant governor of British Columbia.
McCord Museum, M2001X.6.43.8.143.

Lieutenant Governor Henri-Gustave and Margaretta (Lucy) Joly de Lotbinière with their two Chinese servants in Victoria. Domaine Joly de Lotbinière Collection.

The lieutenant governor of British Columbia about to enter the Legislature in 1900 with South African volunteers as a body guard. This photograph by John Wallace Jones is a good illustration of the formal events that helped to make Joly de Lotbinière a popular figure in Victoria. Note the boys in the lower right hand corner, as well as the dignitaries in the background. Library and Archives Canada, Mikan no. 3362081.

Henri Joly de Lotbinière. Painting by Sophie Pemberton in 1906, the last year of Joly de Lotbinière's term as lieutenant governor of British Columbia. Note the prominence of the two medals of the order of St Michael and St George in this rather sombre painting. The medal hanging from the ribbon was worn by Companions of the order, and the star on Joly's chest was for the higher rank of Knight Commander. Royal BC Museum, BC Archives, PDP02263.

Henri-Gustave Joly de Lotbinière at home in Lotbinière. Joly's early years were spent in Paris, and his public career took him to Quebec City, Ottawa, and Victoria, but his masculine identity as well as his social status was closely tied to his seigneury. Bibliothèque et Archives nationales du Québec, P351,S1, P3.

Conclusion

Following his death on November 16, 1908, Sir Henri-Gustave Joly de Lotbinière was buried in the Quebec City suburb of Sillery's Mount Hermon cemetery, overlooking the St Lawrence River. There was no state ceremony, and his grave is marked by a simple column on which the names of his wife and the children who predeceased him are also engraved. The inscription at the base of the column, as well as on the large wall plaque commemorating him in the Anglican Cathedral, reads "Blessed are the pure in heart."[1] In a similar vein, a contemporary article in *Saturday Night* – echoing Machiavelli's aphorism – suggested that Joly may not have been "a great man, but he certainly was a good man, and good in so many ways that he achieved more than is often achieved by greatness."[2] As a politician, Joly was somewhat of a throwback to Britain's Georgian era, when according to Matthew McCormack, "the business of governing was conducted by a class of gentlemen who supposedly possessed the financial means and manly virtues to suppress self-interest in favour of disinterested service."[3] The fact that Joly's public image was as close to sainthood as a politician could hope for reflects an assumption that only an independently wealthy patrician could rise above the pettiness and corruption characteristic of that occupation, and this gave Joly an advantage in the Victorian era, with its emphasis on manly "character,"[4] though it did frustrate his more venal Liberal colleagues. Joly also embodied the hope, to English Canadians in particular, that Confederation would not disintegrate along French–English or East–West lines, but the Riel crisis ended his provincial career, and he avoided debates about imperial federation and the Boer War instead of trying to convince French Canadians to support his imperialistic views.

Given his lack of "greatness," then, why was Joly de Lotbinière "worth a biography," as a colleague once asked me? My answer is that I was less interested in recounting Joly's accomplishments, noteworthy though they were, than in exploring his status both as a transitional figure whose cultural identity combined traditional conservative values with modern liberal ones and as a bicultural figure (by virtue of his mother tongue, his religion, and his marriage) in a country that has constantly faced challenges posed by its dual French-English composition. Furthermore, to echo historian Roderick Barman, I was interested in biography as "an entry way to understanding the structures – social, cultural, political, and economic – of the period in which [Joly] lived."[5] Biography must, of course, privilege human agency, and Joly had to be approached as an individual rather than simply as the product of larger social and cultural forces.[6] To state the obvious, the dominant masculinity that he embodied was of a very different kind than that of his adventurous and impetuous younger brother. But the Joly brothers did have quite different childhood experiences, and Henri-Gustave's years in Paris removed him somewhat from the domineering influence of his restless and demanding father. As Karl Marx wrote, "men make their own history, but they do not make it just as they please; they do not make it under circumstances chosen by themselves, but under circumstances directly encountered, given, and transmitted from the past."[7]

The seigneurial system may have been formally abolished in 1854, but transmitted from the past in places such as Lotbinière was a system of social inequality still based on title to the land itself. In building his reputation as an honourable and principled man, Joly was clearly playing the role of patrician, a way of life that Brian Young describes as "suggestive of honorifics and recognition of high social status, of substantial income from land, of the sustained exercise of civil authority, of leadership in a state church, of crown loyalty and … a sense of national identity permissive of inter-ethnic collaboration." Young adds that "family life would be characterized by patriarchy, estate life, high culture, and childrearing around classical education and male accession to the profession of law."[8] Joly did more than simply collect rents from his landed property, and two of his three sons became engineers rather than lawyers, but his social status certainly conforms to Young's description. Joly insisted that at least one of the parish churches within his seigneury reserve a pew for his family members, even though they were Protestants and this honour had been formally extinguished with the abolition of the seigneurial system. Joly was also quick to assume officer status in the militia, and by the 1880s he was president or vice president of several voluntary societies concerned with agriculture, as well as president of the Society for the Advancement of the Arts and Industry, vice president of the Royal Humane Society of British North America, and vice president of the American Forestry Congress.[9] Finally, honours such as honorary doctorates and a knighthood eventually came his way.[10]

But even though Joly was a social conservative who identified strongly with his mother's seigneurial heritage, he was also a lawyer and businessman strongly influenced by his entrepreneurial and cosmopolitan father's liberal values. He publicly supported Quebec's colonization movement, but he was more committed to agricultural reform, and as an outspoken forest conservationist, he promoted the scientific management of one of the nation's most valuable natural resources. In his role as federal minister of inland revenue, Joly grappled with how to commodify nature more efficiently by introducing standard measures. He also promoted Canadian tobacco production and raised state revenues by clamping down on smuggling and illicit distilling. Above all, as a good liberal Joly stood first and foremost for efficient and parsimonious government, a reflection of his rather cautious management of his own lumber business.

The "new" cultural approach to biography would argue that any attempt to reconcile the apparent contradictions in Joly's life is fruitless because, in the words of Jo Burr Margadant, "the subject of biography is no longer the coherent self but rather a self that is performed to create an impression of coherence or an individual with multiple selves whose different manifestations reflect the passage of time, the demands and options of different settings, or the various ways that others seek to represent that person."[11] As Lois W. Banner argues, however, such a stance "implies a denial of the probability that elements of personality developed in childhood can remain coherent over a lifetime, or that social and cultural modalities that influence personality development can encourage the production of a fixed core within an individual persona."[12] Despite Joly's inconsistencies, there is little evidence that he felt internally conflicted or that his worldview changed substantially over time. Joly may have become more conservative with age, as most people do, but he had never been a radical even in his youth, and he had presented the imperial tie as a defence against centralist forces as early as 1865 in his anti-Confederation pamphlet.

Indeed, the common thread throughout Joly's life and career was his patrician paternalism, beginning with his wife and children and

including the censitaires on his seigneury as well as the employees of
his federal ministry. This paternalism was tempered by a congenial and
conciliatory personality, as shown by his intimate relationship with his
family as well as his diplomatic approach to public life. Joly's sense of
paternalism also helps to explain his dedication to the concept of a collective interest, for Joly advocated strict limits on what he considered to
be the selfish and short-sighted activities of logging companies, as well
as attempting to make employers assume more responsibility for injured workers, opposing the private operation of mental health institutions, and accepting the necessity of state ownership and government
management of the QMOO Railway. In fact, as noted in this book's introduction, there are close parallels between Joly's ideas and the "patrician economic liberalism" of agricultural reformers Sir John Sinclair of
Scotland and John Young of Nova Scotia. According to Daniel Samson
these latter two men were "compelled by a sense of duty to their nation,
their class, and their manhood – much more so than by any faith in the
invisible hand of the market."[13]

Instead of attempting to fit Joly into either a conservative or a liberal
mould, or concluding that he was simply inconsistent ideologically, it
is more constructive to understand how he reconciled his social status
with his political affiliation. Joly's class background did not necessarily
prevent him from becoming a "radical" like his slightly older contemporary, Louis-Antoine Dessaulles, for Dessaulles was also a seigneur.
Dessaulles may have been close to Papineau, but so was the Joly family, and they even associated with Lamennais, who was a major intellectual influence on Dessaulles. In fact, the Saint-Hyacinthe seigneur's
radicalism was largely defined by his anti-clericalism,[14] and this was
a public stance not open to a Protestant with political ambitions in
French-speaking Quebec. But there is also the matter of personality,
for Dessaulles was a journalist and a provocateur by nature, whereas
Joly was a pragmatic social conservative. He certainly disagreed with
the Catholic Church's political interference and the degree to which it
controlled the province's schools system, but he also harboured romantic notions about peasant Catholicism, and he was a conciliator by nature, one who felt duty-bound to challenge religious bigotry in English
Canada.

In many respects, Joly's political ideology was closer to that of moderate Conservatives such as his arch-rival, Adolphe Chapleau. If, as his
biographer states, Chapleau supported gradual change based on tradition, the same was true of Joly, lending support to Jean-Paul Bernard's

claim that Confederation marked the passage to an era when "il n'y avait plus d'alternative idéologique véritable entre le parti libéral et le parti conservateur."[15] From this perspective it was only the intransigent opposition of the Catholic Church that kept the Liberals from power for most of the century. But why, then, did Joly remain a persistent obstacle to a Liberal alliance with Chapleau? He was not politically ambitious enough to be concerned about being cast in the shadow of the dynamic Conservative leader. Indeed, it was the patently ambitious Mercier who constantly flirted with a Bleu alliance.

As fellow *bon vivants*, Mercier and Chapleau were closer to being kindred souls to each other than either was to Joly, whom Laurier's biographer, H. Blair Neatby, rather unfairly dismissed as "rigid and austere."[16] According to Rumilly, "Dans le peuple, on disait toujours: monsieur Joly, par une sorte de déférence instinctive, alors qu'on se permettait bien de dire: Chapleau, ou même: Laurier."[17] Joly's early religious influences should be taken into account, for even though he was diplomatic, sociable, and far from closed-minded – sharing his father's inquiring attitude towards religion and science[18] – he clearly had not jettisoned the puritanical moral code instilled by his reformed Protestant relatives and his schooling in Paris. Contemporaries tended to attribute Joly's strict political standards to his status as a descendant of the old French-Canadian aristocracy, but his insistence on balancing the books and his distaste for the loose political morality of Tarte, Chapleau, Macdonald, and the Conservative Party in general closely paralleled that of George Brown and others of a Calvinist religious persuasion.

Kenneth Munro claims that Chapleau's "refusal to accommodate those who sought purity in politics led to his inability to dominate Quebec or to earn the respect of his English-speaking colleagues."[19] True as this may be, the fact remains that the Conservative politician's corrupt political practices did enable him to unseat Joly as premier, and it was the disapproval of Chapleau's French-speaking ultramontane allies – and not the disrespect of his English-speaking colleagues – that constituted his biggest obstacle in Quebec. In fact, Joly's career suggests that respect from colleagues, be they English-speaking or French-speaking, was not enough to ensure ultimate political success and that high ethical standards could be a major political handicap in Victorian Canada.

Joly's biculturalism was also a two-edged sword. His efforts at national reconciliation during the intensely divisive period between the hanging of Riel and the settlement of the Manitoba schools question earned him a knighthood, but his Protestant faith was a political handicap in

Quebec, and the ultramontane anti-imperialist Henri Bourassa would be the one remembered as the champion of Canadian biculturalism. Although Joly admitted that he did not have a firm idea of how Canada would evolve, and he refused to be drawn into predictions,[20] his persistent hope was that mutual respect between French and English, Catholics and Protestants, as well as adherence to British constitutional principles and a growing sense of Canadian patriotism, would ultimately result in a an economically prosperous and socially stable nation. Joly might today take some comfort in the fact that his hope for national prosperity and stability has been largely fulfilled, but the sad irony is that Canada is more culturally divided and less economically independent than ever, one of the results being that his efforts have been largely forgotten.

Monument to Henri-Gustave Joly de Lotbinière and members of his family
in the Mount Hermon Cemetery of Sillery, Quebec. Domaine Joly de
Lotbinière Collection.

Plaque commemorating Henri-Gustave Joly de Lotbinière and his wife Margaretta Joespha Gowen. Situated at the front of Quebec City's Anglican Cathedral, this plaque faces a stained glass window depicting the Nativity scene and also honouring the couple. Domaine Joly de Lotbinière Collection.

Notes

Preface

1 Geoff Eley, *A Crooked Line: From Cultural History to the History of Society* (Ann Arbor: University of Michigan Press, 2005), 168. On the reasons for the resurgence in biographical writing, see also David Nasaw, "Historians and Biography," *American Historical Review* 114, no. 3 (June 2009): 575–7.

2 See Giovanni Levi, "On Microhistory," in *New Perspectives on Historical Writing*, ed. Peter Burke (University Park: Pennsylvania State University Press, 1991), 96.

3 Jill Lepore, "Historians Who Love Too Much: Reflections on Microhistory and Biography," *Journal of American History* 88, no. 1 (June 2001): 131–2. Lepore also points out (138–41) that in contrast to biographers, microhistorians rarely identify with the main subject of their narratives.

4 Michael E. Gardiner, *Critiques of Everyday Life* (London and New York: Routledge, 2000), 4.

5 Alice Kessler-Harris, "Why Biography?," *American Historical Review* 114, no. 3 (June 2009): 626.

6 On this theme, see Nasaw, "Historians and Biography," 573–5.

7 The fragment theorists simply dismissed French Canada as a pre-Enlightenment Catholic society. See Gad Horowitz, "Conservatism, Liberalism and Socialism in Canada: An Interpretation," *Canadian Journal of Economics and Political Science* 32, no. 2 (May 1965): 143–71, esp. 155, 158–9, 162.

8 The original records are in the Quebec City branch of the Bibliothèque et Archives nationales du Québec, where they have been organized into a number of categories. For reasons of convenience, my research was based largely on the microfilm collection of the same records organized chronologically

that is held by the Library and Archives of Canada (M785–98). The Joly de Lotbinière records include the papers of his parents as well as his brother and grandson.

Introduction

1 Joly's health was too frail to allow him to be involved in the celebration, but he did express apprehensions about it, perhaps because of the way Champlain was overshadowed by the Battle of the Plains of Abraham. Library and Archives Canada [hereafter LAC], MG 27 II C2, R6211-0-4-F, Fonds Henri-Gustave Joly de Lotbinière, Henri-Gustave Joly de Lotbinière, Correspondance, 1863–1908, M795, 8356, Lord Grey to E. G. Joly de Lotbinière, Ottawa, 4 Aug. 1908; H. V. Nelles, *The Art of Nation-Building: Pageantry and Spectacle at Quebec's Tercentenary* (Toronto: University of Toronto Press, 1999).

2 *Daily Telegraph*, 6 Jan. 1908, in LAC, Alain Joly de Lotbinière Papers [hereafter AJL Papers], M797, part 2, 158.

3 John Hamilton to editor, Que., 3 Jan. 1908, in AJL Papers, M797, part 2, 160. See also the *Telegraph* news clipping in ibid., 161.

4 Unidentified news clipping, 4 Jan. 1908, in AJL Papers, M797, part 2, 159.

5 Nor does Hamelin include Joly's voluminous confidential correspondence in his bibliography. Marcel Hamelin, *Les Premières années du parlementarisme québécois (1867–1878)* (Quebec: Les Presses de l'Université Laval, 1974), 1, 5. There is one short booklet on Joly, relying largely on the *Dictionary of Canadian Biography* for its source material. Jacques Lamarche, *Sir H.-G. Joly de Lotbinière* (Montreal: Lidec, 1997). There are also two very useful master's theses: Pierre Trépanier, "L'Administration Joly (1878–1879)" (MA thesis, University of Ottawa, 1972); and Marc Gadoury, "Sir Henri Gustave Joly de Lotbinière: Visionnaire et promoteur de la conservation des forêts, au Québec, à la fin du XIXe siècle" (MA thesis, Laval University, 1998).

6 Yvan Lamonde, *Histoire sociale des idées au Québec, 1760–1896*, vol. 1 (n.p.: Fides, 2000).

7 Jocelyn Letourneau, *A History for the Future: Rewriting Memory and Identity in Quebec* (Montreal: McGill-Queen's University Press, 2004).

8 One exception, though he is a political scientist, is Daniel Salée. See his "Seigneurial Landownership and the Transition to Capitalism in Nineteenth-Century Quebec," *Quebec Studies* 12 (1991): 21–32.

9 Fernande Roy, *Progrès, Harmonie, Liberté: Le libéralisme des milieux d'affaires francophones à Montréal au tournant du siècle* (Montreal: Boréal, 1988), 49–53.

10 Hamelin, *Les Premières années*, 341–3.

11 Éric Bédard, *Les Réformistes: Une génération canadienne-française au milieu du XIXe siècle* (Montreal: Boréal, 2009), 11–27, 81–127, 212–14. On the distinction between civic and ethnic nationalism, see Michel Ducharme, "Penser le Canada: La mise en place des assises intellectuelles de l'État canadien moderne (1838–1840)," *Revue d'histoire de l'Amérique française* 56, no. 3 (Winter 2003): 364–7.

12 See Christian Morissonneau, "La colonisation équivoque," *Recherches sociographiques* 19 (Jan.-Apr. 1978): 33–43; Gabriel Dussault, *Le Curé Labelle: Messianisme, utopie, et colonisation au Québec, 1850–1900* (Montreal: Hurtubise, 1983); and Bernard Proulx, *Le roman du territoire* (Montreal: Université du Québec à Montréal, 1987).

13 Brian Young, *The Politics of Codification: The Lower Canadian Civil Code of 1866* (Montreal: McGill-Queen's University Press, 1994), 117–20, 178, 180; Bruce Curtis, *The Politics of Population: State Formation, Statistics, and the Census of Canada, 1840–1875* (Toronto: University of Toronto Press, 2001), chap. 8.

14 The more committed colonization proponents demanded more rights for the colonists as opposed to the lumber companies that held vast Crown timber leases, but they failed to challenge the principle of those leases or to support the ownership of the timber lands by the colonists, as in Finland and Sweden. See J. I. Little, *Nationalism, Capitalism, and Colonization in Nineteenth-Century Quebec: The Upper St. Francis District* (Montreal: McGill-Queens University Press, 1989), 8–14.

15 Arno J. Mayer, *The Persistence of the Old Regime: Europe to the Great War* (New York: Pantheon Books, 1981); Eugen Weber, *Peasants into Frenchmen: The Modernization of Rural France, 1870–1914* (Stanford, CA: Stanford University Press, 1976). Robert Forster has modified Weber's and Mayer's thesis by arguing that a post-revolutionary elite of *capacités* governed France after 1800, one that represented an amalgam of Ancien Régime nobles and new men of substance whose wealth was drawn from a combination of land ownership, business, and office holding. Robert Forster, "The French Revolution and the 'New' Elite, 1800–1850," in *The American and European Revolutions, 1776–1848* (Iowa City: University of Iowa Press, 1980), ed. Jaroslow Pelenski, 182–207.

16 Alfred Dubuc, "Problems in the Stratification of the Canadian Society from 1760 to 1840," Canadian Historical Association, *Annual Report* (1965), 19–20; Fernand Ouellet, "Le régime seigneuriale," in *Éléments d'histoire sociale du Bas-Canada* (Montreal: Hurtubise HMH, 1972), 101.

17 Benoît Grenier, *Brève histoire du régime seigneuriale* (Montreal: Boréal, 2012), 154.

18 He also mentions the Fleurys de la Gorgendières, Juchereau-Duschenays, Panets, Dionnes, and Carons, as well as the de Lotbinières. Salée, "Seigneurial Landownership," 30.

19 Brian Young, "Patrician Elites and Power in Nineteenth-Century Montreal and Quebec City," in *Who Ran the Cities? City Elites and Urban Power Structures in Europe and North America, 1750–1940*, ed. Ralf Roth and Robert Beachy (Burlington, VT: Ashgate, 2007), 234–5, 237, 245.

20 Cameron Nish, *Les Bourgeois-gentilshommes de la Nouvelle-France, 1729–1748* (Montreal: Fides, 1968). Joly recommended this play to his daughter in 1895. BAnQ, P1000, S3, D1040, Correspondance d'Éthel Joly de Lotbinière, 1894–5, Henri-Gustave Joly de Lotbinière to Ethel, Que., 15 Jan. 1895.

21 Brian Young, "Revisiting Feudal Vestiges in Urban Quebec," in *Transatlantic Subjects: Ideas, Institutions, and Social Experience in Post-Revolutionary British North America*, ed. Nancy Christie, ed. (Montreal: McGill-Queen's University Press, 2008).

22 Quoted in translation in Héléne Leclerc, *Domaine Joly-De Lotbinière* (Montreal: Fides, 2002), 19. The full description was reprinted in L.-O. David, *Les gerbes canadiennes* (Montreal: Librairie Beauchemin, 1921), 99–103.

23 Bédard, *Les Réformistes*, 25.

24 Patrice Dutil, *Devil's Advocate: Godfroy Langlois and the Politics of Liberal Progressivism in Laurier's Quebec* (Montreal: Robert Davies, 1994), 20–1.

25 Giorgi Chittolini, "The 'Private,' the 'Public,' and the State," in "The Origins of the State in Italy, 1300–1600," supplement, *Journal of Modern History* 67 (Dec. 1995): S35–6.

26 Brian Young, *George-Étienne Cartier: Montreal Bourgeois* (Montreal: McGill-Queen's University Press, 1981).

27 Chittolini, "The 'Private,'" S38.

28 Richard Bushman, *The Refinement of America: Persons, Houses, Cities* (New York: Knopf, 1992), xvi–xix.

29 See, for example, Félix Torres, "Du champ des Annales à la biographie: Réflexions sur le retour d'un genre," *Problèmes et méthodes de la biographie* (Paris: Actes du colloque, Sorbonne, 3–4 May 1985), 146–7; and Yvan Lamonde, *Louis-Antoine Dessaulles: Un seigneur libérale et anticléricale* (n.p.: Éditions Fides, 1994), 295–304.

30 McKay's definition of liberalism is essentially the same as Roy's. Ian McKay, "The Liberal Order Framework: A Prospectus for a Reconnaissance of Canadian History," *Canadian Historical Review* 81, no. 4 (2000): 617–45.

31 On Bond Head's paternalism, see Sean Cadigan, "Paternalism and Politics: Sir Francis Bond Head, the Orange Order, and the Election of 1836," *Canadian Historical Review* 72, no. 3 (1991): 320–2; Russell C. Smandych, "Tory Paternalism and the Politics of Penal Reform in Upper Canada, 1830–34: A 'Neo-revisionist' Account of the Kingston Penitentiary," *Criminal Justice History* 12 (1991): 57–84; and Theodore Binnema and Kevin Hutchings, "The Emigrant and the Noble Savage: Sir Francis Bond Head's Romantic Approach to Aboriginal Policy in Upper Canada, 1836–1838," *Journal of Canadian Studies* 39, no. 1 (Winter 2005): 115–38.

32 Daniel Samson, "'The Yoke of Improvement': Sir John Sinclair, John Young, and the Improvement of the Scotlands, New and Old," in *Transatlantic Rebels: Agrarian Radicalism in Comparative Context*, ed. Thomas Summerhill and James C. Scott (East Lansing: Michigan State University Press, 2004), 109–10. According to Jerry Bannister, Canada developed as a separate state rather than being absorbed by the United States because of its strong sense of loyalty to Britain, a loyalty that entailed not only anti-Americanism but also British "conceptions of social order and monarchism." Bannister, "Canada as Counter-Revolution: The Loyalist Order Framework in Canadian History, 1750–1840," in *Liberalism and Hegemony: Debating the Canadian Liberal Revolution*, ed. Jean-François Constant and Michel Ducharme (Toronto: University of Toronto Press, 2009), 99, 104.

33 Heaman notes that when 'conservatives talked of rights, they didn't talk of abstract and universal human rights,' but of 'collective, social, or historical rights.' E.A. Heaman, 'Rights Talk and the Liberal Order Framework,' in *Liberalism and Hegemony*, 155, 162–3.

34 Critics of this definition argue that it overlooks the fact that nineteenth-century liberals such as John Stuart Mill attempted to find a balance between individual liberties and the public good. McKay, in turn, stresses how narrow this "public" was in the eyes of liberals such as Mill, but the fact remains that it transcended the acquisitive individual. Michel Ducharme and Jean-François Constant, "Introduction: A Project of Rule Called Canada – the Liberal Order Framework and Historical Practice," in *Liberalism and Hegemony*, ed. Constant and Ducharme, 8–9; Ian McKay, "Canada as a Long Liberal Revolution: On Writing the History of Actually Existing Canadian Liberalism, 1840s–1940s," in *Liberalism and Hegemony*, ed. Constant and Ducharme, 387–8.

35 Cadigan, "Paternalism and Politics," 320–2.

36 See S. J. R. Noel, *Patrons, Clients, Brokers: Ontario Society and Politics, 1791–1896* (Toronto: University of Toronto Press, 1990).

37 At a corporate level, paternalism survived well into the twentieth century under the guise of welfare capitalism, also known as corporate welfarism. See Margaret McCallum, "Corporate Welfarism in Canada, 1919–39," *Canadian Historical Review* 71, no. 1 (1990): 46–79; and Joan Sangster, "The Softball Solution: Female Workers, Male Managers and the Operation of Paternalism at Westclox, 1923–60," *Labour / Le Travail* 32 (Fall 1993): 167–99.

1. Blood and Soil

1 Library and Archives Canada [hereafter LAC], Fonds Henri-Gustave Joly de Lotbinière [hereafter HGJ Papers], M796, 9556, Canada passport.
2 Charles Langelier, *Souvenirs politiques de 1878 à 1890* (Quebec: Dussault and Proulx, 1909) (CIHM no. 74077), 69.
3 Robert Rumilly, *Histoire de Québec*, vol. 1, *Georges-Étienne Cartier* (Montreal: Éditions Bernard Valiquette, 1942), 189.
4 HGJ Papers, M796, 9534, Diplôme de Bachelier ès Lettres, Université de France; 9536, bar examination certificate; 9559, Queen's Counsel certificate, 29 Mar. 1878.
5 See Louise Dechêne, *Habitants et marchands de Montréal au XVIIe siècle* (Paris: Plon, 1974); and Allan Greer, *Peasant, Lord, and Merchant: Rural Society in Three Quebec Parishes, 1740–1840* (Toronto: University of Toronto Press, 1985).
6 See Lorraine Gadoury, *La noblesse de Nouvelle-France: Familles et alliances* (Ville La Salle, QC: Éditions Hurtubise HMH, 1991); and François-Joseph Ruggiu, "La noblesse du Canada aux XVIIe et XVIIIe siècles," *Histoire, Économie, et Société* 4 (2008): 67–85.
7 The Chartiers were ennobled in the early fifteenth century and added the name de Lotbinière in the following century. Hélène Leclerc, *Domaine Joly-De Lotbinière* (Quebec City: Éditions Fides, 2002), 13.
8 André Vachon, "Chartier de Lotbinière, Louis-Théandre," *Dictionary of Canadian Biography Online*.
9 Abbé Louis L. Paradis, *Les Annales de Lotbinière, 1672–1933* (Quebec: L'Action Catholique, 1933), 13–14; André Vachon, "Chartier de Lotbinière, René-Louis," *Dictionary of Canadian Biography Online*.
10 For details, see Andrée Héroux, "Une région, ses paysages et ses ressources," in *Histoire de Lévis-Lotbinière*, ed. Roch Samson et al. (Sainte-Foy: Les Presses de l'Université Laval, 1996), chap. 1.
11 Paradis, *Les Annales*, 7–12, 15; Vachon, "Chartier de Lotbinière, René-Louis"; LAC, Alain Joly de Lotbinière Papers [hereafter AJL papers], M797, part 2, 17.

12 Paradis, *Les Annales*, 16–17; Andrée Héroux, "Le peuplement et la population," in *Histoire de Lévis-Lotbinière*, ed. Samson et al., 86, 92.

13 Paradis, *Les Annales*, 31–46; Armand Gagné, "Chartier de Lotbinière, Eustache," *Dictionary of Canadian Biography Online*.

14 Confusingly enough, the word *domaine* also applied to all the land on a seigneury that had not been granted, but for the purposes of this study, it will refer only to the land that the seigneur was not obliged to grant upon application by a would-be settler. Richard Colebrook Harris, *The Seigneurial System in Early Canada* (Montreal: McGill-Queen's University Press, 1984), ix, 81–7; Benoît Grenier, *Brève histoire du régime seigneurial* (Montreal: Boréal, 2012), 130–1.

15 Paradis, *Les Annales*, 47–52, 54, 59–68, 74–84; Gagné, "Chartier de Lotbinière, Eustache."

16 Paradis, *Les Annales*, 84, 93–108; F. J. Thorpe and Sylvette Nicolini-Maschino, "Chartier de Lotbinière, Michel, Marquis de Lotbinière," *Dictionary of Canadian Biography Online*.

17 The banquet took place in 1878. The passage was translated by Charles Langelier in his *Souvenirs politiques*, 67–8. As a British officer, Strange very likely would have used the word "vous" rather than "nous" in referring to the French victory.

18 Paradis, *Les Annales*, 119, 135.

19 Members of the Canadian nobility were not recognized as equals by their French peers. Gadoury, *La noblesse de Nouvelle-France*, 52.

20 Paradis, *Les Annales*, 156–8, 172–3; Thorpe and Nicolini-Maschino, "Chartier de Lotbinière, Michel"; information provided by Mylène Richard and Hélène Leclerc.

21 For the parallel with other members of the Canadian nobility, see Colin M. Coates, "French Canadians' Ambivalence to the Empire," in *Canada and the British Empire*, ed. Phillip Buckner (Oxford: Oxford University Press, 2008), 187; and Grenier, *Brève histoire*, 142–4.

22 Paradis, *Les Annales*, 154–5; Marcel Hamelin, "Chartier de Lotbinière, Michel-Eustache-Gaspard-Alain," *Dictionary of Canadian Biography Online*.

23 De Lotbinière commanded the First Battalion Vaudreuil and the Second Battalion Rivière du Chêne of the Vaudreuil Division. Paradis, *Les Annales*, 170–1, 186, 193; L. Homfray Irving, *Officers of the British Forces in Canada during the War of 1812–15* (Wellington, ON: Wellington Tribune Print for the Canadian Military Institute, 1908), 174–5. Legault is clearly mistaken in stating that de Lotbinière's capture by the Americans in 1775 was the last military adventure of his life. Roch Legault, *Une élite en déroute: Les militaires canadiens après la Conquête* (Outremont, QC: Athéna éditions,

2002), 144. On de Lotbinière's role as justice of the peace, see Donald Fyson, *Magistrates, Police, and People: Everyday Criminal Justice in Quebec and Lower Canada, 1764–1837* (Toronto: University of Toronto Press, 2006), 95–7, 105–6.

24 Robert Larin and Yves Drolet, "Les listes de Carleton et de Haldimand. États de la noblesse canadienne en 1767 et 1778," *Histoire sociale / Social History* 41, no. 82 (Nov. 2008): 566–7, 574, 575, 577–9.

25 HGJ Papers, M794, 6078–9, A. C. de Lery Macdonald to HGJ, Montreal, 9 July 1895.

26 Paradis, *Les Annales*, 185–6; Hamelin, "Chartier de Lotbinière, Michel-Eustache-Gaspard-Alain."

27 Fyson, *Magistrates, Police, and People*, 97.

28 One of these three daughters died before de Lotbinière himself, and Julie-Christine was born after this will was drafted. Given that an infant son had also died, she had only two sisters to share the inheritance with. LAC, Fonds Julie-Christine Chartier de Lotbinière [hereafter JCCL Papers], M785, Last will and testament of G.A. Chartier de Lotbinière, 6, 11–13, 16; information provided by Mylène Richard Hélène Leclerc.

29 Paradis, *Les Annales*, 164–5.

30 Paradis, *Les Annales*, 199; Diane Saint-Pierre, "Société, institutions et culture," in *Histoire de Lévis-Lotbinière*, ed. Samson et al., 231.

31 De Lotbinière reported to the surveyor general in 1814 that 580 lots had been granted and that the population had reached 3,400 souls, but the local historian has revealed that this was an exaggeration. Paradis, *Les Annales*, 171, 184–5, 190, 195, 199, 236.

32 Paradis, *Les Annales*, 195–8, 213.

33 JCCL Papers, M785, 38, Dettes de la succession, 1828; 83–6, Partage entre les héritiers de Chartier de Lotbinière, 17 Jan. 1829.

34 On the marriage of sister Marie-Louise-Josephte to Robert Unwood Harwood, see Bettina Bradbury, *Wife to Widow: Lives, Laws, and Politics in Nineteenth-Century Montreal* (Vancouver: UBC Press, 2011), 37, 39, 71, 144–5.

35 Georges Aubin, *Papineau en exil à Paris tome 1, Dictionnaire* (Trois-Pistoles, QC: Éditions Trois-Pistoles, 2007), 142.

36 HGJ Papers, M792, 3852–3, Thos Workman to HGJ, Montreal, 28 Oct. 1887. The marriage took place in the Episcopal Christ Church of Montreal. PGJ Papers, M785, 124–8, 153–4, Marriage contract, 16 Dec. 1828, extract 17 Dec. 1858.

37 LAC, Pierre-Gustave Joly Papers [hereafter PGJ Papers], M785, 122, Nap. de Montebello to Joly, Boston, Oct. 1828.

38 Marcel Hamelin, "Joly de Lotbinière, Sir Henri-Gustave," *Dictionary of*
    Canadian Biography Online; Paradis, *Les Annales*, 255–6; Aubin, *Papineau*
    en exil, tome 1, 139; Pierre-Gustave Joly de Lotbinière, *Voyage en Orient*
    (1839–40): Journal d'un voyageur curieux du monde et d'un pionnier de la
    daguerréotypie, introd. Jacques Desautels, ed. Georges Aubin and Renée
    Blanchet (Ste Foy, QC: Les Presses de l'Université Laval, 2010), 15n18.

39 PGJ Papers, M785, 124–6, Marriage contract, 15 Dec. 1828. On the implica-
    tions of the various contractual arrangements, see Bradbury, *Wife to Widow*,
    chap. 2.

40 On the *lods et ventes* in one seigneury, see Louis Lavallée, *La Prairie en*
    Nouvelle-France, 1647–1760 (Montreal: McGill-Queen's University Press,
    1992), 95.

41 JCCL Papers, M785, 74–95, Partage entre les héritiers de Chartier de
    Lotbinière, 17 Jan. 1829. Alain Chartier de Lotbinière had planned in 1821
    to pass this seigneury on to his eldest daughter, Louise-Josephte. Grenier,
    Brève histoire, 128.

42 Joseph Bouchette, *A Topographical Dictionary of the Province of Lower Canada*
    (London: Longman, Rees, Orme, Brown, Green, and Longman, 1832),
    Lotbinière, seigniory.

43 Roch Samson, "Cuirs, farines, madriers et navires: L'activité préindustri-
    elle et commerciale," in *Histoire de Lévis-Lotbinière*, ed. Samson et al., 179.

44 PGJ Papers, M785, 583–4, survey report by Joseph Hamel and James
    McPhee, 22 Feb. 1836.

45 PGJ Papers, M785, 126, Marriage contract, 15 Dec. 1828; 287–92, Transfer
    of administration and management from Joseph Papineau, n.p., 18 Sept.
    1830; 308–10, Procuration for P. G. Joly by J. C. Chartier de Lotbinière,
    8 Oct. 1830. Few of the widows who inherited seigneuries during the
    French regime assumed active management, particularly after one of their
    sons grew old enough to take over. See Benoît Grenier, "Réflexion sur le
    pouvoir féminin au Canada sous le Régime français: Le cas de la 'seigneur-
    esse' Marie-Catherine Peuvret (1667–1739)," *Revue d'histoire de l'Amérique*
    française 42, no. 84 (Nov. 2009): 299–326.

46 Paradis, *Les Annales*, 256–7.

47 PGJ Papers, M785, 166–7, procuration by Joseph Papineau in favour of
    Lt Col. Fehr de Brunner, 18 Sept. 1829; 629–30, Lt Col. Fehr de Brunner
    to P. G. Joly, Lotbinière, 5 June 1836; M786, 1076–9, Missa Fehr to Pierre-
    Gustave Joly, 29 Oct. 1843. For the Joly–Fehr genannt Brunner genealogy,
    see AJL Papers, M797, part 2, 251.

48 PGJ Papers, M785, 35, Tableau de la superficie des terres concédées dans la
    seigneurie de Lotbinière, 1828; Gilles Boileau, "La paroisse de Lotbinière

lance un cri de détresse," *Histoire Québec* 9, no. 2 (Nov. 2003): 41–4; Andrée Héroux, "La mise en valeur des terroirs," in *Histoire de Lévis-Lotbinière*, ed. Samson et al., 134.

49 PGJ Papers, M785, 171–2, Seigneurial agent's journal, 27 Sept. 1829. On the payment of rents and the accumulation of arrears in La Prairie, see Lavallée, *La Prairie en Nouvelle-France*, 98–101.

50 PGJ Papers, M785, Seigneurial agent's journal, 176, 25 Oct. 1829; 199, 2 June 1830; 176, 25 Oct. 1829; 235, 16 Oct. 1830, 18 Oct. 1830; 241, 5, 7, and 8 March 1831; Héroux, "La mise en valeur," 134–7. As with La Prairie during the French regime, it was difficult to find competent millers for Lotbinière. Lavallée, *La Prairie en Nouvelle France*, 88–93. See also Grenier, *Brève histoire*, 133–5.

51 Those who cut firewood were charged 20 sols per cord, and those who cut lumber either had it seized or were charged. JCCL Papers, M785, Seigneurial agent's journal, 186–9, 3 Jan. 1830, 6 Jan. 1830, 7 Jan. 1830; 192, 15–18 Feb. 1830; 199, 30 May 1830. On the local fishery, see Martine Côté, "Les ressources fluviales et forestière," in *Histoire de Lévis-Lotbinière*, ed. Samson et al., 146–52. On the seigneurs' *droit de pêche*, see Grenier, *Brève histoire*, 91.

52 PGJ Papers, M785, 314–31, Procès-verbal of survey lines between seigneuries of Lotbinière and St-Jean Deschaillons, 1831–2; 410–13, contract between Andrew and John Ritchie of St Jean Chrysostôme and G. P. G. Joly to construct a sawmill, 17 Dec. 1832; 500–3, contract between Alexander Hall and G. P. G. Joly to build a sawmill, 12 Oct. 1834; Leclerc, *Domaine Joly-De Lotbinière*, 14; Héroux, "Le peuplement," 119; Samson, "Cuirs, farines, madriers et navires," 182–3, 187. The mills were about two and a half miles apart. PGJ Papers, M785, 583–4, survey report by Joseph Hamel and James McPhee, 22 Feb. 1836.

53 The failure of at least one farmer to fulfil his contract resulted in the penalty of £4 in 1842. PGJ Papers, M786, 958–9, Obligation résultat de contrat re billots – N. Filteau, 16 Apr. 1842. A similar system developed in the seigneury of Saint-Hyacinthe after 1820, except that it was Quebec lumber merchants who were in charge of logging operations. Christian Dessureault, 'Industrie et société rurale: le cas de la seigneurie Saint-Hyacinthe des origines à 1861,' *Histoire sociale / Social History* 28 (May 1995): 111.

54 The evolution toward subcontracting in the St Maurice watershed in the later nineteenth century resulted in a significant reduction in the size of the crews from an average of 18 working in only sixty *chantiers* in 1860–1 to 5.7 working in many more camps in 1914–15. René Hardy and Normand Séguin, *Forêt et société en Mauricie* (Montreal: Boréal Express, 1984), 91–5. For a good description of how logging crews functioned, see also Richard

Rajala, "The Forest Industry of Eastern Canada: An Overview," accompanying essay to C. S. Silversides, *Broadaxe to Flying Shear: The Mechanization of Forest Harvesting East of the Rockies* (Ottawa: National Museum of Science and Technology, 1997), 128–30.

55 PGJ Papers, M786, 990, Note de Joseph Filteau, n.p., sur entrepreneurs de billots, 1843–4.

56 PGJ Papers, M786, 1491, instructions to Louis Maguenat, 28 July 1847. The annual cut was between 10,000 and 30,000 logs between 1835 and 1850. Côté, "Les ressources," 161–2.

57 The contractors would be paid from £3.10s to £4.4s per 100 twelve-foot logs, depending on diameter. PGJ Papers, M785, 504–11, contract notarized by J. Filteau, 12 Oct. 1834; M786, 1569–74, contract notarized by Mtre. Filteau, Lotbinière, 4 Nov. 1848; 1589–96, contract notarized by Mtre. Filteau, Lotbinière, 24 Nov. 1849. The 1849 contract with forty-two Lotbinière parish farmers and one outsider stipulated the delivery of 9,100 pine and white spruce logs.

58 PGJ Papers, M786, 1490, instructions to Louis Maguenat, seigneurial agent, 28 July 1847.

59 See Benoît Gauthier, "La sous-traitance et l'exploitation forestière en Mauricie (1850–1875)," *Material History Bulletin* 13 (Autumn 1981): 59–67.

60 Serge Courville and Normand Séguin, *Le coût du sol au Québec: Deux études de géographie historique* (Sainte-Foy: Les Presses de l'Université Laval, 1996), 73.

61 Courville and Séguin, *Le coût du sol*, 27. See their p. 13, note 3 for currency conversion ratios.

62 See Lavallée, *La Prairie en Nouvelle-France*, 101.

63 This tax did not apply to land passed on from one generation to the next, but it was sometimes applied to sales of inheritance rights between heirs and even to *donations entre vifs*, namely the transmission of the patrimony to an heir while the parents were still alive. Grenier, *Brève histoire*, 81.

64 Paradis, *Les Annales*, 199–200, 281–2. Gabriel Christie reserved the right to construct mills of any kind on his upper Richelieu seigneuries, and a similar restriction appeared in the Beauharnois contracts after the turn of the nineteenth century, as did the mortmain restriction. Greer claims that even though seigneurs in the lower Richelieu occasionally granted exemptions to build mills, "the increasingly extensive conception of monopolies and reserves set out in concession deeds, tended to discourage quite effectively any impulse habitants may have had to found industrial enterprises on their 'own' land." André Larose, "La seigneurie de Beauharnois, 1729–1867: Les seigneurs, l'espace et l'argent" (PhD dissertation, University of

Ottawa, 1987), 395–8, 402–3; Françoise Noël, 'La gestion des seigneuries de
Gabriel Christie dans la vallée du Richelieu (1760–1845),' *Revue d'histoire
de l'Amérique française* 40, no. 4 (1987): 577, 579; Greer, *Peasant, Lord, and
Merchant*, 133.

65 The same clause appeared in the contracts for île-Jésus. Grenier, *Brève
histoire*, 174–5.

66 Grenier, *Brève histoire*, 76.

67 Essentially the same restrictions applied to Beauharnois and the Jesuit-
owned seigneuries of Saint-Gabriel and Notre-Dame-des-Anges, except
that censitaires were not allowed to cut wood on their own land for
commercial purposes, even after establishing residency and completing
improvements. Larose, "La seigneurie de Beauharnois," 406–8; Grenier,
Brève histoire, 93. Similarly, censitaires on the seigneury of Saint-Hyacinthe
were not allowed to cut pine, except for their own use, and those on the
Christie seigneuries were forbidden from cutting oak or pine, as well as
transporting logs outside the seigneury. Dessureault, 'Industrie et société
rurale,' 111; Noël, 'La gestion des seigneuries,' 577.

68 PGJ Papers, M785, 264–6, Formal land grant contract printed 1830. For the
later contract, see HGJ Papers, M786, 1809–17, document notarized by Er-
rol Boyd Lindsay, n.p., Que., 8 Mar. 1853.

69 Serge Courville, *Quebec: A Historical Geography*, trans. Richard Howard
(Vancouver: UBC Press, 2008), 133–4.

70 Serge Courville, "Tradition or Modernity? The Canadian Seigniory in the
Durham Era," in *Proceedings of the Seventeenth Meeting of the French Colonial
Historical Society, Chicago, May 1991*, ed. Patricia Galloway, 49–50.

71 Bouchette, *Topographical Dictionary*, Lotbinière, seigniory.

72 Paradis, *Les Annales*, 223–4, 256–7. Failure to "tenir feu et lieu" (establish
residency) on the grant within a year would also result in automatic forfeiture, and the land had to be improved without delay.

73 *Le Canadien*, 5 Dec. 1832. On censitaire petitions elsewhere during this era,
see Grenier, *Brève histoire*, 198.

74 The agent's report for the week ending May 26 stated that "a few Scotch
families have gone thither this week." *British Parliamentary Papers, Emigration*, vol. 19 (Shannon, Ireland: Irish University Press, 1969), 197, extracts
from the weekly report made to the Governor-in-Chief by the Chief Agent
for Emigrants at Quebec.

75 On such grievances in general, see Grenier, *Brève histoire*, 169, 173–84.

76 *Le Canadien*, 5 Dec. 1832.

77 The government charged 5 percent of the value, or £432.3.7, for the
commutation. PGJ Papers, M785, 419–22, J. H. Kerr to P. G. Joly, Que., 8

June 1833; 427–8, J. H. Kerr to P. G. Joly, Que., 14 July 1833; 517–18, bill
from J. H. Kerr, 1835; 531–2, petition to Her Majesty for commutation of
Augmentation of Lotbinière, 18 Aug. 1835; 552, news clipping; 553–5, J.
Walcott, civil secretary, to Gustave Joly, Que., 26 Nov. 1835, M786, 1227,
Jos. Bouchette to G. Joly, Montreal, 21 Apr. 1845. Prior to 1840, only nine
seigneurs took advantage of the 1825 legislation providing for commutation. Grenier, *Brève histoire*, 199.

78 *Appendices to the Journals of the Legislative Assembly of Lower Canada* 42
  (1832–3), Appendix Nn.

79 An analysis of notarial contracts uncovered no more than that number for
  the entire decade. Héroux, "Le peuplement," 111.

80 *Appendices to the Journals of the Legislative Assembly of Lower Canada* 42
  (1832–3), Appendix Nn; *Le Canadien*, 5 Dec. 1832.

81 PGJ Papers, M785, 589–602, arrérages des habitants – réglés, 22 Apr. 1836.

82 PGJ Papers, M785, 618–24, procuration de Julie Chartier de Lotbinière à
  Gaspard P. G. Joly, 7 May 1836.

83 PGJ Papers, M785, 574, P. G. Joly to Antoine Joly, Que. 22 Feb. 1836; 625–8,
  3 June 1836, vente de meubles sur la ferme Joly. The quote is from Joly de
  Lotbinière, *Voyage en Orient*, 16.

84 Georges Aubin and Renée Blanchet, eds., *Louis-Joseph Papineau: Lettres à
  Julie* (Sillery, QC: Septentrion, 2000), 458; PGJ Papers, M785, 465–7, John
  Neilson to P. G. Joly (1834).

85 Aubin, *Papineau en exile, tome 1*, 137, 139–40; Aubin and Blanchet, *Louis-
  Joseph Papineau: Lettres à Julie*, 445, 455, 498, 551–2; Renée Blanchet, ed.,
  Julie B. Papineau, une femme patriote: Correspondance, 1823–1862 (Sillery, QC:
  Septentrion, 1997), 232, 241, 243, 245, 246, 254; and numerous references
  in Lactance Papineau, *Journal d'un étudiant en médecine à Paris*, ed. Georges
  Aubin and Renée Blanchet (Montreal: Les Éditions Varia, 2003). For
  references to the Jolys' emotional support of the Papineaus in Paris, see
  Blanchet, *Julie B. Papineau*, 279; Amédée Papineau, *Journal d'un fils de la lib-
  erté, 1838–1855* (Sillery, QC: Septentrion, 1998), 544, 545, 558, 564; Georges
  Aubin, ed., *Papineau en exil à Paris, tome 2, Lettres reçues, 1839–1845* (Trois-
  Pistoles, QC: Éditions Trois-Pistoles, 2007), 206, 428, 434, 437; Georges
  Aubin and Renée Blanchet, eds., *Louis-Joseph Papineau: Lettres à ses enfants,
  tome 11, 1855–1871* (Montreal: Les Éditions Varia, 2004), 567; Aubin and
  Blanchet, *Louis-Joseph Papineau: Lettres à Julie*, 473; and HGJ Papers, M794,
  6060–2, Louis J. A. Papineau to HGJ, Manoir de Monte Bello, 11 May 1895.

86 Joly de Lotbinière, *Voyage en Orient*, 16. Their sister, Kitty Alléon, simply
  refers to Moïse-Salomon as Joly in her letters, but her son would marry his
  daughter in what was a common practice among business families of that

era. John R. Gillis, *A World of Their Own Making: Myth, Ritual, and the Quest for Family Values* (New York: Basic Books, 1996), 64.

87 On this theme, see Graham Dawson, *Soldier Heroes: British Adventure, Empire and the Imagining of Masculinities* (London: Routledge, 1994), chap. 3.

88 Joly was very critical of the much more personal journal published by the poet Alphonse de Lamartine in 1835. Joly de Lotbinière, *Voyage en Orient*, 88–9.

89 Leclerc, *Domaine Joly-De Lotbinière*, 17; M. Christine Boyer, "La Mission Héliographique: Architectural Photographs, Collective Memory and the Patrimony of France, 1851," in Joan M. Schwartz and James R. Ryan, eds., *Picturing Place: Photography and the Geographical Imagination* (London: I. B. Tauris, 2003), 36; Derek Gregory, "Emperors of the Gaze: Photographic Practices and Productions of Space in Egypt, 1839–1914," in *Picturing Place*, 199. For a brief description of Joly's experiences, based on his son's reading of his journal, see HGJ Papers, M793, 4862–3, HGJ to C. W. Galloupe, Que., 31 Jan. 1889.

90 PGJ Papers, M786, 1049, Diploma, Société Orientale, Paris, 1 Mar. 1843.

91 Joly de Lotbinière, *Voyage en Orient*, 28–9, 57.

92 In this letter Joly states that 4,200 francs was the equivalent of £200. Assuming that he meant pounds sterling and that £1 stg = $5 Canadian currency, 1 franc would equal approximately $0.24.

93 PGJ Papers, M785, 127–8, Marriage contract, 15 Dec. 1828.

94 Contrast the business strategy of Barthélemy Joliette, who repeatedly mortgaged the seigneury of Lavaltrie to build mills and roads, as well as when signing logging contracts. Jean-Claude Robert, "Un seigneur entrepreneur, Barthélemy Joliette, et la fondation de la village d'Industrie (Joliette), 1822–1850," *Revue d'histoire de l'Amérique française* 26, no. 3 (1972): 395.

95 JCCL Papers, M785, 115–18, G. Joly to Ma chère Julie, Paris, 29 Apr. 1841.

96 Joly de Lotbinière, *Voyage en Orient*, 24, 26–7.

97 Among other books, Ternaux-Compans wrote *Voyages, relations et mémoires originaux: Pour servir l'histoire de la découverte de l'Amérique* (Paris: A. Bertrand, 1837). See Henry R. Wagner, "Henri Ternaux Compans: The First Collector of Hispanic-Americana," *Review of Inter-American Bibliography* 4, no. 4 (1954): 283–98.

98 PGJ Papers, M786, 845–6, décret, gouvernement de Guyane française concédant terre à société Jules le Chevalier, 15 June 1839; 982–9, Projet d'acte d'une société civile ayant pour objet les études à faire pour la colonisation de la Guyane française, 1843; 994–1003, agreement, Société pour

la colonisation de la Guyanne française, 4 Jan. 1842; 1019–22, agreement between Lechevalier, Joly de Lotbinière, and Tournaux-Compans, 8 Jan. 1843; 1023–6, Cahier des charges, 11 June 1839; 1209–16, Rapport à son exc. le Maréchal Duc de Dalmatie par M. le Comte de Tascher, Paris, 23 Feb. 1843, from *Moniteur Universel*, 16 Mar. 1843.

99 Aubin and Blanchet, *Louis-Joseph Papineau: Lettres à Julie*, 458–9.

100 PGJ Papers, M786, 1061–75, report by H. Sauvage and A. de St Quentin, Paris, 25 Aug. 1843; 1080–1, rupture de contrat de société de colonisation Guyane française, 20 Nov. 1843; 1100–5, Jules Lechevalier to P. G. Joly, 2 May 1844; Aubin, *Papineau en exil, tome 1*, 140. The colonial government's report approving of the project in 1845 stated that the ex-slaves would remain indentured to the company for fifteen years. M786, 1233–5, 31 May 1845, Rapport sur la colonisation de Guyanne française.

101 The fee for titular members was 20 francs a year or a single payment of 200 francs. PGJ Papers, M786, 1274–5, printed prospectus, Institut d'Afrique; 1276, Prince de Rohan-Rochefort to G. Joly (form letter), 1 Dec. 1845.

102 Aubin and Blanchet, *Louis-Joseph Papineau: Lettres à Julie*, 458–9, 473.

103 PGJ Papers, M786, 1240–2, L. J. Papineau to P. G. Joly, Montreal, 15 Oct. 1845; 1388, K. Alléon to P. G. Joly, Paris, 30 Oct. 1846.

104 PGJ Papers, M786, 1248–51, U. Joly to Gustave, Paris, 30 Oct. 1845. Nine hundred forty men were enlisted in eleven units. M786, 1288, Livre d'ordre et retour – Régiment de Lotbinière, 1845–63.

105 Joly himself was a member of the school commission, which voted to establish twelve schools, a considerable reduction in number from the twenty-two reported in 1832. PGJ Papers, M786, 1222, Michel Frenet et al. to Gustave Joly, Lotbinière, 13 Apr. 1845; 1280, A. Gugy to Lt Col. Joly, Montreal, Dec. 1845; Paradis, *Les Annales de Lotbinière*, 407–8.

106 PGJ Papers, M786, 1308–11, contract with William Thurber, millwright, 14 Jan. 1846; 1429–31, contract with George Thurber, millwright, 10 Dec. 1846; 1365–71, contract with Louis Fréchette, 13 Aug. 1846. For the surveyor's plan of Pointe Platon and the wharf, see p. 1440. Joly appears to have improved the wharf in the mid-1850s, for he badgered the government for compensation, which was finally rejected in 1861. See M787, 2262–4, W. B. Robinson to P. G. Joly, Toronto, 24 June 1857; 2768, G. Alleyn to P. G. Joly, Que., 7 Mar. 1861. There would be no government wharf until 1897. Paradis, *Les Annales*, 337–8.

107 PGJ Papers, M786, 1473–5, permission for Valentien Bernier to construct a sawmill, notarized by J. Filteau, 4 Apr. 1847. Even though seigneurs

did not technically have a monopoly over sawmills, they laid claim to the streams that provided the power to operate such mills. Grenier, *Brève histoire*, 193–4.

108 PGJ Papers, M786, 1304–7, H. F. Atkinson to Dear Sir, Spencer Wood, 8 Jan. 1846; 1312–21, Hen'y Atkinson to Gustave Joly, Que., 26 Jan. 1846; 1599–1601, draft document by P. G. Joly, 8 Dec. 1850; 1603–6, P. G. Joly to Mon cher Monsieur, 6 Dec. 1850 [draft]; 1611–12, draft letter to newspaper editor; 1689–1726, draft letters to newspaper editors, 1851; 1759, draft document in favour of North Shore Railway, 5 July 1852; 1767, P. G. Joly to editor of *Quebec Mercury*, Que., 12 July 1852; 1777, Resolutions proposed by a public meeting held in Quebec, 1852; 1785–9, draft letter responding to objections to North Shore Railway.

109 PGJ Papers, M786, 2112–13, F. Evanturel to P. G. Joly, Toronto, 7 June 1856. Joly was a strong critic of the Grand Trunk's close relations with government members, and in 1859 he also criticized Joseph Cauchon's bill for a Quebec–Lake Huron line as a threat to the Quebec-Montreal connection. M786, 2081–95, draft letter to editor of *Le Canadien*, April 1856, and English translation; 2201–4, P. G. Joly to J. Cauchon, Que., 18 Jan. 1859; M787, 2212, J. Cauchon to P. G. Joly, Toronto, 25 Jan. 1859. For details on the failed pre-Confederation efforts to build the North Shore Railway, see Young, *Promoters and Politicians*, chap. 1.

110 The two men were finally reconciled on the Reverend Faucher's initiative in 1860. PGJ Papers, M786, 1478, Ls Legendre to P. G. Joly, 24 May 1847; M787, 2585–7, Ed. Faucher to P. G. Joly, Lotbinière, 13 Sept. 1860; 2602–3, Ed. Faucher to P. G. Joly, 27 Sept. 1860.

111 Paradis, *Les Annales*, 274.

112 PGJ Papers, M786, 1354, U. Joly to Gustave Joly, Paris, 30 July 1846.

113 PGJ Papers, M786, Passeport du Hâvre à Paris, 14 Sept. 1847.

114 PGJ Papers, M786, 1557–66, Report of L. Legendre, D.G.V. (Deputy Grand-Voyer), Lotbinière, 25 Sept. 1848.

115 The seigneurial pew was still in the church when the parish history was published in 1927. Paradis, *Les Annales*, 278–9, 305n1, 343; AJL Papers, M797, part 2, 17, seigneurial rights. Conflicts related to the seigneurial pew and similar honorary privileges were apparently much more common prior to the Conquest. Benoît Grenier, *Seigneurs campagnards de la Nouvelle France: Présence seigneuriale et sociabilité dans la vallée du Saint-Laurent à l'époque préindustrielle* (Rennes: Presse Universitaires de Rennes, 2007), 336–40.

116 The debt was not completely extinguished until 1883. PGJ Papers, M786, 1578, receipt, Paris, 12 Mar. 1849; HGJ Papers, M791, 2829, copied from Edward Hale's Memo of Obligations.

117 Nicholas Green, *The Spectacle of Nature: Landscape and Bourgeois Culture in Nineteenth-Century France* (Manchester: Manchester University Press, 1990), 88.

118 See France Gagnon-Pratte, *L'architecture et la nature à Québec au dix-neuvième siècle: Les villas* (Quebec City: Ministère des Affaires Culturelles, 1980), chap. 3, esp. pp. 111–16.

119 Richard Bushman, *The Refinement of America: Persons, Houses, Cities* (New York: Knopf, 1992), 258–9.

120 Bushman (*Refinement of America*, 131, 244–5, 259–61) points out that these external spaces were also meant to stimulate refined conversation with guests and that architectural books began to pay more attention to the wider setting. Maple House's front lawn was considerably expanded by the wealthy American-born wife of Pierre-Gustave Joly's great-grandson, Alain. Leclerc, *Domaine Joly-De Lotbinière*, 25. For a comparative example, see Colin Coates, "Like 'The Thames towards the Putney': The Appropriation of Landscape in Lower Canada," *Canadian Historical Review* 74, no. 3 (1993): 322–3.

121 Benoît Grenier, "Gentilshommes campagnards de la Nouvelle France, XVIIe–XIXe siècle: Une autre seigneurie laurentienne?" *French Colonial History*, 7 (2006): 21–44; Paradis, *Les Annales*, 272–3; Leclerc, *Domaine Joly-De Lotbinière*, 14, 16. For the location of the *domaine*, see the map in Paradis, *Les Annales*, 44.

122 Grenier, *Seigneurs campagnards*, 52.

123 Grenier, *Brève histoire*, 129.

124 Grenier, *Seigneurs campagnards*, 17–23, 44–53, 330–5, 343–8, 354, 360; Robert de Roquebrune, *Testament of My Childhood*, translated by Felix Walter (Toronto: University of Toronto Press, 1964); Philippe Aubert de Gaspé, *A Man of Sentiment: The Memoirs of Philippe-Joseph Aubert de Gaspé*, trans. Jane Brierly (Montreal: Véhicule Press, 1988); Dechêne, *Habitants et marchands*; Greer, *Peasant, Lord, and Merchant*. For a brief historiographical overview, see Daniel Salée, "Seigneurial Landownership and the Transition to Capitalism in Nineteenth-Century Quebec," *Quebec Studies* 12 (1991): 22.

125 Like Colin Coates, Grenier finds that the habitants were disinclined to cooperate in the construction of local roads or other public works that did not appear to have a direct benefit to them. Grenier, *Seigneurs*

campagnards, 326–7; Colin Coates, *The Metamorphoses of Landscape and Community in Early Quebec* (Montreal: McGill-Queen's University Press, 2000).

126 A second boat was built and put into service the following year. Paradis, *Les Annales,* 283–4; Martine Côté, "Du Grand Tronc au pont de Québec: Les communications," in *Histoire de Lévis-Lotbinière,* ed. Samson et al., 408.

127 PGJ Papers, M786, 1844–5, Requête des habitants du comté de Lotbinière contre le régime seigneurial, ca 1854.

128 Grenier, *Seigneurs campagnards,* 366–8.

129 Coates, *Metamorphoses,* 126–7; Larose, "La Seigneurie de Beauharnois," 336, 343.

130 PGJ Papers, M786, 1489–94, instructions to Louis Maguenat, seigneurial agent, 28 July 1847.

131 For a useful review of the literature applying a Marxist analysis, see David Schulze, 'Rural Manufacture in Lower Canada: Understanding Seigneurial Privilege and the Transition in the Countryside,' *Alternate Routes: A Critical Review* 7 (1984): 134–67.

132 Robert, "Un seigneur entrepreneur." For other examples of seigneurs who established villages, see Serge Courville, *Entre Ville et Campagne: L'essor du village dans les seigneuries du Bas-Canada* (Quebec: Les Presses de l'Université Laval, 1990), 43–6, 82–90.

133 Maude Flamand-Hubert, *Louis Bertrand à L'Isle Verte: Propriété foncière et exploitation des ressources* (Quebec: Presses de l'Université du Québec, 2012), 103–7. Contrast, as well, the seigneurs of Saint-Hyacinthe who generally relied upon local entrepreneurs to establish saw mills and grist mills, entrepreneurs who were then obliged to pay rents to the seigneurs. Dessureault, 'Industrie et société rurale,' 133–4.

134 Joly de Lotbinière, *Voyage en Orient,* 31–4; Aubin, *Papineau en exil, tome 1,* 140–1; PGJ Papers, M786, 1651, draft letter to *Le Canadien,* 4 July [1850?]; 1807, Certificate, Association for the Exhibition of the Industry of All Nations, New York, 1853.

135 PGJ Papers, M786, 1250, U. Joly to Gustave, Paris, 30 Oct. 1845; M787, 2605–10, Cte d'Esprémesnil to P. G. Joly, Paris, 30 Sept. 1860; 2692–8, 14 Jan. 1861; 2714–17, 2 Feb. 1861; 2759–62, P. G. Joly to Cte d'Esprémesnil, 1 Mar. 1861. In March 1844 Lactance Papineau noted in his Paris journal (*Journal d'un étudiant,* 484), that Joly was absent on a "promenade géologique."

136 PGJ Papers, M787, 2978, I. Geoffroy [ ]to P. G. Joly, Paris, 29 Dec. 1861.

137 Christian Dessureault, "L'évolution du régime seigneuriale canadien de 1760 à 1854: essai de synthèse,' in *Le régime seigneuriale au Québec: 150 ans*

après," ed. Alain Laberge and Benoît Grenier (Centre interuniversitaire
d'études québécoises 2009), 36–7.

138 Salée, "Seigneurial Landownership," 26.

2. Family Man

1 To take one example of Joly's kin ties, there are numerous letters from
the 1890s demonstrating the important role he played in redeeming the
troubled son of his cousin, Judge Henri-Elzéar Taschereau of the Supreme
Court of Canada. As for baptisms, various members of the Gowen and
Oliver families (who were close neighbours) were the most favoured,
but three members of the Alléon family in France served by proxy, as did
Jean-Jacques Keller in 1868. Diocese of Quebec, Anglican Cathedral register, 16 Jan. 2011.

2 Britain's gentry and aristocracy were providing a model for intimate family relationships by the early nineteenth century. Catherine Hall, "Home
Sweet Home," in *Histoire de la vie privée,* vol. 4, *De la Révolution à la Grande
Guerre,* ed. Philippe Ariès and Georges Duby (Paris: Éditions du Seuil,
1987), 53–62, 82–5.

3 There is evidence that the couple were living in separate houses by 1861.
Pierre-Gustave Joly de Lotbinière, *Voyage en Orient (1839–40): Journal
d'un voyageur curieux du monde et d'un pionnier de la daguerréotypie,* introd.
Jacques Desautels, ed. Georges Aubin and Renée Blanchet (Ste Foy, QC:
Les Presses de l'Université Laval, 2010), 330n21. In April 1862, Joly's sister
wrote, "Et cette pauvre Julia, tu ne m'en parle plus. Malgré tous ses torts,
je la plains." Library and Archives Canada [hereafter LAC], Fonds Pierre-
Gustave Joly [hereafter PGJ Papers], M787, 3057, K. Alléon to P.G. Joly,
Paris, 9 Apr. 1862.

4 The first indication that Joly had moved to Paris is his sister's letter to
him in January 1865 (PGJ Papers, M787, 3321–3, K. Alléon to P.G. Joly, 26
Jan. 1865). By this time she had her own grandchildren to help care for
because her only son was frequently absent from home on business, and
his wife apparently did not have a strong constitution. See, for example,
PGJ Papers, M787, 2874–6, K. Alléon to P.G. Joly, 9 Aug. 1861.

5 Abbé Louis L. Paradis, *Les Annales de Lotbinière, 1672–1933* (Quebec:
L'Action Catholique, 1933), 296–7; British Columbia Archives, Crease
Family Collection, Susan Crease diary, MS 2879, AO 1847 [hereafter Susan
Crease diary], 18 Oct. 1903; PGJ Papers, M785, 137, Marriage contract, 15
Dec. 1828.

6 The marriage – which Pierre-Gustave Joly described as a love match – took place over his objections. He felt that Savage, who was from a military family in northern Ireland, was rather "wild." Savage died heavily in debt in 1869. PGJ Papers, M786, 2001–4, Henry Savage to P.G. Joly, Que., 17 Oct. 1855; 2115, C.I. Ardouin to P.G. Joly, Que., 11 June 1856; 2138–41, Henry Savage to P.G. Joly, Que., 10 Sept. 1856; 2533–4, H. Savage to P.G. Joly, 6 June 1860; HGJ Papers, M789, 38, A. Winterroth to H.G. Joli [sic], Rochester, NY, 3 Aug. 1869; 42, Church, Munger, and Cooke (attorneys) to HGJ, Rochester, 1 Oct. 1869; Georges Aubin, *Papineau en exil à Paris, tome 1, Dictionnaire* (Trois-Pistoles, QC: Éditions Trois-Pistoles, 2007), 138; Georges Aubin and Renée Blanchet, eds., *Louis-Joseph Papineau: Lettres à Julie* (Sillery, QC: Septentrion, 2000), 729–30.

7 Quoted in Serge Granger, "Les Lotbinière au Cachemire avant la première guerre mondiale," *Synergies Inde* 3 (2008): 134–5.

8 PGJ Papers, M787, 2981, note on Edmond Joly, ca 1862. The printed version can be found on pp. 2985–7.

9 *Montreal Daily Witness*, 20 Feb. 1894.

10 Colin M. Coates, "French Canadians' Ambivalence to the Empire," in *Canada and the British Empire*, ed. Phillip Buckner (Oxford: Oxford University Press, 2008), 192, 194. According to Rasporich, French Canadians were supportive, though not enthusiastically so, of the war effort. A.W. Rasporich, "Imperial Sentiment in the Province of Canada during the Crimean War, 1854–1856," in *The Shield of Achilles: Aspects of Canada in the Victorian Age*, ed. W.L. Morton (Toronto: McClelland and Stewart, 1968), 139–68.

11 LAC, Fonds Henri-Gustave Joly de Lotbinière [hereafter HGJ Papers], M789, 555–7, Edmond Joly to HGJ, Aden, 27 Mar. 1855. These letters have been copied in typescript.

12 HGJ Papers, M789, 557–9, Edmond Joly to HGJ, Alexandria, 6 Apr. [1855].

13 HGJ Papers, M789, 579, Edmond Joly to HGJ, Les tranches devant Balaclava, 7 May 1855; 590, Camp devant Sebastopol, 17 May 1855; 606, Camp devant Sebastopol, 30 May 1855.

14 PGJ Papers, M786, 1911–12, K. Alléon to P.G. Joly, Paris, 1 Mar. 1855; 1946–7, [K. Alléon] to [Pierre-Gustave Joly], Marnes, 26 June 1855; 1958–9, 25 July 1855.

15 PGJ Papers, M876, 1969–71, [K. Alléon] to [P.G. Joly], Marnes, 8 Aug. 1855; 2164–7, K. Alléon to P.G. Joly, Paris, 27 Sept. 1856; 2188–91, Edmond Joly to HGJ, Paris, 18 Dec. 1856; M787, 2208–11, K. Alléon to P.G. Joly, Paris, 21 Jan. 1857.

16 PGJ Papers, M787, 2287, K. Alléon to P.G. Joly, Chatelaine, 4 Sept. 1857.

17 *Montreal Daily Witness,* 20 Feb. 1894; PGJ Papers, M787, 2983, note on Edmond Joly, ca 1862. There is a typed transcription of Edmond's Paris adventures and detailed Indian journal on reel M789. It ends abruptly in late August before he reached Cawnpore.

18 On this theme, see the chapters on General Havelock as public hero in part 2 of Graham Dawson, *Soldier Heroes: British Adventure, Empire and the Imagining of Masculinities* (London: Routledge, 1994).

19 PGJ Papers, M785, 312, Commission for P.G. Joly, 1 Dec. 1830.

20 See Roch Legault, "L'Organisation militaire sous le régime britannique et le rôle assigné à la gentilhommerie canadienne (1760–1815)," *Revue d'histoire de l'Amérique française* 45, no. 2 (1991): 229–49.

21 M. Keller was the school's "proviseur" in 1848. The report cards are in the archives of the Domaine Joly de Lotbinière. See also Georges Aubin, *Papineau en exil à Paris, tome 1, Dictionnaire* (Trois-Pistoles, QC: Éditions Trois-Pistoles, 2007), 141.

22 PGJ Papers, M786, 1182, note to mother; 1183, note to father. There is no date on this document, which is filed in the 1845 section of the correspondence, but a letter from his aunt in October 1846 refers to what is clearly the same trip.

23 Pierre-Gustave Joly ordered 1,000 cigars at a time from Havana. PGJ Papers, M786, 2186, A.E. Bovie [?] to P.G. Joly, Philadelphia, 9 Dec. 1856.

24 PGJ Papers, M786, 13885–8, K. Alléon to P.G. Joly, Paris, 30 Oct. 1846.

25 PGJ Papers, M786, 1389–92, HGJ to mon cher papa. Again there is no date, but this letter precedes one written on 4 Nov. 1846. Joly was still at the Keller Institute in 1850, and he wrote a letter of condolence to the family when Madame Keller died in 1889. HGJ Papers, M793, 5418–25, Jacob Keller to HGJ, Paris, 25 Dec. 1889.

26 PGJ Papers, M786, 1355, U. Joly to P.G. Joly, Paris, 30 July 1846.

27 Hamelin, "Joly de Lotbinière."

28 HGJ Papers, M796, 9533, contract, Atelier de peinture de Poittevin, 1849.

29 PGJ Papers, M786, 2131–4, U. Joly to P.G. Joly, Paris, 28 July 1856.

30 HGJ Papers, M796, 9534, Diploma from Université de France, 7 Aug. 1849.

31 HGJ Papers, M796, 9536, Bar examination certificate, 6 Nov. 1855. It is not clear who Joly studied law with, but a letter from Strachan Bethune of Montreal to his father in 1850 states that "the instruction of your son in the Study & Practice of the legal profession could not be entrusted to an abler person than the gentleman you have selected in Quebec." PGJ Papers, M786, 1655, Bethune to G. Joly, Montreal, 18 July 1850.

32 PGJ Papers, M876, 1828–33, HGJ to cher papa, Lotbinière, 21 Nov. [1853].

33 PGJ Papers, M876, 1959–60, [K. Alléon] to my dear brother [P.G. Joly], Marnes, 25 July 1855; 1971–2, 8 Aug. 1855.

34 HGJ Papers, M792, 4124–5, Rev. A. Bernier to HGJ, Ste Emmélie, 27 Mar. 1888. The task was completed five months later, at a cost of twenty-five cents per mass. M793, 4392, Bernier to HGJ, Lotbinière, 16 Aug. 1888. The curé of Vaudreuil, where Joly's mother was born, replied that he had time to say only forty or fifty. Rev. Godin to HGJ, Vaudreuil, 28 Mar. 1888. See also M792, 3104, HGJ to Hon. A.B. Routhier, Oakland, MD, 30 Aug. 1885; 3852, Thos Workman to HGJ, Montreal, 28 Oct. 1887.

35 Paradis, Les Annales, 329–30; HGJ Papers, M792, 3980, Harry Strange to HGJ, Hampshire [1887]. The last child to be born was baptized Justine de Lotbinière in 1875. Anglican Cathedral, Holy Trinity Church register, recorded in Quebec Vital and Church Records (Drouin Collection), 1621–1967 [hereafter Anglican Cathedral register], 13 Nov. 1875. Accessed via Ancestry.ca.

36 HGJ Papers, M793, 4295–6, Judge J.B. Caron to HGJ, E.G. Joly, Que., 3 July 1888.

37 HGJ Papers, M793, 4853, HGJ to Mrs Campbell, Leclercville, 28 Jan. 1889. Alain's wife also referred to herself simply as Cerise de Lotbinière when writing to her father-in-law from India, and Edmond's son, Alain, had dropped the name Joly by 1950. M793, 5438–45, Cerise de Lotbinière to HGJ [n.d.]; LAC, Alain Joly de Lotbinière Papers, M797, part 2, 277–8, Alain de Lotbinière to My dear Edmond, La Tour de Peilz, Vaud, 14 Feb. 1950.

38 To the English aristocracy, however, the name of the landed estate was more important than that of the family itself. Leonore Davidoff, Megan Doolittle, Janet Fink, and Katherine Holden The Family Story: Blood, Contract and Intimacy, 1830–1960 (London: Longman, 1999), 93–4.

39 LAC, Census of Canada, 1871, Quebec City, St Louis Ward, family 189. Accessed via Ancestry.ca; Joly de Lotbinière, Voyage en Orient, 17n24.

40 PGJ Papers, M787, 2488–90, Jules Tailhau, S.J. , to P.G. Joly, Que., 28 Apr. 1860; 2552–7, Jules Tailhau, S.J., to P.G. Joly, en mer, 29 July 1860.

41 PGJ Papers, M786, 2111, C.A. Heikscher to P.G. Joly, New York, 15 May 1856; 2148–50, C.A. Heikscher to P.G. Joly, New York, 2 Oct. 1856; Philippe-Joseph Aubert de Gaspé, A Man of Sentiment: The Memoirs of Philippe-Joseph Aubert de Gaspé, translated from the 1866 edition by Jane Brierly (Montreal: Véhicule Press, 1988), 178. Gowen had entered into a partnership in 1810 with his brother-in-law, William Hall, engaging in the hat trade and dealing in lumber and foodstuffs. During the War of 1812 they sold hats and uniforms to the military. Michel Monette, "Hall, William," Dictionary of Canadian Biography, vol. 8 (Toronto: University of Toronto Press, 1985), 353.

On Gowen's land speculation activities in the Eastern Townships, see J.I. Little, "Contested Land: Squatters and Agents in the Eastern Townships of Lower Canada," *Canadian Historical Review* 80, no. 3 (1999): 394–5.

42 Benoît Grenier, *Seigneurs campagnards de la Nouvelle France: Présence seigneuriale et sociabilité dans la vallée du Saint-Laurent à l'époque préindustrielle* (Rennes: Presse Universitaires de Rennes, 2007), 158–67.

43 PGJ Papers, M787, 2394–5, HGJ to P.G. Joly, Que., 12 Nov. 1859.

44 HGJ Papers, M793, 5306–7, Cundall [?] to HGJ, Charlottetown, 9 Oct. 1889.

45 HGJ Papers, M790, 1557–8, Lucy Joly to My own darling one, Que., 27 Apr. 1879.

46 John Livesey died of bronchitis at the age of two years and seven months, and Ernest Edgar died four months later, at the age of one year and five months, of "congestion of the brain." Only one of the earlier offspring, Louisa Maud, had died very young, and the cause was "water on the brain" rather than an infectious disease. *Platon Herald / Les Échos du Platon*, vol. 6, undated broadsheet in the Domaine Joly de Lotbinière Archives; Anglican Cathedral register; death register of Mount Hermon Cemetery, Quebec City.

47 HGJ Papers, M790, 1577–84, Lucy Joly to HGJ, Que., 1 May 1877.

48 This arrangement was the norm for Montreal's English-speaking bourgeoisie. Bettina Bradbury, *Wife to Widow: Lives, Laws, and Politics in Nineteenth-Century Montreal* (Vancouver: UBC Press, 2011). 146–9. The contract was not located in the family archives, but its existence is proven by Henri-Gustave's will. HGJ Papers, M795, 7410–22, self-drafted will of Henri-Gustave Joly de Lotbinière, Que., 4 Feb. 1899.

49 HGJ Papers, M790, 1560, Lucy Joly to My own darling one, Quebec, 27 Apr. 1879.

50 HGJ Papers, M794, 6303, Miss J.S. Murray to HGJ, Montreal, 5 Feb. 1896; 6308, Miss Murray to HGJ, n.d.; 6458, Mabel Thomson to HGJ, Cadodgan Gardens SW, 14 Mar. [1896].

51 John Tosh, *Manliness and Masculinities in Nineteenth-Century Britain: Essays on Family, Gender and Empire* (Harlow, UK: Pearson Education, 2005), 36; Bradbury, *Wife to Widow*, 62.

52 Davidoff et al., *The Family Story*, 114–16. See also Amanda Vickery, *The Gentleman's Daughter: Women's Lives in Georgian England* (New Haven: Yale University Press, 1998).

53 HGJ Papers, M794, 6947, HGJ to Edmond, Ottawa, 19 Nov. 1896.

54 Henry James Morgan, ed., *Types of Canadian Women*, vol. 1 (Toronto: William Briggs, 1903), 82; *Platon Herald / Les Échos du Platon*, vol. 6, undated broadsheet in the Domaine Joly de Lotbinière Archives.

55 HGJ Papers, M793, 5508, HGJ to Dearest Lucy, Leclercville, 4 Feb. 1890. On this theme, see Jessica Girard, "Lady Bountiful: Women of the Landed Classes and Rural Philanthropy," *Victorian Studies* 30, no. 2 (1987): 183–210.

56 HGJ Papers, M794, 6862, HGJ to Edmond, Ottawa, 28 Sept. 1896.

57 Susan Crease diary, 15 June 1903.

58 On inheritance under the Coutume de Paris, see Benoît Grenier, *Brève histoire du régime seigneurial* (Montreal: Boréal, 2012), 74.

59 HGJ Papers, M795, 7410–22, self-drafted will of Henri-Gustave Joly de Lotbinière, Que., 4 Feb. 1899. Edmond discharged the annual payments to the other heirs in 1911. For the details, see BAnQQ, AP-G-389, Comptes, 1906–11, 92–105.

60 HGJ Papers, M793, 4298, Rev. T. Adam to HGJ, Bishop's College, Lennox-ville, 4 July 1888; Hazel Boswell, *Town House, Country House: Recollections of a Quebec Childhood*, ed. R.H. Hubbard (Montreal: McGill-Queen's University Press, 1990), 9.

61 On this theme, see Tosh, *Manliness and Masculinities*, 5–6; and J.I. Little, "The Fireside Kingdom: A Mid-Nineteenth-Century Anglican Perspective on Marriage and Parenthood," in *Households of Faith: Family, Gender, and Community in Canada, 1760–1969*, ed. Nancy Christie (Montreal: McGill-Queen's University Press, 2002).

62 HGJ Papers, M790, 1555, Ethel to My Dear Papa, Quebec, 27 Apr. [1879].

63 Boswell had written two other books, but this one was not published until after her death in 1979. For details, see the editor's introduction, which provides the wrong birth years and order for several of the children.

64 Boswell's niece is said to have changed the fictitious names to real ones before submitting the manuscript for publication (*Town House, Country House*, xi), but she presumably decided not to do this for Edmond because his presence was a fictional one.

65 Boswell, *Town House*, 3–5.

66 LAC, Census of Canada, 1871, Quebec City, St Louis Ward, family 189; 1881, Quebec City, St Louis Ward, family 295.

67 *Platon Herald / Les Échos du Platon*, vol. 6.

68 The two younger sons are also listed in the census, but they were serving in the British military outside the country by this time. LAC, Census of Canada, 1891, Quebec City, St Louis Ward, family 243. It would be surpris-ing if the Jolys were not still employing domestic servants, for servants were a distinguishing feature of middle-class status. J.F.C. Harrison, *The Early Victorians 1832–1851* (New York: Praeger, 1971), 109–11.

69 Nancy Christie argues that in Ontario patrician masculinity relied on the control of domestic labour as late as the 1870s. Nancy Christie, "The 'Plague of Servants': Female Household Labour and the Making of Classes

in Upper Canada," in *Transatlantic Subjects: Ideas, Institutions, and Social Experience in Post-Revolutionary British North America* (Montreal: McGill-Queen's University Press, 2008), 104–5.

70 On this theme, see Davidoff et al., *The Family Story*, 29, 81–2.
71 Paradis, *Les Annales*, 346.
72 Paradis, *Les Annales*, 346.
73 HGJ Papers, M792, 3048–50, HGJ to Edmond, Pointe Platon, 3 June 1885.
74 HGJ Papers, M794, 6470–1, Lucy J. de L. to HGJ [n.d.].
75 HGJ Papers, M792, 4179–81, Lucy Joly to Mrs Joly, 26 Apr. 1888; M793, 5614, HGJ to Edmond, Que., 27 Nov. 1890.
76 HGJ Papers, M792, 3274, HGJ to Edmond, Leclercville, 20 Mar. 1886.
77 HGJ Papers, M793, 5402, HGJ to Edmond, Leclercville, 14 Dec. 1889.
78 HGJ Papers, M793, 5512–13, HGJ to Dearest Lucy, Leclercville, 5 Feb. 1890; Jean Hamelin and Michel Paquin, "Irvine, George," *Dictionary of Canadian Biography Online*.
79 HGJ Papers, M793, 5538, HGJ to Edmond, Que., 2 Apr. 1890. Joly was still hoping that Edmond would attract more clients in 1896. M794, 6806–7, HGJ to Edmond, 26 Aug. 1896.
80 HGJ Papers, M793, 5573, HGJ to Edmond, Que., 23 July 1890; 5576, 26 July 1890; 5584–6, 31 July 1890; 5750, 17 July 1893; 5756, 25 July 1893. After Joly's election to Ottawa in 1896, however, Edmond had to remain in Quebec City while his family spent the summer in Bic. HGJ Papers, M794, 6805–7, HGJ to Edmond, Ottawa, 26 Aug. 1896.
81 HGJ Papers, M794, 7929–34, Edmond to HGJ, the Hermitage, 7 Feb. 1906.
82 HGJ Papers, M794, 6854–7, HGJ to Edmond, Vendredi [probably a postscript to 24 Sept. 1896].
83 HGJ Papers, M792, 3029, Adolphe Caron to HGJ, Ottawa, 8 May 1885.
84 HGJ Papers, M792, 3027, Col. E. Hewett to HGJ, R.M. College, 4 May 1885; 3031, HGJ to Col. Hewett, Leclercville, 9 May 1885.
85 HGJ Papers, M792, 3038–42, HGJ to Edmond, Leclercville, 26 May 1885; 3040, HGJ to Edmond, Leclercville, 26 May 1885; 3056, HGJ to Edmond, Pointe Platon, 19 June 1885; 3137, Col. Panet to HGJ, Ottawa, 19 Nov. 1885; 3139–40, Adolphe Caron to HGJ, Ottawa, 19 Nov. 1885; 3174–7, Adolphe Caron to HGJ, Ottawa, 4 Dec. 1885; 3178. Col. Hewett to HGJ, Kingston, 4 Dec. 1885.
86 HGJ Papers, M792, 3353–5, Adolphe Chapleau to HGJ, Que., 14 Sept. 1886. Caron also promised to find employment for one of Joly's in-laws in 1895. M794, 6088–9, Adolphe Caron to HGJ, Ottawa, 6 Aug. 1895.
87 HGJ Papers, M792, 3531–3, A.C. de G. Joly to HGJ, 14 Dec. 1883; 3535–7, Col. Campbell to Alain, Kingston, 1 Dec. [1886]; 3539–41, C. de G. Joly to Col. Campbell, 13 Dec. [1886].

88 HGJ Papers, M792, 3582–4, Marion Campbell to HGJ, King St, 1 Jan. 1887; 3588–9, Col. Campbell to HGJ, [1887].

89 BC Archives, Mf11A, Letters of His Honour Sir Joly de Lotbinière, 1901–6 [hereafter Letters of His Honour], HGJ to Edmond, Victoria, 26 Oct. 1901.

90 Granger, "Les Lotbinière au Cachemire," 136–7.

91 HGJ Papers, M795, 7295, HGJ to Edmond, Ottawa, 22 Nov. 1897. He became a captain in 1895, and the Susan Crease diary refers to him as Captain in 1903 but Major in 1904. Col. William Wood, *The Storied Province of Quebec Past and Present*, vol. 4 (Toronto: Dominion, 1931), 245; Susan Crease diary, 24 May 1903, 14 Oct. 1904.

92 Granger, "Les Lotbinière au Cachemire," 136–7.

93 Boswell, *Town House*, 3–4.

94 HGJ Papers, M792, 3593, Gus to Dear Parents, Royal Military College, Kingston, 6 Jan. 1887.

95 Wood, *The Storied Province*, vol. 4, 245; HGJ Papers, M792, 3980–1, Harry Strange to HGJ, Hampshire [1888]; M793, 4248, Dr Douglas to HGJ, New York, 20 June 1888.

96 HGJ Papers, M793, 4305–7, E. Panet to HJG, Ottawa, 9 July 1888; 4318–19, Sir Adolphe Caron to HGJ, Que., 13 July 1888; 4326, E. Panet to HGJ, Ottawa, 16 July 1888.

97 HGJ Papers, M793, 4562, C.E. Panet to HGJ, 7 Nov. 1888; 4563–6, Gus to mother, Leclercville, 7 Nov. 1888; 4682, Elinor Bland Strange to HJ, Lymington, Hants [n.d., answered 18 Dec.].

98 HGJ Papers, M793, 4704–13, Gus to Ed, Chatham, 23 Dec. 1888.

99 HGJ Papers, M793, 5572, HGJ to Edmond, Que., 23 July 1890; 5607, Pointe Platon, 10 Sept. 1890; BAnQQ, P1000, S3, D1040, Correspondance d'Éthel Joly de Lotbinière, 1894–5 [hereafter EJL Correspondence], HGJ to Ethel, Que., 26 Dec. 1894.

100 Quoted in Granger, "Les Lotbinière au Cachemire," 136.

101 HGJ Papers, M794, 5952–62, Gustave J. de L. to HGJ, Gilgit, 2 Sept. 1894.

102 EJL Correspondence, HGJ to Ethel, Que., 7 Jan. 1895.

103 HGJ Papers, M794, 6889, T. Bland Strange to HGJ, Strangmuir, Oxon, Oct. 1896.

104 HGJ Papers, M794, 7138, HGJ to Edmond, Ottawa, 28 June 1897.

105 HGJ Papers, M795, 7220, HGJ to Edmond, Ottawa, 18 Sept. 1897; 7228, 8 Oct. 1897; 7295, 22 Nov. 1897. On the "Great Frontier Rising" of 1897–8, see T.R. Moreman, *The Army in India and the Development of Frontier Warfare, 1849–1947* (London: MacMillan, 1998), 53–67.

106 Letters of His Honour, HGJ to Edmond, Victoria, 26 Oct. 1901.

107 HGJ Papers, M795, 8173, Lady Mary Minto to HGJ, Government House, Calcutta, 25 Jan. 1907. Granger ("Les Lotbinière au Cachemire," 136) mistakenly states that Gustave spent most of these years on the family seigneury.

108 HGJ Papers, M793, 5048–50, Colonel Percy Lake to HGJ, Grenfell, Alberta, 25 Apr. 1889.

109 Two of the sons-in-law were British officers, and this was a period when, according to John Tosh, the rise of a militaristic hypermasculinity in Britain was reflected in a flight from domesticity. John Tosh, *A Man's Place: Masculinity and the Middle-Class Home in Victorian England* (New Haven: Yale University Press, 1999), chap. 8; and Tosh, *Manliness and Masculinities*, chap. 9.

110 HGJ Papers, M794, 5952–62, Gustave J. de L. to HGJ, Gilgit, 2 Sept. 1894.

111 HGJ Papers, M794, 6073, H. Nanton to HGJ, Dargai, 7 July 1895.

112 HGJ Papers, M794, 6398–400, Mrs M.L. Nanton to HGJ, Toronto, 26 Mar. 1896; Moreman, *The Army in India*, 58–9, 77–8.

113 Letters of His Honour, HGJ to Edmond, Victoria, 20 June 1905; 8 Nov. 1905; 6 Dec. 1905, 12 Jan. 1906.

114 Tosh, *Manliness and Masculinities*, 137.

115 Anglican Cathedral register, 14 Oct. 1891.

116 HGJ Papers, M794, 7155–9, HGJ to Edmond, Ottawa, 16 July 1897.

117 Susan Crease diary, 15 July 1903.

118 HGJ Papers, M793, 5200–3, Harry Strange to HGJ, Royal Artillery Barracks, Woolwich, 1 July 1889.

119 HGJ Papers, M793, 5397, G.W. Stephens to HGJ, Montreal, 10 Dec. 1889; 5402, HGJ to Edmond, Leclercville, 14 Dec. 1889.

120 HGJ Papers, M793, 5561–2, HGJ to Capt. Mills, Que., July 1890.

121 HGJ Papers, M794, 5952–62, Gustave J. de L. to HGJ, Gilgit, 2 Sept. 1894.

122 EJL Correspondence, HGJ to Ethel, Que., 7 Jan. 1895.

123 EJL Correspondence, HGJ to Ethel, Que., 29 Nov. 1894.

124 EJL Correspondence, HGJ to Ethel, Que., 30 Dec. 1894.

125 HGJ Papers, M793, 6014–15, A. Mills to HGJ, Efford Down, Bude Haven, North Cornwall, 7 Jan. 1895; 6052, HGJ to Sir Thomas Dyke Acland of Killarton in Exeter, Que., 6 May 1895.

126 EJL Correspondence, HGJ to Ethel, Que., 25 Feb. 1895.

127 EJL Correspondence, Lucy Joly de Lotbinière to Ethel, Rivière du Chêne, 17 Mar. 1895.

128 EJL Correspondence, Lucy Joly de Lotbinière to Ethel, 4 Mar. [1895].

129 See Young, "Revisiting Feudal Vestiges," 142–3, 146–51.

130 Anglican Cathedral register, 1 Oct. 1881; HGJ Papers, M792, 3051, HGJ to Edmond, Pointe Platon, 3 June 1885. The Boswell family was still spending summers at Pointe Platon as of 1889, when Julia's husband offered to help pay for alterations. M793, 4930–1, St George Boswell to HGJ, 5 Mar. 1889.

131 HGJ Papers, M792, 3286, HGJ to Edmond, Leclercville, 23 Mar. 1886. At an asking price of $11,000, the house remained unsold until 1890, forcing the Jolys to lease it in the meantime. HGJ Papers, M792, 3412, HGJ to Edmond, Leclercville, 10 Nov. 1886; 3629, HGJ to Edmond, Leclercville, 28 Jan. 1887; 5633, HGJ to J. Stevenson, Que., 18 Dec. 1890.

132 HGJ Papers, M792, 3052, Col. Strange to HGJ, 18 June 1885.

133 HGJ Papers, M792, 3287, HGJ to Edmond, Leclercville, 23 Mar. 1886.

134 HGJ Papers, M793, 5517, HGJ to Lucy, Leclercville, 6 Feb. 1890.

135 EJL Correspondence, HGJ to Ethel, Que., 29 Nov. 1894.

136 EJL Correspondence, HGJ to Ethel, Que., 25 Feb. 1895.

137 HGJ Papers, M794, 6649–52, Julia to HGJ, Hattie Bay, Bic, 12 July 1896.

138 HGJ Papers, M793, 4840, draft reply to telegram from Countess de Beau [?], 25 Jan. 1889. The following November Joly asked one of his employees to close Pointe Platon, presumably for the winter. M793, 5377, Jos. Auger to HGJ, Pointe Platon, 26 Nov. 1889.

139 EJL Correspondence, HGJ to Ethel, Que., 4 Feb. 1895.

140 John R. Gillis, A World of Their Own Making: Myth, Ritual, and the Quest for Family Values (New York: Basic Books, 1996), 90.

141 Richard Bushman, The Refinement of America: Persons, Houses, Cities (New York: Knopf, 1992), 256, 270–1.

142 Leclerc, Domaine Joly-De Lotbinière, 16, 38–41. According to Tosh (A Man's Place, 182), by the 1880s in England the study was increasingly emphasized as an escape from femininity. My thanks to Mylène Richard and Hélène Leclerc for the design plans of Maple House and for the personal tour of the house.

143 See, for example, Nancy Cott, The Bonds of Womanhood: "Women's Sphere" in New England, 1780–1835 (New Haven: Yale University Press, 1977), 64–7, 92, 97; Mary Ryan, Cradle of the Middle Class: The Family in Oneida County, New York, 1790–1865 (Cambridge: Cambridge University Press, 1981), 147–53.

144 Leonore Davidoff and Catherine Hall, Family Fortunes: Men and Women of the English Middle Class, 1780–1850 (Chicago: University of Chicago Press, 1987); Gillis, A World of Their Own Making, 72.

145 See John Tosh, A Man's Place: Masculinity and the Middle-Class Home in Victorian England (New Haven and London: Yale University Press, 1999), chap. 7

146 See Martin Francis, "The Domestication of the Male? Recent Research on
     Nineteenth- and Twentieth-Century British Masculinity," *The Historical
     Journal* 45, no. 3 (2002): 648–9; Tosh, *Manliness and Masculinities*, 61–82; and
     Veronica Strong-Boag, "The Less Than Mighty Scot? The Encounter of
     John Campbell Gordon, Earl / Later Marquess of Aberdeen (and Temair)
     1847-1934, with Hegemonic Masculinity," unpublished essay presented to
     the Annual Meeting of the Canadian Historical Association, June 2011.
147 See Davidoff et al., *The Family Story*, 12, 24–5, 52.

3. Seigneur and Lumberman

 1 [G. Amyot], *Deuxième lettre aux électeurs du Comté de Lotbinière* (n.p., n.d.)
    (CIHM no. 798), 2; G. Amyot, Adresse à MM. les Électeurs du Comté de
    Lotbinière (n.p., n.d.) (CIHM no. 886), 15–16.
 2 Albert Soboul, "Persistence of 'Feudalism' in the Rural Society of Nine-
    teenth-Century France," in *Rural Society in France*, ed. Robert Forster and
    Orest Ranum (Baltimore: Johns Hopkins University Press, 1977), 50–71;
    Michael B. Percy and Rick Szostak, "The Political Economy of Seigneurial
    Tenure in Canada East," *Explorations in Economic History* 29 (1992): 61–3.
 3 See J.I. Little, "Colonization and Municipal Reform in Canada East,"
    Histoire sociale / Social History 14 (1981): 94–121.
 4 Library and Archives Canada [hereafter LAC], Fonds Henri-Gustave Joly
    de Lotbinière [hereafter HGJ Papers], M786, 1751, document notarized
    by Errol Boyd Lindsay, n.p., Que., 27 Nov. 1851. Under the seigneurial
    system no part of the domaine, in the strictest sense of the term, could
    be sold. Benoît Grenier, "'Le dernier endroit dans l'univers': À propos
    de l'extinction des rentes seigneuriales au Québec, 1854–1974," *Revue
    d'histoire de l'Amérique française* 64, no. 2 (Autumn 2010): 80.
 5 The seigneur of Beauharnois exercised the same manoeuvre. André
    Larose, "La seigneurie de Beauharnois, 1729–1867: Les seigneurs, l'espace
    et l'argent" (PhD dissertation, University of Ottawa, 1987), 352. On earlier
    attempts to reform the seigneurial system, see Maurice Séguin, "Le
    régime seigneuriale au pays de Québec, 1760–1854," *Revue d'histoire de
    l'Amérique française* 1, no. 3 (1947): 382–404.
 6 Hélène Leclerc, *Domaine Joly-De Lotbinière* (Quebec City: Éditions Fides,
    2002), 15; Marcel Hamelin, "Joly de Lotbinière, Sir Henri-Gustave," *Dic-
    tionary of Canadian Biography Online*.
 7 The "capital" that could be paid off in one instalment was fixed at seven-
    teen years of annual rent, which in turn represented 6 percent of the capi-
    tal. Grenier, "Le dernier endroit," 82. For other accounts of the "abolition"
    of seigneurial tenure, see Brian Young, *The Politics of Codification: The Lower
    Canadian Civil Code of 1866* (Montreal: McGill-Queen's University Press,

1994), 54–60; Benoît Grenier, *Brève histoire du régime seigneuriale* (Montreal: Boréal, 2012), 202–7; and J.I. Little, "Drummond, Lewis Thomas," *Dictionary of Canadian Biography Online.*

8 See, for example, J.I. Little, "Colonization and Municipal Reform in Canada East." *Histoire sociale / Social History* 14 (1981): 113–15. The £75 ($300) a year in cens et rentes that had been stipulated for the 3,000 arpents granted to Henri-Gustave in 1851 was converted to a total payment of $2,500 or, should he so choose, an annual payment of £150 ($600) in constituted rent that could be paid off at any time. HGJ Papers, M786, 1809–17, seigneurial grant by Julie Chartier de Lotbinière to Henri-Gustave Joly, notarized by Errol Boyd Lindsay, Que., 8 Mar. 1853; 1863, commutation document notarized by Errol B. Lindsay, 24 Nov. 1854. Given that the constituted rent was supposed to equal the cens et rentes, it is not clear why the former was double the latter in this case.

9 See Serge Courville, "La crise agricole du Bas-Canada, éléments d'une réflexion géographique (deuxième partie)," Cahiers de Géographie du Québec 24, no. 63 (1980): 401–9.

10 HGJ Papers, M787, 2316–47, Cadastre Abrégé de la Seigneurie de Lotbinière; Jean Benoît, "La question seigneuriale au Bas-Canada, 1850–1867" (MA thesis, Laval University, 1978), 136.

11 LAC, Fonds Pierre-Gustave Joly [hereafter PGJ Papers], M787, 2817–18, draft agreement between P.G. Joly and Louis Gagnon, 26 May 1861; 2867–70, sale of mill lot to Louis Gagnon, 31 July 1861.

12 Andrée Héroux, "Vers une nouvelle vocation: La production laitière," in *Histoire de Lévis-Lotbinière*, ed. Roch Samson et al. (Sainte-Foy: Les Presses de l'Université Laval, 1996), 323–4.

13 Historians have remained somewhat baffled by the fact that the majority of the former censitaires chose to continue paying the annual rent, but Grenier does point out that legal costs for acquiring full title could be higher than the capital involved and that no financial value would be added to the property. Grenier, "Le dernier endroit," 84–5.

14 Abbé Louis L. Paradis, *Les Annales de Lotbinière, 1672–1933* (Quebec City: L'Action Catholique, 1933), 294–6; Jean Benoît, "La question seigneuriale au Bas-Canada, 1850–1867" (MA thesis, Laval University, 1978), 177, 203.

15 It was clearly that symbolic significance that irritated twentieth-century progressive politicians such as T.D. Bouchard. See Grenier, "Le dernier endroit," 84–5, 90–1.

16 Benoît, "La question seigneuriale," 109. Seigneurs had been legally bound to grant concessions to at least two-thirds of the land in their seigneuries.

Serge Courvillle, "Tradition or Modernity? The Canadian Seigniory in the Durham Era," in *Proceedings of the Seventeenth Meeting of the French Colonial Historical Society, Chicago, May 1991*, ed. Patricia Galloway, 49. The ratio occupied by the 360-arpent Lotbinière domaine was similar to that of several other large seigneuries. See Louis Lavallée, *La Prairie en Nouvelle-France, 1647–1760* (Montreal: McGill-Queen's University Press, 1992).

17 Percy and Szostak, "Abolition of Seigneurial Tenure," 65.

18 It appears that other residents' properties were evaluated at less than their true worth, but this was not so in the case of the Jolys. PGJ Papers, M787, 2228, R. Noël to P.G. Joly, Ste Croix, 9 Mar. 1857.

19 This did not prevent the Jolys from appealing the assessment on their wharf three years later. PGJ Papers, M787, 2236–7, P.J.O. Chauveau to P.G. Joly, Montreal, 18 Apr. 1857; 2478–81, HGJ to cher papa, Que., 10 Apr. 1860.

20 HGJ Papers, M797, Receipt, Ste Emmélie de Lotbinière, 9 Jan. 1871.

21 Benoît Grenier, *Seigneurs campagnards de la Nouvelle France: Présence seigneuriale et sociabilité dans la vallée du Saint-Laurent à l'époque préindustrielle* (Rennes: Presse Universitaires de Rennes, 2007), 363–4.

22 Twenty-three of St Édouard's lots were assessed at $100 or less; 215 at between $101 and $1,000; 72 at between $1,001 and $2,000; 7 between $2,001 and $3,000; and only 1 over that amount (at $3,700). HGJ Papers, M797, 10196–207, Evaluation role, St Édouard de Lotbinière, 30 July 1887; Census Reports of Canada, 1881, 1891.

23 Prior to 1835, at least, ownership of several tracts was common practice in the Quebec district, particularly north of the St Lawrence. Gilles Paquet and Jean-Pierre Wallot, "Economic Strategy of the Habitant Landholder: Quebec, 1790–1835," in *Perspectives on Canadian Economic History*, 2nd ed., ed. Douglas McCalla and Michael Huberman (Mississauga: Copp Clark Longman, 1994), 70.

24 HGJ Papers, M795, 8134–5, L.F. Parrot to HGJ, Leclercville, 4 Dec. 1906; LAC, Fonds Alain Joly de Lotbinière [hereafter AJL Papers], M797, part 2, 41, Eugene Bernard, n.p., to Monsieur le Gérant, Leclercville, 10 Jan. 1947. As of 1935, 60,000 ex-censitaires from more than 200 former seigneuries were still paying these rents. Daniel Salée, "Seigneurial Landownership and the Transition to Capitalism in Nineteenth-Century Quebec," *Quebec Studies* 12 (1991): 24–5; Grenier, *Brève histoire*, 207–8.

25 PGJ Papers, M787, 2956–7, C.E. Desroches to P.G. Joly, Riv. du Chêne, 25 Nov. 1861; 2958–61, C.E. Desroches to HGJ, Riv. du Chêne, 29 Nov. 1861; 2962–7, reconnaissance d'occupation illégale de terre, 30 Nov. 1861; 2977, C.E. Desroches to HGJ, Riv. du Chêne, 27 Dec. 1861.

26 Larose, "La seigneurie de Beauharnois," 412–15; HGJ Papers, M793, 5632, HGJ to J. Stevenson, Que., 18 Dec. 1890.
27 HGJ Papers, M797, 10636, Memoir concerning sales conditions, n.d.
28 The major landholder in Wotton township, Jacques Picard, followed the same strategy, ensuring that he would become the longest-serving member of the Legislative Assembly in the province. See Daniel Sevigny, "Le capitalisme et la politique dans une région Québécoise de colonisation: Le cas de Jacques Picard à Wotton, 1828–1905" (MA thesis, Simon Fraser University, 1982).
29 HGJ Papers, M797, 10651–3, Edmond to HGJ, n.d.
30 Courville, "Tradition or Modernity?," 66.
31 HGJ Papers, M792, 4044, R. Moat and Co. to HGJ, Montreal, 17 Feb. 1888; 4045, draft reply. Lotbinière was truly exceptional in this case, for Grenier writes that scarcely ten seigneuries remained in the hands of the original grantees by the time the system was abolished. Grenier, *Brève histoire*, 161.
32 On this theme, see Grenier, *Brève histoire*, 171–3.
33 PGJ Papers, M787, 2890–1, Eliza Thurber to P.G. Joly, Sept. 1861; 3267, C.E. Desroches to P.G. Joly, Riv. du Chêne, 25 Feb. 1863; Paradis, *Les Annales*, 408.
34 Bibliothèque et Archives nationales du Québec à Québec [hereafter BAnQQ], E13, Fonds Éducation, Correspondance Reçue, 1889–163, HGJ to G. Ouimet, Leclercville, 29 Jan. 1889; reply, 4 Feb. 1889.
35 BAnQQ, E13, Fonds Éducation, Correspondance Reçue, 1894–448, HGJ to Ouimet, Que., 9 Mar. 1894.
36 BAnQQ, E13, Fonds Éducation, Correspondance Reçue, 1890–446, HGJ to G. Ouimet, Que., 28 Mar. 1890.
37 HGJ Papers, M792, 3646, J.M. LeMoine to HGJ, Que., 9 Feb. 1887.
38 HGJ Papers, M792, HGJ to LeMoine, Leclercville, 14 Feb. 1887. On the importance of landlords' judicial powers in eighteenth-century England, see E.P. Thompson, *Customs in Common: Studies in Traditional Popular Culture* (New York: New Press, 1991), 46–9.
39 HGJ Papers, M793, 5289, Rev. Bernier to HGJ, Lotbinière, 27 Sept. 1889. For other such requests, see M 793, 5368–9, Rev. Bernier to HGJ, Lotbinière, 24 Nov. 1889.
40 HGJ Papers, M793, HGJ to Lucy, Leclercville, 8 Feb. 1890; 5527–8, 10 Feb. 1890.
41 HGJ Papers, M794, 6744, Alf. Bélanger to HGJ, Mile End (Institut des Sourds-Muets), 12 July 1896.
42 British Columbia Archives, Mf11A, Letters of His Honour Sir Joly de Lotbinière, 1901–6 [hereafter Letters of His Honour], HGJ to Edmond, Victoria, 29 Aug. 1903.

43 HGJ Papers, M792, 38612, Rev. Mr Beaudet to HGJ, Ste Philomène Des-
   chambault, 6 Nov. 1887; 3864, HGJ to Beaudet, Leclercville, 6 Nov. 1887;
   3869–71, Beaudet to HGJ, 8 Nov. 1887; 3882–3, 12 Nov. 1887; 3884–5, 14
   Nov. 1887
44 HGJ Papers, M793, 4381, Ed. H. Laliberté to HGJ, Warwick, 14 Aug. 1888.
   Parrot was the son of the Protestant Louis-Auguste-Frédéric Parrot from
   Valentigny near Montbéliard, who had been appointed seigneurial agent
   before 1837. Paradis, *Les Annales*, 302. For a description of the relationship
   between the Jolys and the Parrots, see Hazel Boswell, *Town House, Country
   House: Recollections of a Quebec Childhood*, ed. R.H. Hubbard (Montreal:
   McGill-Queen's University Press, 1990), 93–9.
45 As a result, Joly sent him $18 four days later. HGJ Papers, M793, 4442–3,
   L. Lemay to HGJ, Ste Croix, 5 Sept. 1888.
46 HGJ Papers, M793, 4597, Rev. Mère Supérieure to HGJ, Bon Pasteur, Lotbinière, 15 Nov. 1888; 5411, 18 Dec. 1889; M797, 10358, notarized donation
   to fabrique of St Édouard, 22 Jan. 1866. The convent had been established
   in 1863. Paradis, *Les Annales*, 289–90.
47 HGJ Papers, M797, 10346–8, notarized donation to Ste Emmélie, 19 Feb.
   1881; 10354–5, draft of notarized donation to St Édouard, 22 Jan. 1870.
48 HGJ Papers, M793, 4219–21, Rev. A. Boucher to HGJ, 5 June 1888; 4450–1,
   Rev. Bernier to HGJ, Lotbinière, 15 Sept. 1888.
49 Boswell, *Town House*, 120–7. Joly himself described a similar event when
   the Rivière du Chêne flooded, but the heroes were "some of the villagers
   who by incredible pluck and skill made two or three trips in a canoe
   across the roaring river – during the few moments that the banks of ice
   held back the water – to bring away the inhabitants (2 families) fr [*sic*] a
   little island that was almost submerged." He added that "the priests stood
   ready to give them extreme unction when they should float to their death."
   BC Archives, Crease Family Collection, Susan Crease diary, MS 2879, AO
   1847, 12 Dec. 1904.
50 The petition was an acknowledgment of Joly's acquisition of government
   funds for the completion of a local bridge. HGJ Papers, M790, 595–6, Address to HGJ, 1878. See also pp. 631–3 for the address to the same effect
   signed by a large number of men and dated Lotbinière, 14 July 1878.
51 HGJ Papers, M791, 2999–3002, Christopher Rae to HGJ, Rivière Bois Claire,
   1 Feb. 1885.
52 HGJ Papers, M794, 7001, Form for a notarized contract before Charles
   Antoine Lemay, n.p.
53 See, for example, M797, 10516–17, sales deed to Damase Lemay, cultiva-
   teur, notarized by Charles-Antoine Lemay, 9 July 1885. The vast majority

of farmers in Lotbinière and surrounding parishes reported cutting firewood to the 1871 census enumerator, but other forest products were much more limited. LAC, Mikan no. 142105, 1871 manuscript census, schedule 7. This was the only census to include raw forest products.

54 HGJ Papers, M795, 7287–90, HGJ to Edmond, Ottawa, 17 Nov. 1897; 7291–2, 20 Nov. 1897; 7294, 22 Nov. 1897; 7309, printed warning to proprietors of Lucieville, Que., 26 Nov. 1897; 7317–18, HGJ to Edmond, Ottawa, 28 Nov. 1897.

55 HGJ Papers, M795, 7299–306, L.F. Parrot to HGJ, Leclercville, 24 Nov. 1897; M797, 10475–8, L.F. Parrot to HGJ, Leclercville, 25 Nov. 1897; M795, 7307–8, Edmond to HGJ, Que., 26 Nov. 1897; 7311–16, petition to HGJ, 27 Nov. 1897; 7319–21, J. Boisvert, MD, to HGJ, Ste Croix, 29 Nov. 1897.

56 HGJ Papers, M795, 7826–7, HGJ to Pierre Blanchet of St Édouard, Pointe Platon, 18 May 1905; 7888, HGJ to Pierre Castonguay of St Édouard, Que., 19 Jan. 1906.

57 He claimed that of eighty-one contracts, there had been only thirteen infractions in his father's time and one in his. AJL Papers, M797, part 2, 65, A. Joly de Lotbinière to Jeffrey Bélanger, 19 May 1939; 73, Ellwood Wilson to A. Joly de Lotbinière, Knowlton, 2 May 1945.

58 HGJ Papers, M793, 5687, H. Mercier to HGJ, Que., 30 Sept. 1891; M795, 8128, Duke of Argyle to HGJ, Kensington Palace, London, 19 Dec. 1906. Joly is described as wearing such a homespun suit in Boswell, *Town House*, 91.

59 BAnQQ, ZQ118, Seigneurie de Lotbinière, Comptes, 1899–1912, Farm Book, 132–5, 242–3.

60 HGJ Papers, M794, 6052–8, HGJ to Sir Thomas Dyke Acland of Killarton in Exeter, Que., 6 May 1895.

61 HGJ Papers, M792, 3560–3, C.H. Farnham to HGJ, Boston, 20 Dec. 1886; M794, 6533–7, Eleanor McNaughton to HGJ, Que., 15 Apr. 1896; M795, 7373–4, H.A. Kennedy to HGJ, The Times Office, 25 May 1898.

62 HGJ Papers, M795, Will drafted by H.G. Joly de Lotbinière, Que., 4 Feb. 1899.

63 Brian Young, "Revisiting Feudal Vestiges in Urban Quebec," in *Transatlantic Subjects: Ideas, Institutions, and Social Experience in Post-Revolutionary British North America*, ed. Nancy Christie (Montreal: McGill-Queen's University Press, 2008), 142.

64 BAnQQ, P351, S6, Edmond-Gustave Joly de Lotbinière Letterbook, 1898–1902 [hereafter EGJ Letterbook], 8, EGJ to Messrs H.M. Price and Co., 18 Oct. 1898; 11, EGJ to Thomas Coulombe, 1 Nov. 1898.

65 EGJ Letterbook, 18–20, EGJ to Honoré Rousseau, 18 Nov. 1898; 43, EGJ to W.H. Nolle, 19 Dec. 1898. A similarly haughty tone was used in a letter to a local resident who had cut some firewood on the Joly property. EGJ Letterbook, 33, EGJ to Mr. Gagnon, 6 Dec. 1898.

66 BAnQQ, Fonds Joly de Lotbinière, Lettres 1901–6 [herafter Lettres 1901–6], 6–7, EGJ to D. Pottinger, 9 May 1901. Edmond also pressed the railway to build a fence to prevent cattle from wandering onto the tracks and to compensate two local station hands for the loss of the two cows they had been keeping to provide milk for their infants. Lettres 1901–6, 101–3, EGJ to D. Pottinger, Pointe Platon, 1 Oct. 1903.

67 Lettres 1901–6, 70, EGJ to Curé de St Édouard, Pointe Platon, 20 July 1903.

68 Jean Hamelin and Yves Roby, *Histoire économique du Québec, 1851–1896* (Montreal: Éditions Fides, 1971), 82–3; J.I. Little, "Public Policy and Private Interest in the Lumber Industry of the Eastern Townships: The Case of C.S. Clark and Company, 1854–81, *Histoire sociale / Social History* 19 (1986): 15; Jean Benoît, "Burstall, John," *Dictionary of Canadian Biography Online.*

69 PGJ Papers, M787, 2301–12, logging contracts, Nov.-Dec. 1857; Normand Séguin, *La conquête du sol au 19e siècle* (Sillery: Boréal Express, 1977); and J.I. Little, *Nationalism, Capitalism, and Colonization in Nineteenth-Century Quebec: The Upper St. Francis District* (Montreal: McGill-Queens University Press, 1989).

70 Hamelin and Roby, *Histoire économique*, 84; PGJ Papers, M787, 2360–71, logging contracts, 28 Oct. 1858; 2354, contract with C.E. Levey, Que., 14 May 1858; 2381, P.G. Joly to Benson Bennett, Que., 13 May 1859; *Dictionary of Timber Terms* (Sydney, Australia: Timber Secretarial Group, n.d.) *www. timber.asn.au/.../tadc/.../dictionaryoftimberterms-historical.pdf. Accessed 25 Feb. 2013.* The number of logs was increased again to 27,400 in 1859. M787, 2384, logging contracts, 22 Oct. 1859.

71 PGJ Papers, M787, 2391–6, HGJ to P.G. Joly, Que., 12 Nov. 1859; 2412–13, C.E. Desroches to P.G. Joly, Riv. Duchêne, 6 Jan. 1860; 2467, J.K. Bethune to P.G. Joly, Montreal, 29 Mar. 1860; 2505–6, C.E. Desroches to P.G. Joly, Riv. Duchêne, 23 Mar. 1860. Joly informed his sister that there had been a cost overrun of 40,000 francs, which would be $16,667 assuming that 1 franc equalled 24 cents. M787, 2477, K. Alléon to P.G. Joly, Nivelles, 4 Apr. 1860. On the steam sawmills of this era, see Graeme Wynn, *Timber Colony: A Historical Geography of Early Nineteenth Century New Brunswick* (Toronto: University of Toronto Press, 1981), 109–11.

72 Joly claimed to be manufacturing 80,000 boards and culls a year in 1860. PGJ Papers, M787, 2535, C.E. Desroches to P.G. Joly, Riv. Duchêne, 6 June

1860; 2538, P.G. Joly to J.C. Peirce and son, 18 June 1860 (draft reply); Manuscript Census, Canada East, 1861, Lotbinière Parish (C1292).

73 PGJ Papers, M787, 2641–2, Blanzy and Co. to P.G. Joly, Boulonge, 24 Nov. 1860; 2647–9, E. Goepfert to P.G. Joly, Rochefort, 30 Nov. 1860; 2655–8, Hailaust and Co. to P.G. Joly, Nantes, 9 Dec. 1860; 2690, Blanzy and Co., 14 Jan. 1861; 2735, Colas, Delongueil and Co. to P.G. Joly, Paris, 17 Feb. 1861; 2915–18, Hailaust and Co. to P.G. Joly, Nantes, 20 Oct. 1861.

74 PGJ Papers, M787, 3122–5, Hailaust and Co. to P.G. Joly, Nantes, 19 July 1862; 3147–9, 9 Sept. 1862.

75 PGJ Papers, M787, 2688, J.A. Peirce and son to P.G. Joly, St Johns, 14 Jan. 1861; 2829, J. Peirce to P.G. Joly, St Johns, 10 June 1861; 2830–1, Léon Chapdelaine to P.G. Joly, St Ours, 12 June 1861; 2837, J.C. Peirce to P.G. Joly, St Johns, 20 June 1861; 2957, C.E. Desroches to HGJ, Rivière du Chêne, 25 Nov. 1861; 2969, 6 Dec. 1861.

76 Hamelin and Roby, *Histoire économique*, 84–5; PGJ Papers, M787, 3091, Laroche and Venner to P.G. Joly, Que., 18 May 1862.

77 PGJ Papers, M787, 3162–72, logging contracts, 16 Oct. 1862; 3303–8, logging contracts, 25 Oct. 1864.

78 On Burstall, see Benoît, "Burstall, John." Joly also appears to have relied on the local market to some extent, for he reported in March 1886 that the ice bridge across the St Lawrence had not taken, with the result that they were left with $3,000 of ash and other wood on their hands. HGJ Papers, M792, 3286–7, HGJ to Edmond, Leclercville, 20 Mar. 1886. Wynn (*Timber Colony*, 116–18) makes a distinction between brokers and agents in the New Brunswick timber trade.

79 HGJ Papers, M797, 10260–5, Leclercville, 13 Nov. 1865. The supply of pine would diminish in future years, for the Canada Census Report of 1881 records only 2,119 pine logs and 43,603 other logs for Lotbinière County as a whole. Canada Census Report, 1881, table 26, 254–5. In 1901 Lotbinière reported 74 m. feet of pine valued at $995, 1811 m. feet of spruce valued at $16,009, and 5409 m. feet of other logs valued at $42,139. Canada Census Report, 1901, table 54, 354–5.

80 On this theme, see Graeme Wynn, "'Deplorably Dark and Demoralized Lumberers'? Rhetoric and Reality in Early Nineteenth-Century New Brunswick," *Journal of Forest History* 24 (October 1980): 168–87; and Richard W. Judd, "Lumbering and the Agricultural Frontier in Aroostook County, Maine," *Journal of Forest History* 28 (Apr. 1984): 63–5.

81 HGJ Papers, M791, 2660, W.C.J. Hall to HGJ, Que., 14 Apr. 1881; 2711, 1 Sept. 1881. See Andrée Desilets, "Hall, George Benson," *Dictionary of*

Canadian Biography Online. The 1871 manuscript census indicates that all the logs processed in the Joly mill were supplied by Fréderic Parrot, Joly's agent. Manuscript Census, Quebec, 1871, Ste. Emmélie Parish, schedule 6 (C10352).

82 Manuscript Census, Quebec, 1871, Ste. Emmélie Parish, schedule 6 (C10352).

83 René Hardy and Normand Séguin, *Forêt et société en Mauricie* (Montreal: Boréal Express/Musée nationale de l'Homme, 1984), 75; Hamelin and Roby, *Histoire économique*, 88–93. For the dramatic impact of this recession on C.S. Clark and Company, see Little, "Public Policy," 18–19.

84 HGJ Papers, M791, 2966–7, HGJ to James Stevenson, Que., 22 Nov. 1884; 2968, reply, Que., 24 Nov. 1884.

85 This sum did not include the houses occupied by the manager, Fritz Parrot, and sixteen others, assessed at $2,960. HGJ Papers, M797, 10695, Property evaluation, Bureau du conseil, Leclercville, 11 Apr. 1883.

86 HGJ Papers, M792, 3070–1, HGJ to Edmond, Leclercville, 8 July 1885.

87 HGJ Papers, M792, 3118, HGJ to Edmond, Pointe Platon, 2 Oct. 1885.

88 HGJ Papers, M792, 3122–3, HGJ to Edmond, Pointe Platon, 15 Oct. 1885.

89 HGJ Papers, M792, 3128–31, HGJ to Edmond, Leclercville, 4 Nov. 1885. The formation of the ice bridge providing access from Leclercville to the railway on the north shore became increasingly rare after 1900. Martine Côté, "Du Grand Tronc au pont de Québec: Les communications," in *Histoire de Lévis-Lotbinière*, ed. Samson et al., 406.

90 Hamelin and Roby, *Histoire économique*, 93–4; HGJ Papers, M792, 3132–5, logging contract, Leclercville, 5 Nov. 1885. When Joly began hiring crews to work directly for him is not clear, but this was reported in the fall of 1889. His foreman had cut 1,500 logs by the end of December. M793, 5381–2, F. Parrot to HGJ, Leclercville, 29 Nov. 1889; 5430, 30 Dec. 1889.

91 HGJ Papers, M792, 3274, HGJ to Edmond, Leclercville, 20 Mar. 1886.

92 HGJ Papers, M792, 3299–300, HGJ to Edmond, Leclercville, 12 May 1886; M797, 10226–41, details of shipments for John Burstall and Co.

93 The figures have been rounded off to the closest dollar amount. HGJ Papers, M797, 10242–57, Que., 1 Dec. 1886, Bennett and Co.

94 HGJ Papers, M792, 3593–4, J. Stevenson to HGJ, Que., 5 Jan. 1887.

95 HGJ Papers, M792, 3606, J. Stevenson to HGJ, Quebec Bank, Que., 15 Jan. 1887.

96 HGJ Papers, M792, 3629–31, HGJ to Edmond, Leclercville, 28 Jan. 1887.

97 HGJ Papers, M792, 3804, Bennett and Co. to HGJ, 26 Sept. 1887; 3833, F. Parrot to HGJ, Leclercville, 8 Oct. 1887.

98 HGJ Papers, M792, 3941–2, sales contract, 1 Dec. 1887; F. Parrot to HGJ, Leclercville, 29 Dec. 1887.

99 HGJ Papers, M792, 3693, A. Bertrand to HGJ, Drummondville, 17 Mar. 1887.

100 With the arrival of the railway, the tanning industry developed particularly quickly in the neighbouring Eastern Townships, where 34 percent of the province's leather was produced in 1871. See Mario Gendron, *Histoire du Piémont des Appalaches: La Montérégie* (Sainte Foy: Les Presses de l'Université Laval, 1999), 192–4.

101 HGJ Papers, M792, 4072–3, Cooke and Sons to Bennett and Co., Whitehall, NY, 25 Feb. 1888; 4084–5, Bennett and Co. to HGJ, Que., 28 Feb. 1888; M793, 4360–1, F. Pagé to HGJ, Lotbinière, 3 Aug. 1888. According to the Canada Census Reports, Lotbinière County produced 2,075 cords of tan bark in 1871; 2,519 in 1881; and 2,017 in 1891.

102 HGJ Papers, M792, 3823, F. Parrot to HGJ, Leclercville, 9 Oct. 1887; 3843, 20 Oct. 1887; 3849, 27 Oct. 1887.

103 HGJ Papers, M792, 3864, HGJ to Rev. Mr Beaudet, Leclercville, 6 Nov. 1887; 3866–8, Bennett and Co. to HGJ, Que., 7 Nov. 1887; 3886, 14 Nov. 1887; 3909, 18 Nov. 1887.

104 HGJ Papers, M792, 3850, F. Parrot to HGJ, Leclercville, 27 Oct. 1887; 3859, Bennett and Co. to HGJ, Que., 3 Nov. 1887.

105 HGJ Papers, M793, 4511, Bennett and Co. to HGJ, Que., 16 Oct. 1888; 4548, 5 Nov. 1888.

106 HGJ Papers, M793, 4418–9, F. Parrot to HGJ, Leclercville, 25 Apr. 1888.

107 Hamelin and Roby, *Histoire économique*, 94; HGJ Papers, M793, 4623–4, J.X. Perrault to HGJ, 22 Nov. 1888. The amount of firewood cut in Lotbinière County declined from 99,766 cords in 1871 to 85,749 in 1881 and 64,002 in 1891. See Canada Census Reports.

108 HGJ Papers, M793, 4883, Bennett and Co. to HGJ, Que., 8 Feb. 1889; 4972, 21 Mar. 1889.

109 HGJ Papers, M793, 5064, M. Marcotte to Eugene Parrot (telegram), South Que., 2 May 1889; 5065, Bennett and Co. to HGJ (telegram), Que., 2 May 1889; 5067–8, 3 May 1889; 5070, 4 May 1889; 5072–5, Edmond to HGJ, Que., 4 May 1889; 5078, Bennett and Co. to HGJ, Que., 7 May 1889; 5104, 15 May 1889; 5157, 10 June 1889; 5190, 31 July 1889; 5218, 14 Aug. 1889; 5259, F. Parrot to HGJ, Leclercville, 20 Sept. 1889; 5264–5, Bennett and Co. to HGJ, Que., 21 Sept. 1889; 5272, 24 Sept. 1889; 5285, 26 Sept. 1889.

110 HGJ Papers, M793, 5211–12, Bennett and Co. to HGJ, Que., 8 Aug. 1889.

111 HGJ Papers, M793, 5563–5, HGJ to Edmond, Pointe Platon, 1 July 1890.

112 HGJ Papers, M793, 5446, HGJ to Edmond, aboard St Louis, Vendredi matin; 5572, HGJ to Edmond, Que., 23 July 1890; 5599, 20 Aug. 1890; 5601, 22 Aug. 1890. Joly also drew up the accounts for the year's operations, a task normally left to the estate manager. M793, 5502, HGJ to Dear little wife, Leclercville, 1 Feb. 1890. There is a rather romantic description of Joly's visit to a timber shanty and log drive, including the dynamiting of a jam, in Boswell, *Town House*, 58–65.

113 HGJ Papers, M793, 5619, J. Stevenson to HGJ, Que., 30 Nov. 1890; 5621–2, reply, Que., 2 Dec. 1890.

114 HGJ Papers, M793, 5631–4, HGJ to J. Stevenson, Que., 18 Dec. 1890; 5635–6, list of advances required, 29 Dec. 1890.

115 HGJ Papers, M793, 5639–40, J. Stevenson to HGJ, Que., 23 Dec. 1890; 5641–2, HGJ to Stevenson, Que., 27 Dec. 1890; 5643–4, Stevenson to HGJ, Que., 30 Dec. 1890.

116 Hamelin and Roby, *Histoire économique*, 96; HGJ Papers, M793, 5755, HGJ to Edmond, Que., 25 July 1893.

117 HGJ Papers, M793, 5731–7, HGJ to Edmond, Chicago, 24 Apr. 1893.

118 HGJ Papers, M793, 5768, HGJ to Edmond, 19 Nov. 1893; Hamelin and Roby, *Histoire économique*, 96–7.

119 HGJ Papers, M793, 5964, HGJ to Edmond, Leclercville, 4 Oct. 1894.

120 HGJ Papers, M794, 6810, HGJ to Edmond, Ottawa, 30 Aug. 1896; BAnQQ, P1000, S3, D1040, Correspondance d'Éthel Joly de Lotbinière, 1894–5, Lucy Joly de Lotbinière to Ethel, Rivière du Chêne, 17 Mar. 1895.

121 HGJ Papers, M794, 6676–7, Edmond to HGJ, Que., 14 July 1896; 6822, HGJ to Edmond, Ottawa, 3 Sept. 1896.

122 HGJ Papers, M794, 6920–2, HGJ to Edmond, Ottawa, 5 Nov. 1896; 6957, 27 Nov. 1896.

123 HGJ Papers, M794, 6936, HGJ to Edmond, Ottawa, 12 Nov. 1896; 6965, 2 Dec. 1896.

124 HGJ Papers, M794, 7016–19, HGJ to Edmond, Ottawa, 28 Feb. 1897.

125 HGJ Papers, M794, 7052, HGJ to Edmond, Ottawa, 5 Apr. 1897.

126 HGJ Papers, M794, 7056–9, HGJ to Edmond, Ottawa, 7 Apr. 1897.

127 HGJ Papers, M794, 7197–9, HGJ to Edmond, Ottawa, 31 Aug. 1897; 7203–4, 4 Sept. 1897.

128 BAnQQ, AP-G-389, Comptes, 1891–1911, Sir Henri Book, 1.

129 EGJ Letterbook, 57, EGJ to Thomas Coulombe, 9 Feb. 1899; HGJ Papers, M795, 7465, HGJ to Edmond, Ottawa, 13 May 1899; 7466, 16 May 1899; 7468–70, 17 May 1899; M796, 9678–81, Formal notice to Government of Canada, 9 May 1899. The rail line was actually an eastward extension of

the Drummond County Railway, but the Intercolonial leased it in 1898
and purchased it a year later. J. Derek Booth, *Railways of Southern Quebec*,
vol. 2 (Toronto: Railfare, 1985), 108–9.

130 EGJ Letterbook, 83, EGJ to D. Pottinger, 29 July 1899; Lettres 1901–6, 7,
EGJ to D. Pottinger, 9 May 1901; Lettres 1901–6, 33–4, EGJ to D. Pottinger,
Pointe Platon, 11 June 1902; 41–2, 21 Aug. 1902. The claim was rejected in
October. Ibid., 43–4, 10 Oct. 1902. See also ibid., 127–8, EGJ to D. Pottinger,
Que., 14 Mar. 1905.

131 HGJ Papers, M795, 7528–9, HGJ to Edmond, Ottawa, 21 Oct. 1899; 7533–6,
23 Oct. 1899; 7542, HGJ to Edmond, Ottawa, 8 Nov. 1899; 7551–3, 20 Nov.
1899.

132 EGJ Letterbook, 117, EGJ to My dear Harry, 22 Jan. 1900; 184, EGJ to
Mrs Lapelleterie Hall, 15 July 1901.

133 Before chemical treatment for insect damage became common, ties had
to be replaced every five to eight years. Donald J. Pisani, "Forests and
Conservation, 1865–1890," in *American Forests: Nature, Culture and Politics*,
ed. Char Miller (Lawrence: University of Kansas Press, 1997), 17.

134 Pisani, "Forests and Conservation," 17; EGJ Letterbook, EGJ to King Bros,
19 Apr. 1901; 185, 26 Nov. 1901; Lettres 1901–6, 28–9, EGJ to Thomas Fee,
11 Dec. 1901. According to the 1901 Canada Census Report, Lotbinière
County produced 61,002 cords of firewood that year, but only 399 railway
ties (a dramatic drop from the 14,218 in 1891), less impressive than the
128,255 fence posts or even the 457 poles for electric wires.

135 EGJ Letterbook, 75, EGJ to H.M. Price and Co., 16 May 1899; 139, EGJ to
H.M. Price and Co., Que., 29 Dec. 1900; Lettres 1901–6, 35–6, EGJ to Thos
Fee and Son, 10 Jan. 1902; 39, EGJ to J.B. Blouin and Son, Pointe Platon,
16 July 1902.

136 EGJ Letterbook, 137–8, EGJ to Jas Hardwell, ass't-gen'l freight agent, 24
Dec. 1900; 141, EGJ to Hardwell, Que., 29 Dec. 1900.

137 EGJ Letterbook, 174, EGJ to Monsieur l'Agent, 19 Apr. 1901.

138 Letters of His Honour, HGJ to Edmond, Victoria, 24 Dec. 1902. Lotbinière
County had produced 2,357,000 shingles in 1890–1, according to the
Canada Census Report of that year.

139 Comtes, 1891–1911, 16–17.

140 Letters of His Honour, HGJ to Edmond, Victoria, 13 Mar. 1902.

141 Letters of His Honour, HGJ to Edmond, Victoria, 22 Nov. 1902.

142 Lettres 1901–6, 106, EGJ to C. Blouin, Que., 28 Jan. 1904. For reasons that
are not clear, the river was still not "ready" in August. Letters of His Honour, HGJ to Edmond, Victoria, 6 Aug. 1903; 29 Aug. 1903.

143 Letters of His Honour, HGJ to Edmond, Victoria, 4 Nov. 1903.

144 Lettres 1901–6, 111, EGJ to C. Blouin, Que., 20 May 1904.

145 Letters of His Honour, HGJ to Edmond, Victoria, 21 Nov. 1903. No pulpwood was reported for Lotbinière County by the 1891 Canada Census
Report, but there were 18,664 cords in 1900–1.

146 HGJ Papers, M795, 7913, Edmond to HGJ, Que., 5 Feb. 1906; M797, 10670–
80, Contract between HGJ, represented by son Edmond, and Joseph
Legendre of St Flavien parish, Lotbinière County, n.d.

147 HGJ Papers, M795, 7889–97, Edmond to HGJ, Que., 23 Jan. 1906.

148 Lettres 1901–6, 129, EGJ to T.C. Burpee, Esq., Pointe Platon, 4 Sept. 1905;
130, EGJ to Cléophas Blouin, Que., 3 Dec. 1905; 132–3, EGJ to Messrs Lee
and Brooks, Alaindale, 3 Dec. 1905.

149 HGJ Papers, M795, 8135–7, L.F. Parrot to HGJ, Leclercville, 4 Dec. 1906.

150 HGJ Papers, M795, 8162–6, L.F. Parrot to Edmond, Leclercville, 21 Jan.
1906; 8167, 23 Jan. 1907.

151 HGJ Papers, M795, 8167–7, L.F. Parrot to Mon cher monsieur, Leclercville, 28 Jan. 1907; 8184–6, 3 Feb. 1907. The final total was 127,000. M795,
8248–50, L.F. Parrot to Mon cher monsieur, Leclercville, 22 Mar. 1907.

152 Quoted in Martine Côté, "Les ressources fluviales et forestières," in
Histoire de Lévis-Lotbinière, ed. Samson et al., 155. On Caldwell's lumber
business, see ibid., 109–10, 157–60.

153 EGJ Letterbook, 34, EGJ to Mon cher Evangeliste, 6 Dec. 1898.

154 EGJ Letterbook, 70–1, EGJ to D. Pottinger, General Manager, ICR, 11 Apr.
1899. Edmond wrote to another interested party in 1900, "Nous ne per-
mettons jamais aux étrangers de faire aucune espèce de bois chez nous."
EGJ Letterbook, 140, EGJ to R. Arsenault, Que., 29 Dec. 1900.

155 See Little, "Public Policy."

156 Joly's grandson would be saddled with a similar burden, being obliged
to pay $11,500 a year in legacies to members of his family at a time when
annual wages totalled $18,423 and insurance was $1,994. BAnQQ, P351,
S4, SS3, Seigneurie de Lotbinière, Comptes, 1911–12, A. Joly de Lotbinière,
16 Mar. 1912.

157 HGJ Papers, M792, 3163, HGJ to Edmond, Leclercville, 29 Nov. 1885.
There are many letters in the Joly papers concerning this topic, for matters were still not completely settled in 1889.

158 HGJ Papers, M793, 4764, James King to HGJ, Que., 5 Jan. 1889; 4765, draft
reply; 4766–8, Abraham Lorrain to HGJ, Stornoway, 7 Jan. 1889; 4771–2,
draft reply, Leclercville, 1 Feb. 1889. On the railway, which failed to reach
Thetford Mines as planned, see Booth, *Railways*, 137; and Côté, "Du

Grand Tronc," 417–18. On the failure of the gold-mining enterprises near Lake Megantic during the late 1860s, see Little, *Nationalism, Capitalism,* 129–30.

159 Salée, "Seigneurial Landownership," 28.

160 HGJ Papers, M796, 8857, unidentified news clipping titled "L'Hon. M. Joly."

161 Grenier, *Seigneurs campagnards,* 365.

162 Nine of the lots were large enough to be farms, including four that were over 100 arpents in size. HGJ Papers, M797, 10450–3, Cadastre for village incorporé de Leclercville, 1876. For the value of manager Parrot's and the sixteen mill employees' properties, see 10695, Bureau de conseil, Leclercville, 11 Apr. 1883.

163 Gérard Bouchard, "Co-intégration et reproduction de la société rurale: Pour un modèle saguenayen de la marginalité," *Recherches Sociographiques* 29, no. 2–3 (1988): 283–310. Andrée Héroux suggests that the main reason average farm sizes decreased in the Lotbinière region between 1830 and 1852 was that farmers worked in the forest industry. She also suggests, however, that mechanization allowed farmers to increase their land holdings during the following half-century while still engaging in seasonal woods labour. Héroux, "La mise en valeur des terroirs," in *Histoire de Lévis-Lotbinière,* ed. Samson et al., 128–9; Andrée Héroux, "Vers une nouvelle vocation: La production laitière," in *Histoire de Lévis-Lotbinière,* ed. Samson et al., 316–17, 318.

164 Between them the two foundries had $8,800 in fixed capital, employed fifty-seven men for eight months of the year, and manufactured 1,772 stoves as well as 1,100 ploughs with a total value of $31,000. LAC, Quebec Manuscript Census, 1871, Lotbinière Parish, schedule 6 (C10353). For the other two parishes see C10352. See also Benoît Gauthier, "La sous-traitance et l'exploitation forestière en Mauricie (1850–1875)," *Material History Bulletin* 13 (Autumn 1981): 61.

165 Thompson, *Customs in Common,* 21, 24.

166 Ian Radforth, *Bush Workers and Bosses: Logging in Northern Ontario, 1900–1980* (Toronto: University of Toronto Press, 1987), 28. See also Chad Gaffield, *Language, Schooling, and Cultural Conflict: The Origins of the French-Language Controversy in Ontario* (Montreal: McGill-Queen's University Press, 1987), 85–92. But Béatrice Craig is more ambivalent, arguing that the lumber industry of the upper St John valley "trapped marginal farmers in an unenviable position as part-time farmers/part-time laborers, but it also directly and indirectly opened new opportunities for

residents who had the required material and human assets. They began to see their farms at least partly as money-making ventures and stepping-stones to social and political power." Béatrice Craig, "Agriculture and the Lumberman's Frontier in the Upper St. John Valley, 1800–70," *Journal of Forest History* 32, no. 3 (July 1988): 137. On the difficult working conditions and weak bargaining position of woods labourers prior to World War I, see also Hardy and Séguin, *Forêt et société*, 114–34.

167 See Jocelyn Morneau, *Petits Pays et Grands Ensembles: Les articulations du monde rural au XIXe siècle. L'exemple du lac Saint-Pierre* (Sainte-Foy: Les Presses de l'Université Laval, 1999), 280–88.

168 Such honours and rituals included priority in receiving communion, walking directly behind the curé in processions, and burial beneath the parish church. See the introduction to Brian Young, "Generation Matters: Two Patrician Families in the History of Quebec," unpublished typescript; and Grenier, *Brève histoire*, 96–7. Thompson (*Customs in Common*, 45–6) also stresses the importance of what he refers to as "public theatre" in promoting the hegemony of the landed gentry.

4. Liberal Deputy

1 Library and Archives Canada [hereafter LAC], Fonds Pierre-Gustave Joly [hereafter PGJ Papers], M786, 1539–41, P.G. Joy to P.J.O. Chauveau [Paris], 10 Mar. 1848.

2 PGJ Papers, M785, 293–4, Capt. Joseph Filteau et al. to P.G. Joly, 28 Sept. 1830; 263c, rough draft letter by Joly listed as c.1830 in the archival index.

3 See C.P. Stacey, *Canada and the British Army, 1846–1871* (Toronto: University of Toronto Press, 1963), 120–3.

4 PGJ Papers, M787, 2994–5, C.E. Desroches to P.G. Joly, Riv. du Chêne, 3 Jan. 1862; 3004, 20 Jan. 1862; 3009, 10 Feb. 1862.

5 PGJ Papers, M787, 3004, C.E. Desroches to P.G. Joly, Riv. du Chêne, 20 Jan. 1862; 3236, H.G. Stebbins and Sons, New York, 19 Jan. 1863; 3224–9, C.A. Heikscher to P.G. Joly, New York, 13 Jan. 1863.

6 PGJ Papers, M787, 3094, C.E. Desroches to P.G. Joly, Riv. du Chêne, 19 May 1862.

7 PGJ Papers, M787, 2994–5, C.E. Desroches to P.G. Joly, Riv. Du Chêne, 3 Jan. 1862; LAC, Fonds Henri-Gustave Joly de Lotbinière [hereafter HGJ Papers], M796, 9538, certificate for captain of militia, First Battalion, Lotbinière, 23 Apr. 1863. Henri-Gustave Joly attended the School of

Military Instruction at Quebec in 1864, earning a second-class certificate by demonstrating that he was able "to command a Company at Battalion Drill" and "to Drill a Company at 'Company Drill.'" M796, 9549, School of Military Instruction certificate, 20 Apr. 1864.

8 PGJ Papers, M786, 1739–40, P.G. Joly to M. le rédacteur, 30 Oct. 1851.

9 Quoted in Marc Gadoury, "Sir Henri Gustave Joly de Lotbinière: Visionnaire et promoteur de la conservation des forêts, au Québec, à la fin du XIXe siècle" (MA thesis, Université Laval, 1998), 38.

10 Diane Saint-Pierre, "Transformation et encadrement de la société," in *Histoire de Lévis-Lotbinière*, ed. Roch Samson et al. (Sainte-Foy: Les Presses de l'Université Laval), 476–7. See also Peter C. Bischoff, *Les Débardeurs au port du Québec: Tableau de luttes syndicales, 1831–1902* (Montreal: Hurtubise, 2009), 74, 79.

11 Abbé Louis L. Paradis, *Les Annales de Lotbinière, 1672–1933* (Quebec: L'Action Catholique, 1933), 296.

12 Concerning the election, Pierre-Gustave Joly's friend Jules Tailhu, S.J., wrote, "Je suppose que les bons offices de Mr Faucher [the parish priest] n'auront pas été inutiles." PGJ Papers, M787, 2879–80, Jules Tailhau, S.J., to P.G. Joly, Paris, 13 Aug. 1861.

13 *Le Canadien*, 3 July 1861, 17 July 1861. O'Farrell had drafted his own electoral list for 1861, but it was obviously rejected by the authorities. PGJ Papers, M787, 2841–3, N.F. Belleau to cher monsieur, Que., 30 June 1861. With roughly the same population size as St Louis (identified simply as Lotbinière in the *Sessional Papers*) in 1861, St Sylvestre had four times as many voters in 1858. Province of Canada, *Sessional Papers*, 1862, no. 24; Canada Parliament, *Parliamentary Debates* (Ottawa: Canadian Library Association, [1956?]) [hereafter HC Debates], 20 Mar. 1868, 130; Paul G. Cornell, *The Alignment of Political Groups in Canada* (Toronto: University of Toronto Press, 1962), 32, 66, 70, 48–9; Jean-Paul Bernard, *Les Rouges: Libéralisme, nationalisme, et anticléricalisme au milieu du XIXe siècle* (Montreal: Les Presses de l'Université du Québec, 1971), 191. According to McQuillan, O'Farrell had drugged the returning officer so that the votes could be counted by one of his partisans. D. Aidan McQuillan, "Beaurivage: The Development of an Irish Ethnic Identity in Rural Quebec, 1820–1860," in *The Untold Story: The Irish in Canada*, ed. Robert O'Driscoll and Lorna Reynolds (Toronto: Celtic Arts of Canada, 1988), 268; D. Aidan McQuillan, "Pouvoir et perception: Une communauté irlandaise au Québec au dix-neuvième siècle," *Recherches sociographiques* 40, no. 2 (1999): 275. See also John Matthew Barlow, "Fear and Loathing in Saint-Sylvestre: The Corrigan Murder Case, 1855–58" (MA thesis, Simon Fraser University, 1998), 85.

14 PGJ Papers, M787, 3051, U. Tessier to P.G. Joly, Que., 8 Apr. 1862; 3071–3, 25 Apr. 1862.

15 See Bruce W. Hodgins, *John Sandfield Macdonald, 1812–1872* (Toronto: University of Toronto Press, 1971), chap. 3. On the breach in Lower Canadian liberalism, see Yvan Lamonde, *Histoire sociale des idées au Québec, 1760–1896* (N.p.: Fides, 2000), chap. 10.

16 J.M.S. Careless, *Brown of the Globe*, vol. 2 (Toronto: Macmillan, 1963), 92–5; Cornell, *Alignment*, 110.

17 LAC, J 02 3, Canada Legislative Debates, 25 Aug. 1863, 44; Careless, *Brown of the Globe*, 96–7; Bernard, *Les Rouges*, 229. François Évanturel, a member of the Sandfield Macdonald–Sicotte ministry, opposed the union with Dorion, and in his effort to take over Quebec City's Liberal voice, *Le Canadien*, he offered to reimburse Joly and his father for the £250 they had invested in the newspaper's shares. HGJ Papers, M787, 3281–3, F. Évanturel to G. Joly, Bureau of Agriculture and Statistics, 2 Apr. 1863; Gérard Laurence, "Évanturel, François," *Dictionary of Canadian Biography Online*.

18 *Le Canadien*, 13 Aug. 1862, 13 Oct. 1862, 17 Oct. 1862. The elder Joly had expressed interest in contesting the Kennebec seat for the Legislative Council, thereby placing his son in an awkward position because he had already promised to support Charles Cormier of Somerset township. Either the elder Joly withdrew from the contest, or he did not receive the necessary nomination to contest the election, which Cormier won, though not with a majority in Lotbinière County. PGJ Papers, M787, 3126, U. Tessier to H.G. Joly, 28 July 1862; 3129, U.J. Tessier to G. Joly, Rimouski, 8 Aug. 1862; 3139, declaration signed by Amable Paré, president, and N. Thibaudeau, secretary, Ste Croix, 1 Sept. 1862; 3141–5, Dr C. Ouellet to G. Joly, Ste Croix, 5 Aug. 1862; *Le Canadien*, 4 Aug. 1862, 6 Aug. 1862, 20 Aug. 1862, 25 Aug. 1862, 6 Sept. 1862, 15 Sept. 1862, 6 Oct. 1862.

19 Canada Legislative Debates, 8 Oct. 1863, 191; Hodgins, *John Sandfield Macdonald*, 70–1; Careless, *Brown of the Globe*, 99–100.

20 Bernard, *Les Rouges*, 250.

21 Ged Martin, "The Case against Confederation," in *The Causes of Canadian Confederation*, ed. Ged Martin (Fredericton: Acadiensis Press, 1990), 20.

22 P.B. Waite's abbreviated *Confederation Debates* includes only Joly's incendiary attack against Cartier as a traitor to his race. P.B. Waite, ed., *The Confederation Debates in the Province of Canada / 1865* (Toronto: McClelland and Stewart, 1963), 96–7. Joly is completely ignored in P.B. Waite, *The Life and Times of Confederation, 1864–1867* (Toronto: University of Toronto Press, 1962), but receives some attention in Ged Martin, *Britain and the Origins of*

Canadian Confederation, 1837–67 (Vancouver: UBC Press, 1995); and Christopher Moore, *1867: How the Fathers Made a Deal* (Toronto: McClelland and Stewart, 1997). Lengthy samples of his eloquent attacks on the Confederation project can be found in Jane Ajzenstat, Paul Romney, Ian Gentles, and William D. Gairdner, eds., *Canada's Founding Debates* (Toronto: Stoddart, 1999), 138–9, 233–4.

23 HGJ Papers, M795, 8363–413, *Discours de Mr H.G. Joly sur la Confédération, Prononcé à la Chambre le 20 Février 1865* (Quebec City: C. Darveau, 1865).

24 Eighth Provincial Parliament of Canada (3rd Session), *Parliamentary Debates on the Subject of the Confederation of the British North American Provinces* (Quebec: Hunter, Rose & Co., Parliamentary Printers, 1865) [hereafter Confederation Debates], 347 [Google Books. http://books.google.ca/books?id=SEg0AAAAIAAJ. Retrieved 7 July 2008].

25 Confederation Debates, 348.

26 Confederation Debates, 349.

27 Confederation Debates, 356.

28 Confederation Debates, 352–4.

29 Confederation Debates, 350.

30 Confederation Debates, 358.

31 Confederation Debates, 360–1.

32 Confederation Debates, 357.

33 HGJ Papers, M795, 8411, *Discours de Mr H.G. Joly.*

34 Confederation Debates, 354.

35 Quoted in Moore, *1867*, 148.

36 Confederation Debates, 384–5. Without providing evidence, Andrée Désilets nevertheless claims that Langevin demolished Joly's argument. Andrée Désilets, *Hector-Louis Langevin, Un Père de la Confédération Canadienne (1826–1906)* (Quebec City: Les Presses de l'Université Laval, 1969), 151.

37 Confederation Debates, 362.

38 Andrew Smith, "Toryism, Classical Liberalism, and Capitalism: The Politics of Taxation and the Struggle for Canadian Confederation," *Canadian Historical Review* 89, no. 1 (Mar. 2008): 1–4, 18–19.

39 Unlike Christopher Dunkin and Joseph Howe, however, Joly did not speak in favour of imperial federation as an alternative to confederation. Martin, "The Case against Confederation," 28.

40 Martin, "The Case against Confederation," 21.

41 See Marcel Hamelin, *Les Premières années du parlementarisme Québécois (1867–1878)* (Québec: Les Presses de l'Université Laval, 1974); and Arthur

Silver, *The French-Canadian Idea of Confederation, 1864–1900* (Toronto: University of Toronto Press, 1982), chap. 2.

42 Quoted in Marcel Hamelin, "Joly de Lotbinière, Sir Henri-Gustave," *Dictionary of Canadian Biography Online*; Hamelin, *Les Premières années*, 17–22; Bernard, *Les Rouges*, 291–3.

43 Bernard, *Les Rouges*, 310; Marcel Hamelin, ed., *Les débats de l'Assemblée Législative* (Quebec City: Assemblée Nationale du Québec, 1974) [hereafter AN Débats], 30 Dec. 1867, 19.

44 HC Debates, 14 Nov. 1867, 15.

45 Norman Ward, "Called to the Bar of the House of Commons," *Canadian Bar Review* 35 (May 1957): 532.

46 Hamelin, *Les Premières années*, 27, 33.

47 AN Débats, 9 Mar. 1869, 137.

48 HGJ Papers, M795, 8443, *L'Événement* (Montreal), 10 Mar. 1869; Hamelin, *Les Premières années*, 25.

49 HGJ Papers, M789, 61, A.A. Dorion to HGJ, Ottawa, 14 Mar. 1871. The Liberal MLAs passed a resolution to the same effect. HGJ Papers, M789, p. 65, 11 Mar. 1871. However, Joly later asked the premier to stop referring to him as the leader of the opposition because it was not united, like the governing party, by the discipline of the ministry. AN Débats, 22 Nov. 1871, 71.

50 Hamelin, *Les Premières années*, 119–30.

51 Robert Rumilly, *Histoire de la Province de Québec*, vol. 1, *Georges-Étienne Cartier* (Montreal: Éditions Bernard Valiquette, 1942), chap. 4; Charles Langelier, *Souvenirs politiques de 1878 à 1890* (Quebec: Dussault and Proulx, 1909) (CIHM no. 74077), 16–17; Laurier LaPierre, "Politics, Race, and Religion in Canada: Joseph Israel Tarte" (PhD dissertation, University of Toronto, 1962), 17–18; HGJ Papers, M789, 99–100, Edward Blake to HGJ, Toronto, 2 Mar. 1872; M795, 8483, news clipping, *Quebec Morning Chronicle*, 8 Mar. 1872; M796, 8988–9, unidentified news clipping [24 Mar. 1876].

52 Désilets, *Hector-Louis Langevin*, 302–3. On the Protestant Defence Alliance, see J.I. Little, *Nationalism, Capitalism, and Colonization in Nineteenth-Century Quebec: The Upper St Francis District* (Montreal: McGill-Queen's University Press, 1989), 136–7, 155, 163. On the Conservatives' association of Joly with Galt and Huntington, see Robert Rumilly, *Histoire de la Province de Québec*, vol. 2, *Le "Coup d'État"* (Montreal: Éditions Bernard Valiquette, 1942), 44.

53 HGJ Papers, M789, 127–8, HGJ to H. Fabre, Que., 29 Jan. 1876.

54 For details, see Désilets, *Hector-Louis Langevin*, 295–300.

55 HGJ Papers, M789, 234–7, Rev. Auclair to HGJ, Que., 21 Nov. 1877.

56 AN *Débats*, 21 Jan. 1868, 51–2.

57 On this issue, see Hamelin, *Les Premières années*, 168–83.

58 See Hamelin, *Les Premières années*, 12–13, 50–9.

59 AN *Débats*, 30 Dec. 1867, 19.

60 AN *Débats*, 19 Mar. 1869, 184, 197.

61 Quoted in Hamelin, *Les Premières années*, 252.

62 AN *Débats*, 13 Nov. 1876, 12–13.

63 Bruce Curtis, *True Government by Choice Men? Inspection, Education, and State Formation in Canada West* (Toronto: University of Toronto Press, 1992).

64 AN *Débats*, 6 Dec. 1876, 110–18.

65 See Hamelin, *Les Premières années*, 246–53. One exception was the radical Arthur Buies. Jacques Lamarche, *Sir H.-G. Joly de Lotbinière* (Montreal: Lidec, 1997), 24.

66 AN *Débats*, 23 Feb. 1869, 75–9; 12 Jan. 1870, 136–7.

67 AN *Débats*, 1 Dec. 1870, 86.

68 AN *Débats*, 9 Dec. 1870, 111; 12 Dec. 1870, 120–1; 14 Dec. 1870, 129.

69 The second reading of the bill was defeated 38–13. AN *Débats*, 22 Dec. 1870, 181–2; 22 Nov. 1871, 70–1.

70 Hamelin, *Les Premières années*, 129.

71 AN *Débats*, 22 Nov. 1872, 62–3, 70–1.

72 AN *Débats*, 29 Nov. 1872, 90; HC Debates, 27 Mar. 1873, 40.

73 AN *Débats*, 5 Dec. 1873, 15; 9 Jan. 1874, 98; Rumilly, *Histoire*, vol. 1, 285.

74 AN *Débats*, 9 Jan. 1874, 100–3; 22 Jan. 1874, 211; 27 Jan. 1874, 250.

75 HGJ Papers, M789, 57–8, HGJ to P. Levasseur, Ste Croix, 17 Jan. 1874. Because the 4 in 1874 closely resembles a 1, this letter has been misfiled.

76 LAC, MG 26 B, Alexander Mackenzie Fonds, Inward Correspondence (M198), 997–1002, Hector Fabre to A. Mackenzie, Que., 11 Oct. 1875.

77 Alexander Mackenzie Fonds, Inward Correspondence, 1009–10, HGJ to A. Mackenzie, Que., 18 Oct. 1875.

78 Alexander Mackenzie Fonds, Letterbooks, vol. 1, 369, A. Mackenzie to HGJ, Ottawa, 26 Oct. 1875.

79 Andrée Désilets, "Cauchon, Joseph-Édouard," *Dictionary of Canadian Biography Online;* Alexander Mackenzie Fonds, Inward Correspondence, 1462–4, HGJ to A. Mackenzie, Que., 6 Dec. 1876.

80 Alexander Mackenzie Fonds, Inward Correspondence, 1510, Letellier to A. Mackenzie, Que., 24 Jan. 1877.

81 HGJ Papers, M789, 166–8, A. Mackenzie to HGJ, Ottawa, 8 Dec. 1876; 179–85, P. Bachand to HGJ, Saint-Hyacinthe, 23 Jan. 1877; 187–8, HGJ to Bachand, Que., 27 Jan. 1877. Cauchon was finally removed from the cabinet in October 1877, when he became lieutenant governor of Manitoba. Désilet, "Cauchon."

82 AN Débats, 13 Dec. 1871, 184; 20 Nov. 1872, 44. For a brief overview, see Hamelin, *Les Premières années*, 281–6.

83 AN Débats, 5 Dec. 1872, 139–40.

84 AN Débats, 9 Dec. 1872, 159; 10 Dec. 1872, 167–8, 172.

85 AN Débats, 16 Dec. 1872, 207–8; 17 Dec. 1872, 213–15.

86 AN Débats, 23 Dec. 1872, 271–4.

87 The following summary is from Hamelin, *Les Premières années*, 139–55.

88 Rumilly, *Histoire*, vol. 1, 320–1.

89 John T. Saywell, *The Office of Lieutenant-Governor: A Study in Canadian Government and Politics* (Toronto: University of Toronto Press, 1957), 115.

90 AN Débats, 4 Dec. 1874, 32–3.

91 Joly was a member of the committee. AN Débats, 4 Dec. 1874, 34–8; 10 Dec. 1874, 69; 11 Dec. 1874, 73–4.

92 Hamelin, *Les Premières années*, 152–3, 223–7; Rumilly, *Histoire*, vol. 1, 339–41.

93 Joly and his Liberal colleague had dissented from the committee's report because they had wished to add a clause stating that Chapleau had played a leading role in the conspiracy. AN Débats, 25 Nov. 1875, 84–6, 101–2; Hamelin, *Les Premières années*, 223–7.

94 The *Morning Chronicle* (7 June 1875, 8 June 1875) reported 1,400, but based on *La Minerve*'s report, Munro – like Rumilly – claims that there were 3,000 people present. Kenneth J. Munro, *The Political Career of Sir Adolphe Chapleau, Premier of Quebec, 1879–1882* (Lewiston, NY: E. Mellen Press, 1992), 38.

95 Rumilly, *Histoire*, vol. 1, 360–8 (the quote is from 368); Hamelin, *Les Premières Années*, 210.

96 Hamelin, *Les Premières années*, 209–23. For accounts of two of Joly's campaign speeches, see *Morning Chronicle*, 7 June 1875, 8 June 1875, 11 June 1875, 23 June 1875. In contrast to the Conservatives, Joly also took a hard line in the case of a colleague, Georges-H. Deschênes, who had confessed to defaming his political adversary during the 1875 election. Hamelin, *Les Premières années*, 297–8.

97 Rumilly, *Histoire*, vol. 1, 372.

98 See also the account of Joly's role in the charges against Langevin concerning contributions to his election campaign of 1872 in Rumilly, *Histoire*, vol. 1, 373–4; and Désilets, *Hector-Louis Langevin*, 292–4.

99 Hamelin, *Les Premières années*, 77–8, 206–7. Essentially the same argument can be found in Éric Bédard, *Les Réformistes: Une génération canadienne-française au milieu du XIXe siècle* (Montreal: Boréal, 2009), 131, 148, 166–7.

100 Hamelin, *Les Premières années*, 80; AN Débats, 6 Dec. 1871, 154–7. In Ottawa in 1869, however, Joly had voted against Dorion's motion to initiate

reciprocity negotiations with the United States because of that country's hostility to Canada. HC Debates, 18 May 1869, 61.

101 On the local agricultural societies, see Andrée Héroux, "Vers une nouvelle vocation: La production laitière," in *Histoire de Lévis-Lotbinière*, ed. Samson et al., 325–6.

102 HGJ Papers, M797, "Excursion dans le Golfe St Laurent et les Provinces Maritimes pendant l'été de 1869"; Daniel Samson, "'The Yoke of Improvement': Sir John Sinclair, John Young, and the Improvement of the Scotlands, New and Old," in *Transatlantic Rebels: Agrarian Radicalism in Comparative Context*, ed. Thomas Summerhill and James C. Scott (East Lansing: Michigan State University Press, 2004), 108–9.

103 Hamelin, "Joly de Lotbinière"; Hamelin, *Les Premières années*, 42–3, 83–5, 161–2; Jean Hamelin and Yves Roby, *Histoire économique de Québec, 1851–1896* (Montreal: Éditions Fides, 1971), 187–9. Marc Perron, *Un grand éducateur agricole: Édouard-A. Barnard* ([Montreal?]: n.p., 1955), chap. 3.

104 Hamelin, *Les Premières années*, 163–4.

105 AN Débats, 10 Jan. 1874, 110.

106 Rather than tariff protection, Joly suggested that no excise should be charged on sugar beets for a ten-year period. HC Debates, 15 Apr. 1873, 77; 25 Apr. 1873, 129, 160; 13 May 1873, 173.

107 AN Débats, 7 Dec. 1875, 146; 21 Dec. 1875, 270–1. For details, see Hamelin, *Les Premières années*, 166–8, 240–2; and Jocelyn Morneau, *Petits Pays et Grands Ensembles: Les articulations du monde rural au XIXe siècle. L'exemple du Lac Saint-Pierre* (Sainte-Foy: Les Presses de l'Université Laval, 1999), 61–4.

108 HGJ Papers, M796, 8989 [unidentified news clipping, 24 Mar. 1876]. Even though 1,195,345 pounds of Quebec tobacco were reported in the 1871 census, and this amount had doubled by 1881, only ten pounds of local product entered Quebec factories in 1875. Jarrett Rudy, *The Freedom to Smoke: Tobacco Consumption and Identity* (Montreal: McGill-Queen's University Press, 2005), 176.

109 AN Débats, 24 Nov. 1869, 10–11. F.G. Marchand spoke in opposition to funding colonization societies, arguing that the monies should go to agricultural societies instead, but there is no record that Joly did so. Hamelin, *Les Premières années*, 92–4. On the colonization railways, see J.I. Little, *Nationalism, Capitalism, and Colonization in Nineteenth-Century Quebec: The Upper St Francis District* (Montreal: McGill-Queen's University Press, 1989), chap. 7.

110 AN Débats, 17 Nov. 1870, 40–1; Hamelin, *Les Premières années*, 94–6.

111 Rumilly argues that the province initially entrusted its interests "à des hommes probes et économiques, qui les gérèrent en pères de famille."

Rumilly, *Histoire*, vol. 1, 151–2. For Joly's critiques, see, for example, AN Débats, 9 Mar. 1869, 137–43; 2 Apr. 1869, 244–5. Joly also assumed the same role of financial watchdog in Ottawa – where he identified himself as an independent – claiming to be perplexed that the governments of Canada, Quebec, and Ontario could all claim budget surpluses when the less expensive pre-Confederation administration ran yearly deficits. HC Debates, 14 May 1869, 54; AN Débats, 30 Nov. 1870, 79.

112 AN Débats, 31 Mar. 1869, 229. Joly repeated this argument in the succeeding sessions. See 3 Dec. 1869, 41; 17 Dec. 1870, 148–50; Hamelin, *Les Premières années*, 319.

113 AN Débats, 21 Dec. 1869, 122–3; 14 Jan. 1870, 136–7.

114 AN Débats, 17 Dec. 1869, 116; 24 Nov. 1869, 10–11; 29 Nov. 1869, 19; 10 Dec. 1869, 75–9.

115 Hamelin, *Les Premières années*, 48–9.

116 AN Débats, 17 Dec. 1870, 148–50.

117 AN Débats, 6 Dec. 1869, 48–50; 9 Dec. 1869, 61, 69–71; 15 Dec. 1869, 97; 17 Dec. 1869, 114.

118 Hamelin, *Les Premières années*, 59–66.

119 AN Débats, 10 Nov. 1870, 17–18; 25 Nov. 1870, 54; 2 Dec. 1870, 88.

120 AN Débats, 9 Dec. 1870, 111–14, 120–1.

121 AN Débats, 12 Dec. 1870, 123. See also Hamelin, *Les Premières années*, 67–71, which takes a strongly pro-Quebec stand.

122 HC Debates, 15 Nov. 1871, 33–4; Hamelin, *Les Premières années*, 70–1, 158–60.

123 AN Débats, 9 Dec. 1870, 109; 20 Dec. 1870, 166. Hamelin (*Les Premières années*, 107) states that in 1869 approximately thirty-five MLAs were directly interested in the construction of colonization railways.

124 HGJ Papers, M789, 70, Secretary of Quebec and Gosford Railway to HGJ, 5 May 1871; 90–5, HGJ to Eugène Chinic, Que., 5 Jan. 1872.

125 Joly's report of February 1872 had been much more optimistic, and Chauveau insisted that the railway would provide a necessary outlet for colonists in the Lac Saint-Jean region. HGJ Papers, M796, 9751–8, Draft of yearly report submitted to shareholders, 27 Feb. 1872; AN Débats, 6 Dec. 1872, 149–51; 26 Dec. 1872, 256–7; 27 Jan. 1875, 176–8; Hamelin, *Les Premières années*, 191–2; Brian Young, *Promoters and Politicians: The North-Shore Railways in the History of Quebec, 1854–85* (Toronto: University of Toronto Press, 1978), 26; Marc Vallières et al., *Histoire de Québec et de sa région*, vol. 2 (Quebec: Les Presses de l'Université Laval, 2008), 1116–18.

126 Young (*Promoters and Politicians*, 61) speculates that Joly may not have been critical of the government's decision to grant land to the railway

companies because he was seeking government approval to extend his own railway.

127 Hamelin, *Les Premières années*, 102–3, 108–9; AN Débats, 27 Jan. 1875, 177; 21 Nov. 1876, 35; HGJ Papers, M789, 83–4, HGJ to W. Henry, Quebec, 26 Dec. 1871; 94–5, HGJ to E. Chinic, Que., 5 Jan. 1872. Joly had purchased 300 shares at ten dollars each in 1870 and ten shares at the same price in 1872. HGJ Papers, M796, 9730–2, shares certificates.

128 AN Débats, 18 Jan. 1875, 133; 27 Jan. 1875, 176–8; 1 Feb. 1875, 196–7; 3 Feb. 1875, 231; 4 Feb. 1875, 238; 5 Feb. 1875, 250; 8 Feb. 1875, 262; 20 Feb. 1875, 343–4. Joly also embarrassed the government by pointing to Sandford Fleming's report that claimed many parts of the North Shore Railway, then under construction with an $80,000 government advance, were faulty and should be rebuilt. AN Débats, 22 Feb. 1875, 359–60. On the troubled history of the railway project from 1870 to 1874, see Young, *Promoters and Politicians*, chap. 5.

129 For details, see Hamelin, *Les Premières années*, 253–72; and Young, *Promoters and Politicians*, 70–83.

130 AN Débats, 14 Dec. 1875, 206, 222–6.

131 AN Débats, 13 Nov. 1876, 13; Young, *Promoters and Politicians*, 83–4.

132 AN Débats, 11 Feb. 1878, 158–9; 20 Feb. 1878, 216; Hamelin, *Les Premières années*, 270–1. In September 1877 the Bank of Montreal had advanced $500,000 to the province at the unusually high rate of 7 percent, with another $500,000 available when needed. Young, *Promoters and Politicians*, 98.

133 AN Débats, 20 Dec. 1876, 161–3; 29 Jan. 1878, 64–5; 30 Jan. 1878, 74; 19 Feb. 1878, 206; Young, *Promoters and Politicians*, 59, 93–7.

134 AN Débats, 26 Feb. 1878, 248.

135 AN Débats, 16 Feb. 1875, 316; 17 Feb. 1875, 325.

136 AN Débats, 19 Nov. 1872, 35; 15 Jan. 1874, 157–8; 29 Jan. 1875, 183–5; 1 Feb. 1875, 201; HC Debates, 11 Mar. 1873, 15.

5. Quebec Premier

1 Robert Rumilly, "Letellier de Saint-Just, Luc," *Dictionary of Canadian Biography Online*. Revenue from woods and forests declined by over 50 percent between 1874–5 and 1878–9. Pierre Trépanier, "L'Administration Joly (1878–1879)" (MA thesis, Université d'Ottawa, 1972), 4. Joly quickly benefited from Letellier's partisanship by being named a Queen's Councillor. Library and Archives Canada [hereafter LAC], Fonds Henri-Gustave

Joly de Lotbinière [hereafter HGJ Papers], M796, 9558, Queen's Council certificate, 11 Mar. 1878.

2 Trépanier, "L'Administration Joly," 9–10; Kenneth J. Munro, *The Political Career of Sir Adolphe Chapleau, Premier of Quebec, 1879–82* (Lewiston, NY: E. Mellen Press, 1992), 46–7.

3 Trépanier, "L'Administration Joly," 14.

4 Robert Rumilly, *Histoire de la Province de Québec*, vol. 2, *Le "Coup d'État"* (Montreal: Éditions Bernard Valiquette, 1942), 133–4; Parlement de Québec, *Débats de Législature de la Province de Québec* [hereafter PQ Débats], 2 Apr. 1884, 335. Mackenzie refused to allow L.H. Holton to leave Ottawa to become provincial treasurer. All Holton could do was extend his sympathy to Joly for "the difficult position in which you are placed." HGJ Papers, M789, 311–13, L.H. Holton to HGJ, Ottawa, 9 Mar. 1878. The pro-Liberal *Montreal Star* was also critical of the dismissal. See G. Amyot, *Adresse à MM. les Électeurs du Comté de Lotbinière* (n.p., n.d.), 23.

5 Saywell, however, is more critical of Boucherville than is Trépanier. See John T. Saywell, *The Office of Lieutenant-Governor: A Study in Canadian Government and Politics* (Toronto: University of Toronto Press, 1957), 115–18, 235–7; and Trépanier, "L'Administration Joly," 52–9.

6 Trépanier, "L'Administration Joly," 14–16.

7 See Charles Langelier, *Souvenirs politiques de 1878 à 1890* (Quebec: Dussault and Proulx, 1909), 64–5; and Saywell, *Office of Lieutenant-Governor*, 118–19.

8 PQ Débats, 12 Feb. 1878, 84–6; Langelier, *Souvenirs politiques*, 55–9.

9 HGJ Papers, M796, 8784, "Aux Électeurs de la Province de Québec," 28 Mar. 1878.

10 HGJ Papers, M796, 8777–83, "Aux Libres et Intélligents Électeurs de Québec."

11 G. Amyot, *Adresse à MM. les Électeurs du Comté de Lotbinière* (n.p., n.d.) (CIHM no. 886), 2–3.

12 HGJ Papers, M789, 334–6, A. Mackenzie to HGJ, Ottawa, 20 Mar. 1878.

13 Amyot, *Adresse*, 19.

14 Langelier, *Souvenirs politiques*, 66; *Le Journal des Trois-Rivières*, 18 Apr. 1878, quoted in Trépanier, "L'Administration Joly," 26.

15 The Soeurs de Charité de l'Asile de la Providence had been unsuccessfully sued by a private competitor for infringement of patent in the production of a spruce gum syrup with "medicinal" qualities. AN Débats, 22 Dec. 1876, 174–80; *Un procès deux fois gagné: le sirop de gomme d'épinette des Soeurs de la Providence n'est pas un imitation* (1880) [CIHM 4856].

16 Amyot, *Adresse*, 14, 19.

17 Trépanier, "L'Administration Joly," 46; HGJ Papers, M796, 8845, "Report of the Remarks Made by the Hon. H.G. Joly, on the 20th December Last."

18 Amyot, *Adresse*, 1, 25–7.

19 [G. Amyot], *Deuxième lettre aux électeurs du Comté de Lotbinière* (n.p., n.d.), 7.

20 Joly asked the archbishop of Quebec to intervene after the curé of St Apollinaire de Lotbinière attacked the Liberals from the church pulpit. HGJ Papers, M789, HGJ to Archbishop of Quebec, Ste Croix, 24 Apr. 1878.

21 H. Blair Neatby, *Laurier and a Liberal Quebec* (Toronto: McClelland and Stewart, 1973), 6–10.

22 HGJ Papers, M789, 327–30, E. Carter to HGJ, Montreal, 13 May 1878; M790, 1983, E. Carter to HGJ, Montreal, 28 July 1879; 2005, Carter to HGJ, Montreal, 20 July 1879.

23 HGJ Papers, M789, 425–7, A.T. Galt to HGJ, Montreal, 20 Apr. 1878.

24 HGJ Papers, M789, 431–3, R.W. Heneker to HGJ, Sherbrooke, 22 Apr. 1878.

25 Rumilly, *Histoire*, vol. 2, 148; Trépanier, "L'Administration Joly," 30–2. See also Munro, *Political Career*, 55–6. Thomas McGreevy reported to John A. Macdonald, nevertheless, that Joly was extremely popular with the English-speaking population of the Quebec district. J.H. Stewart Reid, Kenneth McNaught, and Harry S. Crowe, eds., *A Source-Book of Canadian History* (Toronto: Longmans, 1967), 347.

26 Désilets, *Hector-Louis Langevin*, 317; Amyot, *Adresse*, 12, 16–17.

27 For a colourful account of this contest, see Langelier, *Souvenirs politiques*, 74–81, 88–90.

28 Diane Saint-Pierre, "Transformation et encadrement de société," in *Histoire de Lévis-Lotbinière*, ed. Roch Samson et al. (Sainte-Foy: Les Presses de l'Université Laval, 1996), 481.

29 Trépanier, "L'Administration Joly," 32–6; Rumilly, *Histoire*, vol. 2, 148, 151; AN Débats, 12 June 1878, 23. Edward Carter claimed that he had convinced W.W. Lynch, MLA for Brome, to support Joly, but Lynch remained a Conservative supporter even after Joly wrote, "I can't believe that the first Gov't which has ever had at its head a Protestant in the Prov of Quebec will be defeated at its first step by the vote of Protestants." HGJ Papers, M789, 327–30, E. Carter to HGJ, Montreal, 13 May 1878; 459–62, HGJ to E. Carter, Que., 14 May 1878.

30 *Le Courrier du Canada*, 4 May 1878. Quoted in translation by Ronald Rudin, *Founding Fathers: The Celebration of Champlain and Laval in the Streets of Quebec, 1878–1908* (Toronto: University of Toronto Press, 2003), 46–7.

31 Trépanier, "L'Administration Joly," 11.

32 Trépanier, "L'Administration Joly," 37–40. The Liberals had voted to abolish the Legislative Council in 1878, arguing that it would save $50,000 a year. When the government argued that this would sacrifice the interests of the minority, the Liberals replied that most English-speaking Quebecers opposed the upper house. AN Débats, 6 Feb. 1878, 139–46.

33 Trépanier, "L'Administration Joly," 41–2.

34 Trépanier, "L'Administration Joly," 43–7.

35 Trépanier, "L'Administration Joly," 48–52, 59–60; Saywell, *Office of Lieutenant-Governor*, 234, 239–43.

36 There are sizeable files on the case in the HGJ Papers, M790, M791, and M795. On the complex constitutional and political issues involved, see Trépanier, "L'Administration Joly," 60–5; and Saywell, *Office of Lieutenant-Governor*, 244–8.

37 Young, *Promoters and Politicians*, 108–9.

38 Rumilly, *Histoire*, vol. 2, 191–2; Trépanier, "L'Administration Joly," 65–6.

39 Trépanier, "L'Administration Joly," 89–92. This bridge, which could not be completed because the Legislative Council rejected the bill sanctioning railway expenditures made during the recess, would provide the link to the Canada Central Railway and therefore the crucial access link to western trade. Published letter by H.G. Joly dated 13 Oct. 1879 to editor of *Morning Chronicle*, in HGJ Papers, M796, 9819; Young, *Promoters and Politicians*, 105–6.

40 Rumilly, *Histoire*, vol. 2, 194, 203; Trépanier, "L'Administration Joly," 93; HGJ Papers, M796, 8769–71, flyer of Tarte's speech titled "Délapidation des Fonds Publics, $12,000 pour la Famille Joly!"

41 Trépanier, "L'Administration Joly," 94.

42 Young, *Promoters and Politicians*, 106–7; Trépanier, "L'Administration Joly," 95. Joly had obviously criticized Langelier while still in office, for the latter wrote to him in October 1879, "Il est évident, à la façon dont vous m'avez acceuilli tout-à-l'heure que nos adversaires ont plutôt votre confiance que ceux qui sont vos amis & font en temps & lieu la bataille pour vous." HGJ Papers, M791, 2522, C. Langelier to HGJ, Quebec, 25 Oct. 1879.

43 David E. Smith, *The Invisible Crown: The First Principle of Canadian Government* (Toronto: University of Toronto Press, 1995), 9.

44 Trépanier, "L'Administration Joly," 97–9; Désilets, *Hector-Louis Langevin*, 327–38.

45 Trépanier, "L'Administration Joly," 99–107.

46 André Paradis, "Le sous-financement gouvernemental et son impact sur le développement des asiles francophones au Québec (1845–1918)," *Revue d'histoire de l'Amérique française*, 50, no 4 (Spring 1997): 573–4, 576, 581.

47 PQ Débats, 19 Feb. 1883, 471–2; 28 Mar. 1883, 1327–36; 30 May 1884, 1488;
    30 Mar. 1885, 440; Robert Rumilly, *Histoire de la Province de Québec*, vol. 4,
    Les "Castors" (Montreal: Éditions Bernard Valiquette, 1942), 45–7; Tré-
    panier, "L'Administration Joly," 119–20.
48 HGJ Papers, M789, 469, Copie d'une résolution adopté par le Comité
    Catholique de Conseil de l'Instruction publique, 15 May 1878; AN Débats,
    12 Aug. 1879, 288–9. The Protestant Committee also protested the cuts to
    the McGill Normal School and the salary of the superintendent of public
    instruction. HGJ Papers, M791, 2009, minutes of special meeting of the
    Protestant Committee of the Council of Public Instruction, Quebec, 30 July
    1879.
49 He also pointed out that the inspectors would no longer be political ap-
    pointees because they had to be approved by the Council of Public Instruc-
    tion. HGJ Papers, M791, 2013–20, J.W. Quebec to Gédéon Ouimet, Quebec,
    30 July 1879.
50 Trépanier, "L'Administration Joly," 108–13; Young, *Promoters and Politi-
    cians*, 109–11.
51 See Munro, *Political Career*, 62–3; Peter C. Bischoff, *Les Débardeurs au port de
    Québec: Tableau des luttes syndicales, 1831–1902* (Montreal: Hurtubise, 2009),
    chap. 6; HGJ Papers, M791, 2146, HGJ to Mr Prince, Quebec, 16 Aug. 1879;
    2149, R. Chambers to HGJ, Quebec, 18 Aug. 1879; 2151, reply, 18 Aug.
    1879. There had also been a strike of ship carpenters the previous year,
    one violent enough that three militia regiments had been dispatched from
    Montreal, and Joly had been forced to promise that salary levels would be
    restored. Rumilly, *Histoire*, vol. 2, 153; Bischoff, *Les Débardeurs*, 254–6; HGJ
    Papers, M796, 8885A, Proclamation prohibiting parades, etc; M790, 559, W.
    Rhodes to HGJ, Quebec, 14 June 1878.
52 HGJ Papers, M791, 2215–16, HGJ to Robitaille, Quebec, 29 Aug. 1879; 2225,
    Robitaille to HGJ, Quebec, 29 Aug. 1879; 2229, F. Langelier to HGJ, 29 Aug.
    1879; 2231, HGJ to Robitaille, Que., 30 Aug. 1879; 2232, response, 30 Aug.
    1879; 2241, HGJ to Robitaille, Quebec, 1 Sept. 1879.
53 Trépanier, "L'Administration Joly," 113–18; Munro, *Political Career*, 63. The
    quote is from Trépanier, "L'Administration Joly," 120.
54 HGJ Papers, M796, 8766, "Les Actes de M. Joly."
55 HGJ Papers, M791, F.B. Godin to HGJ, Joliette, 13 Oct. 1879; reply, Quebec,
    17 Oct. 1879.
56 HGJ Papers, M791, 2271, HGJ to Robitaille, Quebec, 5 Sept. 1879; 2275,
    reply, 5 Sept. 1879; 2278, HGJ to Robitaille, Quebec, 8 Sept. 1879; 2331, HGJ
    to P.A. Patterson, Quebec, 12 Sept. 1879; 2341, G. Drolet to HGJ, Que., 12
    Sept. 1879; 2357, J. Poirier to HGJ, Quebec, 16 Sept. 1879; reply, 16 Sept.

1879; 2467, F. Langelier to HGJ, Quebec, 18 Oct. 1879; 2511–14, HGJ to Robitaille, Quebec, 25 Oct. 1879; 2525–38, Provincial Secretary to HGJ, Quebec, 27 Oct. 1879.

57 Trépanier, "L'Administration Joly," 122–32; Munro, *Political Career*, 64–6.

58 HGJ Papers, M791, 2568–70, HGJ to Robitaille, 29 Oct. 1879.

59 Trépanier, "L'Administration Joly," 132–6; Rumilly, *Histoire*, vol. 2, 214–17.

60 PQ Débats, 28 May 1880, 298–301; LAC, Manuscript Census, Quebec, 1871, Quebec City, St Louis Ward.

61 PQ Débats, 28 May 1880, 299–300. On the failure of this industry in Quebec, see Magella Quinn, "Les capitaux français et le Québec, 1855–1900," *RHAF* 24, no. 4 (1971): 559–60.

62 PQ Débats, 14 July 1880, 666–9. Joly did, however, support the colonists of La Patrie near Lake Megantic against the gold-mining operations of the Conservative federal cabinet minister John Henry Pope. See HGJ Papers, M789, 154–6, Petition to Legislative Assembly from colonists of La Patrie, 26 Nov. 1876; AN Débats, 6 Dec. 1876, 105–7; 26 Dec. 1876, 199, 202–4.

63 PQ Débats, 29 Apr. 1881, 353.

64 PQ Débats, 29 Apr. 1881, 359.

65 PQ Débats, 29 Apr. 1881, 362–3.

66 Quinn, "Les capitaux français," 552.

67 PQ Débats, 29 Apr. 1881, 354–5; 2 May 1881, 391–2; 3 May 1881, 4006–10; 21 May 1881, 561; Quinn, "Les capitaux français," 553.

68 PQ Débats, 2 May 1882, 1231–2. The company survived this crisis, in part by focusing increasingly on the urban market. Quinn, "Les capitaux français," 554–7.

69 PQ Débats, 27 May 1881, 614–15; 30 May 1881, 630–5.

70 *Record of the Hon. Mr. Chapleau's Government and the Hon. Mr. Joly's Platform* [n.p., 1881?]. [CIHM 12325] On Laurier's attack against Sénécal in April 1881, see Munro, *Political Career*, 86–8.

71 Munro, *Political Career*, 94; Robert Rumilly, *Histoire de la Province de Québec*, vol. 3, *Chapleau* (Montreal: Éditions Bernard Valiquette, 1942), 117–25.

72 PQ Débats, 10 Mar. 1882, 493. On the negotiations and Joly's critique, see Young, *Promoters and Politicians*, 126–31.

73 Young, *Promoters and Politicians*, 132. For a brief account of the conflict between Chapleau and the Castors, see Munro, *Political Career*, 108–9.

74 PQ Débats, 22 Mar. 1882, 553–4; 569, 24 Mar. 1882; Young, *Promoters and Politicians*, 133; Munro, *Political Career*, 100.

75 PQ Débats, 28 Mar. 1882, 625–6.

76 PQ Débats, 29 Mar. 1882, 694–707.

77 Quoted in Young, *Promoters and Politicians*, 133.

78 Marcel Hamelin, ed., *Les débats de l'Assemblée Législative* (Quebec City: Assemblée Nationale du Québec, 1974), [hereafter AN Débats], 25 Nov. 1875, 101–2.

79 See Rumilly, *Histoire*, vol. 2, 154; Rumilly, *Histoire*, vol. 3, 11–17, 58–63, 85–94, 113, 117–18, 185; and Pierre and Jean Hamelin, "Mercier, Honoré," *Dictionary of Canadian Biography Online*.

80 Rumilly, *Histoire*, vol. 3, 176.

81 PQ Débats, 31 Mar. 1882, 775–6.

82 *L'Électeur*, 14 Dec. 1882. Cited in PQ Débats, 13 May 1884, 1126–7. See also 1128–31.

83 Joly's letter to Beaugrand of 4 Jan. 1884 is quoted in PQ Débats, 13 May 1884, 1131–2. See also Rumilly, *Histoire*, vol. 4, 33–5.

84 PQ Débats, 1 May 1882, 1166–9. The bill was defeated a second time in the upper house, before being passed in June 1884. PQ Débats, 16 Apr. 1884, 598–609; Rumilly, *Histoire*, vol. 4, 48–9, 150–3; Robert Lévesque and Robert Migner, *Le Curé Labelle: Le colonisateur, le politicien, la légende* (Montreal: La Presse, 1979), 88–90.

85 PQ Débats, 15 May 1882, 1313–15.

86 PQ Débats, 16 May 1882, 1375–80. See also 20 May 1882, 1412, 1414, 1433, 1443.

87 Marcel Hamelin, "Joly de Lotbinière, Sir Henri-Gustave," *Dictionary of Canadian Biography Online*; Rumilly, *Histoire*, vol. 3, 18, 57.

88 Rudin, *Founding Fathers*, 47; Hamelin, "Joly de Lotbinière."

89 HGJ Papers, M791, 2802, Goldwin Smith to HGJ, 10 Apr. 1883; 2810, reply, Quebec, 17 Apr. 1883.

90 HGJ Papers, M791, 2825–7, Goldwin Smith to HGJ, Toronto, 6 July 1883; reply, Quebec, 23 July 1883; 2862–3, Goldwin Smith to HGJ, Toronto, 27 Jan. 1884; 2880, Goldwin Smith to HGJ, Toronto, 7 Mar. 1884.

91 LAC, Laurier Papers, C1164, 207942, HGJ to Laurier, Pointe Platon, 4 July 1883.

92 PQ Débats, 22 Jan. 1883, 68–75; Young, *Promoters and Politicians*, 134–5. Joly later claimed to have coined the phrase "better terms" in 1875. PQ Débats, 19 Feb. 1883, 472. Désilets (*Hector-Louis Langevin*, 351) claims that some Liberals continued to look upon Joly as their chief, but there is no evidence that he was interested in reclaiming that mantle.

93 PQ Débats, 13 Mar. 1883, 995–1001.

94 The government introduced a bill in March 1883 that would authorize it to borrow $500,000 towards the deficit. PQ Débats, 27 Mar. 1883, 1205–7; PQ Débats, 31 Mar. 1884, 221–5.

95 HGJ Papers, M791, 2866–7, Dr Rinfret to HGJ, Ottawa, 1 Feb. 1884; 2870–2, HGJ to George Cary, Quebec, 2 Feb. 1884; Young, *Promoters and*

Politicians, 135; Rumilly, *Histoire*, vol. 4, 138. On the Great Eastern, which was never completed, see J. Derek Booth, *Railways of Southern Quebec*, vol. 2 (Toronto: Railfare, 1985), 111–12.

96 HGJ Papers, M791, 2881, H. Mercier to HGJ, Montreal, 20 Mar. 1884; 2888–8A, reply, 24 Mar. 1884; 2895–6, Dr Rinfret to HGJ, Ottawa, 4 Apr. 1884; 2905–6, reply, Quebec, 5 Apr. 1884. In addition to being approached by English-speaking voters in neighbouring Megantic County, Joly was pressured by Blake and Laurier. M791, 2890–1, H.G. Irvine to HGJ, 24 Mar. 1884; 2892–4, draft reply; 2893, Edward Blake to HGJ, Ottawa, 26 Mar. 1884; 2898, W. Laurier to HGJ, Ottawa, 4 Apr. 1884; 2901–2, joint letter to HGJ, Ottawa, 4 Apr. 1884.

97 PQ Débats, 25 Apr. 1884, 766–74, 779–97; Rumilly, *Histoire*, vol. 4, 140–1, 144–5.

98 PQ Débats, 7 Apr. 1884, 430–6; 15 Apr. 1884, 525–6; 24 May 1884, 1347–52; 26 May 1884, 1377–9.

99 PQ Débats, 27 May 1884, 1390–5.

100 PQ Débats, 17 Apr. 1884, 931–6, 968–9.

101 Ottawa had already provided a retroactive subsidy the previous year for the province's investment in construction of the Montreal-Ottawa branch of the QMOO. Young, *Promoters and Politicians*, 135–7.

102 PQ Débats, 6 Mar. 1885, 194.

103 PQ Débats, 4 June 1884, 1643.

104 PQ Débats, 26 Mar. 1884, 504.

105 PQ Débats, 14 Apr. 1885, 814–22.

106 PQ Débats, 20 Apr. 1885, 1047.

107 Langelier, *Souvenirs politiques*, 189.

108 H. Mercier to E. Blake, 4 Jan. 1882, quoted in P.B. Waite, *Canada 1874– 1896, Arduous Destiny* (Toronto: McClelland and Stewart, 1971), 119.

109 M. Hamelin, ed., *Les Mémoires du sénateur Raoul Dandurand, 1861–1942* (Quebec City: Les Presses de l'Université Laval, 1967), 40; Rumilly, *Histoire*, vol. 2, 271.

110 Trépanier, "L'Administration Joly," 21.

111 PQ Débats, 8 July 1878, 119. The quote is from Trépanier, "L'Administration Joly," 109. Joly also rejected a proposal for another police force in 1878. HGJ Papers, M796, 8887–8, "Estimate showing the cost of a small staff," 23 Oct. 1878.

112 Patrice Dutil, *Devil's Advocate: Godfroy Langlois and the Politics of Liberal Progressivism in Laurier's Quebec* (Montreal: Robert Davies, 1994), 27–8.

113 On Mercier and school reform, see Gilles Gallichan, *Honoré Mercier: La politique et la culture* (Sillery, QC: Septentrion, 1994), chap. 5.

114 The response of the former provincial treasurer, Joseph Gibb Robertson, was simply that "if the men worked and were not paid, it was their own

look-out," and the motion was withdrawn. AN Débats, 23 Dec. 1876, 192; Young, *Promoters and Politicians*, 92–3.

115 Trépanier, "L'Administration Joly," 45.

116 PQ Débats, 18 Apr. 1884, 615–19.

117 PQ Débats, 18 Apr. 1884, 619–22; 20 Mar. 1885, 315.

118 PQ Débats, 6 Feb. 1883, 267.

6. Promoter of National Unity

1 Library and Archives Canada [hereafter LAC], Fonds Henri-Gustave Joly de Lotbinière [hereafter HGJ Papers], M796, 9477, Acadian defence subscription; G.F.G. Stanley, "The Caraquet Riots of 1875," *Acadiensis*, 2, no. 1 (1972–3): 21–38.

2 *Morning Chronicle* (Quebec), 8 June 1875.

3 As already noted, Joly had invested in Strange's unprofitable Calgary horse ranch. Unlike other English-speaking officers, Strange had a high opinion of the French-Canadian troops. On Strange and the Riel uprising see M791, 3005, T.B. Strange to HGJ, Calgary, 10 Apr. 1885; 3011–14, T.B. Strange to HGJ, Calgary, 19 Apr. 1885; M792, 3062, T.B. Strange to HGJ, 3062–7, Camp Beaver River, North of Fort Pitt, 20 June 1885; 3078–83, T.B. Strange to HGJ, 8 June 1885. See also Desmond Morton, "Des canadiens errants: French Canadian troops in the North-West campaign of 1885," *Journal of Canadian Studies* 5, no. 3 (Aug. 1970): 28–39.

4 The imperialist link is stressed by Phillip Buckner, who states that "English-Canadian newspapers compared the Canadian campaign against Riel to the recent British campaigns in Egypt and the Sudan." Phillip Buckner, "The Creation of the Dominion of Canada, 1860–1911," in *Canada and the British Empire*, ed. Phillip Buckner (Oxford: Oxford University Press, 2008), 75.

5 Gillian Poulter, *Becoming Native in a Foreign Land: Sport, Visual Culture and Identity in Montreal, 1840–85* (Vancouver: UBC Press, 2009), 216.

6 HGJ Papers, M792, 3040, HGJ to Edmond, Leclercville, 26 May 1885; 3056, HGJ to Edmond, Pointe Platon, 19 June 1885; 3096–8, Henri Delagrave to HGJ, Quebec, 10 Aug. 1885; 3068, formal invitation, Quebec, 23 June 1885; 3069, draft reply, Quebec, 23 June 1885.

7 HGJ Papers, M792, 3141–2, Lotbinière, 24 Nov. 1885; 3144–7, draft reply.

8 HGJ Papers, M792, 3157–61, Dr C. Rinfret to HGJ, Ste Croix, 27 Nov. 1885.

9 HGJ Papers, M792, 3153–4, HGJ to Editor of *Montreal Daily Witness*, Leclercville, 26 Nov. 1885; 3155–6, HGJ to H. Beaugrand, Leclercville, 26 Nov. 1885.

10 Patrice Dutil, *Devil's Advocate: Godfroy Langlois and the Politics of Liberal Progressivism in Laurier's Quebec* (Montreal: Robert Davies, 1994), 54.

11 HGJ Papers, M792, 3195–6, G.W. Stephens to HGJ, Montreal, 11 Dec. 1885. See also 3395, G.W. Stephens to HGJ, Montreal, 30 Oct. 1886.

12 HGJ Papers, M792, 3212–13, Dr. A. Cameron to HGJ, Huntingdon, 23 Dec. 1885.

13 HGJ Papers, M796, 9120, *L'Électeur*, 28 Nov. 1885.

14 HGJ Papers, M796, 9098 [unidentified news clipping]. G.W. Stephens, a former provincial cabinet minister, wrote in rebuttal that Joly's colleagues had begged him not to resign as party leader and that he had "worked harder in the ranks than he did as leader" without ever expressing discontent with Mercier. HGJ Papers, M796, 9099, *Montreal Daily Witness*, 4 Dec. 1885.

15 HGJ Papers, M792, 3182–3, HGJ to Ernest Pacaud, Leclercville, 3 Dec. 1885.

16 HGJ Papers, M792, 3189–90, E. Pacaud to HGJ, 5 Dec. 1885.

17 HGJ Papers, M792, 3191–92, E. Pacaud to HGJ, 5 Dec. 1885.

18 Quoted in Laurier LaPierre, "Politics, Race, and Religion in Canada: Joseph Israel Tarte" (PhD dissertation, University of Toronto, 1962), 149.

19 HGJ Papers, M792, 3186–8, J.D. Edgar to HGJ, Queen's Park, Toronto, 5 Dec. 1885.

20 HGJ Papers, M792, 3197, HGJ to J.D. Edgar, Quebec, 12 Dec. 1885; 3244, HGJ to Dr Rinfret, Leclercville, 6 Feb. 1886; 3377, HGJ to Downie [Oct. 1886]. Joly clearly would not have been pleased with Edgar's attempt to lure into the Liberal Party those Quebec Conservatives who wanted Macdonald to stay Riel's execution. See Paul Stevens, "Edgar, Sir James David," *Dictionary of Canadian Biography Online*.

21 HGJ Papers, M792, 3234, invitation and reply, 3 Feb. 1886.

22 HGJ Paper, M792, 3242, G.V. Housman to HGJ, The Rectory, Que., 6 Feb. 1886. Joly obviously rejoined later, for he resigned once again when he moved to Ottawa in 1896. M794, 6901–2, Dean R.W. Norman to HGJ, Que., 26 Oct. 1896.

23 HGJ Papers, M792, 3303–5, Dr A. Cameron to HGJ, Que., 31 May 1886; 3375–6, Downie of Downie and Lanctot, Advocates, Barristers, to HGJ, Montreal, 3 Oct. 1886; 3377, HGJ to Downie, n.d.; M796, 9164–5 [unidentified news clipping, 28 Aug. 1886].

24 HGJ Papers, M792, 3378 [torn fragment in HGJ's hand].

25 HGJ Papers, M792, 3425, HGJ to Laurier, Leclercville, 15 Nov. 1886; Jocelyn Saint-Pierre, "Langelier, Sir François," *Dictionary of Canadian Biography Online*.

26 HGJ Papers, M792, 3404, O. Ouellette to HGJ, Somerset, 9 Nov. 1886; 3406, draft reply, 11 Nov. 1886; 3421–3, Laurier to HGJ, Arthabaskaville, 12 Nov. 1886; 3425, HGJ to Laurier, Leclercville, 15 Nov. 1886.

27 HGJ Papers, M792, 3434–8, Laurier to HGJ, Arthabaskaville, 17 Nov. 1886.

28 HGJ Papers, M792, 3462, HGJ to Laurier, Leclercville, 21 Nov. 1886.

29 HGJ Papers, M792, 3491, Charles M. Holt to HGJ, Montreal, 27 Nov. 1886.
    Two months later Langelier reiterated the invitation to contest the Megan-
    tic seat. M792, 3600, F. Langelier to HGJ, Que., 11 Jan. 1887.
30 See, for example, HGJ Papers, M792, 3978–9, R. Harris to HGJ, Kingston
    [1888]; M793, 4343, C.B. Mayne to HGJ, Kingston, July 1888. Joly organized
    the provincial agricultural exhibition in 1887. M792, 3784–5, Lord Lansd-
    owne to HGJ, The Citadel, Que., 12 Sept. 1887.
31 HGJ Papers, M792, 3704–5, Joseph Rielle, secretary Montreal Turnpike
    Trust, to HGJ, 19 Mar. 1887; 3706, draft reply, 22 Mar. 1887. See also 4046–7,
    HGJ to P. Levasseur, Leclercville, 18 Feb. 1888; 4048–51, HGJ to Paré [1888].
32 HGJ Papers, M792, 4173, F.G. Marchand to HGJ, St Jean, 23 Apr. 1888;
    M793, 4279–80, A. Paré to HGJ, Nicolet, 1 July 1888; 4311–12, A. Paré to
    HGJ, Nicolet, 12 July 1888; 4329–30, A. Paré to HGJ, Nicolet, 18 July 1888.
33 Col. William Wood, *The Storied Province of Quebec Past and Present* (Toronto:
    Dominion Publishing, 1931), 245.
34 HGJ Papers, M792, 3769–72, E.R. Johnson to HGJ, Magog, 20 Aug. 1887;
    3773–5, George Cloyes to HGJ, 2 Aug. 1887; 3776–7, H. Lovell to HGJ,
    Coaticook, 23 Aug. 1887; 3778–81, S.A. Fisher to HGJ, Knowlton, 29 Aug.
    1887; Bibliothèque et Archives nationales du Québec à Québec [hereafter
    BAnQQ], Fonds F.G. Marchand, P174, S1, P133, HGJ to F.G. Marchand,
    Pointe Platon, 18 Aug. 1887. On Bowen as sheriff, see J.I. Little, *State and So-
    ciety in Transition: The Politics of Institutional Reform in the Eastern Townships,
    1838–1852* (Montreal: McGill-Queen's University Press, 1997), esp. 31–2
35 HGJ Papers, M793, 4545–7, W. Selby Desbarats to HGJ, Que., 5 Nov. 1888;
    4586, H. Mercier to HGJ, Que., 12 Nov. 1888.
36 HGJ Papers, M793, 4609, R. Stevenson to HGJ, Montreal, 19 Nov. 1888;
    4610, draft reply.
37 HGJ Papers, M792, 4012–13, HGJ to Col. Rhodes, 1 Feb. 1888.
38 HGJ Papers, M792, 4231, HGJ to F. Langelier, Pointe Platon, 17 June 1888.
39 HGJ Papers, M792, 4047, HGJ to P. Levasseur, Leclercville, 18 Feb. 1888.
40 HGJ Papers, M793, 4468–9, John McVicar to HGJ, Detroit, 24 Sept. 1888;
    4471–3, rough draft reply by HGJ.
41 See Réal Bélanger, "L'élite politique canadienne-française et l'Empire brit-
    tanique: trois reflets représentatifs canadiennes-françaises (1890–1917),"
    in *Imperial Canada, 1867–1917*, ed. Colin Coates (Edinburgh: University of
    Edinburgh Centre of Canadian Studies, 1997), 122–40.
42 See Donald Wright, "W.D. Lighthall and David Ross McCord: Antimod-
    ernism and English-Canadian Imperialism, 1880s–1918," *Journal of Cana-
    dian Studies* 32, no. 2 (Summer 1997): 137–8.
43 HGJ Papers, M793, 4625, R.R. Dobell to HGJ, Que., 22 Nov. 1888.

44 Marcel Hamelin, ed., *Les débats de l'Assemblée Législative* (Quebec City: Assemblée Nationale du Québec, 1974), 30 Nov. 1870, 79.
45 Parlement de Québec. Débates de Législature de la Province de Québec [hereafter AN Débats], 22 Jan. 1883, 68–75; Young, *Promoters and Politicians*, 134–5. Joly later claimed to have coined the phrase "better terms" in 1875. AN Débats, 19 Feb. 1883, 472.
46 Karuna Mantena, "The Crisis of Liberal Imperialism," *Histoire@Politique. Politique, culture, société* 11 (May-August 2010): 3, http://www.histoire-politique.fr (accessed 27 Mar. 2012).
47 HGJ Papers, M793, 4642–4, HGJ to Dobell, 26 Nov. 1888.
48 HGJ Papers, M796, 9069, official minutes of the annual meeting of the Imperial Federation League in Canada, Hamilton, 11 May 1889; 9073, Special Council Meeting of the Imperial Federation League in Canada, Toronto, 4 Oct. 1889.
49 HGJ Papers, M793, 4954–60, HGJ to Col. Mayne, Leclercville, 19 Mar. 1889; 5024, HGJ to Major Mayne, Leclercville, 11 Apr. 1889.
50 Colin M. Coates, "French Canadians' Ambivalence to the Empire," in *Canada and the British Empire*, ed. Phillip Buckner (Oxford: Oxford University Press, 2008), 194.
51 HGJ Papers, M793, 5000, J.C. Hopkins to HGJ, Toronto, 4 Apr. 1889; 5042–5, HGJ to J.C. Hopkins, Leclercville, 22 Apr. 1889. On Hopkins, see Jeffrey Keshen, "Hopkins, John Castell," *Dictionary of Canadian Biography Online*.
52 HGJ Papers, M793, 5076–7, J.C. Hopkins to HGJ, Toronto, 7 May 1889; 5095–9, HGJ to Hopkins, Leclercville, 11 May 1889.
53 LaPierre, "Politics, Race, and Religion," 187–9; HGJ Papers, M793, 5274, J.C. Hopkins to HGJ, Toronto, 25 Sept. 1889; 5309–10, HGJ to J.C. Hopkins, Que., 11 Oct. 1889; 5316, J.C. Hopkins to HGJ, Toronto, 19 Oct. 1889; 4866, R. Casimir Dickson to HGJ, Ottawa, 31 Jan. 1890; 4868, draft reply, 5 Feb. 1890. In 1894 Joly would refer to imperial federation as "impracticable." M796, 8976, draft copy of speech to National League.
54 Rhodes had also been deputy for Megantic from 1854 to 1858. Born in England in 1821, he had played a leading role in many enterprises, including mining exploration in Quebec's Wolfe and Megantic counties, the Union Bank of Lower Canada, the Quebec and Richmond Railway, the Quebec and Trois-Pistoles Railway, and the North Shore Railway. http://www.assnat.qc.ca/FRA/membres/notices/q-r/rhodw.htm (accessed 20 Dec. 2009). Rhodes's vision was compatible with the Quebec nationalists insofar as he was promoting northern exploration and colonization in the province as a means of offsetting the attraction that the west would have for French Canadians after the completion of the CPR. LAC, R7346–7-7-E, Robert Bell

fonds, General Correspondence, vol. 31, 31–9, Rhodes to Professor Bell of the Geological Survey of Canada, Quebec, 17 Jan. 1885; 4 Feb. 1885. 30 Apr. 1885.
55 HGJ Papers, M793, 4669–71, HGJ to Edmond, Leclercville, 14 Dec. 1888.
56 HGJ Papers, M793, 4673, HGJ to Edmond, 14 Dec. 1888.
57 HGJ Papers, M793, 4697–700, HGJ to editor of *Montreal Daily Witness*, Leclercville, 18 Dec. 1888.
58 HGJ Papers, M793, 4731, Lt Col. William Rhodes to HGJ, Que., 1 Jan. 1889.
59 J.M. LeMoine, *Maple Leaves*, vol. 3, *Canadian History and Quebec Scenery* (Quebec City: Hunter, Rose, 1865), 85–6. Rhodes's outdoorsman image had been captured in a popular series of staged studio photographs published by Notman in 1866. See Poulter, *Becoming Native*, chap. 2.
60 HGJ Papers, M793, 4732, HGJ to Rhodes, Que., 1 Jan. 1889.
61 HGJ Papers, M793, 4814–16, HGJ to Mercier, 17 Jan. 1889.
62 HGJ Papers, M793, 4864–5, St George Boswell to HGJ, 31 Jan. 1889.
63 See Stanley Brice Frost, *McGill University: For the Advancement of Learning*, vol. 1 (Montreal: McGill-Queen's University Press, 1980), 281.
64 HGJ Papers, M793, 4939–40, W. Dawson to HGJ, Montreal, 15 Mar. 1889; 4943, David Ross to HGJ, Que., 18 Mar. 1889; 4964, David Ross to HGJ, Que., 20 Mar. 1889; 4965, HGJ to Ross, Leclercville, 22 Mar. 1889.
65 HGJ Papers, M793, 4970–1, Col. Rhodes to HGJ, Que., 31 Mar. 1889; 4980, HGJ to Sir William Dawson, Leclercville, 27 Mar. 1889.
66 HGJ Papers, M793, 5436–7, HGJ to E. Pacaud, 8 Feb. 1890. Joly's letter appeared in *L'Électeur*, 12 Feb. 1896. See M796, 9174 and 9177, *Morning Chronicle* (Quebec), 13 Feb. 1890. Bishop's also had to defend itself against the charge that it was a second-rate institution. HGJ Papers, M796, 9175, *Morning Chronicle* (Quebec) [31 Jan. 1890].
67 HGJ Papers, M793, 5494–5, E. Pacaud to HGJ, Que., 26 Jan. 1890.
68 See J.R. Miller, *Equal Rights: The Jesuits' Estates Act Controversy* (Montreal: McGill-Queen's University Press, 1979).
69 HGJ Papers, M793, 5452–9, HGJ to editor of *Montreal Daily Witness*, Que., 7 Jan. 1890. On the legal issues involved, see Roy C. Dalton, *The Jesuits' Estates Question, 1760–1888: A Study of the Background for the Agitation of 1889* (Toronto: University of Toronto Press, 1968), 14–20, 159–63.
70 HGJ Papers, M793, 5529–30, HGJ to Goldwin Smith, Que., 12 Mar. 1890; 5532–4, G. Smith to HGJ, Toronto, 15 Mar. 1890; 5535, HGJ to G. Smith, Que., 19 Mar. 1890.
71 HGJ Papers, M793, 5554, F.A. St-Laurent to HGJ, Que., 3 June 1890; 5556, reply, 3 June 1890.
72 HGJ Papers, M793, 5667–9, H. Mercier to HGJ, Que., 31 Jan. 1891.
73 HGJ Papers, M793, 5669, H. Mercier to HGJ, Rome, 5 May 1891.

74 Pierre Dufour and Jean Hamelin, "Mercier, Honoré," *Dictionary of Canadian Biography Online.*

75 HGJ Papers, M793, 5669, H. Mercier to HGJ, Rome, 5 May 1891.

76 HGJ Papers, M793, 5681–2, W. Laurier to HGJ, Ottawa, 4 Sept. 1891.

77 HGJ Papers, M793, 5687, H. Mercier to HGJ, Que., 30 Sept. 1891.

78 Dufour and Hamelin, "Mercier."

79 Joly confided to a correspondent that he would have accepted a seat in a remodelled cabinet. HGJ Papers, M793, 5709, HGJ to J. Ward, 26 Dec. 1891; 5714–16, W. Laurier to HGJ, Arthabaskaville, 9 Jan. 1892; Dutil, *Devil's Advocate*, 29, 65.

80 HGJ Papers, M793, 5714–19, W. Laurier to HGJ, Arthabaskaville, 9 Jan. 1892.

81 LAC, C738, Laurier Papers, vol. 6, 2078–80, HGJ to Laurier, Que., 22 Jan. 1892.

82 HGJ Papers, M793, 5720, HGJ to W. Laurier, Que., 12 Jan 1892.

83 HGJ Papers, M793, 5705–7, J. Ward to HGJ, Montreal, 25 Dec. 1891.

84 HGJ Papers, M793, 5710, HGJ to J. Ward, 26 Dec. 1891.

85 LAC, MG30, D1, Audet's biographical notes, vol. 16, 549–58.

86 Frank Albert Abbott, "The Quebec Winter Carnival of 1894: The Transformation of the City and the Festival in the Nineteenth Century" (MA thesis, University of British Columbia, 1971), ii, 2–3, 10–12, 60. For more on the leisure theme, see Cindy S. Aron, *Working at Play: A History of Vacations in the United States* (Oxford: Oxford University Press, 1999).

87 Abbott, "Quebec Winter Carnival," 62. On the unity of the city's business class, see Frank Abbott, "Cold Cash and Ice Palaces: The Quebec Winter Carnival of 1894," *Canadian Historical Review* 49, no. 2 (1988): 177–82. Joly arranged for free railway transport for costumed Natives from Lorette who took part in the parade, but he neglected to include the grand chief on his list of invited dignitaries. HGJ Papers, M794, 5789–92, HGJ to Grand Chef Maurice Bastien "Ahgnioulen" [sp.?], Que., 23 Jan. 1894; Abbott, "Cold Cash," 190.

88 HGJ Papers, M794, 5808–20, Aberdeen to HGJ, Ottawa, 6 Feb. 1894.

89 The Aberdeens' sleigh was pulled through the streets to the recently built Chateau Frontenac by members of various snowshoe clubs. John T. Saywell, ed., *The Canadian Journal of Lady Aberdeen, 1893–1898* (Toronto: Champlain Society, 1960), 64, 67.

90 Abbott, "Cold Cash," 174–5, 184; HGJ Papers, M794, 5827–9, B. Letellier to HGJ, Que., 9 Feb. 1894.

91 See HGJ Papers, M793, 5762, A.C. Campbell to HGJ, Toronto, 30 Aug. 1893; 5773, HGJ to Horace Archambault, Dec. 1893; 5777–9, J.J. Maclaren to HGJ, Toronto, 15 Jan. 1894. Laurier initially had Tarte, now a Liberal MP, in

mind but had been informed that his vocal support of remedial legislation in the Manitoba Schools Question had made him unpopular in Ontario. LaPierre, "Politics, Race, and Religion," 273. Tarte was at this time
working towards having Mowat commit to running for federal office as
a means of overcoming radical Protestant opinion in that province. K.M.
McLaughlin, "Race, Religion and Politics: The Election of 1896 in Canada" (PhD dissertation, University of Toronto, 1974), 186. Miller (*Equal
Rights*, 171–2) stresses the differences between the ERA and the PPA. On
the PPA, see J.T. Watt, "Anti-Catholic Nativism in Canada: The Protestant
Protective Association," *Canadian Historical Review* 68 (1967): 45–58.

92 Saywell, ed., Canadian Journal, 67.
93 HGJ Papers, M794, 5832–4, E. Pacaud to HGJ, Que., 11 Feb. 1894.
94 HGJ Papers, M794, 5787, Edward Blake to HGJ, Toronto, 22 Jan. 1894;
    5793, Edward Blake to HGJ, Toronto, 26 Jan. 1894. Charles Langelier
    reminded Joly that the Quebec government had donated $10,000 towards
    the reconstruction of the university after much of it had been destroyed
    by fire. M794, 5821–3, C. Langelier to HGJ, Que., 7 Feb. 1894.
95 HGJ Papers, M794, 5795–7, J.J. Maclaren to HGJ, Toronto, 29 Jan. 1894;
    Jean-Marie Lebel, "Tassé, Joseph," *Dictionary of Canadian Biography Online*.
96 *Montreal Daily Witness*, 15 Jan. 1894. On Papineau and his wife, Mary
    Westcott, see Françoise Noël, *Family Life and Sociability in Upper and Lower
    Canada, 1780–1870* (Montreal: McGill-Queen's University Press, 2003).
97 HGJ Papers, M794, John J. Maclaren to HGJ, Toronto, 30 Jan. 1894; 5801, F.
    Pedley to HGJ, Toronto, 1 July 1894. The phrase "truly national spirit" ap-
    pears in the rough draft of a speech Joly delivered to the National League
    in Quebec shortly after his Ontario visit, in which he denied that he had
    assumed the role of Protestant minority representative and suggested that
    educated English Quebecers should make some effort to learn French. (I
    was unable to find any information on this organization). HGJ Papers,
    M796, 8971, 8973, 8975.
98 The address of welcome mistakenly referred to Joly's "efforts to bring
    about a Confederation of the Provinces." HGJ Papers, M794, 5838–9, An
    Address of Welcome to the Hon. H.G. Joly de Lotbinière, Kingston, 21
    Feb. 1894. Judging from the coverage by the 10 Mar. 1894 edition of Lon-
    don, Ontario's *Catholic Record*, Joly's Toronto speech was essentially the
    same as the one in Kingston. See HGJ Papers, M796, 8970.
99 HGJ Papers, M796, 8968–9, *Daily British Whig* (Kingston), 23 Feb. 1894.
100 Ontario's Equal Rights Association published Sellar's pamphlet in 1889,
    and 1916 saw the publication of his book, *The Tragedy of Quebec: The
    Expulsion of Its Protestant Farmers*. This book was reprinted with Robert

Hill's introduction by the University of Toronto Press in 1974. For a brief critical analysis, see J.I. Little, "Watching the Frontier Disappear: English-Speaking Reaction to the French-Canadian Colonization Movement in the Eastern Townships, 1844–90," *Journal of Canadian Studies* 15, no. 4 (1980–1): 107–8.

101　HGJ Papers, M796, 8968–9, *Daily British Whig* (Kingston), 23 Feb. 1894.

102　British Columbia Archives, Mf 11A, Letters of His Honour Sir Joly de Lotbinière, 1901–6, HGJ to Edmond, Victoria, 6 Dec. 1901; HGJ Papers, M794, 5848, Aberdeen to HGJ, Ottawa, 3 Mar. 1894; 5852–5, D.R. Cameron to HGJ, Kingston, 5 Mar. 1894.

103　HGJ Papers, M794, 5856–8, HGJ to Lord Aberdeen, Que., 7 Mar. 1894.

104　HGJ Papers, M794, 5860–1, Aug. Dupuis to HGJ, Village des Aulnaies, 20 Mar. 1894; draft reply.

105　HGJ Papers, M796, 8983, *Montreal Daily Witness*, 20 Feb. 1894. For Sellar's response to Joly's Toronto speech, see his "Defence of the Quebec Minority" in HGJ Papers, M796, 8981.

106　Jacques Lamarche, *Sir H.-G. Joly de Lotbinière* (Montreal: Lidec, 1997), 52.

107　Marcel Hamelin, ed., *Les mémoires du Sénateur Raoul Dandurand (1861–1942)* (Quebec City: Les Presses de l'Université Laval, 1967), 85, 88.

108　BAnQQ, F.G. Marchand Fonds, P174, S1, P135, HGJ to F.G. Marchand, Ottawa, 16 May 1897; P136, HGJ to F.G. Marchand, Ottawa, 30 July 1899.

109　HGJ Papers, M794, 5990–5, W. Laurier to HGJ, Arthabaskaville, 16 Nov. 1894.

110　HGJ Papers, M794, 6022–4, HGJ to Editor of *Montreal Daily Witness*, Que., 9 Feb. 1895.

111　In fact, this meant that in rural Manitoba, where most of the French Canadians lived in parishes in which they constituted the majority, the religious exercises were Catholic. Robert Comeau, "La question des écoles du Manitoba – Un nouvel éclairage," *Revue d'histoire de l'Amérique française* 33, no. 1 (1979): 3–23.

112　*Montreal Daily Witness*, 28 Nov. 1894.

113　Quoted in Paul Crunican, *Priests and Politicians: Manitoba Schools and the Election of 1896* (Toronto: University of Toronto Press, 1974), 60–1.

114　HGJ Papers, M794, 6047–50, HGJ to Monseigneur Langevin, Que., 3 May 1895; Crunican, *Priests and Politicians*, 88–9.

115　HGJ Papers, M794, 6060–2, Louis J.A. Papineau to HGJ, Manoir de Monte Bello, 11 May 1895.

116　HGJ Papers, M794, 6064–9, HGJ to Mr Papineau, Pointe Platon, 21 May 1895. Joly also objected to the claim in a book by the Bishop of Springfield

that the Church of Rome "is to be classed with Calvinism and Lutheran-
ism" and to the book's "other heresies & schisms which pervert and
corrupt the truth and rend the body of Christ." Joly also remarked, "I
look up to Religion as a source of peace and do not find much of it in
these controversial books." HGJ Papers, M794, 6123–4, HGJ to Rev. G.H.
Parker, Que., 27 Dec. 1895.

117 HGJ Papers, M794, 6591, W.A. Marsh to HGJ, Que., 9 May 1896.

118 HGJ Papers, M794, 6070, Lord Ripon to HGJ, 24 May 1895. For an account
of the dinner offered in Joly's honour by Quebec City's Union Club, see
Morning Chronicle (Quebec), 4 July 1895, clipping in HGJ Papers, M796,
8881.

119 David Cannadine, *Ornamentalism: How the British Saw the Empire* (London:
Penguin, 2001), 86–7.

120 HGJ Papers, M794, 6041–4, Ishbel Aberdeen to HGJ, Ottawa, 6 Apr. 1895.

121 HGJ Papers, M794, HGJ to Dr Rinfret, 6243, Que., 17 Jan. 1896. For the
petition, see 6029–3.

122 See Jeffrey Simpson, *The Spoils of Power: The Politics of Patronage* (Toronto:
Collins, 1988), 120.

123 *L'Électeur*, 12 Feb. 1895, in HGJ Papers, M796, 8935.

124 Ronald Rudin, *Founding Fathers: The Celebration of Champlain and Laval
in the Streets of Quebec, 1878–1908* (Toronto: University of Toronto Press,
2003), 70–2.

125 Joly had, however, rejected the invitation to be president on the grounds
that the distribution of funds inevitably resulted in disappointment for
some participants. He explained, "I do not wish to assume any hostile
position towards those with whom I have worked so happily in the past."
BAnQQ, P73, Fonds George Moore Fairchild, AP-F-3-4, HGJ to Fairchild,
Pointe Platon, 14 Aug. 1895; 30 Aug. 1895.

126 HGJ Papers, M794, 6264–6, Lady Aberdeen to HGJ, Ottawa, 24 Jan. 1896;
6270–7, 28 Jan. 1896. On the Aberdeens' futile efforts at this time, see Crunican, *Priests and Politicians*, 179–83.

127 LAC, MG27, I, B5, Aberdeen Papers, Correspondence, vol. 2, 636–42, HGJ
to Lady Aberdeen, Que., 3 Feb. 1896.

128 See McLaughlin, "Race, Religion and Politics," 314–15.

129 LAC, MG27, I, B5, Aberdeen Papers, Correspondence, vol. 2, 636–42, HGJ
to Lady Aberdeen, Que., 3 Feb. 1896.

130 HGJ Papers, M794, 6451, J.S. Willison to HGJ, Toronto, 12 Mar. 1896; HGJ
to Editor of the "Globe," Que., 14 Mar. 1896.

131 Quoted in Crunican, *Priests and Politicians*, 253–4.

132 McLaughlin, "Race, Religion, and Politics," 322–4, 328–9.

133 HGJ Papers, M794, 6635–41, Arthur Delisle to HGJ, Montreal, 3 July 1896.

134 Quoted in translation in J.H. Stewart Reid, Kenneth McNaught, and Harry S. Crowe, eds., *A Source-Book of Canadian History* (Toronto: Longmans, 1967), 360.

135 Crunican, *Priests and Politicians*, 331, 333.

136 *Morning Chronicle* (Quebec), 15 June 1896.

137 *Morning Chronicle* (Quebec), 16 June 1896.

138 *L'Électeur*, 15 June 1896. The quote is from Crunican, *Priests and Politicians*, 282.

139 Saywell, *Canadian Journal*, 347.

140 Mgr L.N. Bégin to HGJ, St Evariste de Forsyth, 15 June 1896, in *Documents Pour Servir à l'Intélligence de la Question des Écoles du Manitoba* (Rome: A. Befani, 1896), 125–6.

141 McLaughlin, "Race, Religion, and Politics," chap. 9; A.I. Silver, *The French-Canadian Idea of Confederation, 1864–1900* (Toronto: University of Toronto Press, 1982), chap. 9. The fact that the Acadians of New Brunswick voted Conservative despite the inroads the Liberal Party had been making among them suggests that their minority status made them more sensitive than the Quebecers to the situation of the French-speaking Manitobans. See J.I. Little, "New Brunswick Reaction to the Manitoba Schools' Questions," *Acadiensis* 1, no. 2 (1971): 43–58.

142 Saywell, *Canadian Journal*, 347. The coverage by the Liberal *L'Électeur* and Conservative *Morning Chronicle* suggests that in Portneuf the schools question was by far the dominant one in the many *assemblées contradictoires*.

143 Crunican, *Priests and Politicians*, 333.

144 See J.R. Miller, "Anti-Catholic Thought in Victorian Canada," *Canadian Historical Review* 66, no. 4 (1985): esp. 477.

145 But the popular vote in 1896 for the Liberals in Ontario almost equalled that for the Conservatives. J.M. Beck, *Pendulum of Power: Canada's Federal Elections* (Scarborough, ON: Prentice-Hall, 1968), 80, 96.

7. Forest Conservationist

1 Library and Archives Canada [hereafter LAC], Pierre-Gustave Joly Papers [hereafter PGJ Papers], M787, 2405, G. Tailhau, S.J., to P.G. Joly, ca 1860.

2 On the origins of the forest conservation movement in the United States, see Donald J. Pisani, "Forests and Conservation, 1865–1890," in *American Forests: Nature, Culture and Politics*, ed. Char Miller (Lawrence: University of Kansas Press, 1997). On its Canadian origins, see R. Peter Gillis and

Thomas R. Roach, *Lost Initiatives: Canada's Forest Industries, Forest Policy and Forest Conservation* (New York: Greenwood Press, 1986).

3 On this theme, see Michel F. Girard, "Conservation and the Gospel of Efficiency: Un modèle de gestion de l'environnement venu d'Europe?" *Histoire sociale/Social History* 23, no. 45 (May 1990): 63–80.

4 René Hardy and Normand Séguin, *Forêt et société en Mauricie. La formation de la région de Trois-Rivières, 1830–1930* (Montreal: Boréal Express, 1984), 17–21; Guy Gaudreau, *L'Exploitation des forêts publiques au Québec, 1842– 1905* (Quebec: Institut québécois de recherche sur la culture, 1986), 13–18, 21–2.

5 Donald MacKay, *Heritage Lost: The Crisis in Canada's Forests* (Toronto: Macmillan, 1985), 25. One exception was the introduction of a ground rent of fifty cents per acre in 1851. Gaudreau, *L'Exploitation*, 19–21.

6 Richard Judd, *Common Lands, Common People: The Origins of Conservation in Northern New England* (Cambridge, MA: Harvard University Press, 1997).

7 Article reprinted in *Eastern Townships Gazette and Shefford County Advertiser* (Granby), 24 Dec. 1862.

8 Marcel Hamelin, ed., *Les débats de l'Assemblée législative* (Quebec City: Assemblée Nationale du Québec, 1974) [hereafter AN Débats], 18 Dec. 1873, 75–6. Colin Coates notes that wood had become scarce close to settlements even in the early eighteenth century and that deforestation had seriously damaged the landscape by the 1820s. Colin Coates, *The Metamorphoses of Landscape and Community in Early Quebec* (Montreal: McGill-Queen's University Press, 2000), 36, 129. In 1872 the former superintendent of education, Jean-Baptiste Meilleur, expressed a similar concern. Marc Gadoury, "Sir Henri Gustave Joly de Lotbinière: Visionnaire et promoteur de la conservation des forêts, au Québec, à la fin du XIXe siècle" (MA thesis, Laval University, 1998), 27–8. On the firewood problem in Trois-Rivières, see Hardy and Séguin, *Forêt et société*, 188–9.

9 Gillis and Roach, *Lost Initiatives*, 109–10.

10 AN Débats, 18 Dec. 1873, 75–7.

11 Marcel Hamelin, *Les Premières années du parlementarisme Québécois (1867– 1878)* (Québec: Les Presses de l'Université Laval, 1974), 186. For a case study of the government's ineffectiveness in managing the Crown timber, see J.I. Little, "Public Policy and Private Interest in the Lumber Industry of the Eastern Townships: the Case of C.S. Clark and Company, 1854–1881," *Histoire sociale/Social History* 19 (May 1986): 9–37.

12 AN Débats, 9 Dec. 1871, 178; 8 Nov. 1872, 8–10; 13 Dec. 1872, 193.

13 Hamelin, *Les Premières années*, 187.

14 Hardy and Séguin, *Forêt et société*, 21.

15 AN Débats, 9 Dec. 1873, 49–51.

16 Hamelin, *Les Premières années*, 184; AN Débats, 19 Nov. 1872, 37–8. Joly, in turn, claimed credit as the originator of the idea. AN Débats, 9 Dec. 1872, 159.

17 AN Débats, 5 Dec. 1873, 13–14; 9 Dec. 1873, 48–50. Rumilly is clearly mistaken in stating that Joly indulged in academic jousts while Tremblay, who first levied the charge, took an aggressive role in this debate. Robert Rumilly, *Histoire de la Province de Québec*, vol. 1, *Georges-Étienne Cartier* (Montreal: Éditions Bernard Valiquette, 1942), 288.

18 AN Débats, 9 Dec. 1873, 53–6.

19 Hardy and Séguin, *Forêt et société*, 80–2.

20 Canada. Parliament. *Sessional Papers*, 1878, no. 11, pt. 8, no. 9, Report of the Minister of Agriculture for 1877, appendix no. 1, Report on Forestry and Forests of Canada, by H.G. Joly [hereafter Joly Report, 1877], 1–5.

21 LAC, Fonds Henri-Gustave Joly de Lotbinière [hereafter HGJ Papers], M793, 5740, HGJ to Edmond, Leclercville, 22 May 1893; 5742–4, Pointe Platon, 22 May 1893.

22 The italicized phrase appears as such in the original. Joly Report, 1877, 5–9. On the forest fire problem, see René Hardy, "Exploitation forestière et environnment au Québec, 1850–1920," *Zeitschrift der Gesellschaft für Kanada-Studien* 27, no. 2 (1995): 69, 72; and Stephen J. Pyne, "Mon pays, c'est le feu. Le Québec, le Canada, les forêts et le feu," *Globe. Revue internationale d'études québécoises* 9, no. 1 (2006): 141–75.

23 Paul-André Linteau, René Durocher, and Jean-Claude Robert, *Quebec: A History, 1867–1929*, trans. Robert Chodos (Toronto: Lorimer, 1983), 112.

24 Joly Report, 1877, 10–14.

25 Joly was referring to the Société pour le Reboisement de la Province de Québec, formed in 1872, of which he himself was vice president. Despite its name, members who came from the Quebec City elite were simply pledged to plant a small number of trees in the old parishes in order to act as examples for the local farmers. Gadoury, "Sir Henri Gustave," 28–9.

26 Joly Report, 1877, 15–20; *La Gazette des Campagnes*, 22 Aug. 1878–12 Dec. 1878.

27 On Little, who published pamphlets on the subject in 1872 and 1876, see Gillis and Roach, *Lost Initiatives*, 34–5.

28 He agreed, however, not to press for a vote on his resolutions, but to allow them to stand as recommendations only. AN Débats, 11 Feb. 1878, 158; 21 Feb. 1878, 224–7.

29 Hon. H.G. Joly, *Forest Tree Culture, from a Paper in the Montreal Horticultural Society's Report for 1880* (Montreal: Witness Printing House, 1881), 3–12. A

year later, Joly presented an update on his experiences with black walnut in particular, reporting that he had sown about 10,000 in his nursery the previous fall. Hon. H.G. Joly, *The Returns of Forest Tree Culture: A Paper from the Report of the Montreal Horticultural and Fruit Grower's Association* (Montreal: Witness Printing House, 1882), 7.

30 AN Débats, 11 Apr. 1882, 1015–27.

31 AN Débats, 11 Apr. 1882, 1032–3; 4 May 1882, 1257–60, 1265.

32 *Proceedings of the American Forestry Congress at Its Sessions Held at Cincinnati, Ohio, in April, 1882, and at Montreal, Canada, in August, 1882* (Washington, DC: Printed for the Society, 1883), 15, 22, 24, 25.

33 For brief accounts of the Cincinnati meeting, see MacKay, *Heritage Lost*, 28–32; and Gillis and Roach, *Lost Initiatives*, 35–6.

34 Gillis and Roach, *Lost Initiatives*, 36–41; Gadoury, "Sir Henri Gustave," 55–7. On the conflict between colonists and lumber companies, see Hardy and Séguin, *Forêt et société*, 152–6.

35 HGJ Papers, M796, 9678–81, Notarized notice to Government of Canada, 9 May 1899.

36 He also complained that the railway refused to take responsibility for a fire that it had caused the previous year. Edmond Joly de Lotbinière's comments in *Canadian Forestry Association: Report of the Fourth Annual Meeting, 1903*, 26–7, 46–8.

37 BAnQQ, P351, S4, SS3, Seigneurie de Lotbinière, Comptes, 1911–12, A. Joly de Lotbinière, 16 Mar. 1912.

38 Parlement de Québec. Débats de Législature de la Province de Québec [hereafter PQ Débats], 22 Jan. 1883, 73–4.

39 PQ Débats, 14 Feb. 1883, 317–18.

40 PQ Débats, 21 Mar. 1883, 1130–1; 26 Mar. 1883, 1188–90; Gillis and Roach, *Lost Initiatives*, 42, 111–12.

41 For Joly's role at the St Paul meeting, see *Proceedings of the American Forestry Congress at Its Sessions Held at St. Paul, Minn., in August, 1883* (Washington, DC: n.p., 1884), 1, 16, 17, 29–30, 44–5.

42 Gillis and Roach, *Lost Initiatives*, 40.

43 Other Canadians who delivered papers were William Little, A.T. Drummond, and J.K. Ward. *Proceedings of the American Forestry Congress at Its Meeting Held in Boston, September, 1885* (Washington: Judd and Detweiller, 1886), v–vii, 36–40, 79–80.

44 Gadoury, "Sir Henri Gustave," 59. Joly had launched another small initiative as president of the number two Lotbinière agricultural society. In 1879 the society's program announced that it would offer prizes for the most beautiful tree plantations, both ornamental and utilitarian, planted that

spring or fall. Trees would be judged by their vigour and form rather than their size. Gadoury, "Sir Henri Gustave," 48.

45 PQ Débats, 15 May 1882, 1335–7. On the depletion of trees for fuel and fences in the seigneury of La Prairie during the French regime, see Louis Lavallée, *La Prairie en Nouvelle-France, 1647–1760: Étude d'histoire sociale* (Montreal: McGill-Queen's University Press, 1992), 175.

46 In 1885 Joly ordered, on behalf of the corporation of Quebec City, 189 maples, 60 balsam firs, and 33 red spruces. In 1896 he was asked to preside over the ceremony in Quebec City where approximately 250 trees were to be planted along rue St Louis. HGJ Papers, M792, 3035–6, bill drafted by Auguste Dupuis, Village des Aulnaies, 18 May 1885; M794, 6571–2, A. Sylvestre to HGJ, Quebec, 5 May 1896. For further details, see Gadoury, "Sir Henri Gustave," 60–4; and Hardy, "Exploitation forestière," 71–2.

47 H.G. Joly, "The Study of Forestry as an Important Contributor to Practical Education," State Horticultural Society, *Annual Report*, 236–8 (read at the St Paul meeting of the American Forestry Congress, August 8, 1883).

48 BAnQQ, E13, Fonds Éducation, Correspondance Reçue, 1883–108, Circulaire aux commissaires et syndics et aux instituteurs et institutrice, au sujet de la plantation des arbres, Que., 16 Apr. 1892.

49 Pisani, "Forests and Conservation," 23–5.

50 BAnQQ, E13, Fonds Éducation, Correspondance Reçue, 1883–108, 1894–2147, HGJ to Protestant Committee of Council of Public Instruction, Que., 20 Sept. 1894; Secretary to HGJ, 9 Oct. 1894; secretary to inspectors Taylor and McGregor, Que., 2 June 1895.

51 H.G. Joly de Lotbinière, "La Fête des Arbres," *La Revue Nationale* 1, no. 3 (Apr. 1895): 221–6.

52 Joly de Lotbinière, "La Fête des Arbres."

53 Abbé Gingras, "Reboisement: Hommage à l'Hon. H.-G. Joly," *La Verité*, 9 May 1885, in HGJ Papers, M786, 9157–8.

54 Gadoury, "Sir Henri Gustave," 59–60, 64–5, 67; HGJ Papers, M793, 4243, C.B. Mayne to HGJ, Kingston, July 1888; 4733–6, R.J. Harrington to HGJ, McGill College, Montreal, 2 Jan. 1889.

55 HGJ Papers, M792, 4192–3, M.W. Kirwan to HGJ, Somerset, 8 May 1888.

56 Gadoury, "Sir Henri Gustave," 66.

57 Joly also reiterated his call for the classification of public lands, strict regulations on the minimum size of logs, more effective fire protection, and the maintenance of export duties on saw logs. H.G. Joly de Lotbinière, "Forestry in Canada," *Annual Report of the Montreal Horticultural Society and Fruit-Growers' Association of the Province of Quebec* 14 (1889): 146–9.

58 HGJ Papers, M793, 5545, HGJ to Edmond, Quebec, 6 Apr. 1890; 5597–8, HGJ to Edmond, Pointe Platon, 20 Aug. 1890.

59 J.M. LeMoine, ed., *Maple Leaves*, vol. 4 (Quebec City: L.J. Demers, 1894), 308–22; *Proceedings of the American Forestry Association at the Summer Meeting, held in Quebec, September 2–5, 1890* (Washington, DC: Secretary's Office, 1891), 68–70.

60 Col. William Wood, *The Storied Province of Quebec Past and Present* (Toronto: Dominion Publishing, 1931), 245.

61 HGJ Papers, M794, 6006–8, A.G. Lang to J.M. Lemoine, Pres., Royal Society of Canada, Loch Tay, 27 Nov. 1894.

62 Existing timber licences remained in place in these parks. See Bruce W. Hodgins, Jamie Benidickson, and Peter Gillis, "The Ontario and Quebec Experiments with Forest Reserves, 1883–1930," *Journal of Forest History* 26, no. 1 (1982): 23–4.

63 HGJ Papers, M794, 6908, Lord Aberdeen to HGJ, Coldstream Ranch, Vernon, BC, 26 Oct. 1896.

64 HGJ Papers, M794, 6102–7, Mary C. Simpson Ross to HGJ, the Manor House, Beaurivage, 14 Oct. 1895. For other cases, see M794, 6092, Jules Tessier to HGJ, Lac St Joseph, 1 Sept. 1895; 6300–2, Hiram Calvin to HGJ, Ottawa, 5 Feb. 1896; 6375, A.C. Reesor to HGJ, Locust Hill, Ont., 28 Feb. 1896; 7082–3, HGJ to Edmond, Ottawa, 11 May 1897.

65 The letter was translated by Joly's son Edmond, who included it in his address to the Canadian Forestry Association in 1902. See E.G. Joly de Lotbinière, "The Danger Threatening the Crown Lands Forests of the Province of Quebec," in *Canadian Forestry Association, Report of the Third Annual Meeting* (Ottawa, 1902), 107–8.

66 *Victoria Daily Colonist*, 14 July 1900, 7. Much of the pulpwood sold on the export market was supplied by Quebec farmers and settlers. Pulpwood cut in Quebec increased from approximately a fifth of sawn lumber production in 1900 to three-fifths in 1910, doubling or nearly doubling each decade between 1900 and 1930. Linteau, Durocher, and Robert, *Quebec: A History*, 389; Gillis and Roach, *Lost Initiatives*, 107–9. For a detailed history of the industry, see Jean-Pierre Charland, *Les pâtes et papiers au Québec, 1880–1980: Technologies, travail et travailleurs* (Quebec City: Institut Québécois de Recherche sur la Culture, 1990).

67 See Gillis and Roach, *Lost Initiatives*, 54–8; MacKay, *Heritage Lost*, 46–9; and Girard, *L'écologisme retrouvé*, 32–4.

68 British Columbia Archives, Mf 11A, Letters of His Honour Sir Joly de Lotbinière, 1901–6 [hereafter Letters of His Honour], HGJ to Edmond, Victoria, 6 Dec. 1901.

69 Wood, *The Storied Province*, 245.

70 Thomas Roach and Richard Judd, "A Man for All Seasons: Frank John Dixie Barnjum, Conservationist, Pulpwood Embargoist and Speculator!" *Acadiensis* 20, no. 2 (1991): 132–7, 143–4.

71 Letters of His Honour, HGJ to Edmond, Victoria, 13 Feb. 1902; 16 Feb. 1902. In January 1900 the Quebec government imposed a charge of $1.90 per cord on pulpwood that was to be exported, but reduced it to sixty-five cents the following June. Ontario had actually imposed the manufacturing condition on raw logs cut on Crown lands in 1898 and on pulpwood in 1900. Joly de Lotbinière, "The Danger Threatening," 106; Gillis and Roach, *Lost Initiatives*, 85–6.

72 Letters of His Honour, HGJ to Edmond, Victoria, 24 Feb. 1902.

73 Letters of His Honour, HGJ to Edmond, Victoria, 13 Mar. 1902.

74 Joly de Lotbinière, "The Danger Threatening," 107.

75 Letters of His Honour, HGJ to Edmond, Victoria, 28 Nov. 1902.

76 Letters of His Honour, HGJ to Edmond, Victoria, 6 Dec. 1902.

77 Letters of His Honour, HGJ to Edmond, Victoria [n.d.; the first four pages of the letter are missing]; HGJ to Edmond, 23 Jan. 1906. Quebec would not impose the manufacturing condition on pulpwood until 1910. On the reasons, see Gillis and Roach, *Lost Initiatives*, 107–9.

78 *Canadian Forestry Association: Report of the Third Annual Meeting*, 102–3.

79 Letters of His Honour, HGJ to Edmond, Victoria, 25 Apr. 1905.

80 See Girard, *L'écologisme retrouvé*, 36–9.

81 Girard is clearly mistaken in assuming that the elder Joly attended the conference, given that he was still in Victoria in January. HGJ Papers, M795, 7909–11, Edmond to HGJ, Quebec, 5 Feb. 1906; Letters of His Honour, HGJ to Edmond, Victoria, 12 Feb. 1906; Janet Foster, *Working for Wildlife: The Beginning of Preservation in Canada*, 2nd ed. (Toronto: University of Toronto Press, 1998), 34–5.

82 E.G. Joly de Lotbinière, "Compulsory Timber Reserves on Settlers' Lands," *Canadian Forestry Convention, Held at Montreal, 11 and 12 March 1908* (Quebec: Department of Lands and Forests, 1908), 12.

83 Joly de Lotbinière, "Compulsory Timber Reserves," 13–14.

84 HGJ Papers, M795, 7737, G.W. Stephens to HGJ, Montreal, 28 Mar. 1903; 7739–41, Summary of Stephens's report in Joly's handwriting; 7743, G.W. Stephens to HGJ, Montreal, 1 Apr. 1903; 7745–6, Joly's notes on Stephens's report; Gillis and Roach, *Lost Initiatives*, 114.

85 The forest reserve policy followed the recommendation of the Colonization Commission. Ironically, these reserves were gradually dismantled after the formation of the Quebec Forestry Service in 1909, but Joly would

have taken comfort in the implementation that same year of the manu-facturing condition for pulpwood cut on Crown lands. MacKay, *Heritage Lost*, 49, 52–3; Gillis and Roach, *Lost Initiatives*, 114–23; Hodgins, Benidick-son, and Gillis, "The Ontario and Quebec Experiments," 27–31.

86 Pisani, "Forests and Conservation," 25–8.

87 Donald Worster, *Nature's Economy: A History of Ecological Ideas*, 2nd ed. (Cambridge: Cambridge University Press, 1994), 266–8.

88 PGJ Papers, M787, 2356, L.N. Sicotte to J.W. Dunscome, Toronto, 20 May 1858; Hardy, "Exploitation forestière," 74; Sylvain Gingras, *Hunting and Fishing in Quebec: A Century of Sport* (St-Raymond, QC: Les Éditions Rapides Blancs, 1994), 191–3.

89 Girard, *L'écologisme retrouvé*, 23–6.

90 PQ Débats, 11 Apr. 1882, 1011–14.

91 For a brief discussion of Marsh, see Worster, *Nature's Economy*, 268–9. Janet Foster (*Working for Wildlife*, 12) points out that during the nineteenth century wildlife "was seldom viewed in terms of conservation or preser-vation. It was generally viewed as a food supply, a source of recreation through fishing and hunting and, much later, as a substantial producer of tourist revenues."

92 British Columbia Archives, Crease Family Collection, Susan Crease diary, MS 2879, AO 1847, 11 Dec. 1904.

93 PQ Débats, 13 Apr. 1885, 750–1.

94 *Histoire et Nature du Domaine Joly-De Lotbinière* (Fondation du Domaine Joly-De Lotbinière, 2006), 1.

95 Joly de Lotbinière, "Forestry in Canada," 150.

96 Gadoury, "Sir Henri Gustave," 78–81. To his acquaintances, Joly also shipped Lombardy poplars and maples. HGJ Papers, M793, 4246, Dr Douglas to HGJ, New York, 20 June 1888; 4550, Mrs Matilda Smith to HGJ, Kent, 6 Nov. 1888.

97 Joly, *Forest Tree Culture*, 6; Henri G. Joly de Lotbinière, "Eastern Forest Trees Grown at Victoria, B.C., From Seed," *The British Pacific* 1 (1902): 4 [my thanks to Howard Smith for this article].

98 Doug Owram, "Progress, Science, and Religion: Exploring Victorian Thought in Canada," in *Thinkers and Dreamers: Historical Essays in Honour of Carl Berger*, ed. Gerald Friesen and Doug Owram (Toronto: University of Toronto Press, 2011), 231–2.

99 On natural history in Quebec, see Girard, *L'écologisme retrouvé*, 20–1; and Raymond Duchesne and Paul Carle, "L'ordre des choses: Cabinets et musées d'histoire naturelles au Québec (1824–1900)," *Revue d'histoire de l'Amérique française* 44, no. 1 (1990): 3–30.

100 Joly, *Forest Tree Culture*, 3. Joly repeated much the same words in the *Gazette des Campagnes* in 1881. Gadoury, "Sir Henri Gustave," 2.
101 J.G.A. Creighton, "French Canadian Life and Character," in *Picturesque Canada*, vol. 1, ed. George Monro Grant (Toronto: Belden, 1882), 80–1.
102 Gadoury, "Sir Henri Gustave," 74–6, 81.
103 Brian Young, "Generation Matters: Two Patrician Families in the History of Quebec," unpublished typescript, 309.
104 Joly also sent western species such as the large-leaved maple (*Acer macrophylum*) to the east. Joly de Lotbinière, "Eastern Forest Trees," 3–4; Gadoury, "Sir Hector Gustave," 82–3; Letters of His Honour, HGJ to Edmond, Victoria, 13 Mar. 1902; 30 May 1902.
105 *Daily Colonist* (Victoria), 17 Nov. 1908.
106 Gadoury, "Sir Henri Gustave," 88–9.

8. Laurier Cabinet Minister

1 *L'Électeur*, 27 June 1896.
2 See John T. Saywell, "The Cabinet of 1896," in *Cabinet Formation and Bicultural Relations: Seven Case Studies*, ed. Frederick W. Gibson (Ottawa: Queen's Printer, 1970), 37–45. Saywell notes that because of his Protestantism, "many papers preferred not to include Joly as a true member of the French Canadian society" (40).
3 Library and Archives Canada [hereafter LAC], Fonds Henri-Gustave Joly [hereafter HGJ Papers], M794, 6676–7, Edmond to HGJ, Que., 14 July 1896.
4 HGJ Papers, M791, 2766–8, HGJ to O. Mowat, Que., 23 Dec. 1882.
5 On the early development of the Canadian commodities inspection and weights and measure systems, see Bruce Curtis, "From the Moral Thermometer to Money: Metrological Reform in Pre-Confederation Canada," *Social Studies of Science* 28, no. 4 (1998): 557–66. The question of how to grade various types of wheat did not emerge until after Joly had left Ottawa. See John F. Varty, "On Protein, Prairie Wheat, and Good Bread: Rationalizing Technologies and the Canadian State, 1912–1935," *Canadian Historical Review* 85, no. 4 (2004): 721–53.
6 HGJ Papers, M794, 6815–17, HGJ to Edmond, Ottawa, 30 Aug. 1896; Canada Parliament, *Parliamentary Debates* (Ottawa: Canadian Library Association, [1956?]) [hereafter HC Debates], 14 Sept. 1896, 1033.
7 HGJ Papers, M794, 6653–5, Camille Germain to HGJ, Cap Santé, 12 July 1896.
8 HGJ Papers, M794, 6695, E. Duggan to HGJ, Que., 15 July 1896.

9 HGJ Papers, M794, 6668, G.B. Hall to HGJ, Que., 13 July 1896; 6693, Thos. Davidson to HGJ, Quebec, 15 July 1896; LAC, Sir Wilfrid Laurier Fonds [hereafter Laurier Papers], C743, vol. 21, 7492A-B, HGJ to Laurier, Ottawa, 25 Sept. 1896; C748, vol. 43, 14095C-F, HGJ to Laurier, Ottawa, 22 Apr. 1897; C764, 31648A-B, HGJ to Laurier, Ottawa, 23 Mar. 1899. During the months leading up to the election, Tupper had padded the civil service with Conservative Party stalwarts. Jeffrey Simpson, *Spoils of Power: The Politics of Patronage* (Toronto: Collins, 1988), 106.

10 HC Debates, 7 May 1897, 1654.

11 Simpson, *Spoils of Power*, 104–6; HC Debates, 29 Sept. 1896, 1902.

12 W.L. Morton, "The Cabinet of 1867," in *Cabinet Formation and Bicultural Relations*, ed. F.W. Gibson (Ottawa: Queen's Printer, 1970), 3.

13 HC Debates, 31 Mar. 1873, 47; 8 May 1873, 157.

14 Parlement de Québec, *Débats de Législature de la Province de Québec*, 20 Dec. 1877, 10.

15 HC Debates, 28 Aug. 1896, 296; Laurier Papers, C745, vol. 28, 9475A, undated newspaper clipping; HGJ Papers, M794, 6823, HGJ to Edmond, Ottawa, 3 Sept. 1896.

16 Gordon Stewart, "Political Patronage under Macdonald and Laurier, 1878–1911," *American Review of Canadian Studies* 10, no. 1 (1980): 3–4.

17 The quote is from Stewart, 'Political Patronage,' 7.

18 Quoted in Stewart, "Political Patronage," 10–12. I have corrected the obvious spelling mistakes in these names.

19 HGJ Papers, M794, 6948, HGJ to Edmond, Ottawa, 19 Nov. 1896.

20 Laurier Papers, C745, vol. 28, 9444B-F, C.F. McIsaac to Laurier, Antigonish, 30 Nov. 1896; 9444G, HGJ to C.F. McIsaac, Ottawa, 19 Nov. 1896.

21 HGJ Papers, M794, 6966, HGJ to Edmond, Ottawa, 2 Dec. 1896.

22 HGJ Papers, M794, 6971–3, HGJ to Edmond, Ottawa, 7 Dec. 1896.

23 Laurier Papers, C745, vol. 28, 9444A, HGJ to Laurier, Ottawa, 2 Dec. 1896.

24 John T. Saywell, "Introduction," *The Canadian Journal of Lady Aberdeen, 1893–1898* (Toronto: Champlain Society, 1960), lxxxi–lxxxii.

25 Laurier Papers, C745, vol. 28, 9475B-E, HGJ to Laurier, Ottawa, 3 Dec. 1896.

26 Laurier Papers, C744, vol. 27, 9254A-B, HGJ to William Mulock, Ottawa, 28 Nov. 1896.

27 Laurier Papers, C745, vol. 28, 9475C-E, HGJ to Laurier, Ottawa, 3 Dec. 1896; HC Debates, 18 May 1897, 2188. Joly also argued that accepting a ministerial salary "cannot be done without giving the lie to our solemn pledges to the people." Laurier Papers, C750, vol. 48, 15431A, HGJ to Fitzpatrick, Ottawa, 31 May 1897.

28 See Laurier Papers, C746, vol. 32, 10813A-D, HGJ to Laurier, Ottawa, 9 Jan. 1897; 10813E, T.C. Gaboury to Laurier, Bresson, 31 Dec. 1896.

29 Laurier Papers, C748, vol. 39, 12989A-J, HGJ to Laurier, Ottawa, 12 Mar. 1897.

30 Laurier Papers, C747, vol. 39, 12898–9, Jno. A. Macdonell to HGJ, Winnipeg, 10 Mar. 1897.

31 Laurier Papers, C750, vol. 48, 15449A, HGJ to Laurier, Ottawa, 1 June 1897.

32 Laurier Papers, C746, vol. 34, 10907A, HGJ to Laurier, Ottawa, 12 Jan. 1897. A Board of Examiners independent of party control had been established by the Civil Service Act of 1882, but its minimal standards meant that it did not represent a challenge to patronage appointments. Ken Rasmussen, "Administrative Reform and the Quest for Bureaucratic Autonomy, 1867–1919," *Journal of Canadian Studies* 29, no. 3 (1994): 53–4.

33 Laurier Papers, C748, vol. 41, 13352A-C, HGJ to Laurier, Ottawa, 22 Mar. 1897. See also vol. 43, 14095B, HGJ to Laurier, Ottawa, 22 Apr. 1897.

34 HC Debates, 17 June 1897, 3783–4; HGJ Papers, M794, 7129, HGJ to Edmond, Ottawa, 8 June 1897.

35 Simpson, *Spoils of Power*, 116.

36 HGJ Papers, M794, 7030–2, HGJ to Edmond, Ottawa, 6 Mar. 1897; 7987–90, HGJ to Edmond, Ottawa, 12 May 1897; 7091, F.G. Marchand to HGJ, St Jean, 14 May 1897; 7127–8, HGJ to Edmond, Ottawa, 8 June 1897.

37 Marcel Hamelin, "Joly de Lotbinière, Henri-Gustave," *Dictionary of Canadian Biography Online*; HC Debates, 7 May 1897, 1653.

38 HGJ Papers, M795, 7243–5, HGJ to Edmond, Ottawa, 14 Oct. 1897; 7247–8, HGJ to Edmond, Ottawa, 15 Oct. 1897; H. Blair Neatby, *Laurier and a Liberal Quebec* (Toronto: McClelland and Stewart, 1973), 133; Laurier LaPierre, "Politics, Race, and Religion in Canada: Joseph Israel Tarte" (PhD dissertation, University of Toronto, 1962), 303–6, 308, 524–6.

39 Neatby, *Laurier*, 131–6; LaPierre, "Politics, Race, and Religion," 372–83, 528.

40 LaPierre, "Politics, Race, and Religion," 357, 523–4.

41 HGJ Papers, M795, 7351–3, Lord Aberdeen to HGJ, Government House, 5 Feb. 1898; Saywell, "Introduction," lxxxii–lxxxiii.

42 John G. Sproat, *"The Best Men": Liberal Reformers in the Gilded Age* (New York: Oxford University Press, 1968), 257; Robert A.J. McDonald, "The Quest for 'Modern Administration': British Columbia's Civil Service, 1870s to 1940s," *BC Studies* 161 (Spring 2009): 9–10.

43 Rasmussen, "Administrative Reform," 50–4; Laurier Papers, C746, vol. 33, 10907A, HGJ to Laurier, Ottawa, 12 Jan. 1897; HC Debates, 27 Apr. 1897, 2251–2.

44 Rasmussen, "Administrative Reform," 46–7.

45 Rasmussen ("Administrative Reform," 48) states that "patronage began to represent a serious impediment to efficiency" with the rapid expansion of the civil service during the Laurier boom.

46 Stewart, "Political Patronage," 13–18. McDonald ("The Quest," 12) argues that the traditional patronage system survived in British Columbia until the 1940s because the province "remained a geographically fractured region of local communities."

47 HGJ Papers, M795, 7560, HGJ to Fritz, Ottawa, 2 Feb. 1900; 7568–70, HGJ to Fritz, Ottawa, 15 May 1900. The winning candidate, Edmond Fortier, is identified as a Liberal in the *Canadian Directory of Parliament, 1867–1967* (Ottawa: Public Archives of Canada, 1968), but Joly supported a man named Boisvert in the by-election. Fortier was re-elected five times.

48 HC Debates, 19 Apr. 1898, 3294–9; Jarrett Rudy, *The Freedom to Smoke: Tobacco Consumption and Identity* (Montreal: McGill-Queen's University Press, 2005), chap. 3.

49 HC Debates, 19 June 1897, 4073–4.

50 HC Debates, 18 May 1897, 2152–3, 2156. Joly attributed the subsequent decline in illegal distilling to this tactic. HC Debates, 25 May 1900, 6052.

51 Laurier Papers, C759, vol. 87, 26839, Thomas Davidson to Laurier, Que., 29 Sept. 1898; 26840, Laurier to Davidson, 1 Oct. 1898; C760, vol. 87, 26985A-C, HGJ to Laurier, Ottawa, 4 Oct. 1898.

52 HC Debates, 22 Mar. 1899, 215.

53 The Quebec Civil Code required that the parish priests read aloud the text of the law on illegal sales of alcohol each year after the election of church-wardens and that it also be read to parishioners after morning mass the first three Sundays of September. J.U. Baudry, *Code des curés, marguillers et paroissiens accompagné de notes historiques et critiques* (Montreal: n.p., 1870), 275–6. My thanks to Frank Abbott for this reference.

54 Joly also suggested that representatives of the mine workers and farmers should be allowed to inspect the weigh scales at collieries and grain elevators. HC Debates, 11 Mar. 1898, 1497–1502; 18 Mar. 1898, 1827, 1834–6; 5 Apr. 1898, 2675; 1 June 1898, 5725.

55 The former Conservative controller of revenue, M. Wood, opposed Joly's recommendations, claiming that they would undermine national standards. HC Debates, 18 May 1897, 2169–73.

56 A permissive act had been passed but not proclaimed in Canada in 1871. HGJ Papers, M793, 4481–3, Sandford Fleming to HGJ, Ottawa, 26 Sept. 1888; Curtis, "From the Moral Thermometer," 565; *Victoria Daily Colonist*, 14 July 1900.

57 Patricia E. Roy, *A White Man's Province: British Columbia Politicians and Chinese and Japanese Immigrants, 1858–1914* (Vancouver: UBC Press, 1989), 66–9, 87, 96.

58 HGJ Papers, M794, 6833–6, HGJ to Edmond, Ottawa, 8 Sept. 1896.

59 HGJ Papers, M794, 6821, HGJ to Edmond, Ottawa, 3 Sept. 1896; 6824, HGJ to Edmond, Ottawa, 3 Sept. 1896; 6829–30, Major General Ruger to HGJ, Niagara Falls, 6 Sept. 1896; 6843–5, HGJ to Edmond, Ottawa, 19 Sept. 1896; 6855, HGJ to Edmond, Vendredi; Keith Walden, *Becoming Modern in Toronto: The Industrial Exhibition and the Shaping of a Late Victorian Culture* (Toronto: University of Toronto Press, 1997), 151–2; *Memoirs of the Viceroy Li Hung Chang* (London: Constable, 1913); and Samuel C. Chu and Kwang-Ching Liu, eds., *Li Hung-chang and China's Early Modernization* (Armonk, NY: M.E. Sharpe, 1994).

60 Roy, *White Man's Province*, 97.

61 HC Debates, 16 Sept. 1896, 1165–70.

62 HGJ Papers, M795, 7255–68, D. Mills to HGJ, Devonport, 20 Oct [1897].

63 Roy, *A White Man's Province*, 98. See, for example, HGJ Papers, M795, 7516–18, Acting Deputy Minister, Department of Trade and Commerce, to HGJ, Ottawa, 24 July 1899.

64 LAC, MG27, I, B5, Aberdeen Papers, Correspondance, vol. 2, 644–5, HGJ to Lady Aberdeen, Ottawa, 15 Jan. 1897.

65 Laurier Papers, C768, vol. 124, 37271–3, HGJ to Laurier, 8 Sept. 1898.

66 See, for example, the observation by a Conservative MP in HC Debates, 27 Apr. 1899, 2255.

67 HGJ Papers, M795, 7564–5, C. Langelier to HGJ, Que., 12 Mar. 1900; 7573–4, C. Langelier to Laurier, Ottawa, 18 May 1900.

68 HC Debates, 25 May 1900, 6051–2, 6060–1.

69 HC Debates, 25 May 1900, 6047–9.

70 Simpson, *Spoils of Power*, 101, 121. S.J.R. Noel also defends what he refers to as the "culture of clientalism" in this country. S.J.R. Noel, *Patrons, Clients, Brokers: Ontario Society and Politics, 1791–1896* (Toronto: University of Toronto Press, 1990). But Stewart ("Political Patronage," 20) argues, on the other hand, that the patronage system "constricted any incipient structural accommodation between the two racial blocs." See also Gordon T. Stewart, *The Origins of Canadian Politics: A Comparative Approach* (Vancouver: UBC Press, 1986), 96–101.

71 Simpson, *Spoils of Power*, 110–11, 198; LaPierre, "Politics, Race and Religion," 526.

72 Simpson, *Spoils of Power*, 101, 112–13.

9. Lieutenant Governor of British Columbia

1 Margaret Ormsby, *British Columbia: A History* (n.p.: Macmillan, 1958), 336;
   Bryan Palmer, *Working-Class Experience: The Rise and Reconstitution of Canadian Labour, 1800–1980* (Toronto: Butterworth, 1983), 155–6.
2 See Robert A.J. McDonald, "Victoria, Vancouver, and the Economic Development of British Columbia, 1886–1914," in *British Columbia: Historical
   Readings*, ed. W. Peter Ward and Robert A.J. McDonald (Vancouver: Douglas and McIntyre, 1981), 369–95.
3 Ian McKay, "The Liberal Order Framework: A Prospectus for a Reconnaissance of Canadian History," *Canadian Historical Review* 81, no. 4 (Dec.
   2000): 617–45.
4 Jacques Monet, *The Canadian Crown* (Toronto: Clarke, Irwin, 1979), 40–2.
5 See David E. Smith, *The Invisible Crown: The First Principle of Canadian Government* (Toronto: University of Toronto Press, 1995), 9.
6 Monet, *Canadian Crown*, 42–5, 64–5.
7 *Vancouver Province*, 19 June 1897.
8 The *Victoria Colonist*'s Ottawa correspondent reported that "the Tarte
   faction here has long been anxious to crowd Sir Henri out of the cabinet."
   Victoria Daily Colonist, 21 June 1900.
9 Library and Archives Canada [hereafter LAC], Fonds Henry-Gustave Joly
   de Lotbinière [hereafter HGJ Papers], M789, 307–10, Hon. C. Cornwall to
   HGJ, The Senate, 9 Mar. 1878.
10 Forrest D. Pass, "Agrarian Commonwealth, or Entrepôt of the Orient?
   Competing Conceptions of Canada and the BC Terms of Union Debate
   of 1871," *Journal of the Canadian Historical Association*, n.s., 17, no. 1 (2006):
   36–7.
11 Quoted in *Vancouver World*, 30 June 1900.
12 John T. Saywell, *The Office of Lieutenant-Governor: A Study in Canadian Government and Politics* (Toronto: University of Toronto Press, 1957), 24–5, 28.
13 Laurier to D.J. Munn, Esq., Ottawa, 25 June 1900. My thanks to John
   Moreau of Calgary, who owns this letter.
14 *Victoria Daily Colonist*, 23 June 1900.
15 Victoria *Times*, 23 June 1900, 11 July 1900.
16 *Vancouver World*, 21 June 1900.
17 British Columbia Archives [hereafter BCA], GR441, Premiers' Papers, Correspondence Inward, Private, box 15, Horace F. Evans to James Dunsmuir,
   Rossland, 4 July 1900.
18 The column from the Ottawa correspondent in the same issue of the *Colonist* stated that Joly's appointment was "considered as a wise step on the

government's part" because the appointment of a local Liberal would have accentuated the province's political confusion.

19 See David Cannadine, *Ornamentalism: How the British Saw the Empire* (London: Penguin, 2001), 31, 100.

20 Cannadine, *Ornamentalism*, 122.

21 *Victoria Daily Colonist*, 30 June 1900. Saywell (*Office of Lieutenant-Governor*, 28) clearly exaggerates, therefore, in stating that Joly's appointment caused widespread criticism in British Columbia.

22 See Terry Reksten, *"More English than the English": A Very Social History of Victoria* (Victoria: Orca Publishing, 1986); Valerie Green, *Above Stairs: Social Life in Upper Class Victoria, 1843–1918* (Victoria: Sono Nis Press, 1995); and Carole Gerson, *A Purer Taste: The Writing and Reading of Fiction in English in 19th Century Canada* (Toronto: University of Toronto Press, 1989), chap. 8.

23 See Daniel Marshall, "An Early Rural Revolt: The Introduction of the Canadian System of Tariffs to British Columbia, 1871–4," in *Beyond the City Limits: Rural History in British Columbia*, ed. R.W. Sandwell (Vancouver: UBC Press, 1999), 47–61.

24 Ormsby, *British Columbia*, chap. 11.

25 Martin Robin, *The Rush for Spoils: The Company Province, 1871–1933* (Toronto: McClelland and Stewart, 1972), 69.

26 Peter Jeffrey Brock, "Fighting Joe Martin in British Columbia" (MA thesis, Simon Fraser University, 1976), 18; Saywell, *Office of Lieutenant-Governor*, 132–3. Details of McInnes's record as lieutenant governor can also be found in George F.G. Stanley, "A 'Constitutional Crisis' in British Columbia," *Canadian Journal of Economics and Political Science* 21, no. 3 (1955): 281–92.

27 See Brock, "Fighting Joe Martin," 23–30, 37–9; Saywell, *Office of Lieutenant-Governor*, 134–6.

28 Saywell, *Office of Lieutenant-Governor*, 136–7; Brock, "Fighting Joe Martin," 39–42.

29 See Saywell, *Office of Lieutenant-Governor*, 136–7, 251–6; Robin, *Rush for Spoils*, 69–74; Brock, "Fighting Joe Martin," 44–55; and *Victoria Daily Colonist*, 26 June 1900.

30 Victoria *Times*, 19 June 1900; *Vancouver World*, 29 June 1900.

31 See, for example, the correspondence printed in Victoria *Times*, 5 July 1900.

32 Saywell, *Office of Lieutenant-Governor*, 139, 249.

33 Victoria *Times*, 22 June 1900.

34 Brock, "Fighting Joe Martin," 61–8.

35 LAC, Sir Wilfrid Laurier Fonds [hereafter Laurier Papers], C788, 59505–7, Laurier to HGJ, Ottawa, 25 Oct. 1901.

36 Saywell, *Office of Lieutenant-Governor*, 140–1; Laurier Papers, C788, HGJ to Laurier, Victoria, 30 Oct. 1901.

37 HGJ Papers, M795, 7694–8, D.W. Higgins to HGJ, Victoria, 8 Mar. 1902; Robin, *Rush for Spoils*, 74–80; Brock, "Fighting Joe Martin," 75–86.

38 BCA, Mf11A, Letters of His Honour Sir Joly de Lotbinière, 1901–6 [hereafter HGJ Letters], HGJ to Edmond, Victoria, 13 Mar. 1902.

39 Peter Robert Hunt, "The Political Career of Sir Richard McBride" (MA thesis, University of British Columbia, 1953), 16–17.

40 Saywell, *Office of Lieutenant-Governor*, 140–1; Robin, *Rush for Spoils*, 80–4; Victoria *Times*, 14 May 1903, 15 May 1903, 18 May 1903, 19 May 1903, 27 May 1903, 28 May 1903; *Victoria Daily Colonist*, 28 May 1903.

41 Quoted in Robin, *Rush for Spoils*, 84. See also Saywell, *Office of Lieutenant-Governor*, 141–3; and *Victoria Daily Colonist*, 29 May 1903, 30 May 1903.

42 Quoted in Saywell, *Office of Lieutenant-Governor*, 142.

43 The *World* supported the claims of W.W.B. McInnes, a former member of the Prior government who was also the son of the former lieutenant governor, to form a new ministry. *Vancouver World*, 30 May 1903.

44 The premier's secretary, R.E. Gosnell, later wrote that McBride had succumbed to pressure from Joly. Hunt ("The Political Career," 24–6) rejects Gosnell's claim, though without providing solid evidence to the contrary.

45 *Victoria Daily Colonist*, 2 June 1903.

46 *Victoria Daily Colonist*, 3 June 1903.

47 McBride was thirty-two years old in 1903, the youngest premier in the country. Brian Ray Douglas Smith, "Sir Richard McBride: A Study in the Conservative Party of British Columbia, 1903–1916" (MA thesis, Queen's University, 1959), 1, 18–19.

48 BCA, HGJ Letters, HGJ to Edmond, Victoria, 12 Oct. 1903.

49 *Vancouver World*, 2 June 1903.

50 Victoria *Times*, 1 June 1903.

51 Victoria *Times*, 2 June 1903, 5 June 1903. The Vancouver *Province* also referred to McBride's "regrettable display of bad faith towards ... old associates." Quoted in Hunt, "The Political Career," 27.

52 Robin, *Rush for Spoils*, 85–6.

53 Brock, "Fighting Joe Martin," 88. The Victoria *Times* finally admitted that even if a Liberal had been chosen to form a ministry, the breach in the party "would have remained as wide as ever." Victoria *Times*, 3 June 1903, 5 June 1903. Elected in 1903 were twenty-two Conservatives, seventeen Liberals, two Socialists, and one Labour supporter. Robin, *Rush for Spoils*, 90.

54 Brock, "Fighting Joe Martin," 121–5.
55 Saywell, *Office of Lieutenant-Governor*, 38.
56 Hunt, "The Political Career," 30–1; Smith, "Sir Richard McBride," 35. Joly kept an extensive newspaper file on this minor crisis. See HGJ Papers, M796, 9247–63.
57 McBride would pull the same trick three years later under Joly's successor. Saywell, *Office of Lieutenant-Governor*, 159.
58 See the correspondence in BCA, GR441, British Columbia Premiers' Papers, Series IX: Letterbooks (official), 1883–1916, vol. 389.
59 BCA, GR441, British Columbia Premiers' Papers, Series IV: Private correspondence, 1903–15, box 74, HGJ to McBride, Victoria, 9 July 1893; box 76, vol. 365, no. 133, HGJ to McBride, 30 June 1903.
60 BCA, HGJ Letters, HGJ to Edmond, Victoria, 17 Jan. 1904.
61 BCA, HGJ Letters, HGJ to Edmond, 22 Mar. 1906.
62 BCA, E/D/J68, Joly de Lotbinière, Sir Henri Gustave, Correspondence Outward, 1901, 1905–7, HGJ to McBride, Pointe Platon, 22 Aug. 1906.
63 HGJ Papers, M795, 8338, McBride to HGJ, Victoria, 8 Aug. 1907.
64 BCA, GR443, British Columbia, Lieutenant-Governor, 1896–1919, Letterbook Copies of Correspondence Outward [hereafter Correspondence Outward], vol. 4, p. 416, HGJ to Acting Provincial Secretary, Oct. 1901. The resolutions appear to have been principally concerned with the prevention of forest fires. GR443, Lieutenant-Governors' Papers, Miscellaneous Correspondence Inward, box 61, file 5, H. Bostock to HGJ, Vancouver, 28 Oct. 1901.
65 Correspondence Outward, vol. 7, p. 270, acting private secretary to R.H. Campbell [n.d.]; p. 295, 21 Dec. 1904.
66 Correspondence Outward, vol. 6, p. 80, HGJ to Secretary of State in Ottawa [1903]. Yoho and Glacier national parks had been established at ten square miles each in 1886, but Yoho was expanded to 828 square miles in 1901, and Glacier to 700 square miles in 1903. Janet Foster, *Working for Wildlife: The Beginnings of Preservation in Canada*, 2nd ed. (Toronto: University of Toronto Press, 1998), 31.
67 See Robert Howard Marris, "'Pretty Sleek and Fat': The Genesis of Forest Policy in British Columbia, 1903–1914" (MA thesis, University of British Columbia, 1979), 5–9; and McDonald, "Victoria, Vancouver," 381–3.
68 BCA, HGJ Letters, HGJ to Edmond, Victoria, 11 Nov. 1902. On Joly's support for the manufacturing condition, see also HGJ to Edmond, Victoria, 16 Feb. 1902.

69 *Victoria Daily Colonist*, 14 July 1900.

70 No more pulpwood leases were granted after 1903, but holders of crown timber leases paid fifteen cents per acre if they operated a sawmill and twenty-five cents if they did not. Marris, "Pretty Sleek and Fat," 22–4.

71 BCA, HGJ Letters, HGJ to Edmond, Victoria, 22 Nov. 1902.

72 Marris, "Pretty Sleek and Fat," 20–4, 28; R. Peter Gillis and Thomas R. Roach, *Lost Initiatives: Canada's Forest Industries, Forest Policy and Forest Conservation* (Westport, CT: Greenwood Press, 1986), 135.

73 Marris, "Pretty Sleek and Fat," 24–31, 111–12; Robin, *Rush for Spoils*, 92–3; Gillis and Roach, *Lost Initiatives*, 140–1; Stephen Gray, "Forest Policy and Administration in British Columbia, 1912–1928" (MA thesis, Simon Fraser University, 1982), 20–1.

74 In addition, the McBride government had in 1903 quadrupled the tax on all timber cut on lands not subject to royalty, with this amount to be rebated if the logs were processed within the province. Gray, "Forest Policy," 120.

75 Gray, "Forest Policy," 20.

76 Gray, "Forest Policy," 118–20, 151; Marris, "Pretty Sleek and Fat," 31–2, 112–14.

77 Gray, "Forest Policy," 2–5.

78 Quebec was arguably more of a model than Ontario because it generally took a more active approach to forestry and forest reserve management, one inspired to some extent by Europe. Gillis and Roach, *Lost Initiatives*, 107–18, 139, 145; René Hardy and Normand Séguin, *Forêt et société en Mauricie* (Montreal: Boréal Express, 1984), 22–3; Gray, "Forest Policy," 55.

79 HGJ Papers, M795, 7868–9, McBride to HGJ, Victoria [1906]; 8082–3, McBride to HGJ, Victoria, 16 Aug. 1906.

80 BCA, E/D/J68, HGJ, Correspondence Outward, HGJ to McBride, Quebec, 10 Dec. 1906.

81 Quoted in *Vancouver World*, 30 June 1900.

82 Quoted in *Vancouver World*, 28 June 1900.

83 Laurier Papers, C777, 46717, HGJ to Laurier, Ottawa, 21 June 1900.

84 Patricia E. Roy, *A White Man's Province: British Columbia Politicians and Chinese and Japanese Immigrants, 1858–1914* (Vancouver: UBC Press, 1989), 100–2; Peter Ward, *White Canada Forever: Popular Attitudes and Public Policy towards Orientals in British Columbia* (Montreal: McGill-Queen's University Press, 1978, reprint 2002), 59–60.

85 But Ottawa generally allowed the Natal Act to remain in force each year until the last possible minute. Roy, *White Man's Province*, 92–3, 98, 103–6, 133, 163; Ward, *White Canada*, 55–9.

86 Roy, *White Man's Province*, 159–64, 181–2.
87 This tax had been recommended by the 1901 royal commission. Roy, *White Man's Province*, 109, 118–19, 150, 153–6, 172; Ward, *White Canada*, 61.
88 Smith, "Sir Richard McBride," 37, 44; Roy, *White Man's Province*, 164.
89 Roy, *White Man's Province*, 100.
90 BCA, E/D/J68, HGJ, Correspondence Outward, HGJ to McBride, Pointe Platon, 22 Aug. 1906; HGJ to McBride, Quebec, 14 Dec. 1907.
91 BCA, GR443, Lieutenant-Governors' Papers, Miscellaneous correspondence inward, HGJ to Ivan Ponomareff et autres, Victoria, 23 Oct. 1902 (typescript draft, accents as in original).
92 BCA, GR441, Premiers' Papers, Correspondence Inward, Private, box 19, file 95, HGJ to James Dunsmuir, Victoria [1902]. Joly, not surprisingly, did approve of the project to settle a group of Alsatians in the province, claiming that they were "well deserving of the good reputation which they have earned, for their industry, their perseverance, and high moral qualities." Box 21, file 1, HGJ to Col. Prior, Victoria, 4 Apr. 1903; Series IX: Letterbooks (official), 1883–1916, vol. 385, p. 661, Premier to HGJ, 6 Apr. 1903.
93 Saywell observes that this was true of many lieutenant governors. *Office of Lieutenant-Governor*, 188–9.
94 Laurier Papers, C788, 59638, Victoria, 30 Oct. 1901.
95 Laurier Papers, C788, 59639–40, Laurier to HGJ, Ottawa, 8 Nov. 1901; C789, 60023–6, HGJ to Laurier, Victoria, 18 Nov. 1901.
96 BCA, GR441, Premiers' Papers, Correspondence Inward, Private, box 78, unnumbered file, HGJ to McBride, Victoria [n.d.]; Harold Percival Johns, "British Columbia's Campaign for Better Terms, 1871–1907" (MA thesis, University of British Columbia, 1935), 123–6.
97 Smith, "Sir Richard McBride," 35–6, 39–45; Hunt, "The Political Career," 45–54; Robin, *Rush for Spoils*, 90–2.
98 BCA, E/D/J68, HGJ, Correspondence Outward, HGJ to McBride, Government House, 5 Mar. 1906.
99 Ormsby, *British Columbia*, 345–6; Smith, "Sir Richard McBride," 55–80; Hunt, "The Political Career," 54–66, 81–103; Robin, *Rush for Spoils*, 99–104.
100 HGJ Papers, M795, 7862–9, McBride to HGJ, Victoria [1906].
101 BCA, HGJ, E/D/J68, Correspondence Outward, HGJ to McBride, Quebec, 6 Nov. 1906. Joly later wrote to McBride (10 Dec. 1906) concerning the conference: "As to separation fight to the death against those who mention the word."
102 Edmond Joly wrote to Laurier in confidence that his father was "deeply interested in his work & all that concerns the welfare of the Province & would be happy to continue in office for a few years more." Five months

later Joly wrote to Edmond, "Of course, you understand that it is out of the question for me to communicate with Sir Wilfrid, or to allow any one to communicate with him, on my behalf. I am here, and wait." Laurier Papers, C823, 98075, Edmond Joly to Laurier, Pointe-Platon, 1 June 1905; 98078, reply, 3 June 1905; BCA, HGJ Letters, HGJ to Edmond, Victoria, 8 Nov. 1905. Although John A. Macdonald always refused to renew lieutenant governors' commissions, Laurier reappointed three. Saywell, *Office of Lieutenant-Governor*, 232.

103 Laurier Papers, C819, 94605, W.W. Columbia to Laurier, Victoria, 9 Feb. 1905; 94606, Laurier to My dear Lord Bishop, Ottawa, 18 Feb. 1905.

104 See BCA, MS 2879, Crease Family Collection, AO 1847, Susan Crease Diary, 2 June 1904, 15 June 1904; Barbara Powell, "Sarah Crease and Susan Crease," in *The Small Details of Life: Twenty Diaries by Women in Canada, 1830–1996*, ed. Kathryn Carter (Toronto: University of Toronto Press, 2002), 152–3. The biographer of Susan's mother, Sarah, claims that the unmarried Susan, then in her early forties, was having "a passionate yet platonic affair" with Joly, but her diary suggests only a strong sense of admiration for the elderly widower. Kathryn Bridge, *Henry and Self: The Private Life of Sarah Crease, 1826–1922* (Victoria: Sono Nis Press, 1996), 104.

105 Laurier Papers, C808, 81833, W.T. to Laurier, n.d. Laurier gave the same reply to Templeman as to the bishop. Laurier Papers, C808, 81834, Ottawa, 18 Feb. 1905.

106 See S.W. Jackman, *The Men at Cary Castle: A Series of Portrait Sketches of the Lieutenant-Governors of British Columbia from 1871 to 1971* (Victoria, BC: Morriss Printing, 1972), 79–82; and Joseph Pope, *The Tour of the Their Royal Highnesses the Duke and Duchess of Cornwall and York through the Dominion of Canada in the Year 1901* (Ottawa: S.E. Dawson, 1903), chap. 5.

107 William M. Kuhn, *Democratic Royalism: The Transformation of the British Monarchy, 1861–1914* (London: Macmillan, 1996).

108 Phillip Buckner, "Casting Daylight upon Magic: Deconstructing the Royal Tour of 1901 to Canada," in *The British World: Diaspora, Culture and Identity*, ed. Carl Bridge and Kent Fedorowich (London: Frank Cass, 2003), 158–89. See also Robert M. Stamp, *Kings, Queens and Canadians: A Celebration of Canada's Infatuation with the British Royal Family* (Markham, ON: Fitzhenry and Whiteside, 1987).

109 Bruce Curtis, "The 'Most Splendid Pageant Ever Seen': Grandeur, the Domestic, and Condescension in Lord Durham's Political Theatre," *Canadian Historical Review* 89, no. 1 (Mar. 2008): 55–88.

110 Walter Bagehot, *The English Constitution*, republication of 1915 edition (Ithaca, NY: Cornell University Press, 1963), 90.

111 In the fall of 1902, for example, Joly opened exhibitions in Kamloops, Ashcroft, New Westminster, and Victoria. BCA, HGJ Letters, HGJ to Edmond, Victoria, 28 Sept. 1902. For one of many studies that point to the influence of the British landed elite in British Columbia, see Mary-Ellen Kelm, "Touring with Trouncer: Community, Adaptation, and Identities," *BC Studies* 131 (Autumn 2001): 63–70.

112 Cannadine, *Ornamentalism*, 131.

113 Laurier mistakenly assumed that the exhibition was to be in Victoria. Laurier Papers, C823, 98074, Laurier to HGJ, Ottawa, 8 June 1905; C824, 98753–4, HGJ to Laurier, 20 June 1905.

114 Laurier Papers, C831, 106755, Laurier to HGJ, Ottawa, 1 Feb. 1906; 106928–9, HGJ to R.W. Scott, Victoria, 8 Feb. 1906 (coded telegram). Joly was not replaced by James Dunsmuir until late May.

115 See, for example, *Victoria Daily Colonist*, 12 May 1906, and its excerpt from the Vancouver *News-Advertiser*, 17 May 1906.

116 HGJ Papers, M795, 7878–81, Charles Hibbert Tupper to HGJ [10 Jan. 1906].

117 HGJ Papers, M795, 8097–8, Mayor Morley to HGJ, Victoria, 8 Nov. 1906.

118 *Vancouver World*, 16 Nov. 1908.

119 Victoria *Times*, 16 Nov. 1908; *Victoria Daily Colonist*, 17 Nov. 1908.

120 The other two occasions were in Quebec in 1878 and 1891. Monet, *Canadian Crown*, 55–6.

121 Escott M. Reid, "The Rise of National Parties in Canada," in *Party Politics in Canada*, ed. Hugh G. Thorburn (Scarborough: Prentice-Hall, 1967), 21.

122 Robert A.J. McDonald, "Sir Charles Hibbert Tupper and the Political Culture of British Columbia, 1903–1924," *BC Studies* 149 (Spring 2006): 65–6.

123 Robert McDonald, "'Variants of Liberalism' and the Liberal Order Framework," in *Liberalism and Hegemony: Debating the Canadian Liberal Revolution*, eds. Jean-François Constant and Michel Ducharme (Toronto: University of Toronto Press, 2009), 325–6; Gordon T. Stewart, *The Origins of Canadian Politics: A Comparative Approach* (Vancouver: UBC Press, 1986).

124 See Tina Loo, *Making Law, Order, and Authority in British Columbia, 1821–1871* (Toronto: University of Toronto Press, 1994), 3–17.

125 HGJ Papers, M795, 8091–2, HGJ to Captain Tatlow, Pointe Platon, 23 Sept. 1906.

126 See David E. Smith, *The Invisible Crown: The First Principle of Canadian Government* (Toronto: University of Toronto Press, 1995), 11.

127 McKay, "Liberal Order," 624, 632–3.

128 See, for example, John Douglas Belshaw, "Provincial Politics, 1871–1916," in *The Pacific Province: A History of British Columbia*, ed. Hugh J.M. Johnston (Vancouver: Douglas and McIntyre, 1996), 137–8, 145, 149–50, which completely ignores Joly.

129 McDonald's main argument is that McKay overlooks more popular
	varieties of liberalism that found expression in resistance to monopolistic
	abuses of power. McDonald, "Variants of Liberalism," 327–40.
130 Cannadine, *Ornamentalism*, 31, 34, 38.
131 McKay, "Liberal Order," 640. Monet argues that Lord Sydenham and
	Lord Metcalfe were unable to win the popular support of the French
	Canadians during the 1840s in large part because – in contrast to the
	more successful Sir Charles Bagot and Lord Elgin – they "sprang from a
	bourgeois liberal *milieu*, and neither had married." Jacques Monet, "The
	Personal and Living Bond, 1839–1849," in *The Shield of Achilles: Aspects
	of Canada in the Victorian Age*, ed. W.L. Morton (Toronto: McClelland and
	Stewart, 1968), 91.

Conclusion

1 Contrast the practice of families such as the McCords, with their sar-
	cophagus in Montreal's Mount Royal Cemetery providing ample space
	for epitaphs that record their histories and civic virtues. Brian Young,
	"Generation Matters: Two Patrician Families in the History of Quebec,"
	unpublished typescript, 377–80.
2 Quoted in S.W. Jackman, *The Men at Cary Castle* (Victoria: Morriss Print-
	ing, 1972), 83. As early as 1883, the journalist P.A.J. Voyer claimed that
	Joly had never succumbed to – nor had even been tempted to succumb
	to – "la tentation." *Biographies des Hons. MM. Mercier, Joly, Irvine, Marchand*
	(Trois-Rivières: 1883), 24.
3 Matthew McCormack, ed., *Public Men: Masculinity and Politics in Modern
	Britain* (New York: Palgrave Macmillan, 2007), 188.
4 McCormack, *Public Men*, 189.
5 Roderick J. Barman, "Biography as History," *Journal of the Canadian His-
	torical Association*, n.s., 21, no. 2 (2009): 69.
6 For a critique of the approach by Pierre Bourdieu and Michel de Certeau,
	see Barman, "Biography as History," 68–9.
7 Karl Marx, *The Eighteenth Brumaire of Louis Napoleon*, quoted in David
	Nasaw, "Historians and Biography," *American Historical Review* 114, no. 3
	(June 2009): 578.
8 Young, "Generation Matters," 86.
9 Voyer, *Biographies*, 25; R. Peter Gillis and Thomas R. Roach, *Lost Initiatives:
	Canada's Forest Industries, Forest Policy and Forest Conservation* (New York:
	Greenwood Press, 1986), 37.

10 On the role of the volunteer militia, voluntary societies, and honours in reinforcing status, see Brian Young, "Patrician Elites and Power in Nineteenth-Century Montreal and Quebec City," in *Who Ran the Cities? City Elites and Urban Power Structures in Europe and North America, 1750–1940*, ed. Ralf Roth and Robert Beachy (Burlington, VT: Ashgate, 2007), 240–5.

11 Quoted in Nasaw, "Historians and Biography," 576.

12 Lois W. Banner, "Biography as History," *American Historical Review* 114, no. 3 (June 2009): 581.

13 Daniel Samson, "'The Yoke of Improvement': Sir John Sinclair, John Young, and the Improvement of the Scotlands, New and Old," in *Transatlantic Rebels: Agrarian Radicalism in Comparative Context*, ed. Thomas Summerhill and James C. Scott (East Lansing: Michigan State University Press, 2004), 89, 101.

14 Yvan Lamonde, *Louis-Antoine Dessaules: Un seigneur libéral et anticlerical* (n.p.: Fides, 1994), 300–1.

15 Kenneth J. Munro, *The Political Career of Sir Adolphe Chapleau, Premier of Quebec, 1879–1882* (Lewiston, NY: E. Mellen Press, 1992), 82; Jean-Paul Bernard, *Les Rouges: Libéralisme, nationalisme, et anticléricalisme au milieu du XIXe siècle* (Montreal: Les Presses de l'Université du Québec, 1971), 320.

16 H. Blair Neatby, *Laurier and a Liberal Quebec* (Toronto: McClelland and Stewart, 1973), 18.

17 Robert Rumilly, *Histoire de la Province de Québec*, vol. 1 (Montreal: Éditions Bernard Valiquette, 1942), 361.

18 For examples of Joly's interest in Buddhism, mesmerism, and Christian theological issues, see Library and Archives Canada, MG27 II C2, Fonds Henri-Gustave Joly de Lotbinière [hereafter HGJ Papers], M792, 3373, Rev. S.M. Kellogg to HGJ, Toronto, 27 Sept. 1886; 3591, HGJ to Major Mayne, Leclercville, 4 Jan. 1887; M793, 4848–50, William Bennett to HGJ, Que., 27 Jan. 1889; 4860–1, H. Petry to HGJ, Lennoxville, 30 Jan. 1889; M793, 5504, HGJ to Lucy [Leclercville], 2 Feb. [1890].

19 Munro, *Political Career*, xii.

20 See, for example, HGJ Papers, M793, 5110–11, HGJ to Tillotson and Sons, Leclercville, 17 May 1899.

Bibliography

Manuscript Sources

Bibliothèque et archives Nationales du Québec à Montréal
Fonds Famille Mercier (P74–1.1/19–3)

Bibliothèque et archives Nationales du Québec à Québec
Correspondance d'Éthel Joly de Lotbinière, 1894–5 (P1000, S3, D1040)
Edmond-Gustave Joly de Lotbinière Letterbook, 1898–1902 (P351, S6)
Fonds Éducation, Correspondance Reçue (E13)
Fonds F.G. Marchand (P174)
Fonds George Moore Fairchild (P73)
Fonds Joly de Lotbinière, Comptes, 1891–1911, Sir Henri Book (AP-G-389)
Fonds Joly de Lotbinière, Comptes, 1906–11 (AP-G-389)
Fonds Joly de Lotbinière, Lettres, 1901–6 (AP-G-389)
Seigneurie de Lotbinière, Comptes, 1899–1912 (ZQ118)
Seigneurie de Lotbinière, Comptes, 1911–12 (P351, S4, SS3)

British Columbia Archives

British Columbia Premier's Papers, Correspondence Inward, Private, 1900–3;
    Series IV: Private correspondence, 1903–15; Series IX: Letterbooks (official),
    1883–1916; Series XII: Letterbooks (personal, 1903), vol. 409 (McBride),
    (GR441)
Crease Family Collection, Susan Crease diary (MS 2879, microfilm AO 1847)
Joly de Lotbinière, Sir Henri Gustave, Correspondence Outward, 1901, 1905–7
    (E/D/J68)
Letters of His Honour Sir Joly de Lotbinière, 1901–6, loaned by his grandson,
    Alain Joly de Lotbinière (mf 11A)

Lieutenant-Governors' Papers, Miscellaneous correspondence inward; Let-
    terbook Copies of Correspondence Outward, 1896–1919 (GR443)

Library and Archives of Canada

Aberdeen Papers, Correspondence, vol. 2 (MG27, I, B5)
Alain Joly de Lotbinière Fonds (R1733–0-0-F, microfilm reels M797–8)
Alexander Mackenzie Fonds, Inward Correspondence (M198), 1875–7; Let-
    terbooks, vol. 1, 1875 (MG 26 B)
Audet's biographical notes, vol. 16 (MG30, D1)
Census of Canada, Province of Quebec, 1871, 1881, 1891. Accessed via Ances-
    try.ca
Edmond-Gustave Joly de Lotbinière Fonds (R9827–0-0-F, microfilm reel M789)
Henri-Gustave Joly de Lotbinière Fonds, Henri-Gustave Joly de Lotbinière,
    Correspondance, 1863–1908 (R6211–0-4-F, microfilm reels M789–97)
Manuscript Census, Canada East, 1861, Lotbinière Parish (microfilm reel C1292)
Manuscript Census, Quebec, 1871, Lotbinière Parish and Ste. Emmélie Parish
    Schedule 6 (microfilm reel C10353); Quebec City, St Louis Ward (microfilm
    reel C10097)
Pierre-Gustave Joly and Julie-Christine Chartier de Lotbinière Fonds (micro-
    film reels M785–8)
Robert Bell fonds, General Correspondence, vol. 31 (R7346–7-7-E)
Sir Wilfrid Laurier Fonds (MG26-G)

Miscellaneous

Anglican Cathedral, Diocese of Quebec, Holy Trinity Church register, re-
    corded in Quebec Vital and Church Records (Drouin Collection), 1621–1967.
    Accessed via Ancestry.ca
Domaine Joly de Lotbinière archives, library inventory

Printed Primary Sources

Amyot, G. *Adresse à MM. les Électeurs du Comté de Lotbinière* (n.p., n.d.) (CIHM
    no. 886).
Amyot, G. *Deuxième lettre aux électeurs du Comté de Lotbinière* (n.p., n.d.) (CIHM
    no. 798).
Appendices to the Journals of the Legislative Assembly of Lower Canada 30 (1821),
    Appendix U; 42 (1832–3), Appendix Nn.
Aubin, Georges, ed. *Louis-Joseph Papineau: Lettres à ses enfants*. Vol. 11, *1855–
    1871*. Montreal: Les Éditions Varia, 2004.

Aubin, Georges, ed. *Papineau en exil à Paris*. Vol. 1, *Dictionnaire*. [Trois-Pistoles, QC]: Éditions Trois-Pistoles, 2007.

Aubin, Georges, ed. *Papineau en exil à Paris*. Vol. 2, *Lettres reçues, 1839–1845*. Trois-Pistoles, QC: Éditions Trois-Pistoles, 2007.

Aubin, Georges, and Renée Blanchet, eds. *Louis-Joseph Papineau: Lettres à Julie*. Sillery, QC: Septentrion, 2000.

Bagehot, Walter. *The English Constitution / by Walter Bagehot: With an Introduction by R.H.S. Crossman*. Ithaca, NY: Cornell University Press, 1963.

Baudry, J.U. *Code des curés, marguillers et paroissiens accompagné de notes historiques et critiques*. Montreal: n.p., 1870.

Blanchet, Renée, ed. *Julie B. Papineau, une femme patriote: Correspondance, 1823–1862*. Sillery, QC: Septentrion, 1997.

Bouchette, Joseph. *A Topographical Dictionary of the Province of Lower Canada*. London: Longman, Rees, Orme, Brown, Green, and Longman, 1832.

British Parliamentary Papers, Emigration. Vol. 19. Shannon, Ireland: Irish University Press, 1969.

Canada. *Census Reports*, 1851–1901.

Canada. House of Commons Debates, 1896–1900 (Library and Archives Canada).

Canada. Parliament. *Parliamentary Debates, 1867–74*. Ottawa: Canadian Library Association, [1956?].

Canada. Parliament. *Sessional Papers*, 1878, no. 11, pt. 8, no. 9. Report of the Minister of Agriculture for 1877, appendix no. 1, Report on Forestry and Forests of Canada, by H.G. Joly.

Canada. Parliamentary Debates, 1862–4 (Library and Archives Canada).

Canadian Forestry Association. Report of the Fourth Annual Meeting, 1903.

Creighton, J.G.A. "French Canadian Life and Character." In *Picturesque Canada*, vol. 1, ed. George Monro Grant. Toronto: Belden, 1882.

Discours de Mr H.G. Joly sur la Confédération, Prononcé à la Chambre le 20 Février 1865. Quebec City: C. Darveau, 1865.

Documents Pour Servir à l'Intélligence de la Question des Écoles du Manitoba. Rome: A. Befani, 1896.

Eighth Provincial Parliament of Canada (3rd Session). *Parliamentary Debates on the Subject of the Confederation of the British North American Provinces*. Quebec City: Hunter, Rose & Co., Parliamentary Printers, 1865. Google Books, http://books.google.ca/books?id=SEg0AAAAIAAJ. Accessed 7 July 2008.

Aubert de Gaspé, Philippe. *A Man of Sentiment: The Memoirs of Philippe-Joseph Aubert de Gaspé*. Trans. Jane Brierly. Montreal: Véhicule Press, 1988.

Hamelin, Marcel, ed. *Les débats de l'Assemblée Législative, 1867–1878*. Quebec City: Assemblée Nationale du Québec, 1974.

Joly de Lotbinière, E.G. "Compulsory Timber Reserves on Settlers' Lands." *Canadian Forestry Convention, Held at Montreal, 11 and 12 March 1908*. Quebec: Department of Lands and Forests, 1908.

Joly de Lotbinière, E.G. "The Danger Threatening the Crown Lands Forests of the Province of Quebec." In *Canadian Forestry Association, Report of the Third Annual Meeting*. Ottawa, 1902.

Joly de Lotbinière, H.G. "Eastern Forest Trees Grown at Victoria, B.C., from Seed." *British Pacific* 1 (1902): 3–4.

Joly de Lotbinière, H.G. "La Fête des Arbres." *La Revue Nationale* 1, no. 3 (Apr. 1895): 221–6.

Joly de Lotbinière, H.G. *Forest Tree Culture, from a Paper in the Montreal Horticultural Society's Report for 1880*. Montreal: Witness Printing House, 1881.

Joly de Lotbinière, H.G. "Forestry in Canada." *Annual Report of the Montreal Horticultural Society and Fruit-Growers' Association of the Province of Quebec* 14 (1889): 146–9.

Joly de Lotbinière, H.G. *The Returns of Forest Tree Culture: A Paper from the Report of the Montreal Horticultural and Fruit Grower's Association*. Montreal: Witness Printing House, 1882.

Joly de Lotbinière, H.G. "The Study of Forestry as an Important Contributor to Practical Education." State Horticultural Society, *Annual Report*, 236–8. Read at the St Paul meeting of the American Forestry Congress, Aug. 8, 1883.

Joly de Lotbinière, Pierre-Gustave. *Voyage en Orient (1839–40): Journal d'un voyageur curieux du monde et d'un pionnier de la daguerréotypie*, introd. Jacques Desautels, ed. Georges Aubin and Renée Blanchet. [Ste Foy, QC]: Les Presses de l'Université Laval, 2010.

Journals of the Legislative Assembly, Province of Quebec, 1879.

Langelier, Charles. *Souvenirs politiques de 1878 à 1890*. Quebec City: Dussault and Proulx, 1909 (CIHM no. 74077).

Lemoine, J.M. *Maple Leaves*. Vol. 3, *Canadian History and Quebec Scenery*. Quebec City: Hunter, Rose, 1865.

Lemoine, J.M. *Maple Leaves*. Vol. 4. Quebec City: L.J. Demers, 1894.

Lettres des curés des paroisses respectives du Bas-Canada dont il est fait mention dans la cinquième Rapport du Comité Spécial sur les Terres incultes de la Couronne. Chambre d'Assemblée, 15 Feb. 1823 (CIHM 21143).

Memoirs of the Viceroy Li Hung Chang. London: Constable, 1913.

Papineau, Amédée. *Journal d'un fils de la liberté, 1838–1855*. Sillery, QC: Septentrion, 1998.

Papineau, Lactance. *Journal d'un étudiant en médecine à Paris*, ed. Georges Aubin and Renée Blanchet. Montreal: Les Éditions Varia, 2003.

Parlement de Québec. *Débats de Législature de la Province de Québec*, 1877–85.

Pope, Joseph. *The Tour of the Their Royal Highnesses the Duke and Duchess of Cornwall and York through the Dominion of Canada in the Year 1901.* Ottawa: S.E. Dawson, 1903.

Proceedings of the American Forestry Congress at Its Sessions Held at Cincinnati, Ohio, in April, 1882, and at Montreal, Canada, in August, 1882. Washington, DC: Printed for the Society, 1883.

Proceedings of the American Forestry Congress at Its Sessions Held at St. Paul, Minn., in August, 1883. Washington, DC: n.p., 1884.

Proceedings of the American Forestry Congress at Its Meeting Held in Boston, September, 1885. Washington, DC: Judd and Detweiller, 1886.

Proceedings of the American Forestry Association at the Summer Meeting, Held in Quebec, September 2–5, 1890. Washington, DC: Secretary's Office, 1891.

Un procès deux fois gagné: le sirop de gomme d'épinette des Soeurs de la Providence n'est pas un imitation (1880) (CIHM 4856).

Province of Canada. *Sessional Papers*, 1862, no. 24.

Record of the Hon. Mr. Chapleau's Government and the Hon. Mr. Joly's Platform. N.p., [1881?] (CIHM 12325).

de Roquebrune, Robert. *Testament of My Childhood.* Trans. Felix Walter. Toronto: University of Toronto Press, 1964.

Sellar, Robert. *The Tragedy of Quebec: The Expulsion of Its Protestant Farmers.* 1916. Toronto: University of Toronto Press, 1974.

Voyer, P.A.J. *Biographies des Hons. MM. Mercier, Joly, Irvine, Marchand, de MM. Stephens, Gagnon, Shehyn, Watts, Rinfret, McShane, Bernatchez, Demers, Bernard, Cameron et Laberge.* Trois-Rivières: n.p., 1883 (CIHM 9247).

Waite, P.B., ed. *The Confederation Debates in the Province of Canada / 1865.* Toronto: McClelland and Stewart, 1963.

Newspapers

Le Canadien (Quebec City), 1862
Daily British Whig (Kingston), 1894
Daily Colonist (Victoria), 1900–8
Daily Times (Victoria), 1900–3, 1908
L'Électeur (Quebec City), 1882, 1885, 1895, 1896
L'Événement (Montreal), 1869
La Gazette des Campagnes, 1878, 1881
Montreal Daily Witness, 1885, 1890, 1894
Platon Herald / Les Échos du Platon, vol. 6, undated broadsheet in the Domaine Joly de Lotbinière Archives
Quebec Morning Chronicle, 1872, 1875, 1890, 1895, 1896

Vancouver Province, 1897
Vancouver World, 1900, 1903, 1908
La Verité, 1885

Published Secondary Sources

Abbott, Frank. "Cold Cash and Ice Palaces: The Quebec Winter Carnival of 1894." *Canadian Historical Review* 69, no. 2 (1988): 167–202. http://dx.doi.org/10.3138/CHR-069-02-02.

Ajzenstat, Jane, Paul Romney, Ian Gentles, and William D. Gairdner, eds. *Canada's Founding Debates*. Toronto: Stoddart, 1999.

Aron, Cindy S. *Working at Play: A History of Vacations in the United States*. Oxford: Oxford University Press, 1999.

Banner, Lois W. "Biography as History." *American Historical Review* 114, no. 3 (June 2009): 579–86. http://dx.doi.org/10.1086/ahr.114.3.579.

Bannister, Jerry. "Canada as Counter-Revolution: The Loyalist Order Framework in Canadian History, 1750–1840." In *Liberalism and Hegemony: Debating the Canadian Liberal Revolution*, ed. Jean-François Constant and Michel Ducharme. Toronto: University of Toronto Press, 2009.

Barker-Benfield, G.J. *The Culture of Sensibility: Sex and Society in Eighteenth-Century Britain*. Chicago: University of Chicago Press, 1992.

Barman, Roderick J. "Biography as History." *Journal of the Canadian Historical Association* 21, no. 2 (2010): 61–75. http://dx.doi.org/10.7202/1003088ar.

Beck, J.M. *Pendulum of Power: Canada's Federal Elections*. Scarborough, ON: Prentice-Hall, 1968.

Bédard, Éric. *Les Réformistes: Une génération canadienne-française au milieu du XIXe siècle*. Montreal: Boréal, 2009.

Bélanger, Réal. "L'élite politique canadienne-française et l'Empire brittanique: trois reflets représentatifs canadiennes-françaises (1890-1917)." In *Imperial Canada, 1867-1917*, ed. Colin M. Coates. Edinburgh: University of Edinburgh Centre of Canadian Studies, 1997.

Belshaw, John Douglas. "Provincial Politics, 1871–1916." In *The Pacific Province: A History of British Columbia*, ed. Hugh J.M. Johnston. Vancouver: Douglas and McIntyre, 1996.

Benoît, Jean. "Burstall, John." *Dictionary of Canadian Biography Online*.

Bernard, Jean-Paul. *Les Rouges: Libéralisme, nationalisme, et anticléricalisme au milieu du XIXe siècle*. Montreal: Les Presses de l'Université du Québec, 1971.

Binnema, Theodore, and Kevin Hutchings. "The Emigrant and the Noble Savage: Sir Francis Bond Head's Romantic Approach to Aboriginal Policy in Upper Canada, 1836–1838." *Journal of Canadian Studies. Revue d'Etudes Canadiennes* 39, no. 1 (Winter 2005): 115–38.

Bischoff, Peter C. *Les Débardeurs au port du Québec: Tableau de luttes syndicales, 1831–1902*. Montreal: Hurtubise, 2009.

Boileau, Gilles. "La paroisse de Lotbinière lance un cri de détresse." *Histoire Québec* 9, no. 2 (Nov. 2003): 41–5.

Booth, J. Derek. *Railways of Southern Quebec*. Vol. 2. Toronto: Railfare, 1985.

Boswell, Hazel. *Town House, Country House: Recollections of a Quebec Childhood*, ed. R.H. Hubbard. Montreal: McGill-Queen's University Press, 1990.

Bouchard, Gérard. "Co-intégration et reproduction de la société rurale: Pour un modèle saguenayen de la marginalité." *Recherches Sociographiques* 29, no. 2–3 (1988): 283–310. http://dx.doi.org/10.7202/056370ar.

Boyer, M. Christine. "La Mission Héliographique: Architectural Photographs, Collective Memory and the Patrimony of France, 1851." In *Picturing Place: Photography and the Geographical Imagination*, ed. Joan M. Schwartz and James R. Ryan. London: I.B. Tauris, 2003.

Bradbury, Bettina. *Wife to Widow: Lives, Laws, and Politics in Nineteenth-Century Montreal*. Vancouver: UBC Press, 2011.

Bridge, Kathryn. *Henry and Self: The Private Life of Sarah Crease, 1826–1922*. Victoria: Sono Nis Press, 1996.

Buckner, Phillip. "Casting Daylight upon Magic: Deconstructing the Royal Tour of 1901 to Canada." In *The British World: Diaspora, Culture and Identity*, ed. Carl Bridge and Kent Fedorowich. London: Frank Cass, 2003. http://dx.doi.org/10.1080/03086530310001705656

Bushman, Richard. *The Refinement of America: Persons, Houses, Cities*. New York: Knopf, 1992.

Cadigan, Sean. "Paternalism and Politics: Sir Francis Bond Head, the Orange Order, and the Election of 1836." *Canadian Historical Review* 72, no. 3 (1991): 319–47. http://dx.doi.org/10.3138/CHR-072-03-02.

Canadian Directory of Parliament, 1867–1967. Ottawa: Public Archives of Canada, 1968.

Cannadine, David. *Ornamentalism: How the British Saw the Empire*. London: Penguin, 2001.

Careless, J.M.S. *Brown of the Globe*. Vol. 2. Toronto: Macmillan, 1963.

Charland, Jean-Pierre. *Les pâtes et papiers au Québec, 1880–1980: Technologies, travail et travailleurs*. Quebec City: Institut Québécois de Recherche sur la Culture, 1990.

Chittolini, Giorgi. "The 'Private,' the 'Public,' and the State." *Journal of Modern History* 67, no. S1 (Dec. 1995): S34–S61. http://dx.doi.org/10.1086/245008.

Christie, Nancy. "The 'Plague of Servants': Female Household Labour and the Making of Classes in Upper Canada." In *Transatlantic Subjects: Ideas, Institutions, and Social Experience in Post-Revolutionary British North America*, ed. Nancy Christie. Montreal: McGill-Queen's University Press, 2008.

Chu, Samuel C., and Kwang-Ching Liu, eds. *Li Hung-chang and China's Early Modernization*. Armonk, NY: M.E. Sharpe, 1994.

Coates, Colin M. "French Canadians' Ambivalence to the Empire." In *Canada and the British Empire*, ed. Phillip Buckner. Oxford: Oxford University Press, 2008.

Coates, Colin M. "Like 'the Thames towards the Putney': The Appropriation of Landscape in Lower Canada." *Canadian Historical Review* 74, no. 3 (1993): 317–43. http://dx.doi.org/10.3138/CHR-074-03-01.

Coates, Colin M. *The Metamorphoses of Landscape and Community in Early Quebec*. Montreal: McGill-Queen's University Press, 2000.

Comeault, Gilbert L. "La question des écoles du Manitoba – Un nouvel éclairage." *Revue d'Histoire de l'Amerique Francaise* 33, no. 1 (1979): 3–23. http://dx.doi.org/10.7202/303748ar.

Cornell, Paul G. *The Alignment of Political Groups in Canada*. Toronto: University of Toronto Press, 1949. http://dx.doi.org/10.3138/CHR-030-01-02

Cott, Nancy. *The Bonds of Womanhood: "Women's Sphere" in New England, 1780–1835*. New Haven: Yale University Press, 1977.

Courville, Serge. "La crise agricole du Bas-Canada, éléments d'une réflexion géographique (deuxième partie)." *Cahiers de Geographie de Quebec* 24, no. 63 (1980): 385–428. http://dx.doi.org/10.7202/021487ar.

Courville, Serge. *Entre Ville et Campagne: L'essor du village dans les seigneuries du Bas-Canada*. Quebec: Les Presses de l'Université Laval, 1990.

Courville, Serge. *Quebec: A Historical Geography*. Trans. Richard Howard. Vancouver: UBC Press, 2008.

Courville, Serge. "Tradition or Modernity? The Canadian Seigniory in the Durham Era." In *Proceedings of the Seventeenth Meeting of the French Colonial Historical Society, Chicago, May 1991*, ed. Patricia Galloway.

Courville, Serge, and Normand Séguin. *Le coût du sol au Québec: Deux études de géographie historique*. Sainte-Foy: Les Presses de l'Université Laval, 1996.

Craig, Béatrice. "Agriculture and the Lumberman's Frontier in the Upper St. John Valley, 1800–70." *Journal of Forest History* 32, no. 3 (July 1988): 125–37. http://dx.doi.org/10.2307/4005171.

Crunican, Paul. *Priests and Politicians: Manitoba Schools and the Election of 1896*. Toronto: University of Toronto Press, 1974.

Curtis, Bruce. "From the Moral Thermometer to Money: Metrological Reform in Pre-Confederation Canada." *Social Studies of Science* 28, no. 4 (1998): 547–70. http://dx.doi.org/10.1177/030631298028004002.

Curtis, Bruce. "The 'Most Splendid Pageant Ever Seen': Grandeur, the Domestic, and Condescension in Lord Durham's Political Theatre." *Canadian Historical Review* 89, no. 1 (Mar. 2008): 55–88. http://dx.doi.org/10.3138/chr.89.1.55.

Curtis, Bruce. *The Politics of Population: State Formation, Statistics, and the Census of Canada, 1840–1875*. Toronto: University of Toronto Press, 2001.

Curtis, Bruce. *True Government by Choice Men? Inspection, Education, and State Formation in Canada West*. Toronto: University of Toronto Press, 1992.

Dalton, Roy C. *The Jesuits' Estates Question, 1760–1888: A Study of the Background for the Agitation of 1889*. Toronto: University of Toronto Press, 1968.

Davidoff, Leonore, and Catherine Hall. *Family Fortunes: Men and Women of the English Middle Class, 1780–1850*. Chicago: University of Chicago Press, 1987.

Davidoff, Leonore, Megan Doolittle, Janet Fink, and Katherine Holden. *The Family Story: Blood, Contract and Intimacy, 1830–1960*. London: Longman, 1999.

Dawson, Graham. *Soldier Heroes: British Adventure, Empire and the Imagining of Masculinities*. London: Routledge, 1994.

Dechêne, Louise. *Habitants et marchands de Montréal au XVIIe siècle*. Paris: Plon, 1974.

Desilets, Andrée. "Cauchon, Joseph-Édouard." *Dictionary of Canadian Biography Online*.

Desilets, Andrée . "Hall, George Benson." *Dictionary of Canadian Biography Online*.

Desilets, Andrée. *Hector-Louis Langevin, Un Père de la Confédération Canadienne (1826–1906)*. Quebec City: Les Presses de l'Université Laval, 1969.

Dessureault, Christian. "L'évolution du régime seigneuriale canadien de 1760 à 1854: essai de synthèse." In *Le régime seigneuriale au Québec: 150 ans après*, ed. Alain Laberge and Benoît Grenier. Centre interuniversitaire d'études québécoises, 2009.

Dessureault, Christian. "Industrie et société rurale: le cas de la seigneurie Saint-Hyacinthe des origines à 1861." *Histoire sociale / Social History*, 28 (May 1995): 99-136.

Douville, Raymond. "Trois seigneuries sans seigneurs." *Les Cahiers des Dix* 16 (1951): 133–70.

Dubuc, Alfred. "Problems in the Stratification of the Canadian Society from 1760 to 1840." Canadian Historical Association, *Annual Report*, 1965, 13–29.

Ducharme, Michel. "Penser le Canada: La mise en place des assises intellectuelles de l'État canadien moderne (1838–1840)." *Revue d'Histoire de l'Amerique Francaise* 56, no. 3 (Winter 2003): 357–86. http://dx.doi.org/10.7202/007618ar.

Ducharme, Michel, and Jean-François Constant. "Introduction: A Project of Rule Called Canada – The Liberal Order Framework and Historical Practice." In *Liberalism and Hegemony: Debating the Canadian Liberal Revolution*, ed. Michel Ducharme and Jean-François Constant. Toronto: University of Toronto Press, 2009.

Duchesne, Raymond, and Paul Carle. "L'ordre des choses: Cabinets et musées d'histoire naturelles au Québec (1824–1900)." *Revue d'Histoire de l'Amerique Francaise* 44, no. 1 (1990): 3–30. http://dx.doi.org/10.7202/304861ar.

Dufour, Pierre, and Jean Hamelin. "Mercier, Honoré." *Dictionary of Canadian Biography Online*.

Dussault, Gabriel. *Le Curé Labelle: Messianisme, utopie, et colonisation au Québec, 1850–1900*. Montreal: Hurtubise, 1983.

Dutil, Patrice. *Devil's Advocate: Godfroy Langlois and the Politics of Liberal Progressivism in Laurier's Quebec*. Montreal: Robert Davies, 1994.

Eley, Geoff. *A Crooked Line: From Cultural History to the History of Society*. Ann Arbor: University of Michigan Press, 2005.

Fecteau, Jean-Marie. *La liberté du pauvre: Sur la régulation de crime et de la pauvreté au XIXe siècle québécois*. Montreal: VLB, 2004.

Flamand-Hubert, Maude. *Louis Bertrand à L'Isle-Verte: Propriété foncière et exploitation des ressources, 1811-1871*. Quebec: Presses de l'Université du Québec, 2012.

Forster, Robert. "The French Revolution and the 'New' Elite, 1800–1850." In *The American and European Revolutions, 1776–1848*, ed. Jaroslow Pelenski. Iowa City: University of Iowa Press, 1980.

Foster, Janet. *Working for Wildlife: The Beginning of Preservation in Canada*. 2nd ed. Toronto: University of Toronto Press, 1998.

Francis, Martin. "The Domestication of the Male? Recent Research on Nineteenth- and Twentieth-Century British Masculinity." *Historical Journal* (Cambridge, England) 45, no. 3 (2002): 637–52. http://dx.doi.org/10.1017/S0018246X02002583.

Frost, Stanley Brice. *McGill University: For the Advancement of Learning*. Vol. 1. Montreal: McGill-Queen's University Press, 1980.

Fyson, Donald. *Magistrates, Police, and People: Everyday Criminal Justice in Quebec and Lower Canada, 1764–1837*. Toronto: University of Toronto Press, 2006.

Gadoury, Lorraine. *La noblesse de Nouvelle-France: Familles et alliances*. Ville La Salle, QC: Éditions Hurtubise HMH, 1991.

Gaffield, Chad. *Language, Schooling, and Cultural Conflict: The Origins of the French-Language Controversy in Ontario*. Montreal: McGill-Queen's University Press, 1988. http://dx.doi.org/10.1177/036319908801300126

Gagné, Armand. "Chartier de Lotbinière, Eustache." *Dictionary of Canadian Biography Online*.

Gagnon-Pratte, France. *L'architecture et la nature à Québec au dix-neuvième siècle: Les villas*. Quebec City: Ministère des Affaires Culturelles, 1980.

Gallichan, Gilles. *Honoré Mercier: La politique et la culture*. Sillery, QC: Septentrion, 1994.

Gardiner, Michael E. *Critiques of Everyday Life*. London: Routledge, 2000.

Gaudreau, Guy. *L'Exploitation des forêts publiques au Québec, 1842–1905*. Quebec City: Institut québécois de recherche sur la culture, 1986.

Gauthier, Benoît. "La sous-traitance et l'exploitation forestière en Mauricie (1850–1875)." *Material History Bulletin* 13 (Autumn 1981): 59–67.

Gendron, Mario. *Histoire du Piémont des Appalaches: La Montérégie*. Sainte Foy: Les Presses de l'Université Laval, 1999.

Gerson, Carole. *A Purer Taste: The Writing and Reading of Fiction in English in 19th Century Canada*. Toronto: University of Toronto Press, 1989.

Gillis, John R. *A World of Their Own Making: Myth, Ritual, and the Quest for Family Values*. New York: Basic Books, 1996.

Gillis, R. Peter, and Thomas R. Roach. *Lost Initiatives: Canada's Forest Industries, Forest Policy and Forest Conservation*. New York: Greenwood Press, 1986.

Gingras, Sylvain. *Hunting and Fishing in Quebec: A Century of Sport. St-Raymond*. QC: Les Éditions Rapides Blancs, 1994.

Girard, Jessica. "Lady Bountiful: Women of the Landed Classes and Rural Philanthropy." *Victorian Studies* 30, no. 2 (1987): 183–210.

Girard, Michel F. "Conservation and the Gospel of Efficiency: Un modèle de gestion de l'environnement venu d'Europe?" *Histoire sociale / Social History* 23, no. 45 (May 1990): 63–80.

Granger, Serge. "Les Lotbinière au Cachemire avant la première guerre mondiale." *Synergies Inde* 3 (2008): 129–40.

Green, Nicholas. *The Spectacle of Nature: Landscape and Bourgeois Culture in Nineteenth-Century France*. Manchester: Manchester University Press, 1990.

Green, Valerie. *Above Stairs: Social Life in Upper Class Victoria, 1843–1918*. Victoria: Sono Nis Press, 1995.

Greer, Allan. *Peasant, Lord, and Merchant: Rural Society in Three Quebec Parishes, 1740–1840*. Toronto: University of Toronto Press, 1985.

Gregory, Derek. "Emperors of the Gaze: Photographic Practices and Productions of Space in Egypt, 1839–1914." In *Picturing Place: Photography and the Geographical Imagination*, ed. Joan M. Schwartz and James R. Ryan. London: I.B. Tauris, 2003.

Grenier, Benoît. *Brève histoire du régime seigneurial*. Montreal: Boréal, 2012.

Grenier, Benoît. "'Le dernier endroit dans l'univers': À propos de l'extinction des rentes seigneuriales au Québec, 1854–1974." *Revue d'Histoire de l'Amerique Francaise* 64, no. 2 (Autumn 2010): 75–98.

Grenier, Benoît. "Élites seigneuriales, élites municipales: le pouvoir à l'heure de l'abolition." In *Les figures du pouvoir à travers le temps: formes pratiques et intérêts des groups élitaires au Québec, XVIIe-XXe siècles*, ed. Thierry Nootens and Jean-René Thuot. Quebec: Les Presses de l'Université Laval, 2012.

Grenier, Benoît. "Gentilshommes campagnards de la Nouvelle France, XVIIe–XIXe siècle: Une autre seigneurie laurentienne?" *French Colonial History* 7, no. 1 (2006): 21–43. http://dx.doi.org/10.1353/fch.2006.0004.

Grenier, Benoît. "Réflexion sur le pouvoir féminin au Canada sous le Régime français: Le cas de la 'seigneuresse' Marie-Catherine Peuvret (1667–1739)." *Revue d'Histoire de l'Amerique Francaise* 42, no. 84 (Nov. 2009): 299–326.

Grenier, Benoît. *Seigneurs campagnards de la Nouvelle France: Présence seigneuriale et sociabilité dans la vallée du Saint-Laurent à l'époque préindustrielle.* Rennes: Presse Universitaires de Rennes, 2007.

Hall, Catherine. "Home Sweet Home." In *Histoire de la vie privée*. Vol. 4, *De la Révolution à la Grande Guerre*, ed. Philippe Ariès and Georges Duby. Paris: Éditions du Seuil, 1987.

Hamelin, Jean, and Michel Paquin. "Irvine, George." *Dictionary of Canadian Biography Online.*

Hamelin, Jean, and Yves Roby. *Histoire économique du Québec, 1851–1896*. Montreal: Éditions Fides, 1971.

Hamelin, Marcel. "Chartier de Lotbinière, Michel-Eustache-Gaspard-Alain." *Dictionary of Canadian Biography Online.*

Hamelin, Marcel. "Joly de Lotbinière, Sir Henri-Gustave." *Dictionary of Canadian Biography Online.*

Hamelin, Marcel, ed. *Les Mémoires du sénateur Raoul Dandurand, 1861–1942.* Quebec City: Les Presses de l'Université Laval, 1967.

Hamelin, Marcel. *Les Premières années du parlementarisme Québécois (1867–1878).* Quebec City: Les Presses de l'Université Laval, 1974.

Hardy, René. "Exploitation forestière et environnment au Québec, 1850–1920." *Zeitschrift der Gesellschaft für Kanada-Studien* 27, no. 2 (1995): 63–79.

Hardy, René, and Normand Séguin. *Forêt et société en Mauricie.* Montreal: Boréal Express / Musée nationale de l'Homme, 1984.

Harris, Richard Colebrook. *The Seigneurial System in Early Canada.* Montreal: McGill-Queen's University Press, 1984.

Harrison, J.F.C. *The Early Victorians, 1832–1851.* New York: Praeger, 1971.

Heaman, E.A. "Rights Talk and the Liberal Order Framework." In *Liberalism and Hegemony: Debating the Canadian Liberal Revolution*, ed. Jean-François Constant and Michel Ducharme. Toronto: University of Toronto Press, 2009.

Histoire et Nature du Domaine Joly-De Lotbinière. Fondation du Domaine Joly-De Lotbinière, 2006.

Hodgins, Bruce W. *John Sandfield Macdonald, 1812–1872*. Toronto: University of Toronto Press, 1971.

Hodgins, Bruce W., Jamie Benidickson, and Peter Gillis. "The Ontario and Quebec Experiments with Forest Reserves, 1883–1930." *Journal of Forest History* 26, no. 1 (1982): 20–33. http://dx.doi.org/10.2307/4004566.

Horowitz, Gad. "Conservatism, Liberalism and Socialism in Canada: An Interpretation." *Canadian Journal of Economics and Political Science* 32, no. 2 (May 1966): 143–71. http://dx.doi.org/10.2307/139794.

Irving, L. Homfray. *Officers of the British Forces in Canada during the War of 1812–15*. Wellington, ON: Wellington Tribune Print for the Canadian Military Institute, 1908.

Jackman, S.W. *The Men at Cary Castle: A Series of Portrait Sketches of the Lieutenant-Governors of British Columbia from 1871 to 1971*. Victoria, BC: Morriss Printing, 1972.

Jedwab, Jack. "Stephens, George Washington." *Dictionary of Canadian Biography Online*.

Judd, Richard. *Common Lands, Common People: The Origins of Conservation in Northern New England*. Cambridge, MA: Harvard University Press, 1997.

Judd, Richard. "Lumbering and the Agricultural Frontier in Aroostook County, Maine." *Journal of Forest History* 28 (Apr. 1984): 165–80.

Kelm, Mary-Ellen. "Touring with Trouncer: Community, Adaptation, and Identities." *BC Studies* 131 (Autumn 2001): 63–70.

Keshen, Jeffrey. "Hopkins, John Castell." *Dictionary of Canadian Biography Online*.

Kessler-Harris, Alice. "Why Biography?" *American Historical Review* 114, no. 3 (June 2009): 625–30. http://dx.doi.org/10.1086/ahr.114.3.625.

Kuhn, William M. *Democratic Royalism: The Transformation of the British Monarchy, 1861–1914*. London: Macmillan, 1996.

Lamarche, Jacques. *Sir H.-G. Joly de Lotbinière*. Montreal: Lidec, 1997.

Lamonde, Yvan. *Histoire sociale des idées au Québec, 1760–1896*. Vol. 1. N.p.: Fides, 2000.

Lamonde, Yvan. *Louis-Antoine Dessaules: Un seigneur libérale et anticlerical*. N.p.: Fides, 1994.

Lanlancette, Mario. "Description et analyse du rapport pêche/seigneurie à l'Île aux Coudres au XVIIIe siècle." In *Évolution et éclatement du monde rurale: France-Québec, XVIIe-XXe siècles*, ed. Joseph Goy and Jean-Pierre Wallot. Montreal: Presses de l'Université de Montréal, 1986.

Larin, Robert, and Yves Drolet. "Les listes de Carleton et de Haldimand. États de la noblesse canadienne en 1767 et 1778." *Histoire sociale / Social History* 41, no. 82 (Nov. 2008): 563–603

Laurence, Gérard. "Évanturel, François." *Dictionary of Canadian Biography Online*.

Lavallée, Louis. *La Prairie en Nouvelle-France, 1647–1760*. Montreal: McGill-Queen's University Press, 1992.

Lebel, Jean-Marie. "Tassé, Joseph." *Dictionary of Canadian Biography Online*.

Leclerc, Héléne. *Domaine Joly-De Lotbinière*. Quebec City: Éditions Fides, 2002.

Legault, Roch. "L'Organisation militaire sous le régime britannique et le rôle assigné à la gentilhommerie canadienne (1760–1815)." *Revue d'Histoire de l'Amerique Francaise* 45, no. 2 (1991): 229–49. http://dx.doi.org/10.7202/304967ar.

Legault, Roch. *Une élite en déroute: Les militaires canadiens après la Conquête*. Outremont, QC: Athéna éditions, 2002.

Lepore, Jill. "Historians Who Love Too Much: Reflections on Microhistory and Biography." *Journal of American History* 88, no. 1 (June 2001): 129–44. http://dx.doi.org/10.2307/2674921.

Letourneau, Jocelyn. *A History for the Future: Rewriting Memory and Identity in Quebec*. Montreal: McGill-Queen's University Press, 2004.

Letourneau, Jocelyn. *Le Québec, les Québécois: Un parcours historique*. Montreal: Éditions Fides, 2004.

Lévesque, Robert, and Robert Migner. *Le Curé Labelle: Le colonisateur, le politicien, la légende*. Montreal: La Presse, 1979.

Levi, Giovanni. "On Microhistory." In *New Perspectives on Historical Writing*, ed. Peter Burke. University Park: Pennsylvania State University Press, 1991.

Linteau, Paul-André, René Durocher, and Jean-Claude Robert. *Quebec: A History, 1867–1929*. Trans. Robert Chodos. Toronto: Lorimer, 1983.

Little, J.I. "Colonization and Municipal Reform in Canada East." *Histoire sociale / Social History* 14 (1981): 94–121.

Little, J.I. "Contested Land: Squatters and Agents in the Eastern Townships of Lower Canada." *Canadian Historical Review* 80, no. 3 (1999): 381–414. http://dx.doi.org/10.3138/CHR.80.3.381.

Little, J.I. "Drummond, Lewis Thomas." *Dictionary of Canadian Biography Online*.

Little, J.I. "The Fireside Kingdom: A Mid-Nineteenth-Century Anglican Perspective on Marriage and Parenthood." In *Households of Faith: Family, Gender, and Community in Canada, 1760–1969*, ed. Nancy Christie. Montreal: McGill-Queen's University Press, 2002.

Little, J.I. *Nationalism, Capitalism, and Colonization in Nineteenth-Century Quebec: The Upper St. Francis District.* Montreal: McGill-Queens University Press, 1989.

Little, J.I. "New Brunswick Reaction to the Manitoba Schools' Questions." *Acadiensis* 1, no. 2 (1971): 43–58.

Little, J.I. "Public Policy and Private Interest in the Lumber Industry of the Eastern Townships: The Case of C.S. Clark and Company, 1854–81." *Histoire sociale / Social History* 19 (1986): 9–37.

Little, J.I. *State and Society in Transition: The Politics of Institutional Reform in the Eastern Townships, 1838–1852.* Montreal: McGill-Queen's University Press, 1997.

Little, J.I. "Watching the Frontier Disappear: English-Speaking Reaction to the French-Canadian Colonization Movement in the Eastern Townships, 1844–90." *Journal of Canadian Studies* 15, no. 4 (1980–1): 93–111.

Loo, Tina. *Making Law, Order, and Authority in British Columbia, 1821–1871.* Toronto: University of Toronto Press, 1994.

MacBeath, George. "Joybert (Joibert) de Soulanges et de Marson, Pierre de." *Dictionary of Canadian Biography Online.*

MacKay, Donald. *Heritage Lost: The Crisis in Canada's Forests.* Toronto: Macmillan, 1985.

McCallum, Margaret. "Corporate Welfarism in Canada, 1919–39." *Canadian Historical Review* 71, no. 1 (1990): 46–79. http://dx.doi.org/10.3138/CHR-071-01-02.

McCormack, Matthew, ed. *Public Men: Masculinity and Politics in Modern Britain.* New York: Palgrave Macmillan, 2007.

McDonald, Robert A.J. "The Quest for 'Modern Administration': British Columbia's Civil Service, 1870s to 1940s." *BC Studies* 161 (Spring 2009): 9–34.

McDonald, Robert A.J. "Sir Charles Hibbert Tupper and the Political Culture of British Columbia, 1903–1924." *BC Studies* 149 (Spring 2006): 63–86.

McDonald, Robert A.J. "'Variants of Liberalism' and the Liberal Order Framework." In *Liberalism and Hegemony: Debating the Canadian Liberal Revolution*, ed. Jean-François Constant and Michel Ducharme. Toronto: University of Toronto Press, 2009.

McDonald, Robert A.J. "Victoria, Vancouver, and the Economic Development of British Columbia, 1886–1914." In *British Columbia: Historical Readings*, ed. W. Peter Ward and Robert A.J. McDonald. Vancouver: Douglas and McIntyre, 1981.

McKay, Ian. "The Liberal Order Framework: A Prospectus for a Reconnaissance of Canadian History." *Canadian Historical Review* 81, no. 4 (2000): 617–45. http://dx.doi.org/10.3138/CHR.81.4.617.

McNairn, Jeffrey L. *The Capacity to Judge: Public Opinion and Deliberative Democracy in Upper Canada, 1791–1854.* Toronto: University of Toronto Press, 2000.

McQuillan, D. "Pouvoir et perception: Une communauté irlandaise au Québec au dix-neuvième siècle." *Recherches Sociographiques* 40, no. 2 (1999): 263–83. http://dx.doi.org/10.7202/057279ar.

McQuillan, D. Aidan. "Beaurivage: The Development of an Irish Ethnic Identity in Rural Quebec, 1820–1860." In *The Untold Story: The Irish in Canada,* ed. Robert O'Driscoll and Lorna Reynolds. Toronto: Celtic Arts of Canada, 1988.

Mantena, Karuna. "The Crisis of Liberal Imperialism." *Histoire@Politique. Politique, culture, société* 11 (May–Aug. 2010). http://www.histoire-politique.fr. Accessed 27 Mar. 2012.

Marshall, Daniel. "An Early Rural Revolt: The Introduction of the Canadian System of Tariffs to British Columbia, 1871–4." In *Beyond the City Limits: Rural History in British Columbia,* ed. R.W. Sandwell. Vancouver: UBC Press, 1999.

Martin, Ged. *Britain and the Origins of Canadian Confederation, 1837–67.* Vancouver: UBC Press, 1995.

Martin, Ged. "The Case against Confederation." In *The Causes of Canadian Confederation,* ed. Ged Martin. Fredericton: Acadiensis Press, 1990.

Mayer, Arno J. *The Persistence of the Old Regime: Europe to the Great War.* New York: Pantheon Books, 1981.

Miller, J.R. "Anti-Catholic Thought in Victorian Canada." *Canadian Historical Review* 66, no. 4 (1985): 474–94. http://dx.doi.org/10.3138/CHR-066-04-03.

Miller, J.R. *Equal Rights: The Jesuits' Estates Act Controversy.* Montreal: McGill-Queen's University Press, 1979.

Monet, Jacques. *The Canadian Crown.* Toronto: Clarke, Irwin, 1979.

Monet, Jacques. "The Personal and Living Bond, 1839–1849." In *The Shield of Achilles: Aspects of Canada in the Victorian Age,* ed. W.L. Morton. Toronto: McClelland and Stewart, 1968.

Monette, Michel. "Hall, William." In *Dictionary of Canadian Biography Online.*

Moore, Christopher. *1867: How the Fathers Made a Deal.* Toronto: McClelland and Stewart, 1997.

Moreman, T.R. *The Army in India and the Development of Frontier Warfare, 1849–1947.* London: MacMillan, 1998. http://dx.doi.org/10.1057/9780230374621

Morgan, Henry James, ed. *Types of Canadian Women.* Vol. 1. Toronto: William Briggs, 1903.

Morissonneau, Christian. "La colonisation équivoque." *Recherches Sociographiques* 19, no. 1 (Jan.–Apr. 1978): 33–43. http://dx.doi.org/10.7202/055772ar.

Morneau, Jocelyn. *Petits Pays et Grands Ensembles: Les articulations du monde rural au XIXe siècle. L'exemple du Lac Saint-Pierre.* Sainte-Foy: Les Presses de l'Université Laval, 1999.

Morton, Desmond. "Des canadiens errants: French Canadian Troops in the North-West Campaign of 1885." *Journal of Canadian Studies. Revue d'Etudes Canadiennes* 5, no. 3 (Aug. 1970): 28–39.

Morton, W.L. "The Cabinet of 1867." In *Cabinet Formation and Bicultural Relations*, ed. F.W. Gibson. Ottawa: Queen's Printer, 1970.

Munro, Kenneth J. *The Political Career of Sir Adolphe Chapleau, Premier of Quebec, 1879–1882.* Lewiston, NY: E. Mellen Press, 1992.

Nasaw, David. "Introduction: Historians and Biography." *American Historical Review* 114, no. 3 (June 2009): 573–8. http://dx.doi.org/10.1086/ahr.114.3.573.

Nash, Roderick. *Wilderness and the American Mind.* New Haven, CT: Yale University Press, 1967.

Neatby, H. Blair. *Laurier and a Liberal Quebec.* Toronto: McClelland and Stewart, 1973.

Nelles, H.V. *The Art of Nation-Building: Pageantry and Spectacle at Quebec's Tercentenary.* Toronto: University of Toronto Press, 1999.

Nish, Cameron. *Les Bourgeois-gentilshommes de la Nouvelle-France, 1729–1748.* Montreal: Fides, 1968.

Noël, Françoise. *Family Life and Sociability in Upper and Lower Canada, 1780–1870.* Montreal: McGill-Queen's University Press, 2003.

Noël, Françoise. "La gestion des seigneuries de Gabriel Christie dans la vallée du Richelieu (1760-1845)." *Revue d'histoire de l'Amérique française*, 40, no. 4 (1987): 561-82.

Noel, S.J.R. *Patrons, Clients, Brokers: Ontario Society and Politics, 1791–1896.* Toronto: University of Toronto Press, 1990.

Nootens, Thierry. "'Nous ne voulons pas que nos héritiers soient à la merci des tiens': Famille, patrimoine et entreprise chez les Rolland, 1880–1980." *Revue d'Histoire de l'Amerique Francaise* 61, no. 1 (2007): 5–36. http://dx.doi.org/10.7202/016872ar.

Ormsby, Margaret. *British Columbia: A History.* N.p.: Macmillan, 1958.

Ouellet, Fernand. "Le régime seigneuriale." In *Éléments d'histoire sociale du Bas-Canada*, ed. Fernand Ouellet. Montreal: Hurtubise HMH, 1972.

Owram, Doug. "Progress, Science, and Religion: Exploring Victorian Thought in Canada." In *Thinkers and Dreamers: Historical Essays in Honour of Carl Berger*, ed. Gerald Friesen and Doug Owram, 225–44. Toronto: University of Toronto Press, 2011.

Palmer, Bryan. *Working-Class Experience: The Rise and Reconstitution of Canadian Labour, 1800–1980.* Toronto: Butterworth, 1983.

Paquet, Gilles, and Jean-Pierre Wallot. "Economic Strategy of the Habitant Landholder: Quebec, 1790–1835." In *Perspectives on Canadian Economic History*, 2nd ed., ed. Douglas McCalla and Michael Huberman. Mississauga: Copp Clark Longman, 1994.

Paradis, André. "Le sous-financement gouvernemental et son impact sur le développement des asiles francophones au Québec (1845-1918)." *Revue d'histoire de l'Amérique française* 50, no 4 (Spring 1997): 571-98.

Paradis, Louis L. *Les Annales de Lotbinière, 1672–1933*. Quebec City: L'Action Catholique, 1933.

Pass, Forrest D. "Agrarian Commonwealth, or Entrepôt of the Orient? Competing Conceptions of Canada and the BC Terms of Union Debate of 1871." *Journal of the Canadian Historical Association*, n.s., 17, no. 1 (2006): 25–53.

Percy, Michael B., and Rick Szostak. "The Political Economy of the Abolition of Seigneurial Tenure in Canada East." *Explorations in Economic History* 29, no. 1 (1992): 51–68. http://dx.doi.org/10.1016/0014-4983(92)90032-R.

Perron, Marc. *Un grand éducateur agricole: Édouard-A. Barnard*. [Montreal?]: n.p., 1955.

Pisani, Donald J. "Forests and Conservation, 1865–1890." In *American Forests: Nature, Culture and Politics*, ed. Char Miller. Lawrence: University of Kansas Press, 1997.

Poulter, Gillian. *Becoming Native in a Foreign Land: Sport, Visual Culture and Identity in Montreal, 1840–85*. Vancouver: UBC Press, 2009.

Powell, Barbara. "Sarah Crease and Susan Crease." In *The Small Details of Life: Twenty Diaries by Women in Canada, 1830–1996*, ed. Kathryn Carter. Toronto: University of Toronto Press, 2002.

Pyne, Stephen J. "Mon pays, c'est le feu. Le Québec, le Canada, les forêts et le feu." *GLOBE: Revue Internationale d'Etudes Quebecoises* 9, no. 1 (2006): 141–75. http://dx.doi.org/10.7202/1000801ar.

Proulx, Bernard. *Le roman du territoire*. Montreal: Université du Québec à Montréal, 1987.

Quinn, Magella. "Les capitaux français et le Québec, 1855–1900." *Revue d'Histoire de l'Amerique Francaise* 24, no. 4 (1971): 527–66. http://dx.doi.org/10.7202/303019ar.

Radforth, Ian. *Bush Workers and Bosses: Logging in Northern Ontario, 1900–1980*. Toronto: University of Toronto Press, 1987.

Rajala, Richard. "The Forest Industry of Eastern Canada: An Overview." Accompanying essay to C.R. Silversides, *Broadaxe to Flying Shear: The Mechanization of Forest Harvesting East of the Rockies* (Ottawa: National Museum of Science and Technology, 1997), 121–54.

Rasmussen, Ken. "Administrative Reform and the Quest for Bureaucratic Autonomy, 1867–1919." *Journal of Canadian Studies. Revue d'Etudes Canadiennes* 29, no. 3 (1994): 45–62.

Rasporich, A.W. "Imperial Sentiment in the Province of Canada during the Crimean War, 1854–1856." In *The Shield of Achilles: Aspects of Canada in the Victorian Age*, ed. W.L. Morton. Toronto: McClelland and Stewart, 1968.

Rawls, John. *The Law of Peoples with "The Idea of Public Reason Revisited."* Cambridge, MA: Harvard University Press, 1999.

Reid, Escott M. "The Rise of National Parties in Canada." In *Party Politics in Canada*, ed. Hugh G. Thorburn. Scarborough: Prentice-Hall, 1967.

Reid, J.H. Stewart, Kenneth McNaught, and Harry S. Crowe, eds. *A Source-Book of Canadian History: Selected Documents and Personal Papers*. Toronto: Longmans, 1964.

Reksten, Terry. *"More English than the English": A Very Social History of Victoria.* Victoria: Orca Publishing, 1986.

"Rhodes, Col. William." http://www.assnat.qc.ca/fr/deputes/rhodes-william-5071/biographie.html Accessed 20 Dec. 2009.

Roach, Thomas, and Richard Judd. "A Man for All Seasons: Frank John Dixie Barnjum, Conservationist, Pulpwood Embargoist and Speculator!" *Acadiensis* 20, no. 2 (1991): 129–44.

Robert, Jean-Claude. "Un seigneur entrepreneur, Barthélemy Joliette, et la fondation de la village d'Industrie (Joliette), 1822–1850." *Revue d'Histoire de l'Amerique Francaise* 26, no. 3 (1972): 375–95. http://dx.doi.org/10.7202/303193ar.

Robin, Martin. *The Rush for Spoils: The Company Province, 1871–1933.* Toronto: McClelland and Stewart, 1972.

Roy, Fernande. *Progrès, Harmonie, Liberté: Le libéralisme des milieux d'affaires francophones à Montréal au tournant du siècle.* Montreal: Boréal, 1988.

Roy, Patricia E. *A White Man's Province: British Columbia Politicians and Chinese and Japanese Immigrants, 1858–1914.* Vancouver: UBC Press, 1989.

Rudin, Ronald. *Founding Fathers: The Celebration of Champlain and Laval in the Streets of Quebec, 1878–1908.* Toronto: University of Toronto Press, 2003.

Rudy, Jarret. *The Freedom to Smoke: Tobacco Consumption and Identity.* Montreal: McGill-Queen's University Press, 2005.

Ruggiu, François-Joseph. "La noblesse du Canada aux XVIIe et XVIIIe siècles." *Histoire, Economie et Société* 4 (2008): 67–85. http://dx.doi.org/10.3917/hes.084.0067.

Rumilly, Robert. *Histoire de la Province de Québec.* Vol. 1–4. Montreal: Éditions Bernard Valiquette, 1942.

Rumilly, Robert . "Letellier de Saint-Just, Luc." *Dictionary of Canadian Biography Online.*

Ryan, Mary. *Cradle of the Middle Class: The Family in Oneida County, New York, 1790–1865.* Cambridge: Cambridge University Press, 1981.

Saint-Pierre, Jocelyn. "Langelier, Sir François." *Dictionary of Canadian Biography Online.*

Salée, Daniel. "Seigneurial Landownership and the Transition to Capitalism in Nineteenth-Century Quebec." *Quebec Studies* 12 (1991): 21–32.

Samson, Daniel. "'The Yoke of Improvement': Sir John Sinclair, John Young, and the Improvement of the Scotlands, New and Old." In *Transatlantic Rebels: Agrarian Radicalism in Comparative Context*, ed. Thomas Summerhill and James C. Scott. East Lansing: Michigan State University Press, 2004.

Samson, Roch, Andrée Héroux, Diane Saint-Pierre, and Martine Côté. *Histoire de Lévis-Lotbinière.* Sainte-Foy: Les Presses de l'Université Laval, 1996.

Sangster, Joan. "The Softball Solution: Female Workers, Male Managers and the Operation of Paternalism at Westclox, 1923–60." *Labour / Le Travail* 32 (Fall 1993): 167. http://dx.doi.org/10.2307/25143730.

Saywell, John T. "The Cabinet of 1896." In *Cabinet Formation and Bicultural Relations: Seven Case Studies*, ed. Frederick W. Gibson. Ottawa: Queen's Printer, 1970.

Saywell, John T., ed. *The Canadian Journal of Lady Aberdeen, 1893–1898.* Toronto: The Champlain Society, 1960.

Saywell, John T. *The Office of Lieutenant-Governor: A Study in Canadian Government and Politics.* Toronto: University of Toronto Press, 1957.

Schulze, David. "Rural Manufacture in Lower Canada: Understanding Seigneurial Privilege and the Transition in the Countryside." *Alternate Routes: Critical Review* 7 (1984): 134–67.

Séguin, Maurice. "Le régime seigneuriale au pays de Québec, 1760–1854." *Revue d'Histoire de l'Amerique Francaise* 1, no. 3 (1947): 382–404. http://dx.doi.org/10.7202/801387ar.

Séguin, Normand. *La conquête du sol au 19e siècle.* Sillery: Boréal Express, 1977.

Silver, Arthur. *The French-Canadian Idea of Confederation, 1864–1900.* Toronto: University of Toronto Press, 1982.

Simpson, Jeffrey. *The Spoils of Power: The Politics of Patronage.* Toronto: Collins, 1988.

Smandych, Russell C. "Tory Paternalism and the Politics of Penal Reform in Upper Canada, 1830–34: A 'Neo-revisionist' Account of the Kingston Penitentiary." *Criminal Justice History* 12 (1991): 57–84.

Smith, Andrew. "Toryism, Classical Liberalism, and Capitalism: The Politics of Taxation and the Struggle for Canadian Confederation." *Canadian Historical Review* 89, no. 1 (Mar. 2008): 1–25. http://dx.doi.org/10.3138/chr.89.1.1.

Smith, David E. *The Invisible Crown: The First Principle of Canadian Government.* Toronto: University of Toronto Press, 1995.

Soboul, Albert. "Persistence of 'Feudalism' in the Rural Society of Nineteenth-Century France." In *Rural Society in France: Selections from the Annales: Économies, Sociétés, Civilisations,* ed. Robert Forster and Orest Ranum, trans. Elborg Forster and Patricia M. Ranum. Baltimore: Johns Hopkins University Press, 1977.

Sproat, John G. *"The Best Men": Liberal Reformers in the Gilded Age.* New York: Oxford University Press, 1968.

Stacey, C.P. *Canada and the British Army, 1846–1871.* Toronto: University of Toronto Press, 1963.

Stamp, Robert M. *Kings, Queens and Canadians: A Celebration of Canada's Infatuation with the British Royal Family.* Markham, ON: Fitzhenry and Whiteside, 1987.

Stanley, G.F.G. "A 'Constitutional Crisis' in British Columbia." *Canadian Journal of Economics and Political Science* 21, no. 3 (1955): 281–92. http://dx.doi.org/10.2307/138200.

Stanley, G.F.G. "The Caraquet Riots of 1875." *Acadiensis* 2, no. 1 (1972–3): 21–38.

Stevens, Paul. "Edgar, Sir James David." *Dictionary of Canadian Biography Online.*

Stewart, Gordon T. *The Origins of Canadian Politics: A Comparative Approach.* Vancouver: UBC Press, 1986.

Stewart, Gordon T. "Political Patronage under Macdonald and Laurier, 1878–1911." *American Review of Canadian Studies* 10, no. 1 (1980): 3–26. http://dx.doi.org/10.1080/02722018009481170.

Thompson, E.P. *Customs in Common: Studies in Traditional Popular Culture.* New York: New Press, 1991.

Thorpe, F.J., and Sylvette Nicolini-Maschino. "Chartier de Lotbinière, Michel, Marquis de Lotbinière." *Dictionary of Canadian Biography Online*

Torres, Félix. "Du champ des Annales à la biographie: Réflexions sur le retour d'un genre." *Problèmes et méthodes de la biographie.* Paris: Actes du colloque, Sorbonne, 3–4 May 1985.

Tosh, John. *A Man's Place: Masculinity and the Middle-Class Home in Victorian England.* New Haven: Yale University Press, 1999.

Tosh, John. *Manliness and Masculinities in Nineteenth-Century Britain: Essays on Family, Gender and Empire.* Harlow, UK: Pearson Education, 2005.

Vachon, André. "Chartier de Lotbinière, Louis-Théandre." *Dictionary of Canadian Biography Online.*

Vallières, Marc, Yvon Desloges, Fernand Harvey, Andrée Héroux, Reginald Auger, Sophie-Laurence Lamontagne; avec la collaboration d'André

Charbonneau. *Histoire de Québec et de sa région*. Vol. 2. Quebec City: Les Presses de l'Université Laval, 2008.

Varty, John F. "On Protein, Prairie Wheat, and Good Bread: Rationalizing Technologies and the Canadian State, 1912–1935." *Canadian Historical Review* 85, no. 4 (2004): 721–53.

Wagner, Henry R. "Henri Ternaux Compans: The First Collector of Hispanic-Americana." *Review of Inter-American Bibliography* 4, no. 4 (1954): 283–98.

Waite, P.B. *Canada 1874–1896, Arduous Destiny*. Toronto: McClelland and Stewart, 1971.

Waite, P.B. *The Life and Times of Confederation, 1864–1867*. Toronto: University of Toronto Press, 1962.

Walden, Keith. *Becoming Modern in Toronto: The Industrial Exhibition and the Shaping of a Late Victorian Culture*. Toronto: University of Toronto Press, 1997.

Ward, Norman. "Called to the Bar of the House of Commons." *Canadian Bar Review* 35 (May 1957): 529–46.

Ward, Peter. *White Canada Forever: Popular Attitudes and Public Policy towards Orientals in British Columbia*. Montreal: McGill-Queen's University Press, 1978, reprint 2002.

Watt, J.T. "Anti-Catholic Nativism in Canada: The Protestant Protective Association." *Canadian Historical Review* 48, no. 1 (1967): 45–58. http://dx.doi.org/10.3138/CHR-048-01-03.

Weber, Eugen. *Peasants into Frenchmen: The Modernization of Rural France, 1870–1914*. Stanford: Stanford University Press, 1976.

Wood, Col. William. *The Storied Province of Quebec Past and Present*. Vol. 4. Toronto: Dominion Publishing, 1931.

Worster, Donald. *Nature's Economy: A History of Ecological Ideas*. 2nd ed. Cambridge: Cambridge University Press, 1994.

Wynn, Graeme. "'Deplorably Dark and Demoralized Lumberers'? Rhetoric and Reality in Early Nineteenth-Century New Brunswick." *Journal of Forest History* 24, no. 4 (Oct. 1980): 168–87. http://dx.doi.org/10.2307/4004443.

Wynn, Graeme. *Timber Colony: A Historical Geography of Early Nineteenth Century New Brunswick*. Toronto: University of Toronto Press, 1981.

Young, Brian. *Brian Young, George-Étienne Cartier: Montreal Bourgeois*. Montreal: McGill-Queen's University Press, 1981.

Young, Brian. "Patrician Elites and Power in Nineteenth-Century Montreal and Quebec City." In *Who Ran the Cities? City Elites and Urban Power Structures in Europe and North America, 1750–1940*, ed. Ralf Roth and Robert Beachy. Burlington, VT: Ashgate, 2007.

Young, Brian. *The Politics of Codification: The Lower Canadian Civil Code of 1866.* Montreal: McGill-Queen's University Press, 1994.

Young, Brian. *Promoters and Politicians: The North-Shore Railways in the History of Quebec, 1854–85.* Toronto: University of Toronto Press, 1978.

Young, Brian. "Revisiting Feudal Vestiges in Urban Quebec." In *Transatlantic Subjects: Ideas, Institutions, and Social Experience in Post-Revolutionary British North America*, ed. Nancy Christie. Montreal: McGill-Queen's University Press, 2008.

Young, Brian. "Thinking about Power in Post-Rebellion Quebec, 1837–1867." In *Quebec Questions: Quebec Studies for the Twenty-First Century*, ed. Stéphan Gervais, Christopher Kirby, and Jarrett Rudy. Don Mills, ON: Oxford University Press, 2011.

Unpublished Secondary Sources

Abbott, Frank Albert. "The Quebec Winter Carnival of 1894: The Transformation of the City and the Festival in the Nineteenth Century." MA thesis, University of British Columbia, 1971.

Barlow, John Matthew. "Fear and Loathing in Saint-Sylvestre: The Corrigan Murder Case, 1855–58." MA thesis, Simon Fraser University, 1998.

Benoît, Jean. "La question seigneuriale au Bas-Canada, 1850–1867." MA thesis, Laval University, 1978.

Brock, Peter Jeffrey. "Fighting Joe Martin in British Columbia." MA thesis, Simon Fraser University, 1976.

Christie, Nancy. "Families, Private Life and the Emergence of Liberalism in Canada." Typescript kindly provided by the author.

Gadoury, Marc. "Sir Henri Gustave Joly de Lotbinière: Visionnaire et promoteur de la conservation des forêts, au Québec, à la fin du XIXe siècle." MA thesis, Laval University, 1998.

Gray, Stephen. "Forest Policy and Administration in British Columbia, 1912–1928." MA thesis, Simon Fraser University, 1982.

Hunt, Peter Robert. "The Political Career of Sir Richard McBride." MA thesis, University of British Columbia, 1953.

Johns, Harold Percival. "British Columbia's Campaign for Better Terms, 1871–1907." MA thesis, University of British Columbia, 1935.

LaPierre, Laurier. "Politics, Race, and Religion in Canada: Joseph Israel Tarte." PhD dissertation, University of Toronto, 1962.

Larose, André. "La seigneurie de Beauharnois, 1729–1867: Les seigneurs, l'espace et l'argent." PhD dissertation, University of Ottawa, 1987.

Marris, Robert Howard. "'Pretty Sleek and Fat': The Genesis of Forest Policy
    in British Columbia, 1903–1914." MA thesis, University of British Columbia,
    1979.
McLaughlin, K.M. "Race, Religion and Politics: The Election of 1896 in
    Canada." PhD dissertation, University of Toronto, 1974.
Sevigny, Daniel. "Le capitalisme et la politique dans une région Québécoise
    de colonisation: Le cas de Jacques Picard à Wotton, 1828–1905." MA thesis,
    Simon Fraser University, 1982.
Smith, Brian Ray Douglas. "Sir Richard McBride: A Study in the Conservative
    Party of British Columbia, 1903–1916." MA thesis, Queen's University, 1959.
Strong-Boag, Veronica. "The Less Than Mighty Scot? The Encounter of
    John Campbell Gordon, Earl / Later Marquess of Aberdeen (and Temair)
    1847–1934, with Hegemonic Masculinity." Presented to the Annual Meeting
    of the Canadian Historical Association, June 2011.
Strong-Boag, Veronica. "Liberal Hearts and Coronets: The Lives and Times of
    Ishbel Marjoribanks Gordon and John Campbell Gordon, the Aberdeens."
    Typescript kindly provided by the author.
Trépanier, Pierre. "L'Administration Joly (1878–1879)." MA thesis, University
    of Ottawa, 1972.
Young, Brian. "Generation Matters: Two Patrician Families in the History of
    Quebec." Typescript kindly provided by the author.

Index

O'Farrell, John, 102
Ontario, Henri-Gustave Joly de
Lotbinière's tour of, 167–9, 176
ornamentalism, 217
Ouimet, Gédéon, 112, 116, 180

Pacaud, Ernest, 154, 162, 165, 167
pageantry and ceremony, 233–5.
See also ornamentalism
Panet, Colonel E., 56
Papineau, Amédée, 167–8, 172
Papineau, Joseph, 19–20, 21–2
Papineau, Louis-Joseph, 20–1, 26,
27, 30, 101
Parent, Simon-Napoléon, 196
Parrot, Fritz, 77, 78, 91, 283n44,
287n85
Parti nationale, 108–9, 152, 154, 157
paternalism/charity, 9, 12, 50, 64, 71,
75–6, 78, 80–1, 87, 95, 96, 124, 148,
189, 237, 245–6, 256n38, 328n27
patricianism. *See* Joly de Lotbinière,
Sir Henri-Gustave, patrician
elite/status
La Patrie, 141–2
patronage. *See* corruption, political;
Joly de Lotbinière, Henri-Gustave,
patronage
Perrault, Joseph, 106
pew, seigneurial, 32, 95, 244, 266n115
Picturesque Canada, 199
Pinchot, Gifford, 196
Pointe Platon, 31, 32, 53, 59, 83, 86,
154, 197, 199, 228, 232, 265n106.
See also Lotbinière seigneury;
manor house
police, provincial, 108, 120, 132,
147, 309n111
Portneuf, 31, 32, 122, 170, 173–5
passim, 202, 232

Price, Herbert and Co., 35, 80, 88,
89, 180
Prior, Colonel Edward G., 221,
223, 236
Privy Council, Judicial Committee
of, 121, 133, 134, 174, 214
Programme catholique, 108
Protestant Defence Alliance, 109, 130
Protestant Protective Association,
167, 168
Provincial Rights Association of
British Columbia, 216
pulpwood/pulp and paper industry,
90, 192–5 *passim*, 226, 227, 324n66,
325n71, 325n77, 336n70

Quebec Bank, 82–9 *passim*
Quebec City property/residence, 21,
29, 50, 52, 62
Queen's University, 169

railways: Canadian Pacific, 140, 144,
146, 213, 218, 220, 221; Canadian
Northern, 220; Columbia and
Western, 221; Drummond County,
206; Esquimalt and Nanaimo,
220; Grand Trunk, 31, 107; Grand
Trunk Pacific, 232; Great Eastern,
144; Great Northern, 218; Intercolonial (ICR), 81, 88, 89, 90, 92, 186,
289n129; Lotbinière and Megantic,
89, 93, 291n158; Montreal Colonization, 123; North Shore, 31, 107,
122–3, 144; Quebec, Montreal,
Ottawa, and Occidental (QMOO),
123, 133, 134, 136, 138–40 *passim*,
305n39, 309n101; 145–6; wooden,
117, 122
railway ties, 88, 89, 90, 290n133
Red Toryism, xi